The Illustrated Book of World History

The Illustrated Book of

World History

Margaret Sharman and Derek Wilson

Evans Brothers Limited

Published by Evans Brothers Limited
Montague House, Russell Square,
London WC1B 5BX

© Evans Brothers Limited 1977

This edition first published 1977
originally published in two volumes as Worldspan

Printed in Great Britain by Morrison & Gibb Ltd, Edinburgh

ISBN 0 237 44827 0   PRA 4868

Contents

List of Maps

Acknowledgements

Several people have very kindly read chapters in this book and advised me on points of history. I should especially like to thank Richard Leakey and Jean Brown for information on East African prehistory; James Kirkman and Neville Chittick on the Arab and Portuguese periods in East Africa; Dr Ahmed Salim for reading the chapters on Islam; and E.W. Young for drawing me sketch-maps to show the difficulties the Atlantic explorers had to face.

Most of my other helpers I have not met—they are the authors of the dozens of books which I read while writing this history.

Margaret Sharman 1977

I have to thank many people for help and guidance in the production of my manuscript. To two Headmasters of Lenana School go my thanks for permission to embroil myself in a labour not directly connected with my teaching duties. Many colleagues at the school advised on various points, especially Mr P. Ayerst who put a mere historian right on many points of scientific detail. The publishers have laboured hard to dress the bare bones of the text with suitable illustrations and to give the whole book its attractive format. My wife thundered her way through 80,000 words on an inadequate portable typewriter—and all for love. To everyone involved—thank you.

D.A. Wilson 1977

Illustrations Maurice Wilson

Maps Edgar Holloway

Picture-maps, charts and diagrams
Leslie Haywood

For permission to reproduce copyright illustrations, the authors and publishers gratefully acknowledge the following:

Academy of Sciences, Leningrad; page 262 (above)
Ashmolean Museum; page 44

Baghdad Museum; page 30
Biblioteca Nazionale, Florence; page 175
Curators of the Bodleian Library; page 123, taken from MSS Marsh 144
BPC Publishing Limited. From Story of Africa and its Explorers, edited R. Brown page 320 (below)
British Institute of History and Archaeology in East Africa; pages 148, 313
British Rail; page 207 (below)
Trustees of the British Museum; pages 16 (above), 23 (above), 26, 27, 31, 37 (below right), 41, 46, 53 (bottom), 56, 59, 65, 66 (above), 72, 90 (above), 102, 108, 109 (above), 114, 117 (below), 124, 127, 132, 150, 153 (above), 158, 181, 186 (above), 191, 198 (below), 209 (below), 210, 222, 231, 261, 314, 318

Cadbury Brothers Ltd.; page 211 (above)
Camera Press; page 353, 358 (right), 365, 368
Church Missionary Society; page 317
Common Ground (1951) Ltd.; page 266 (below)
Commonwealth War Graves Commission; page 329
Contemporary Films; page 275 (below)
Crown Copyright; page 156 (bottom)

Daily Sketch and Oxfam; page 355
De Beers Consolidated Mines Ltd.; page 297 (above)

East African Railways and Harbours; page 325
École Française D'Archéologie D'Athènes; page 90 (below)
Editions Payot, Paris; page 22 (bottom), taken from La Chase Prehistorique by Lindner

Fotofast; page 200 (above)

John Hancock Mutual Life Insurance Company; page 239
Harpers Weekly; page 269
Heinemann Educational Books Ltd.; pages 195 (below), 196 (above), 197
The Executors of the late Mary Houston; page 38, taken from Ancient Egyptian, Mesopotamian and Persian Costume, by Mary Houston

Every effort has been made to trace the owners of copyrights,
but we take this opportunity of tendering our apologies
to any owner whose copyright may have been unwittingly
infringed.

List of Colour illustrations with acknowledgements

Preface

To Henry Ford history was 'bunk'; to Karl Marx it was the inevitable movement of human society towards the international worker state; to the Venerable Bede it was the record of God's dealings with men. But what is it to us? Does it matter much? Isn't reading history just another hobby like rock-climbing or keeping tropical fish? No, our world is too small for us to indulge that attitude. Inevitably we all make assumptions, about ourselves and about other peoples' histories and the way we react to that knowledge.

Unfortunately, history has long been taught from a jingoistic standpoint. There are certain milestones of prestige, economic, political or cultural—the Roman Empire, Britain in the Industrial Revolution, France under Bonaparte, the Golden Age of Spain or the Inca civilizations of Peru. Children learn how their own country developed socially and politically—an inevitable progression highlighting military victories and acts of imperialism while neglecting the implication of their defeats.

Such a view of history is narrow and misleading. The media confront us daily with our own history and both past and present are manipulated. The fact that Napoleon, Churchill, Stalin or John F. Kennedy said such and such does not invest their words with either eternal wisdom or relevance. The fact that a sequence of events occurred in the 1930's does not mean that given similar circumstances, the sequence would repeat itself in the 1970's or '80's.

Life for the individual, as for society, is a process of constant change, continuing struggle and frequent adaptation to other individuals and societies. Utopia will never be reached. And it is precisely because life is so that we ought to study history, and study it without preconceived ideas. History is about people. It tells us what men and women, either individually or in groups,

have done to and for each other. It should help us to understand those who have gone before us. If we can do that, we shall understand ourselves better and that will take us a long way to solving our problems.

In coming to terms with our world we need to know something of our own past and the past of other cultures. To understand the way people in other lands live it is necessary to know not only what they believe, how they earn their living, what kind of government they have now, but also something of their past development. And we need to set our own history alongside theirs, to compare them and to see how each was influenced by the other. Mankind has travelled to the present by many varied paths. Between our common origins in primeval Africa or Asia and our present age of rapid communications and close international relationships there stand three million years during which the world's races developed their own cultures in greater or lesser degrees of isolation.

Yet the fact remains that peoples of other times and places were much like us. They experienced love and hate, joy and suffering, greed and self-sacrifice, achievement and despair, success and failure. They too puzzled about the meaning of life, and either died before they solved that puzzle or found religions and philosophies which provided answers that satisfied them. So, when we are studying the history of other peoples or that of primitive Man, we cannot think of them as a different species, like animals in a zoo—objects of curiosity to be looked at from a position of superiority; they are *us* as we would have been if we had lived in the same time and place. Today the youngest school child learns things about the universe that the wisest adults of the sixteenth century did not know; conversely, even if they were less informed about the 'outside' world, each man and woman in a sixteenth-century village knew a lot more than most of us about how to weave cloth, preserve meat or make pottery.

These are some of the beliefs and assumptions that underlie this book. In it we have tried to tell the exciting and absorbing story of humanity in a way which will not only help readers to fill gaps in their own knowledge but also inspire them to make fresh discoveries for themselves. We have tried to do two things: to provide a framework of world history from the origins of Mankind to the present day; and to tell the story of each region *in its own terms*, and not from an insular standpoint. To do this we have had to stand back and take a fresh look at the international past. In world terms what were the most important events and who were the most significant people? Certainly not the Wars of the Roses, nor Culloden nor Henry VIII nor even Nelson. In the long view of history the discovery of electricity made more impact than Marlborough's victory at Blenheim and the world owes more (for ill or good) to Karl Marx than the Duke of Wellington.

The result, we hope, has been a fresh and up-to-date approach to world history. We have outlined the development of all the major world civilizations and pointed out those aspects of them that have lasting influence. We hope that as you read these pages you will gain a bird's-eye view of the whole panorama of human activity—and find it enjoyable. Studying history means making discoveries and discoveries should always be fun. It is fascinating to learn how archaeologists gradually pieced together the story of our earliest forbears. It is amazing to realize just how much Greek thinkers added to our knowledge of the universe in the space of a few centuries. Try to imagine how wealthy and powerful the Moghul emperors of India were; what it meant to transform Japan from a feudal nation to a modern, industrialized state within thirty years; how devastating was the effect of the First World War on Europe when most of her young men were killed or wounded.

All of us are adding to history all the time. One day the twentieth century will be 'ancient history' and people will read about the way we lived and the legacy we left to them. What will they say of us? 'Well, they must have been like us in some ways, but they knew nothing about inter-galactic travel. And how primitive their methods of communication were! They had to rely on things called radios, televisions and telephones. They were very unsophisticated; perhaps it was because they spent most of their time fighting wars.' Let us hope that our age will be better understood. But we cannot expect later generations to be sympathetic if we are not prepared to understand those who preceded us. History is about people, people bound together—past, present and future—in the common destiny of one species on an insignificant planet among the countless millions of spinning spheres. We call it humanity.

Derek Wilson 1977

In the Beginning

The Earth was spinning in space *millions* of years before there were any living plants or animals on it.

200
million
years ago

There were plants, animals and birds on Earth *millions* of years before men appeared. Some of the animals were very strange, and died out long ago.

2
million
years
ago

There were also — the apes.

Some of the apes, after countless generations and more millions of years, became man-like. Many kinds of man-apes (we call them 'hominids') lived on earth at the same time. Only the more cunning ones survived. Their brains became larger, and their intelligence grew.

The scientific words used to describe ancient apes and hominids come from Latin and Greek. Here are some of the English meanings:

Australopithecus = southern ape
Homo sapiens = 'thinking' man
Homo erectus = upright man

13

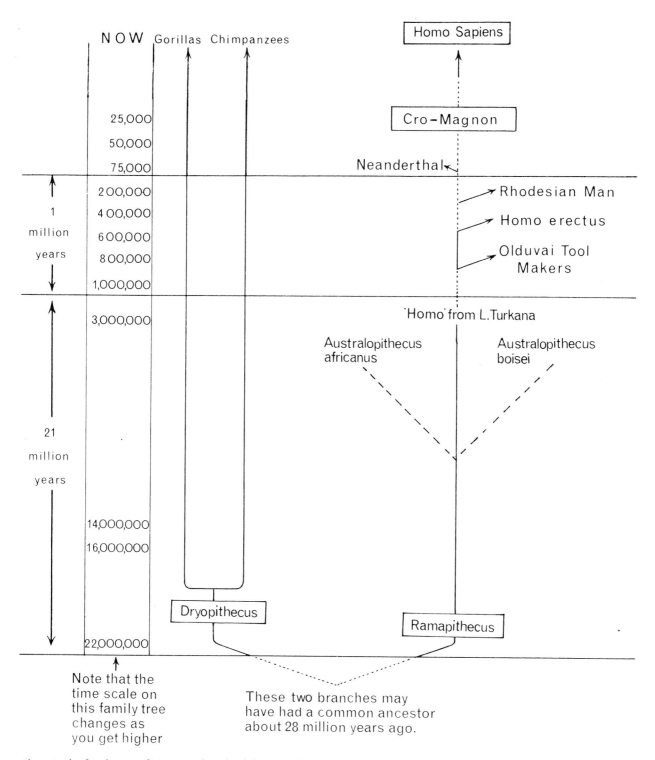

NOW Gorillas Chimpanzees

Homo Sapiens

25,000

50,000

75,000

Cro-Magnon

Neanderthal

1 million years

200,000 → Rhodesian Man

400,000 → Homo erectus

600,000

800,000 → Olduvai Tool Makers

1,000,000

3,000,000 'Homo' from L. Turkana

Australopithecus africanus

Australopithecus boisei

21 million years

14,000,000

16,000,000

Dryopithecus

Ramapithecus

22,000,000

Note that the time scale on this family tree changes as you get higher

These two branches may have had a common ancestor about 28 million years ago.

Above is the family tree of Man stretching back for more than 22 million years. At the bottom are the very earliest types of men and at the top *Homo sapiens*—modern Man. The relationship between Man and the Gorilla and Chimpanzee is shown; the arrows jutting out from the main branch indicate some of the types of Man to have become extinct; the dotted line shows the most distant stages of human development about which little is known.

14

Part I The First Men

Chapter 1 The Ancestors of Man

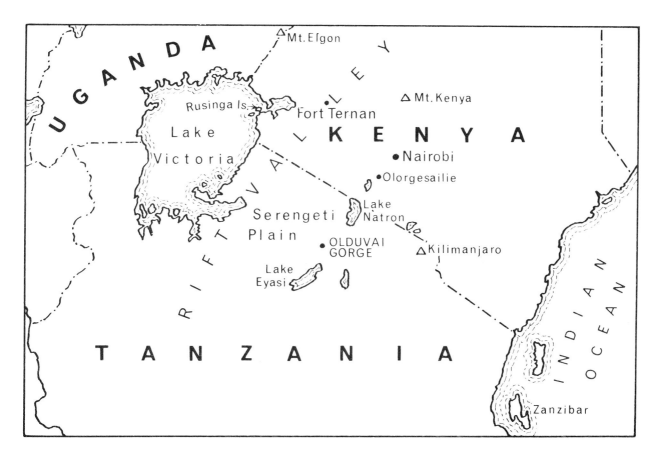

In 1859 a scientist named Charles Darwin published a book called *The Origin of Species*. In this book, he put forward the theory that all creatures on Earth had developed from more primitive forms. The book shocked the Christian world. Previously most Christians had believed in the Genesis story in the Bible, which says that every creature was created in its present form. But gradually the idea of 'evolution' (change and development over many years) was accepted; and in the last 100 years we have found out a great deal about the creatures that inhabited the Earth thousands and even millions of years ago.

But 100 years has not been long enough to find out about *all* the stages that took place. Palaeontologists are searching all the time for more clues to Man's ancestors. Perhaps even before you finish reading this book, we may be told about some new discovery.

The Cradle of Man
We now believe that Africa was the starting-place of Man. The early apes, and hundreds of

other different kinds of animals, first lived in Africa, probably around what is now the Rift Valley and Lake Victoria. Millions of years ago, some of them went northwards into Europe and Asia. Here their descendants went through similar stages of development to those who were left behind in Africa.

Near the Equator, in Central and West Africa, there were thick forests; in East Africa, near the Great Lakes, the forest was not so thick as in lands to the west. And this 'savannah' country (grassland with scattered trees and bushes) of Eastern Africa may have been Man's first home. There is plenty of evidence that East Africa in those days had much more surface water than it does to day. Many places where bones and stone tools have been found are nowadays far from water, whereas when these sites were occupied by hominids, they were near lakes and rivers. Indeed, some sites are high up on the slopes of what is now the Great Rift Valley, overlooking Lakes Elmenteita and Nakuru far below. Three million years ago, Lake Victoria was an enormous inland sea. Now much of N. Africa is desert.

Fortunately for the palaeontologists, the Great Rift Valley was still taking shape long after hominids started to roam about East Africa. There were earthquakes which caused the ground to tilt, and dust from erupting volcanoes covered a wide area of land. So dust and earth covered the places where the hominids had left their stone weapons and tools, and the bones of the animals they had eaten. It is these animal bones, weapons and tools — and in some cases the bones of the hominids themselves — that present-day palaeontologists are now finding in East Africa. In many other parts of the world, including West Africa, much of the evidence about early Man has been lost for ever, because geological conditions and events were not so favourable.

Dryopithecus africanus

Our earliest East African evidence comes from a small creature's skull, squashed sideways by the weight of the covering earth. This little creature has been named 'Dryopithecus', and his skull was found on Rusinga Island, at the north-eastern end of Lake Victoria, in present-day Kenya.

These animals may sometimes have left the forests and scrambled around on open ground; they are the forerunners of our apes. The canine teeth (the pointed teeth on each side of the four

Fossils

Fossils are the result of long burial by ash or rock. A small animal, or a skull, or even a leaf may be completely covered by earth or water. In time the perishable part is washed away and the space is filled by minerals from the surrounding earth. The mineral substances harden, leaving the shape of the original specimen. The fossil bird above, *Archaeopteryx lithographica*, was fossilised in limestone and water about 180 million years ago.

Of course only a very few bones or leaves become covered with suitable kinds of earth to turn them into fossils. Most animal and vegetable remains just rot away.

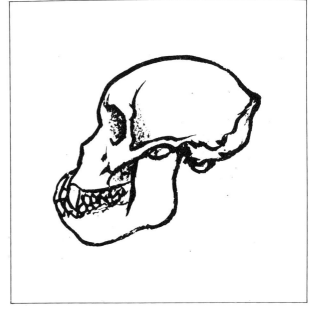

Skull of Dryopithecus africanus

front 'incisors', the cutting teeth) were long, as in most animals. They could be used for tearing flesh, or stripping the bark off trees. Our human canine teeth are very little different in length from the rest of our teeth. This is one of the signs palaeontologists look for when they are deciding whether a skull belongs to an ape or to a near-man.

Ramapithecus

Not far away from Lake Victoria, there is a very small prehistoric site called Fort Ternan. (Prehistory is the time before there were any written records.) Here there are thousands of fossils (ancient bones and traces of bones preserved in the Earth) in a very small area, no larger than an average classroom. They are all between 12,000,000 and 14,000,000 years old. Dr L. S. B. Leakey was a well-known Kenya palaeontologist who worked on the prehistory of the Earth for many years. Dr Leakey believed that there was once a watering-place at Fort Ternan, where animals came to drink. At some point in time the land was covered with ash from an erupting volcano, and some of the bones of the animals who lived there were preserved until now. Most of the bones on this site are of small animals, but there is evidence of one more man-like than the rest. He is called *Ramapithecus*. This kind of hominid may in fact have been a very, very remote ancestor of us all. They also lived between 12,000,000 and 14,000,000 years ago. We do not know what they looked like, because the palaeontologists have so far found only jawbones. The canine teeth were smaller than those of true apes, yet these creatures were still more like apes than men. *Ramapithecus* and other man-like creatures have also been found as far away as India and China, so already these animals had wandered far. The name *Ramapithecus* was first given to a skull found in India, and the Kenya skulls belong to the same kind of hominid. These creatures probably existed in a forested area stretching right across Arabia and into the Far East.

Australopithecus boisei

There is a gap in our knowledge of hominids here until about 3,000,000 years ago—though isolated remains exist within this period. The next kind of hominid we know about from finds in East Africa is today called **Australopithecus boisei** (*A. boisei* for short). A skull was discovered by Mrs Mary Leakey when she was

Dryopithecus africanus, remains of skull found in Kenya

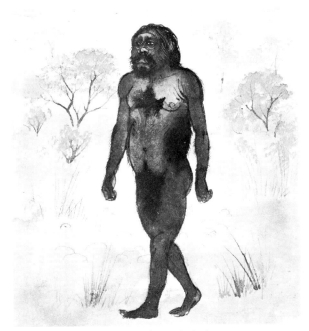

Reconstruction of Australopithecus boisei

looking for prehistoric evidence in Olduvai Gorge, in Tanzania.

In the days when *A. boisei* lived, the cool waters or rivers and lakes attracted many birds and animals to Olduvai. *A. boisei* ate small animals when he could catch them; he also ate vegetable foods, and he developed a huge jaw for grinding up tough stringy leaves and stems. Although the skull that was found belonged to quite a young hominid (whose 'wisdom-teeth' had only just come through his gums*), his huge molar teeth were already worn down because of constant chewing. He has been nicknamed 'Nutcracker Man'. He belongs to a family of African hominids all of which are called 'Australopithecines'. They lived in scattered places in East and South Africa. The Olduvai skull is about 1¾ million years old; since 1969 many other Australopithecine remains have been found near Lake Turkana, some of them up to 3 million years old.

The Australopithecines were probably hairy all over; they were short and strong, with low foreheads and deep-set eyes. They had very strong muscles on both sides of the head, a sloping brow, and a brain of about one-third the size of ours.

The skull Mrs Leakey found at Olduvai was incomplete: there was no bottom jaw. So it was great good fortune that 50 miles away, near Lake Natron, there lay on a shelf of rock a bottom jaw belonging to another Nutcracker Man. The two fossils together show us how Nutcracker Man's skull differed from ours.

Dr Leakey
Ranged in front of Dr Leakey are the skulls of *Australopithecus africanus* (left), *A. boisei* (centre) and that of a modern ape (right).

*In humans these teeth, at the back of the jaw, normally appear when we are 18–20 years old.

Australopithecus with animals in the background
Here are some of the animals that roamed over the African plains and were even found in Europe and Asia nearly 2 million years ago. There are crocodiles and hippos in the lake. An odd-looking, elephant-like animal and a pig graze in the background.

Australopithecus habilis

Olduvai Gorge had further surprises in store for palaeontologists, for they found the broken fragments of the skull of a very young hominid. With painstaking care the pieces were stuck together to form the back part of the head. Later a lower jaw, and the bones of a hand were found. Dr. Leakey was certain that this was a true ancestor of Man, and called it *Homo habilis*, 'the man with ability'. The shape of the skull is very like ours, the teeth are in the same positions on the jaw as ours are; the finger bones show that this creature could grasp an object as we do, between finger and thumb. Later finds seem to show that this was a type of Australopithecine, and so today it is known as *A. habilis*. *A. habilis* and *A. boisei* both lived in Africa about 1 million years ago. *A. boisei* died out somewhere between that date and the coming of *Homo sapiens*. He could not compete against the later men, with their larger brains and greater ability.

Recently found skulls in the Lake Turkana area seem to indicate that a true *Homo* ancestor existed 3 million years ago, but more research is needed before we have any definite information.

Homo erectus

After another long gap in time, we find that a new hominid has taken the place of the earlier ones. His face was still very ape-like, but his leg and thigh bones show that he could stand up straight. This hominid is one member of a world-wide family which has been called *Homo erectus*, the 'upright man'. *Homo erectus* was much cleverer than any of the Australopithecines. He was capable of patiently spending hours chipping away at pieces of stone and bone in order to make for himself a really efficient weapon or tool. One type of tool we find in very large quantities — it is called a 'hand-axe', though in fact it was not used like a modern axe, but as a knife and scraper. From then onwards for thousands of years, hominids used hand-axes for all sorts of jobs that required a sharp-edged or pointed tool. Before long, these men had also learned how to make spear-heads, which they tied to long wooden handles. They hunted in groups, and with great cunning; they had a primitive form of speech. Their brains were about the size of the smallest of ours today. In Europe and parts of Asia, some of these groups of people could use fire, but they had not

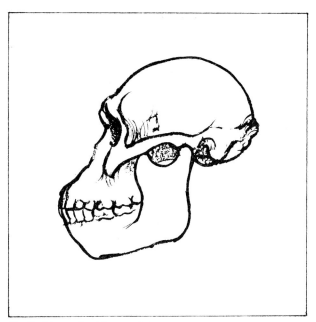

Skull of Australopithecus africanus

'Man the toolmaker'

What makes a man different from an ape? A long time ago people used to say 'Man is a tool-maker'; but many apes can make simple tools (an ape can hold a stick in a very similar way to man). There is no really good definition of the difference between an ape and early man. Perhaps we can say that man is a creature that uses tools to make other tools.

The human hand can control the movement of comparatively delicate objects.

yet discovered how to make it for themselves. Having fire meant that they could relax at night in caves and shelters, knowing that the glowing wood at the entrance would keep away wild animals.

At Olduvai, the first hand-axes are found in 'Bed 2', just above the remains of *A. habilis* and Nutcracker Man (see below). The higher up we look in the layers of earth, the better the axes we find.

Olorgesailie, near Nairobi, and Isimila near Iringa in Tanzania, are two of the greatest known sources of stone weapons and tools of that period in the world. In both places, lakes which existed perhaps 100,000 years ago, used to be the watering places of bands of these nomadic, hunting people. There are thousands of animal bones alongside the tools, but no skulls or human bones have been found so far.

Side by side with the hunters there lived giant wild pigs, and some queer elephant-like animals, giraffes and hippos, all long since extinct. Antelopes and little three-toed horses galloped across the plains, and were sometimes caught by the hunters, who probably entangled their legs with stone balls wrapped in skins, and tied together with leather strips or 'thongs'. This very useful weapon is still used today, and is called a 'bolas' by the Spanish-speaking hunters of South America.

Homo erectus lived all over Africa, Europe and Asia, and everywhere he made beautiful hand-axes, and later spear-heads and even arrow heads out of stone.

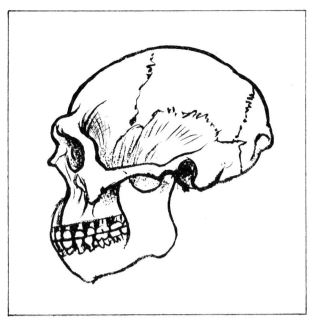

Skull of Homo erectus

How a gorge-site like Olduvai may be formed

I   1,750,000 years ago: hominids leave thigh bones of animals, fish bones and round pebble tools near a lake.

II The lake floods and covers the tools and bones and later retreats. This happens many times.

III Other animals use the lakeside and leave *their* bones and tools above those of the first hominids.

IV Eventually, many layers of ash and mud about 95 metres thick are deposited.

V After severe earth movements a river is formed; it wears away the soil. Steep banks appear on both sides of the river.

VI The river dries up, leaving a deep gorge. Some of the ancient bones and tools are washed away by the river. Others are exposed in the sides of the gorge after rain and soil erosion.

These were found at Olduvai Gorge:

hand-axes, stone balls, cleavers etc; bones of an animal like a white rhino, an extinct buffalo and antelopes caught in an ancient swamp. *Homo erectus* lived here

hand-axes, choppers, scrapers and cleavers

bones of elephant-like animal with downward curving tusks

skulls of *Australopithecus boisei* and *A. habilis*; circle of loosely piled stones which may have been a 'wind-break'

(4a)

(Top of Bed 2)

(Bottom)

1,650,000 years ago

1,750,000 years ago

LAVA — 1,850,000 years ago

BEDS

Other early hominids

If you look at the diagram on p. 14, you will see that the next step in human evolution is 'Rhodesian Man'. He was given this name because his skull was found in Northern Rhodesia (now Zambia). But he, or other hominids very like him, also lived in many other places. Rhodesian Man was nearer to us than *Homo erectus* was. He had straight legs and could walk with a long stride, as we do. His brain was nearly as big as ours, but his skull shows that he had great ridges over his eyes, as well as a backward-sloping forehead.

'Neanderthal Man' (named after the Neander Valley in Europe in which his bones were first found) comes almost at the top of our family tree. Traces of him have been found all over Europe and the Near East. Neanderthal Man was powerful and broad, with heavy brow-ridges and a receding chin. He was intelligent, and skilled with his hands. He had a very large brain. Like *H. erectus*, he lived in Africa, Asia and Europe. He hunted the mammoth (a kind of hairy elephant), and the woolly rhinoceros, both of which were common in Europe and Asia. He relied for his meat on smaller kinds of animals like deer, pig and wild sheep. Some Neanderthal skulls seem to be almost man-like; others are much more like those of apes. Perhaps the more man-like ones are the result of breeding

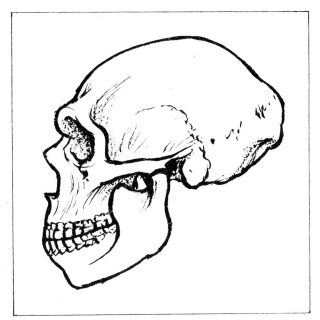

Skull of Neanderthal Man

with European and Asian hominids who were as advanced as Rhodesian Man. We do not yet know.

Long before Neanderthal Men disappeared for ever, another and more important creature was also making tools and weapons, and hunting the same kinds of animals for his food. He is the only hominid who has not yet died out. His name is *Homo sapiens*.

Men of the 'Stone Age'

In order to live at all men must have water. Without water plants could not grow and without plants there would be no animals and no men. You will always find stone-age sites near rivers or lakes, where the vegetation and animal life were at their richest, and bones most easily fossilized.

Chapter 2 Homo Sapiens

As you can see from the diagram on p. 14, it is not possible for us to say 'this is exactly the way in which man evolved', because we have gaps in our knowledge. All we can say is that from the many different hominids, one kind was, so to speak, 'the winner'. During the centuries, men in different climates developed the different characteristics that we call 'race'. But all the races of Man belong to the same species, or type – *Homo sapiens*.

Early *Homo sapiens* (we will now just call them 'men') made weapons and tools of flint, stone, bone, ivory, wood and horn. He caught fish with bone harpoons; he used scrapers for cleaning animal hides, and sewed them together with bone needles to make clothes, and even small boats.

Cro-Magnon Man and cave art
The Cro-Magnon people were taller and probably stronger than modern men. They believed in magic and were superstitious. We think they drew animals and people on cave walls as a magic spell to give them good fortune in hunting.

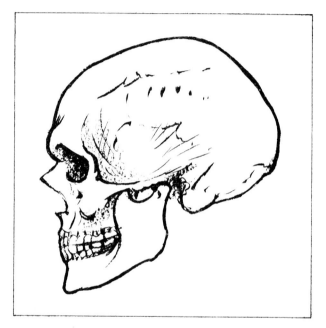

Skull of Cro-Magnon Man

There were very few people living in each continent. The way of life of ancient men did not allow them to live for very long, and most of them died before they were 30. In the days before medicines of any kind, and when wild animals killed men for food, their 'expectation of life', that is the length of time they could expect to live, was not very high.

Man is an inventor. He likes to find out about the things around him. His enquiring mind has led him to discover more about the universe than Nutcracker Man ever learnt—although he has only been on Earth a fraction of the time that Nutcracker Man was here. His first really big discovery was how to make fire by striking sparks into wood shavings and dried leaves. After that, each new invention led to another. Now that everybody could make fire when and where he liked, men (or more likely, women) made pots to put on the fire. The old way of roasting meat on sticks, or between stones was wasteful, and much of the fat and the nourishing juices were lost. Soon the clay pots were in every hut, some reserved for cooking, and others for storing water, grain, honey, milk or berries.

A long time later the hunters captured some of the wild dogs that lived in the bush country, and trained them to help catch larger animals. Hunting, and collecting wild wheat, berries and leaves took up most of their time.

In North Africa parts of the Sahara became inhabited during the fertile periods of ancient times. Here early men hunted all the animals that today live much farther south—ostriches, giraffes, elephants, and buffalo. We know this because they painted pictures of these animals on the walls of caves and rocks.

By about 10,000 B.C., the Sahara area had started to dry up, and men were forced to follow the more fertile valleys either to the north or to the south. The southern part of Africa gradually became cut off from the north by a wide belt of rock and sand. In the north-east, the mighty river Nile attracted many of the refugees from the drying Sahara. They joined the people who already lived by the river banks, and together built huts, and hunted for their food.

As far as we know, nobody had the idea of actually sowing grasses for grain until about 9000 B.C. By that time *Homo sapiens* may have been on the Earth for as long as 100,000 years. The first grain planters probably lived in Asia. They improved the quality of the wild crop by

Pottery
Wood, leather and woven grasses do not survive as well as bone and stone, so we are not always certain about which kinds of people plaited baskets or made wooden bowls. But we do know that baskets were made before pots. Some baskets were plastered with mud inside so that flour, small berries and seeds did not fall through. When people started making pots of clay only, without the basket-work outside, they often made patterns on them imitating basket-work plaiting.

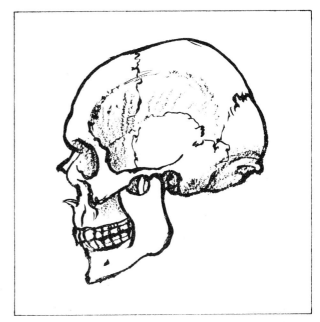

Skull of Homo sapiens
Comparison of this diagram with the preceeding ones illustrates how the shape of the human skull has adapted and changed as a result of evolution.

23

1. In very early times men took handfuls of seed and just threw them on to the' ground. Much of the seed which was 'broadcast' like this was eaten by birds, so it was not a very good method of sowing. (But it was still used in many parts of the world until quite recently.)

2. Some people improved on this method by making holes in the ground with a pointed stick, but this was very slow.

3. Then the hoe was invented, which cut up and loosened the soil, on to which the seed was dropped.

4. The first ploughs were just pieces of bone or wood with long handles and the farmers pulled them along the ground making a furrow, a long cut in the ground, into which they dropped the seed.

5. When cattle were tame enough to pull ploughs, farmers could prepare a much larger area of ground in a day and so could enlarge their fields and grow more food.

Early Agriculture

6. Improvements were invented to make the job of a farm-worker easier at harvest time. Sickles were made out of sharpened flint or bone with a wooden handle. Later came the idea of using a curved bone and the sickle became the shape it is today.

planting only the biggest and best seeds each year. While they tended the crops, they had to live near the fields. So small settlements grew near to fertile ground.

The hunters still went after wild animals for meat, but even they were soon able to stay at home for longer periods, because the new farmers had learnt how to build stockades, protective places made of wood, in which to keep wild animals, and fatten them for food. They could then choose the beast they wanted to kill, and they could eat meat even when the wild herds had migrated elsewhere. So a new occupation was invented—that of a herdsman. As time went by, the domestic animals improved in the same way as the grain improved for the agriculturalists—by clever selection and breeding.

Men were now able to 'control their environment', that is, their surroundings and the conditions under which they lived. They no longer had to live at the mercy of wild animals, storms and cold, or famine. The coming of agriculture meant that they need no longer be nomads. They built permanent houses to shelter them from the weather, wore clothing to keep out the cold, stored grain to eat all the year round, and made efficient weapons for protection. The groups of people grew, as one group joined another to share their crops. Only a few people had to grow food; the rest could hunt, or make tools, or repair houses, or sew skins. Men began to specialize in the jobs they were best at, and as they now had more leisure, they became more skilled. They decorated their pots with coloured paint, and with interesting patterns. They carved wood and ivory into beautiful shapes, and set precious stones into gold to make decorative drinking vessels, jewellery and ornaments. Each community had its own special ways of decorating pottery. Archaeologists can tell how old a society is by the type of pottery the people made or imported.

When the villagers had a surplus of goods (that is, more than enough for their own needs), they exchanged them with the next village for *their* surplus goods. This was the beginnings of trade, and competition between the villages led to each craftsman trying to become more skilled than his neighbour. The basket-weavers developed their art and invented the weaving of cloth. In Asia and North Africa they used the fibres of a kind of grass called flax—the first grass grown not for its grain, or flour, but for

Boats
Tree trunks were probably the first form of boats used by man. He could get across streams and rivers by simply sitting astride a log. Early settlers used to hollow out the trunks to make canoes, and string logs together to make rafts. In countries where there were no large trees available, rafts were made from reeds or rushes. In time, animal skins were stretched over a framework of wood.

clothing. The new settlements became self-supporting. Some of them were on the very brink of becoming what we now call 'civilized'.

25

Part II Early Civilizations
Chapter 3 Mesopotamia

We are now going to jump in time to about 3500 B.C., when the earliest civilizations we know about were already flourishing. Up to that date, archaeologists rely on examining bones, tools and weapons, baskets, and pots, in order to find out about man's past. But from around 3500 B.C. their work is helped enormously by a great invention—writing. Prehistory now becomes history, because for the first time we have actual records from the people themselves.

Writing

It may be that much early writing was only concerned with such things as lists of kings, lists of goods in a storeroom, the measurements of fields, and so on. But from this time onwards men relied less and less on memory, and more and more on written records. Of course, if someone living 6000 years *later* than us—in about A.D. 8000—were to find a page of your exercise book, he would not (if he were wise!) immediately assume that everything written in it was true; the same applies to all the written evidence from the past. The writer of a letter may have been wrongly informed; an account of a battle is almost always one-sided; and an inscription cut in stone or metal praising a king may have been written more to flatter than to tell the truth. Therefore, historians read all these writings with an open mind, hoping that some other evidence—perhaps the discovery of a ruined building, or a weapon, or a second piece of writing—will agree with the evidence they already have.

So—the early civilizations had writing: that was an enormous step forward. Without it, perhaps they would not have been civilizations at all.

Writing

The earliest kind of writing was in pictures so at first people could only write down information about *things*. Then gradually pictures came to mean abstract words as well—for instance, a picture of a leg might mean 'walk' or 'travel' as well as being the symbol for the leg itself. The people of Sumeria and the Near East simplified the pictures into horizontal and vertical strokes. This is called cuneiform writing.

The Egyptians wrote on a kind of paper made of papyrus stems, with a pen cut from the hard part of a feather—a quill—and ink. We call their writing hieroglyphics.

This is what the two kinds of writing looked like in about 2000 B.C.

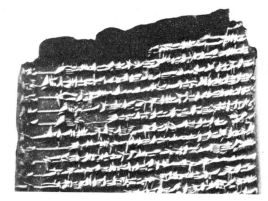

Above: Cuneiform. *Below:* Hieroglyphics

Learning to live together

We know that in several places around the Mediterranean Sea, and in the area we now call the 'Fertile Crescent', between Palestine and the Persian Gulf, people lived together in large towns, with well-built houses, good drainage, and sometimes town walls to protect them from their nomadic neighbours. (Many communities have remained as nomads, or as small village dwellers, right up to the present.)

In these towns, each person had his own rights in the community, and to protect their rights, they had to have laws. The farmers had to know where their fields ended, and where their neighbours' fields began; the tax-collectors had to have rules about how to calculate each man's contribution to the state; there had to be some way of stopping crimes like theft or murder. This was the beginning of government, and of laws — laws that everyone helped to keep, so that they could all live peacefully together in these large communities.

The gods look on

The lives of people in all the early civilizations were coloured by their religion. 'Religion' means 'binding together'. And religious ideas have to do with the way people live together, as well as their feelings about their god or gods. Primitive religions were all concerned with nature — there was a god of the sun, a god (or goddess) of the moon, a sea-god, a fire-god, a god of thunder, and so on. The gods were all around, on this Earth.

Then people began to believe in a life beyond this Earth, a life after death. And so they thought it was important to bury people in the right way, to ensure that their souls lived on. It is because of these burial customs that we know so much about the lives of people in the early civilizations — and indeed in some of the village communities as well. For most of these people did not simply bury the dead body. They included in the graves the dead person's goods — his pottery, his ornaments, his furniture, and his weapons. Much of the early pottery and ornaments you can see in museums today was once part of the grave-furniture of ancient people.

Sumeria — the land between two rivers

In about 3500 B.C., there were many small towns in the land between the two rivers called Tigris and Euphrates, in Mesopotamia. Nowadays the

Metals

Gold was probably the first metal used by ancient peoples because it was easy to find, in tiny bits, among river sand and even just lying on the surface of the earth. It is a very soft metal, suitable for making cups, plates and ornaments but not for tools and weapons.

A much more useful metal was copper, which people had started to use for knife blades and tools by about 5000 B.C. As people from one civilization began to have contact with other groups quite early on, they became aware of the existence of different metals such as copper. The bison pictured above is of copper and comes from Sumeria, dating from about 2300 B.C.

Copper when alloyed with tin is called bronze. Bronze is a harder metal than copper by itself, but not as hard as iron. People had found lumps of iron that had come from meteorites — a phenomenon the Egyptians called 'the metal from the sky'.

It is comparatively rare to find metal exposed in rocks or in the sand, so gold, copper and iron are usually mined.

Burial Scene, 4500 B.C.

area round the Persian Gulf is desert or semi-desert, and the ruins of the old towns are buried in sand; but 5500 years ago the towns were situated in a broad, fertile plain at one end of the Fertile Crescent. Each town in the plain had its own ruler, but all the towns were loosely connected, all speaking the same language and obeying the same laws. The rulers often quarrelled with each other, but their towns also carried on a lively trade. The whole country we call Sumeria, and one of its most important towns was called Ur.

The river Euphrates was the life-blood of Sumeria. The Tigris was not so navigable. Fishing boats, pleasure boats and barges loaded with cargo sailed up the Euphrates to the towns north of Ur, linking them all together. The river was the main highroad for the transport of market produce – barley and dates, goat-cheese and wine. In winter, when the two rivers flooded the plain, the effects on the farmlands could be disastrous. One of the first great works in which all the towns joined was the building of canals and ditches to control the overflowing waters. Without canals, the fields would have been waterlogged, the water uncontrolled, and the crops completely ruined. After this, every year when the waters went down, the land was ready for planting the Sumerians' staple crop, barley. (Wheat did not grow well in the land of the two rivers, because the ground was very salty.) Once the barley crop had ripened, men and women cut it with flint-and-wood sickles, and piled the golden grain on to heavy wooden carts. These were probably the first wheeled vehicles in the world, and their solid wheels clattered along the stone-paved streets of the towns as the tame oxen pulled them to the store-rooms, or to the market stalls.

Just outside the walls of Ur, archaeologists have found some very interesting graves, dating from about 3200 B.C. There are 16 of them, and they are known as 'royal' graves, although we are not absolutely certain that they were the graves of kings and queens.

The Sumerian burial customs were unusual: the priests and the people brought their dead king (we will assume he was a king) on a chariot to the top of a long sloping roadway, or ramp, which led to the underground tomb. They carried him down the ramp, through large limestone-lined chambers, into the burial place itself. His drinking cups and bowls were put on the ground

Clothing
The early Sumerians wore clothes made of lambs' skins. Then later they wove woollen cloth, and wore a kind of skirt with fringes. The women wore a one-piece dress leaving one shoulder bare. Sometimes they added a shawl with a jewelled pin. In old statues and pictures kings and gods are sometimes shown wearing a long robe, fastened on one shoulder.

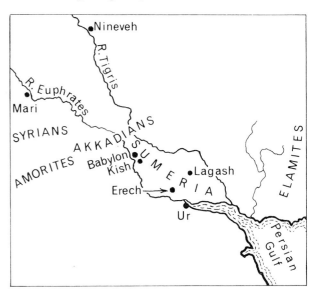

Ur
Ur was once a busy town and port on the shores of the Persian Gulf. But year by year the rivers brought fresh earth down from the highlands, and the sea built up ridges of sand along the coast. Ur was left high and dry, with its wharves and boat-sheds far inland.

Compare this map with a modern map of Iraq. You will see that Ur is now buried under an uninhabited desert about 150 miles from the sea. The sand of the desert has completely swallowed it up, and the only people who go to Ur now are archaeologists and historians. Ur might have been forgotten completely, had it not been mentioned many times in the Old Testament of the Bible. This encouraged archaeologists to dig in the sands for traces of the old cities of Sumeria. All our knowledge of Sumeria has been gained during this present century.

nearby. Then a curious (and to us, horrible) ceremony took place. Dozens of young men and women, all dressed in their best clothes, wearing gold and silver ornaments, and jewels made of precious stones, came down the ramp into the tomb. To the music of a harp they took their places in the chambers of the tomb. The king's chariot, decorated with gold and precious stones, was backed down the ramp, and the groom and driver led in the asses which had pulled the king's body from his palace to the tomb. Six of the king's soldiers, wearing their copper helmets, and with their copper daggers in their belts, marched down the ramp, and lined up near the opening. Then when everyone was ready, someone filled over 60 little cups with poison, one cup for each person. All these people, the attendants of the king in his lifetime, had come into the pit to die, so that they could continue to serve the king in his future life. In accepting the honour of becoming a king's or queen's servant or lady's-maid, a young man or woman knew that one day he or she might have to die by this kind of suicide.

Archaeologists can reconstruct the lives of ancient peoples from bones, broken pottery, beads, and even grains of wheat! So from these graves, we get a picture not only of the burial customs of the Sumerians, but also of the way they dressed, the musical instruments they played, their games, their food, and their chariots.

As we have seen, the thousands of ordinary citizens of Ur, Erech, Lagash, Kish, Mari, and all the other towns in the plain, lived the busy life of thriving agricultural communities. The town was the centre where all the produce from the neighbouring farms, and all the work of the craftsmen, were exchanged by barter. It was also the home of the scholars, among them mathematicians who worked out the number of days in a year, and who divided the day into hours, minutes, and even seconds. We still use the old Sumerian system, with its divisions based on 12's and 60's.

King Sargon

After about 500 years of civilization, the townsmen of Sumeria started to be worried by threats from outside their borders. The years were not always peaceful, and nomads from beyond the

Wheels

Perhaps the invention of the wheel began when someone rolled a log under a heavy object, in order to move it from one place to another. The oldest wheel discovered so far comes from Sumeria, and dates back to 3000 B.C. It was made of three pieces of wood joined together. Painted clay models found in the Near East show that the spoked wheel has been known to mankind since about 2500 B.C. The Egyptians were using spoked wheels (as in the bottom picture above) from about 1500 B.C. They made chariots much lighter and faster.

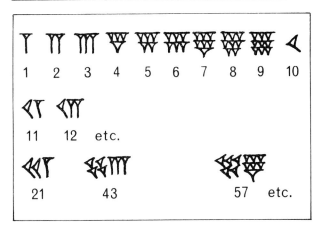

Sumerian numerals

29

rivers often tried to raid the rich cities. The townspeople built stout walls to keep them out, and they organized an army—the first in the world—for their defence. But to the north of Sumeria lived a people called the Akkadians. They copied the Sumerians' idea of an army, and in time they became stronger than the Sumerians. They invaded the country and took the whole land for themselves. They united the two kingdoms under one ruler. This meant that all the various towns owed allegiance, or loyalty, to the same king; they no longer had local quarrels about water-rights, or claims to fertile land, as they used to do in the days when there were many kings. But the taxes forced on them by the new rulers were far higher than they had been in the past.

The first Akkadian king of Sumeria was called Sargon, and he ruled from the northern town of Babylon in about 2380 B.C. The Akkadians were not as advanced as the Sumerians, but they wisely adopted the existing laws and system of government. They employed Sumerians as clerks in the government offices, and they used Sumerian writing, changing it to suit their own quite different language. The two peoples gradually came to accept one another as partners in one country. Both languages were spoken in the towns; but Sumerian very gradually died out. In time it was only used as a religious language in the temples.

Sumeria's Golden Age

In about 2150 B.C., 200 years after Sargon died, a great king named Ur-Nammu ruled in Sumeria. He was one of the strongest and most just rulers the Sumerians had ever known. This was the 'Golden Age' of Sumeria, and a time of great prosperity. Ur-Nammu made Ur his capital, and there he built a magnificent temple, called a ziggurat. At the top of the ziggurat the priests kept the most holy shrine of the moon-god, where every year a New Year's ceremony was held with great rejoicing.

Ur-Nammu dismissed dishonest officials, looked after the poor, and forced traders to use honest weights and measures. There were Halls of Justice at the gateway of the temple, where the king's representative heard court cases, and the complaints of the people. It was usual for the judge to 'sit in the gate to give judgement' in the ancient world. Religion, government, law and political power were all linked together,

Bronze mask, perhaps of King Sargon

and the Sumerians must have thought of them all as parts of one whole.

The priests, law-givers, and government servants were the most highly educated men in the community. The priests were greatly respected because they seemed to know all the right magic words to bring rain, or to stop plague, or to send away the swarms of locusts that sometimes ate the crops. Of course the priests could do none of these things, but they could use their knowledge of the weather, or of astronomy, to predict when rain, or famine, or a flood would come. They were the first real scientists in the world. Some of them were the first doctors, who no doubt relied on magic a good deal, but who also

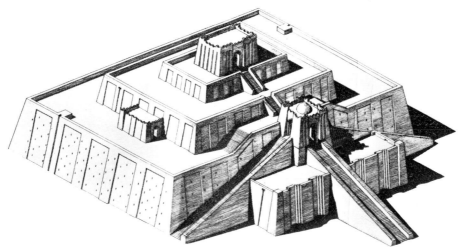

Ziggurat, present-day ruins and reconstruction

The centre part of the ziggurat at Ur was made of solid mud-brick. The outer walls were mud-brick with bitumen (tar) to bind them together. (There were no suitable rocks in Sumeria, so all stone for building had to be imported. The Sumerians used mud-brick for most of their buildings.)

The three staircases each had 100 steps, leading to the lower platform. The walls were painted black and red, with blue tiles on the walls of the topmost shrine.

We think the priests planted trees and flowers on the terraces, and that the slits in the walls were drainage holes for the water, which would otherwise have caused the centre of the ziggurat to swell and crumble.

used herbs, poultices, and ointments. They even performed surgical operations – though we cannot say how many of their patients lived!

The Babylonians

Then suddenly everything changed. Two new tribes, called the Elamites and the Amorites, invaded Sumeria. The ancient ways of the southern Sumerians were taken over by their conquerors, who recognized that the people in these old towns were superior in knowledge and in art and in government. But in the north, the Sumerians refused to submit to the foreigners' rule, and they set up a king of their own at Babylon.

King Hammurabi

The sixth king of the new Babylonian line was called Hammurabi. He reigned in about 1780 B.C. He took his armies into southern Sumeria, and he conquered the Amorite and Elamite kings. He reunited the country into one great kingdom, stretching from Nineveh to the Persian

Gulf, and from the Elamite Mountains in the east to the borders of Syria. From this time onwards we call the Sumerians 'Babylonians', because the capital city was Babylon. The old capital, Ur, gradually lost importance until it became just a small market town.

In the wars against the Amorites and Elamites, Hammurabi destroyed a great many of Sumeria's ancient buildings; but when peace was restored he organized the rebuilding of towns, and encouraged the farmers to clear the canals and waterworks. He built a marvellous new ziggurat in Babylon—the legendary 'Tower of Babel' mentioned in the Bible. In the book of Genesis we read that the labourers working on the Tower spoke many different languages. Certainly by then the Babylonians were a very mixed people, and no doubt they were using slave-labour from other countries as well.

Hammurabi also built schools, where young scholars copied texts, telling them how to be good citizens. The exercise books of Babylonia were squares of dried mud, or clay. The boys wrote on the clay with their wedge-shaped 'pens'. (The Latin for 'wedge' is *cuneus* from which we get the word 'cuneiform'.) The hardened clay was thrown away afterwards, and some of the exercises were found hundreds of years later, in the ruins of the old Babylonian towns.

One of these exercises said: 'He who shall excel in tablet-writing shall shine like the sun'. The schoolboys' task was by no means easy, for whereas we have between 20 and 30 letters in our alphabets, *they* had to learn between 600 and 700 different symbols! Hammurabi himself was a fine letter-writer, and we have found many writings on literature and science dating from his time.

Hammurabi's tablet
Here are some of the laws which scribes wrote on stone for all to read. Some were very harsh.

If a house falls down and kills someone, the builder's son shall die.

If a man steals from the temple, he must pay back ten times the value of the stolen article.

If a man breaks your tooth, you may break his in return.

A careless or spendthrift wife, [one who spends too much money], may be made into a slave, or drowned.

If a carrier loses a man's goods, the man may claim five times the value of the goods.

If a doctor kills his patient while using a bronze knife, his hand shall be cut off.

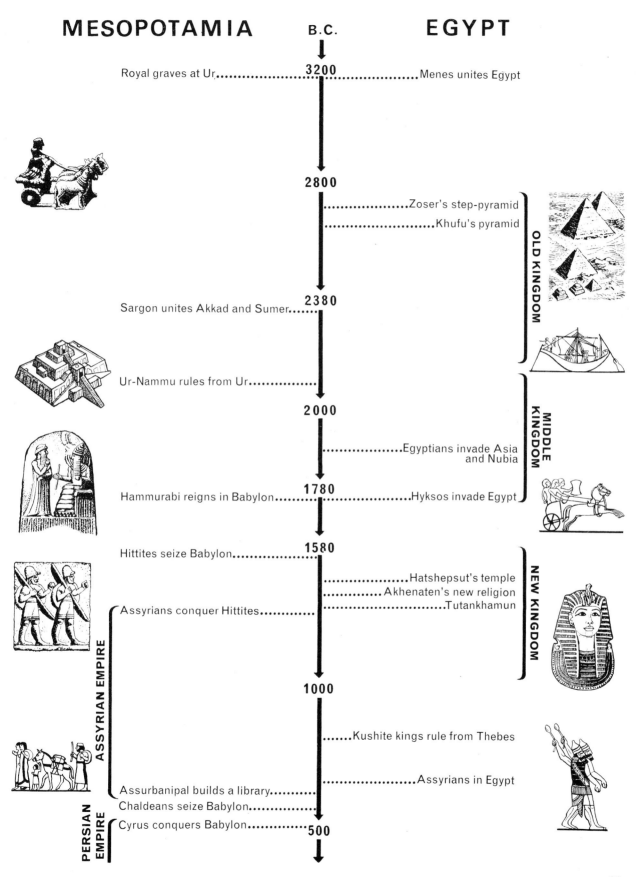

MESOPOTAMIA

B.C.

EGYPT

Royal graves at Ur.....................	**3200** ....Menes unites Egypt
	2800
	.................Zoser's step-pyramid
	.................Khufu's pyramid
	OLD KINGDOM
Sargon unites Akkad and Sumer......	**2380**
Ur-Nammu rules from Ur...............	
	2000
	.................Egyptians invade Asia and Nubia
	MIDDLE KINGDOM
Hammurabi reigns in Babylon..........	**1780** ....Hyksos invade Egypt
Hittites seize Babylon...................	**1580**
	.................Hatshepsut's temple
	.................Akhenaten's new religion
Assyrians conquer Hittites.............	.................Tutankhamun
	NEW KINGDOM
ASSYRIAN EMPIRE	**1000**
	......Kushite kings rule from Thebes
	.................Assyrians in Egypt
Assurbanipal builds a library..........	
Chaldeans seize Babylon...............	
PERSIAN EMPIRE Cyrus conquers Babylon.............	**500**

33

Chapter 4 The Land of Egypt

The various peoples living by the banks of the Nile were divided into 'clans', each with its own animal-sign. There was a jackal clan, a falcon clan (a falcon is a bird of prey like a hawk), a crocodile clan, and so on. (Some of the inhabitants of Africa still have a clan-system.) By about 3500 B.C., the Egyptian villages had grown into towns, linked together by the river Nile. The sacred clan-animals became the gods of the different towns. The whole country was now divided into two kingdoms: the kingdoms of Upper Egypt and Lower Egypt.

Riverside farmers

In the north, the Lower Nile valley had a warm, fairly wet climate, and here the people grazed cattle, sheep and goats on the broad meadows between the marshes and streams. Upper Egypt was very much drier, and it needed a lot of tremendously hard work to keep the desert from creeping on and on into the cultivated lands and destroying them. (Many of the fields that the ancient Egyptians once ploughed are now just sand.) The problem in Egypt was how to keep the fields watered; in Sumeria it was the other way round—canals had to be built to drain the water away. So in Egypt the yearly Nile floods

Egypt

Egypt, in ancient times, could be defended easily. To the north there was the sea, and to the north-east a desert over which any invaders would have to march for three days without water. Upper Egypt was bordered on both sides by barren cliffs and desert. In the south the Nubians (Egypt's southern African neighbours) could not get their boats past the waterfalls that we call Cataracts. At first the Egyptian boundary was at the First Cataract, and an armed fort guarded it from attack. Later in Egypt's history, the boundary was extended to the Second and Third Cataracts.

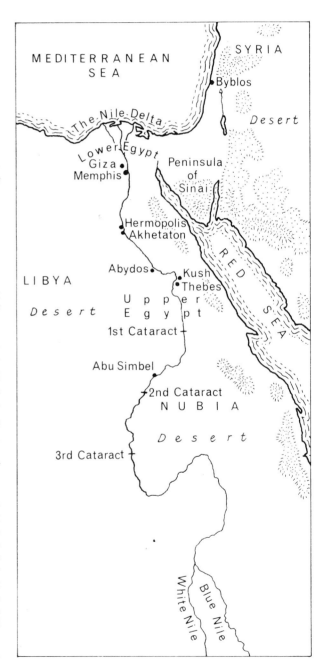

were welcomed with relief, for they brought fresh fertile soil to the land, and moisture for the spring planting.

There are two main branches of the Nile; the two rivers called the White and the Blue Nile meet at Khartoum in the Sudan. In July, August and September, the rains that fall near Lake Victoria swell the White Nile, and the snows on the Ethiopian mountains melt into the Blue Nile. The High Nile Festival, a time of great rejoicing, marked the beginning of the floods in ancient times. Then the farmers waited for the land to reappear, so that in November they could plant their crops in the rich black soil.

Besides grain, which grew plentifully, the farmers planted lentils and beans, onions, leeks and cucumbers. They used domestic animals to tread the seeds into the thick mud. The fields were separated from each other by little hard-mud walls, a foot or two high. They had to be rebuilt every November, and records were kept to show where each man's boundaries lay: here was the beginning of geometry—can you see why?

In the farm enclosures, farmers kept ducks, geese, hens and cows for fattening. Almost all the countrymen lived by farming. Some of them owned their own farms, but most were paid labourers. Even so, it was possible for everyone to live a reasonably happy (though hard-working) life during the peaceful periods of Egypt's long history.

Egypt becomes one kingdom

In about 3200 B.C., a powerful king united the two kingdoms, and became the sole ruler of Upper and Lower Egypt. We call this king Menes, though the deeds he is supposed to have done may really have been the work of several different kings. Menes belonged to the falcon clan, and the falcon became the symbol of kingship in Egypt for the next 3000 years. This falcon-god was called Horus.

Menes built Memphis as the capital of his new, united country. He dammed the Nile to control the yearly flooding, so that the water was distributed more evenly over the land, and for a longer period. Already Egypt was a land rich in farm products; in the wonderful work of goldsmiths and coppersmiths; in art and in culture. The state was well organized and well run.

Much later, the kings of Egypt were called 'Pharaoh' by the people; but nowadays we

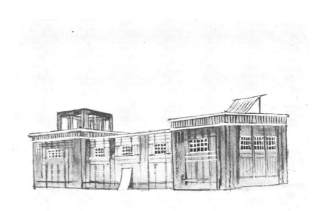

Egyptian house

Those who could afford to do so built themselves spacious houses of mud-brick and wood, with courtyards, pools and green gardens. For the next 3000 years, Egypt remained at this civilized level, in a way which the world has never seen since. Egyptian houses, temples, statues, paintings and tombs are among the most splendid ever created. Art and literature reached a very high standard.

Note that a nation does not have to have machines and electrical or atomic power to be civilized. At first the word just meant 'living in cities'.

The Narmer Palette

This is one of the oldest surviving pieces of carving from Dynastic Egypt. It shows Pharaoh Narmer (who may be the same as Menes) holding an enemy by the hair and striking him. This became a familiar attitude in later pictures of Pharaohs. The falcon sits near the king, and at the bottom lie dead enemy soldiers. Narmer here wears the White Crown of Upper Egypt. On the other side of the slate (not pictured here) he is wearing the Red Crown of Lower Egypt.

generally apply this name to all the rulers, from Menes onwards.

In a sense, the Pharaoh was not the most important person in the land, for he owed his throne to his queen. In ancient Egypt women were very highly respected, and all property was inherited through them. The Pharaoh was the husband of the queen, and did not rule because he himself had a right to the throne; he was the father of the next heiress, and *her* husband became the next Pharaoh. This meant that if a Pharaoh wanted his son to rule after him, the young man had to marry his own sister. And if a Pharaoh's wife died, he often married his own daughter in order to remain the rightful ruler.

Nevertheless, the Egyptian people honoured the Pharaoh, and not his wife, as the head of the country. They thought of him as a god whom they could actually touch and see. Besides having Horus as his own 'personal' god, he was to the Egyptians the living representation of the sun-god, Re, without whom there would be no life. When a Pharaoh died, they said that he joined the sun on its daily journey across the sky.

The Egyptians were a people who respected tradition, and throughout these 3000 years they did not change their way of life very much. So we can talk about their religion and their customs in a general way, and what we say will apply (with only minor variations) for any part of their 3000 years of civilization.

Priests and gods

The religion of the ancient Egyptians is difficult for us to understand—there seem to be so many different gods and goddesses. One reason for this is that when Menes united the clans, all their various gods had to have some part in the new religion and government. Later, other gods were 'imported' from foreign lands, and these were worshipped together with the old gods. The Egyptians were a very religious people, and their gods brought comfort and hope, and strength to endure the terrible years when the Nile did not flood properly, and there was famine. In countries south of Egypt, the kings were the 'rain-makers', who were supposed to be able to control the weather; in Egypt, where it hardly ever rained, the Pharaoh was the 'controller of the Nile'.

Next to the Pharaoh, the priests became the most important people in the land, not only because they talked to the gods, but also because

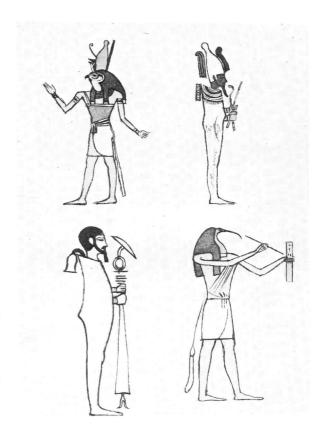

Gods of Egypt

There were hundreds of gods in Egypt, all with their functions and duties. Some of the most important are:

Horus; (top left) the falcon-headed god, was the Pharaoh's own god and is often seen wearing the Double Crown of Egypt.

Osiris; (top right) murdered by his brother, his body was cut up and scattered through the land. Isis, his sister-wife, collected the pieces together and buried them. Osiris was the god of the next world and the judge of souls.

Ptah; (bottom left) was a powerful god often shown wearing a Pharaoh's beard. He was the protector of craftsmen.

Thoth; (bottom right) the ibis-headed god of wisdom, learning, medicine, magic and all the skills practised by the priests.

Anubis; the jackal watched over all the ritual concerned with the dead.

they could predict flood or famine. As in Sumeria, they in fact did this by observation—that is they noticed how the stars and planets behaved, they noticed how the river flooded every year at about the same time (when the stars were in the same place in the sky), and they used this knowledge to tell people when to sow their crops. The farmers, and even the more educated townspeople, thought the priests had learnt their wisdom directly from the gods.

It was from these wise men that the Pharaohs learnt how to govern the country. A Pharaoh's training was very thorough. He had lessons in reading and writing; he was taught to hunt, to throw the light spear called a javelin, and to fight with sword and shield; and he was instructed in the details of his religion. The Egyptians liked to think that their Pharaoh was as wise and as fit as possible. They said of one of them that he could 'shoot at a metal target of one palm's thickness and pierce it in such a way that his arrow would stick out on the other side'. And of another Pharaoh: 'There is nothing that he did not know, he was Thoth in everything.'

Writing

Egyptians were already familiar with writing in the days of Pharaoh Menes. They had simply copied the Sumerians' idea of drawing little pictures of whatever they wanted to record. But whereas the Sumerians simplified their picture-writing very early, the Egyptians continued to write in pictures for centuries.

Each little picture originally stood for one word, or for one idea. Scribes (professional writers or clerks) recorded the major events of a Pharaoh's reign, and even the daily lives of the noblemen. Sculptors and artists recorded their history on the walls of temples and tombs. The quotations in this chapter and in Chapter 5 come from these inscriptions.

Later the Egyptians did develop a simpler form of writing, though they still used many of the same pictures. Instead of writing a different picture for each word, they used pictures to represent sounds as well as ideas. It is as if in English we wrote the word *idol* by drawing pictures of an eye and a doll, like this:

Later still, many of the pictures stood for single letters, or combinations of letters, almost like our alphabet — so then they had pictures which were words, pictures which were sounds, and pictures which stood for letters, all in one piece of writing. This is what makes hieroglyphics, as these kinds of symbols are called, so difficult for us to read.

Papyrus

The papyrus plant had many uses in ancient Egypt. The stems were cut and bound together to make baskets and containers, and were even used in building the pleasure-boats, fishing-boats and ferries which sailed on the Nile. The stalks were also hammered into a pulp to make a kind of paper. (*Papyrus* comes from the old Greek name for the plant: from it we get our word 'paper'.)

The papyrus lakes of Egypt have disappeared now. The level of the surrounding land dropped, and the sea came in, killing the plants. Other lakes which existed in the days of the ancient kingdoms have since dried up.

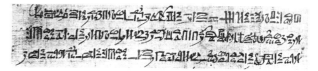

Hieratic script

For more 'day-to-day' writing — lists, or letters, the Egyptians sometimes used a much simpler and more flowing form of writing called 'hieratic'.

Besides learning to write, the Egyptians learnt to count and to reckon. They were very good at this, as we can see when we look at the monuments and pyramids they built. Their mathematicians, without our knowledge of algebra or trigonometry, worked out angles and heights to a fraction of a centimetre.

Noblemen sent their children to school when they were about seven years old. They became the priests, the doctors, the scribes, and the tax-collectors of Egypt. To maintain a high standard, the children were made to work very hard. An Egyptian proverb said: 'A youngster's ear is on his back; he listens when he is beaten.'

Craftsmen, artists and peasants

The upper classes, then, were all literate and often educated. Just below them in the social scale came the craftsmen, most of whom were not literate. The sculptors carved enormous granite statues of the Pharaohs, their queens, and the gods; the goldsmiths, coppersmiths and gem-cutters made beautiful delicate jewellery for rich noblemen and their wives to wear, and cups, bowls and ornaments for their houses. Builders hardened mud-bricks in the sun, and built spacious houses and temples. Gardeners planted trees and dug ornamental pools in the noblemen's gardens. Carpenters carved wood, brought all the way from Lebanon in Syria, and made furniture, which they often inlaid with precious stones, or covered with sheets of thin gold.

Most of the Egyptians—the ordinary peasants—did not have any of these things. They worked in the fields, repaired canals, fed the animals, took their rations of food in payment, and went home at night to their crowded little mud huts.

Dynastic Egypt

Right at the end of Egypt's long civilization, a priest named Manetho was ordered by his Pharaoh to write down the history of the country from the very beginning. Manetho very reasonably divided the rulers up into families, and called each line of rulers of the same family a dynasty. We still use his divisions now, because modern scholars have found that they are remarkably accurate. Menes, according to this list, was the first king of the First Dynasty, and Manetho himself lived during the Thirty-first Dynasty. We also divide the 3000 years up into 'kingdoms'. We call the three periods of Egypt's greatness:

The Old Kingdom	about 2800–2180 B.C.
The Middle Kingdom	about 2130–1780 B.C.
The New Kingdom	1580–1080 B.C.

The gaps between the kingdoms were periods in which weak Pharaohs allowed the country to fall into disorder and civil war, and invading armies took control.

In the next chapter we will see how Egypt was a country concerned with its own affairs in the Old Kingdom, and how gradually the people came into contact with other civilizations and peoples beyond their borders.

Egyptian Dress

Egyptian clothing was made of linen so finely woven that it might have been silk. Both men and women wore simple garments. The Pharaoh, the nobles and the officials all wore a short belted skirt, folded and pleated, sometimes into a stiff triangular 'apron' in front. Later on the fashion was to wear the skirt longer. Men often wore a striped cloth on their heads.

On ceremonial occasions the Pharaoh wore the Double Crown on his head, and a false beard was strapped to his chin. When he was not wearing the Crown, he wore an ornament called a 'uraeus'. It was shaped like the heads of two snakes, the cobra and the viper.

Women wore a long garment reaching the ankles, pleated and folded according to the latest fashion. Both men and women wore wigs in public. Women used cosmetics, and outlined their eyes with powdered malachite—a form of copper-ore—as protection against too much sun, and against eye-disease.

Labourers and slaves sometimes wore a loincloth round the waist; but many of them were completely naked.

Chapter 5 The Three Kingdoms

The Old Kingdom c.2800 – 2180 B.C.
The Egyptians of later ages came to think of the Old Kingdom as the Golden Age, when Egypt was at her most glorious. The state was highly organized, and there were many officials working in the government offices. The country was divided up into 20 'nomes' or districts, and administered by officials called 'nomarchs', all of whom were under the control of the central government at Memphis. The nomarchs were responsible for seeing that the canals were kept in order, and that the people paid their taxes regularly.

Taxes were paid 'in kind', that is in goods not money, and tax-collectors had the difficult job of receiving cattle, grain, tools, carvings and flax from each wage-earner in every home. Money – that is, coins with a certain fixed value – had not yet been invented. Early trade in the Nile Valley was carried on by barter. People exchanged property with each other. Later, the Egyptians adopted a system whereby every article to be exchanged had a fixed 'price'. A spiral or twist of copper was used as a measure, or unit. Thus a cow might be worth 40 units, and would buy (say) 4 lengths of fine linen, each worth 10 units. The units *themselves* were not used for buying and selling. The Egyptians did not think of the much simpler plan of using them as money.

The pyramids
Much of the wealth of the country went into the building of huge tombs for the Pharaohs. They were buried with all their property around them, for, like the Sumerians, the Egyptians believed that in the next world the Pharaoh would need his furniture and clothes, his servants and his food (though in Egyptian graves, the servants were represented by statues).

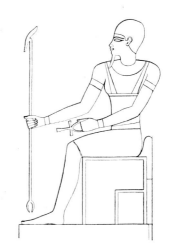

Zoser's step-pyramid and the god Imhotep
The step-pyramid of the Third Dynasty Pharaoh Zoser was designed by a nobleman named Imhotep. He was the 'Chief of the Works of the King of Upper and Lower Egypt'. The Egyptians remembered Imhotep for centuries because of his skill in medicine, and his knowledge of literature. They even worshipped him as the god of medicine, and associated him with Thoth, god of wisdom. Pilgrims went to his burial place for thousands of years, bringing mummified ibises to his grave as gifts.

Menes' grave was a flat square tomb called a 'mastaba'. Later rulers built other smaller squares on top of the mastaba, making a tall structure which we call a 'step-pyramid'. They look rather like ziggurats, but they were tombs, not temples.

The pyramids at Giza, near Cairo, tombs of the Old Kingdom Pharaohs Khufu, Kaefre and Menkaure*, were the next development in tomb design. The steps of a mastaba were filled in to make a smooth slope, which was coated with white limestone. Most of the limestone has gone now, so we have no proper idea of the effect these shining white pyramids had on the people living 4000 years ago. They must have been dazzling in the harsh Egyptian sunlight.

The Pharaoh himself watched his tomb being built, and his people often had to labour for as long as 20 years to ensure that their god-king would 'live for ever'. It was important to *them*, because of his relationship with the sun-god. So every winter season, some of the labourers rowed boats carrying great blocks of granite up the river from quarries in the eastern hills; others dragged the blocks from the banks of the Nile to the site of the new pyramid. The mere size of the work is astonishing to us today. These men cut stones with knives that were made only of soft bronze, with harder inset cutting-edges; and the stones themselves were so hard that they have lasted until now without 'weathering'. They had no pulleys, or cranes for lifting, and no mechanical engines. They put all the huge stone blocks into place with the help of wooden rollers and levers only. Yet they built the pyramids so accurately that it would be hard for us (with all our machines) to better them.

Until the nineteenth century A.D., when the Americans began to construct 'skyscrapers', Khufu's pyramid was the highest building in the world. His son Khaefre built the famous Sphinx next to his pyramid; the face of the Sphinx is probably a portrait of the king.

Since the Pharaoh had absolute authority, he was able to command his subjects to work for him on the time-consuming task of building his pyramid. He was their god, and they could not complain. His councillors and officials were often members of his own family, and the Vizier (a sort of Prime Minister) was often his eldest son.

---

*They are sometimes called Cheops, Chephren and Mycerinus, because this is how the Greeks later spelt their names.

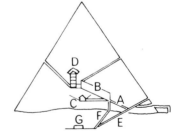

A Ascending gallery
B Grand gallery
C Queen's Chamber
D King's Chamber
E Descending gallery
F 'Well'-escape route
G Unfinished Chamber

The pyramids of Giza and the Sphinx
These are the pyramids we know so well today. But they are by no means the only ones still standing in Egypt. In ancient times there were pyramids stretching for 100 miles up the Nile. The picture at the top shows the Sphinx with the pyramids behind before the site was excavated in A.D. 1925. Below it, the full splendour of the Sphinx can be seen after the removal of thousands of tons of sand and earth.

A cross-section of Khufu's pyramid shows that it is not all hollow. The King's Chamber was shut off by workmen with huge granite blocks, pushed up into the gallery marked B. They then 'escaped' down the tunnels marked F and E, which they blocked up behind them.

Each nome was administered in much the same way, often by members of one family.

In the Old Kingdom, the whole of Egypt was working for the Pharaoh. To us, now, this seems an incredible way of life. But it certainly united the country and made it prosperous.

Once the state of Egypt had been organized, and was running smoothly, the Pharaohs began to look beyond their borders. In the north there were already small towns on the eastern shores of the Mediterranean. The land known as Lebanon was famous for its beautiful trees, and as early as the Second Dynasty (about 3000 B.C.) the townsmen of Byblos, on the coast, exported wood to Egypt. (Egypt had very little wood of her own.)

The copper on which Egypt's prosperity depended, and the precious stone called turquoise for ornaments, came from Sinai, across the Red Sea. This desert land was so hot and uncomfortable to live in, that the Egyptians used only slaves or criminals as their miners. Thousands of them died in the terrible heat, and there was always a demand for fresh slaves. Most of these unfortunate people came from the south and west. Egyptian slave-raiders crossed the borders into Nubia and Libya, and drove their African captives to the waiting ships on the Red Sea. Towards the end of the Old Kingdom, caravans were travelling deep into the heart of Africa, and may even have reached the Congo forest.

Then the Kingdom collapsed completely. The nomarchs became too powerful for the Pharaohs to control properly; royal authority became weaker, and finally the Kingdom came to an end, as each nomarch tried to gain more territory for himself. 'The land trembled . . . all the people were in terror, the villages were in panic, fear entered into their limbs.'

Mummy

Pyramids, mummies, sun-worship and building in stone were all 'invented' just before the Old Kingdom began. A mummy (so named from an Arabic word meaning 'tar') is a dead body which has been embalmed.

The Egyptians soaked the bodies of their Pharaohs and important nobles in ointments, and bound them in linen, before putting them into their tombs. Many of these bodies have been found wonderfully preserved in the hot dry air of Upper Egyptian pyramids and rock-graves. The graves were on the western side of the river, towards the setting sun. New Kingdom Pharaohs and officials were buried in the Theban hills.

The Middle Kingdom c.2130–1780 B.C.

Surprisingly, Egypt survived 50 years of unrest and disturbances, and arose again, almost as splendid as before. The new Pharaohs of the Eleventh Dynasty built their capital at Thebes, in Upper Egypt; and because of this, Amun, the god of Thebes, became powerful. He was declared equal to Re, and all Middle Kingdom Pharaohs now worshipped Amun-Re, even though in the Twelfth Dynasty the court returned to Memphis once more. The priests of Amun were delighted, for their wealth and prosperity were greatly increased.

The noblemen of the land were more important than they had been in the Old Kingdom. They built themselves elaborately decorated tombs, in which painters drew pictures showing the way they lived. It is because of these pictures—many of which can still be seen in Egypt—that we have such a good idea of the lives of the ancient Egyptians. During this

41

period, the Pharaohs were buried in very modest pyramids, often built only of mud-brick.

Pharaohs and noblemen of the Middle Kingdom prided themselves on being kind and tolerant. It was a duty of the rich to feed the poor, and tomb-inscriptions like this are common:

> 'I grew corn, I loved Neper the grain god. In every valley the Nile greeted me. None hungered or thirsted during my reign.'

That was written in a Pharaoh's tomb: we can also read how noblemen comforted widows and looked after orphans, and how judges were upright in their decisions, and free from dishonesty. At the time of the Middle Kingdom, people believed that there was a life after death only for those who had been good on earth.

Now that less of the Pharaohs' time was occupied with pyramid-building, they could instead find out what was happening in the rest of the world. 'Travel' in ancient times either meant trading expeditions, or it meant armed invasion. The Middle Kingdom Pharaohs tried both. Their trading caravans travelled far into Nubia in search of gold; and their 'Byblos ships'* sailed across the Mediterranean to Crete for pottery and to Syria for wood and cloth, and to Punt for spices and plants, wild animals and ivory. Nobody knows exactly where Punt was. It may have been a name for many different ports in the Indian Ocean and the Red Sea, or it may have been a name for the coast of Somaliland.

As often happens, along with increased trade went a desire to gain more control over other countries. A Pharaoh of the Twelfth Dynasty, Senusret III, ordered his nomarchs to raise an army for him. It probably consisted of about 20,000 men. He armed them with bows and arrows, spears, clubs and shields, and personally led them by boat across the Mediterranean to present-day Palestine. When they returned, after claiming their conquests for Egypt, they left envoys behind to represent the Pharaoh. Other troops were sent south during this dynasty, far into Nubia. They set up fortresses along the trade routes, and left a permanent guard of soldiers to protect them. Only genuine African traders were now allowed north of the First Cataract. To the west of Egypt, soldiers were constantly on the look-out for raiding Libyans.

*The people of Byblos built sea-going ships for the Egyptians, in exchange for farm produce and metal goods.

Kushites
Round about the time of the Eleventh and Twelfth Dynasties (Middle Kingdom) a new people arrived in Upper Nubia, south of the Second Cataract. The Kushites were very much influenced by the Egyptians. When the Egyptians left their lands in the seventh century B.C., they built their own capital Napata. They copied the Egyptian architecture and worshipped Egyptian gods. At the end of Egypt's history, Kushite kings ruled Upper Egypt as well as Kush.

Whenever they could, they turned them out of the oases in the desert, or captured them and made them work in the copper mines.

All the spoils of these campaigns were brought back to Egypt. Some were given as tribute to the gods, and so the priestly possessions grew even larger. Nomads living beyond the borders of Egypt heard of this marvellous kingdom, where there was so much wealth. It sounded to them like 'a land of plenty'. In times of drought and famine they crossed the terrible deserts as refugees, asking only to be allowed to live peacefully, and graze their flocks on the rich meadows of Egypt. These people were Semites from Palestine and North Arabia, and because of their arrival, many Semitic words enriched the Egyptian language.

The Hyksos kings

By about 1800 B.C., many of these Asian and Arabian refugees had come into Egypt to settle. Soon they were powerful enough to take over for themselves some of the rich lands of the Nile delta. Then more Asians poured in from the north-east, armed with iron weapons, and driving iron chariots drawn by horses. This was the very first time horses and wheeled vehicles had been used in Egypt, although the Sumerians had had them for over a thousand years. We call these Asiatic invaders the 'Hyksos'. They took over the whole of Lower Egypt, and although native Pharaohs continued to rule in the south, they had no real power. We do not know very much about the 200 years of Hyksos control, because they did not keep records, nor did they build tombs or temples inscribed with hieroglyphics. They ruled in Egypt at roughly the same time as the Babylonians were supreme in the lands of Mesopotamia.

The New Kingdom 1580–1080 B.C.
At last there arose a leader strong enough to drive out the Hyksos, and revive the old Egyptian ways and customs. The new Pharaohs recognized the importance of chariots and horses and bronze armour, and the weapons they now used to restore law and order were all copies of the Hyksos ones. When there was a firm government again, they marched into Palestine, Syria and Mesopotamia in an attempt to drive the hated Hyksos well away from their borders. Parts of all these countries came under Egyptian rule, and it is very likely that during part of its history Crete, and perhaps Cyprus also, had to pay homage to the Pharaoh. From now onwards Egypt had a regular army, in peace as well as in war. Nubia was colonized, and the Pharaoh appointed as his representatives there the 'royal sons of Kush'. These men were responsible for the administration of the south, and for organizing the great trade caravans.

The conquest of new lands meant that even more wealth flowed into Egypt. All the subject kings had to send yearly tribute to the Pharaoh. Sometimes also, the messengers of foreign lands brought costly presents, in order to persuade the Egyptians to trade with them. We hear that:

'. . . while he (the Pharaoh) was hunting elephants, envoys from Babylon brought him gifts of lapis-lazuli, and from the heart of Asia Minor the great king of the Hittites sent silver and precious stones'. (Lapis-lazuli is a deep blue semi-precious stone.)

Trade flourished; Nubians from the south brought gold and ivory, the hard wood called ebony, leopard skins and ostrich feathers to Thebes, and exchanged them for the superb work of the Egyptian craftsmen and artists. They also brought slaves to work in the copper-mines, and to become the household servants, dancers and musicians in rich Egyptian homes.

Egyptian ships once more sailed up the east coast of the Mediterranean to Byblos, and returned with cargoes of 'cedar of Lebanon'. Sea-going ships brought back from Crete and Greece barrels of olives and wine, and bales of cloth. Hatshepsut, a queen of the Eighteenth Dynasty, imported from Punt:

'. . . fresh myrrh trees, ebony and pure ivory, with green gold of Emu, with cinnamon wood, with two kinds of incense, eye-cosmetic, with apes, monkeys, dogs, and the skins of the southern panther.'

A ship of Queen Hatshepsut being laden with treasures from Punt

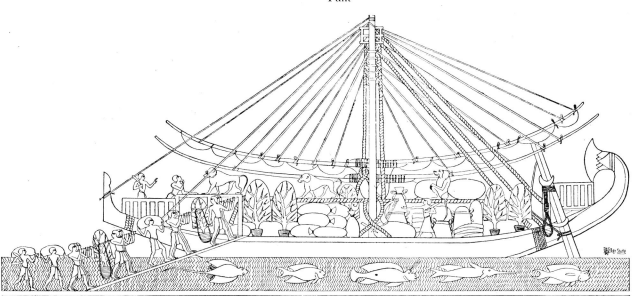

She wrote this inscription on the walls of her temple at Thebes, and planted the myrrh trees in the temple gardens.

Temples and rock-tombs

Huge sums of money were constantly being spent on the temples, and on paying priests to continue with prayers and offerings for the Pharaohs of the past. The burial customs changed in the New Kingdom, and labourers now cut great caves out of the rocks in the Theban hills. The walls were covered with inscriptions, and all the rooms were filled with furniture, clothing, food, flowers and statues. Then the cave-mouth was closed with rocks and plaster, and disguised to make it as unnoticeable as possible. Tomb-robbery was by now a great 'occupation' in Egypt, and watchmen were constantly on the look-out for thieves. Hardly any of the rich furnishings or jewels – or even the mummies themselves – were left untouched. There may of course still be graves that have not been found at all, but it is doubtful.

Rich people in Egypt during the New Kingdom lived in great luxury. They held parties, went for excursions on the river, were entertained by musicians and dancers, and hunted for wild animals or game-birds. There was plenty of food and drink for them, some of it imported. They had no wish to change their lives, and very little curiosity about peoples living outside Egypt. If a new god was introduced from abroad, they accepted him, but continued to worship the old gods as well.

Pharaoh Akhenaten, in about 1375 B.C., tried to introduce a new god called Aten as the sole god of Egypt. After his death the angry priests of Amun tore down his shrines, and re-established the old gods. They were too powerful, and too fond of power, to allow such a basic change.

So on the whole, Egyptian customs had not differed much since the Giza pyramids were built – and to a man living in Queen Hatshepsut's reign, that was a thousand years ago.

The end of the New Kingdom

In spite of increasing contact with the peoples

Tutankhamun's mask
One tomb that robbers did not strip was that of a young Pharaoh named Tutankhamun, who reigned in about 1360 B.C. The tomb was found only 54 years ago, and in it were magnificent pieces of furniture, jewellery, pottery, statues and weapons. The Pharaoh's mummy was still undamaged. A mask of gold and lapis-lazuli covered his face, and his body was encased in a series of three golden coffins or caskets, one inside the other, carved in the shape of a man, and richly decorated. All this treasure was buried 'for ever', which tells us how very wealthy the country must have been. The contents of the tomb are now on show in the Cairo Museum.

of the outside world, Egypt was still reluctant to learn new ways. The scribes copied out old inscriptions instead of inventing new ones, and although the Egyptians used many words borrowed from their neighbours, they did not change their writing very much. It seems to us that they could easily have made the next important step and invented an alphabet, but they never did so.

Even their attempts at colonizing other countries became half-hearted, and they were finally turned out of all the lands they had conquered. All real progress now took place in the new vigorous nations north and east of Egypt – countries which were later to conquer Egypt completely, and bring an end to the ancient civilization for ever.

Chapter 6 Nations of the Near East

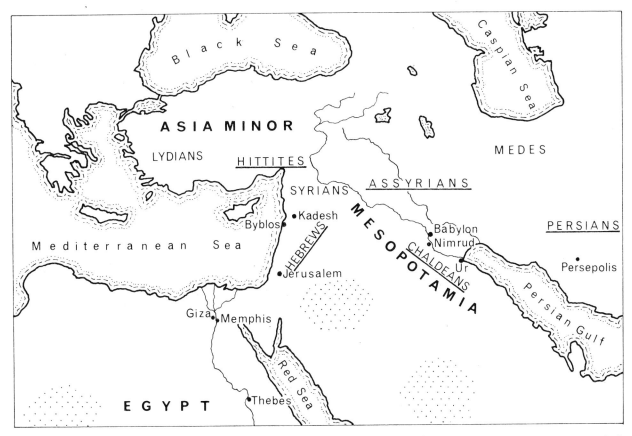

Map of the Ancient Near East
During the time of the New Kingdom in Egypt, the most powerful nations of the Near East were, in turn, the Hittites, the Assyrians, and the Persians. The Hebrews, as we shall see, were less powerful. They are important to us for a completely different reason.

THE HITTITES were a tough warrior nation. They were the first great western peoples to use horses—long before the Hyksos invasion of Egypt. Their soldiers poured into Babylon in about 1580 B.C., and 30 years later Egypt had to make a treaty with them.

THE ASSYRIANS were in many ways like the Babylonians, speaking a closely related language, and using the same cuneiform script for their writing. They too invaded Babylon, and broke the power of the Hittites. Their troops were well-disciplined, and for 700 years they were very much feared because of their great cruelty.

Sennacherib, who ruled the Assyrians from 705–681 B.C., was a terrible destroyer. Here is an ancient description of the damage he was

Egyptians fighting Hittites at Kadesh

Rameses II, pharaoh of Egypt, fought king Muwatallis of the Hittites in 1285 B.C., at the Battle of Kadesh. The Hittites struck the first blow, but the Egyptians said this was not fair, as they were not ready! Rameses boasted about this battle for the rest of his life, and he ordered hundreds of inscriptions, praising his courage, to be carved on all his new buildings; but we also have an account of the battle in cuneiform, written by the Hittites. The battle really ended when both sides agreed to stop, but Rameses had to sign a treaty with Muwatallis' son. Then, to seal the agreement, he married one of the Hittite princesses.

proud of having done in Babylon:

'Through the midst of that city I dug canals; I flooded the site with water: so that in days to come the place of that city, its temples and gods shall not be remembered, I completely blotted it out with flood-water.'

The Assyrians laid siege to Jerusalem, the capital of the Hebrews, with a new kind of weapon—a battering-ram on wheels. This was a heavy beam with an iron head used for breaking down walls or gates. In 667 B.C. they conquered Egypt, and divided the land into 22 districts under Assyrian governors. Right at the end of the great Assyrian empire there ruled a king named Assurbanipal. He came to the throne in 668 B.C. He was a well-educated and wise man, anxious that his country should live in peace. He collected all the old Sumerian texts he could find, and made a library which contained 22,000 tablets. Many of these tablets were found recently in the ruins of Assurbanipal's palace, and have since been studied by our scholars.

THE CHALDEANS retook Babylon, and rebuilt it. Then another people conquered both the Assyrians and the Chaldeans. They were

THE PERSIANS, a people with a new religion called Zoroastrianism (after its founder Zoroaster), who swept across Asia Minor in five short years. Egypt and Babylonia were among the countries which became Persian provinces, or *satrapies*, ruled by governors called satraps.

The Persians 550–520 B.C.

Cyrus the Great, King of Persia, was perhaps the wisest of all Emperors. He found that the towns he conquered were in many ways more civilized than his own, so he allowed them to continue with their own customs. He did not interfere with their government, or with their religion. As long as the conquered nations were loyal to Persia, paid their taxes, and sent soldiers to fight in his armies, they could live as they liked. The Babylonians, the Egyptians, the Syrians and the Lidyans were no match for the expert Persian archers. All these countries had to pay tribute to the Persians — a people they all thought of as 'barbarians'.

The Chaldeans had built a mighty wall round three sides of the new Babylon, and the waters of the river Euphrates guarded the fourth side. But Cyrus, according to one story, dug a channel and diverted the river away from the city. His armies entered Babylon by crossing over the dry river-bed without a fight. In Babylon, Cyrus found hundreds of Hebrew slaves, sons and daughters of the prisoners taken when Nebuchadnezzar, Chaldean king of Babylon, captured Judah, 50 years earlier. Cyrus allowed them to go free, and some of them made the long journey back to Jerusalem.

Cyrus's son, Cambyses, had to make a treaty with the king of Arabia before he could take his soldiers over the burning desert to conquer the Egyptians. The Arabians, in return for peace in their own lands, supplied him with camels, to carry men and equipment and precious water. The Persian troops entered Egypt, and soon captured Memphis. The Egyptians had already managed to drive out the Assyrians, but now there was no strong Pharaoh to bind the country together, and keep out the new invaders.

But the new occupation was not entirely bad for Egypt. The Persians realized that a contented satrapy was better than a discontented one, so they worked hard to raise the standard of living in Egypt. Once more there was a healthy trade with Asia, and the neglected temples and statues and monuments were repaired.

Now that they had gained a large part of the ancient civilized world, the Persians started to learn from the peoples they had conquered. They adapted the old Sumerian cuneiform writing, and made from it a simplified syllabary* of

*A syllabary is a set of symbols representing syllables or parts of a word.

only 41 symbols — a great advance on the hundreds of symbols the Sumerian school-children had had to learn. We owe our knowledge of Sumerian literature to Assurbanipal the Assyrian, but we discovered how to interpret their writing because of the Persians. For King Darius I, who followed Cambyses, ordered a huge inscription to be cut in a rock. In order that everyone would be able to understand it, the sculptors engraved the inscription three times — in Persian, in Sumerian, and in another eastern

Zoroaster

We do not know very much about Zoroaster, the founder of the Persian religion. He probably lived in about 600 B.C. In this religion there were two gods, Ahura Mazda, all-good, lover of truth, and god of purity and light; and his opposite, Ahriman, who was the creator of evil. Zoroaster taught that all men should be on the side of good. Evil to him was to be conquered by fighting against it continuously.

Zoroaster hated the old Persian beliefs, which included the burning of animals to keep the gods contented. His religious ideas spread right across Asia from the Aegean Sea to India. In India today we have the last remaining worshippers of his god — they are the Parsees.

47

Persepolis

Cyrus's grandson, Darius I, brought together masons, carpenters, goldsmiths and iron-workers from Egypt, Babylon, Assyria and Greece to build his capital city, Persepolis.

He was immensely rich, and he produced gold coins for use in trading. (He had copied the idea of money from the Lydians.) He also started a banking system, and our word 'cheque' comes from Persia.

---

language called Susian. This triple inscription was deciphered in the nineteenth century A.D. Linguists trained to decipher scripts and who could read ancient Persian worked out the meaning of the parallel text in Sumerian. So now they had plenty of clues to help them translate the tablets they had found in the ruins of Assurbanipal's library.

Besides taking over cuneiform writing from the Sumerians, the Persians also used the Egyptian calendar, and their scholars learnt Egyptian astronomy and medicine. The artists copied Assyrian sculpture, and the builders built temples and columns like those of the Egyptians. The Persians were great imitators, and their own capital city benefited from the centuries-old knowledge of earlier civilizations.

In order to reach their satrapies more easily, the Persians built excellent roads. One road stretched all the way from Egypt, through Babylon to India. On these roads there were staging-posts or stopping-places where messengers were given fresh horses and food.

In Dynastic Egypt, some of the Pharaohs tried to build a permanent canal between the Red Sea and the Nile. For lack of proper attention, it was always falling into disuse. Now the Persians rebuilt it, and widened it to allow two huge rowing galleys to pass each other. By using the canal, traders could reach Punt by boat without having a long walk overland to the Red Sea.

But an empire created so quickly depended very much on the quality of its leaders. The army consisted mainly of foreign soldiers, though the king himself had a bodyguard of Persians called 'The Immortals'. The foreign soldiers naturally felt more loyalty for their own countries than for Persia, and could only be kept obedient by strict discipline. Persia needed time, and a series of strong kings, for her new satrapies to settle down. But as we shall see in Chapter

8, only 40 years after the Persians captured Memphis, a new king tried to enlarge the empire by further conquests to the west. He wrongly believed that the Persians were too strong for any enemy to resist.

The Jewish People and their religion

We have already talked about a people called the Hebrews, who also lived in Asia Minor at this time. They are not remembered for their conquests, or their worldly power. They were

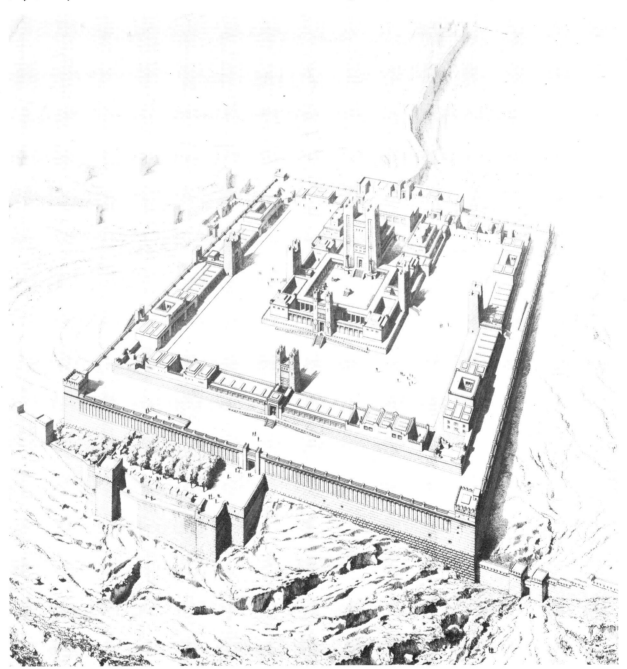

The Jewish Temple at Jerusalem

During the migration from Egypt the Jews used a kind of tent, called the Tabernacle, as their holy place; it housed the Ark containing the Covenant of the Law. Later this tent became the model for the great Temple of King Solomon who built it about 950 B.C. King Nebuchadnezzar of Babylon destroyed it in 486 B.C.

After the Babylonian captivity had ended in 539 B.C. the Second Temple was built. (The picture above is a reproduction of it.) About 20 B.C. Herod, King of the Jews, rebuilt this Temple on a larger and grander scale, but it was destroyed finally when the soldiers of the Roman Emperor Titus captured the city in A.D. 70.

quite unlike the Hittites, the Assyrians, or the Persians, for they did not try to enlarge their territory, or enslave other peoples. Yet in the history of the world they have played a great part: they have left us a religion which is a living faith for millions of people today—and from which two other present-day world religions stemmed.

The Hebrews (or Israelites) were a small nomadic tribe who came to settle in southern Palestine. During the early part of their history, the Pharaohs enslaved them as labourers for building temples and statues; according to Biblical tradition, Moses led them out of this capitivity and into the wilderness where they wandered for 40 years with their flocks through Arabia and up towards Mesopotamia and Palestine. During this time Moses was their leader through whom God made a Covenant with the Hebrews. The main tenets of this Covenant were the Ten Commandments, the first two were

> Thou shalt have no other gods but me
> Thou shalt not make to thyself any graven image . . .

In these statements are contained the essence of the first truly monotheistic religion and the laws which make up the backbone of modern Judaism as well as Christianity. Moses guided the Hebrews in the practice of their new Faith; much of Deuteronomy is believed to be his.

The various Arabian nomads worshipped thousands of different mountain spirits as did other tribes. The concept of a god without physical existence but who is everywhere and in the heart of each individual was, thus, difficult to grasp. Akhenaten, an Eighteenth Dynasty Pharaoh of Egypt, had had the idea of a single god, but even he used the image of the sun to symbolize him. The widespread habit of idol worship is illustrated by the Hebrews' own faithless construction of the Golden Calf whilst Moses communed with God.

At the end of his life Moses pointed out to the Israelites the rich plains of Canaan in Palestine, and told them that God had led them into the Promised Land. The Israelites settled in Palestine, and they lived side by side with the Canaanites, who already had towns and villages there. Some Israelites remained tent-dwellers until about 1000 B.C., when a warrior-king

named David captured the Canaanite town of Jerusalem and made it the capital of a new united country. The Israelites and the Canaanites became one people. King David ruled over the whole of present-day Palestine, and grew rich by trading with Egypt and Babylonia, and by allowing these countries to use his ports.

In 700 B.C. Israel fell to the Assyrians, and then Jerusalem itself was captured by the Chaldeans in 588 B.C. We have already seen how Cyrus, King of Persia, took Babylon, and allowed the Israelites to go home again. During the unsettled times when Assyrians and Chaldeans were overrunning the country, the only thing that kept the Israelites united was their faith in Yahweh. Many times some of them had returned to worshipping other gods, particularly the 'baals' of the Canaanites. But their prophets (people who had a religious conviction that they could save their country from destruction) demanded that the Israelites return to the worship of Yahweh. They condemned the rich landlords, and told the people that Yahweh was punishing them for their sins by allowing their enemies to triumph.

Judaism was a personal religion. That is to say, every man went on believing in the power of Yahweh, even when he was far from his own country. In other lands, a man who went to live away from home would adopt the gods of his new town. The Israelites did not do this. Some of their finest writings show that even in captivity they continued to believe in Yahweh. From that time right up to the present, the Jews (as they are now called) have been a scattered people, rather than a 'nation', united only in their faith. Since 1948 some of them have created a national state, Israel, including what used to be the old land of Canaan, and call themselves Israelis.

The Bible begins with an account of the beginning of the world. In this story, God made the world in six days, and rested on the seventh day. In remembrance of this, the Jews kept (and still keep) Saturday as a holy day, on which they do no work. The idea of a holy day was copied by people of other religions, and even by people with no religion at all. So today we have one day in the week on which shops and offices are closed, and religious services are held. For Christians, and many non-Christians, the day of rest is Sunday.

Chapter 7 Far Eastern Religions

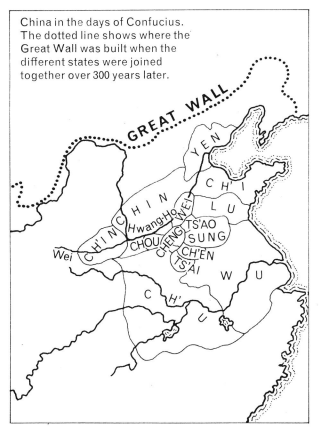

China in the days of Confucius. The dotted line shows where the Great Wall was built when the different states were joined together over 300 years later.

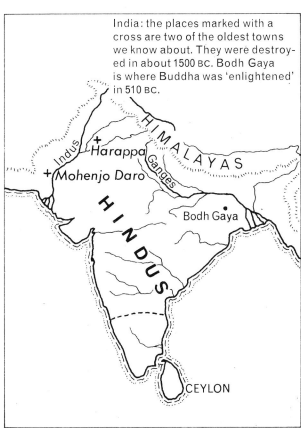

India: the places marked with a cross are two of the oldest towns we know about. They were destroyed in about 1500 BC. Bodh Gaya is where Buddha was 'enlightened' in 510 BC.

(1) CHINA

On the east coast of China, the first towns and villages were grouped along the river Hwang-Ho at about the time of Egypt's Middle Kingdom. (Look up the date of this on p. 38.) And although the Chinese did not build great temples or statues, as the Egyptians did, they already had all the basic characteristics of civilization which we have seen in North Africa and Mesopotamia.

The Chinese had their own system of writing, which by 1500 B.C. was so well developed that it must have been invented much earlier. They wrote down the names of their kings, and the lists of their crops, on pieces of bone, some of which have been found and read by our scholars. Chinese writing started as simple pictures, but was 'formalized' into a most elaborate system of 'characters' or symbols, which are used to this day. These characters are also really very complicated pictures.

Chinese wheelwrights (wheel makers) about 1700 B.C. built some of the earliest known wheels with spokes; and so their carts were lighter and

51

more comfortable than the Sumerian ones, with their heavy, solid wheels. The most commonly used animal for drawing carts, or even for riding, was the water-buffalo; though rulers and nobles used horses for their war-chariots. When a king died, his chariots and horses were buried with him in a deep pit, a custom which reminds us very much of the royal graves at Ur.

There was one other completely new discovery that the Chinese made—they found out how to spin the threads made by a certain kind of caterpillar called a silk-worm. They made clothes out of this spun thread, which we call 'silk', and by the 8th century B.C. they even used it as a fabric on which they painted pictures, or practised their beautiful writing with brushes and a kind of ink.

Travel outside China was very difficult—to the west are deserts and mountains, to the south, thick jungle-forest and mountains; and to the east the sea—but in spite of this, new ideas and inventions did sometimes travel between China and the west, particularly to and from India, the second of the two early eastern civilizations. The Chinese welcomed new ideas in astronomy from India, Persia, and even from as far away as Babylon.

Character

This is how the character for the word 'bright' probably developed:

The Chinese wrote first on bone, then they used bamboo strips. Later, they painted characters on silk panels.

Yang-Yin

The Chinese believed that all things could be represented by two forces, the Yang and the Yin. The Yang was heaven, male, hard, clear, bright; the Yin was earth, female, soft, dark. The two lived in harmony together, as their symbol shows. The Yang and the Yin together make a complete circle.

The Great Wall of China

Once China had been united, the emperor, Shih-Huang-Ti, built a 1,500 mile wall along the northern boundary, to keep out raiding nomads. It was built of earth and stone, with a roadway of bricks all along the top. At intervals there were watchtowers, where guards lit warning fires in times of danger.

Shih-Huang-Ti wanted his people to forget the past. He ordered all books, except those about medicine or agriculture, or divination, to be publicly burnt. Anyone who disobeyed was either burnt alive, or branded with a hot iron, and sent to work on the Great Wall.

The country was mainly agricultural, and the Chinese did not build great cities as other civilizations did. The nobles and lords built fortified castles, and their servants and tradesmen were grouped round the castles, outside the walls in a 'market' area. Everybody depended on everybody else, in a chain which led from the poorest slave or peasant, right up to the kings themselves. There was great respect for every kind of authority: a father was the master of his children, a lord had control over the lives of his servants, and the king had absolute power over all.

But the area over which a king ruled was limited. In time many states grew up in China, each with its own organization. For centuries the different states struggled against each other, and it was not until about 220 B.C. that China was united into one great empire.

Chinese religion and thought

The Chinese were a practical people, cheerful and hard-working. Their gods had always been the gods of nature: the soil, trees, mountains and streams. They used to regulate their daily lives by *divination*—that is, they tried to find out about the future. The Chinese method of divination was to write symbols on pieces of bone and then to break the bone to see where the cracks would come. They respected and revered the family, past, present and future. Each house had a little altar in one corner, and here the whole household prayed to the ancestors, whose names were written down and remembered for ever. The greatest sin a Chinese could commit was to dishonour his ancestors, by behaving in a manner they would have disapproved of. The family tradition thus had to continue so that each person who 'joined his ancestors' could be respected by his children and his children's children. So it was important to have children, and to bring them up to be well-behaved. Ancestor-worship was a good influence on behaviour, and it kept families together.

In ancient China, men loved to learn. The Chinese idea of a well-educated man was one who could write poetry, play music, paint, and talk intelligently. There were many schools where young men could go to listen to the words of wise teachers. Some of these teachers became famous, and their teachings have been remembered until the present day. One of them was a man named Kung-fu-tze, whom we call Confucius.

Halley's Comet
A few years before Shih-Huang-Ti's reign, the Chinese astronomers recorded the appearance of a great 'heavenly body'. We think this was the comet we now know as 'Halley's Comet'. In A.D. 1704 an English scientist named Edmund Halley discovered from old records that there is a comet which can be seen from our earth every 75 years. Its next appearance is due in 1985.

Confucius

53

The teachings of Confucius (552–479 B.C.)

Confucius was not a leader of religion, and he did not teach people about God, or a life after death. One of his pupils once asked him about this, and he replied, 'We have not yet learnt to know life. How can we know of death?' His teachings were about good government and social behaviour. The relationships between a man and his son, a ruler and his subjects, a husband and his wife, and an older and younger brother, should be the same; on the one hand kindness and thoughtfulness, and on the other, respect and obedience. Confucius believed that men should behave in society as they did in their own homes – the whole nation was one big family. 'Never do to others what you would not like them to do to you.' A good man, Confucius said, does not worry if his goodness is not noticed; he is more concerned with seeing goodness in other people.

Confucius thought that ceremonies and customs were important, and that the old Chinese traditions should be preserved. As a reward for honesty and right living, men might expect to have health and happiness in *this* life.

The Chinese listened to his words, and after his death his disciples (or followers) wrote them down. In time Confucianism became the state 'religion', and government servants had to pass examinations in the teachings of Kung-fu-tze before they could be promoted.

(2) INDIA

At about the time of Zoroaster in Persia (the sixth century B.C.), new ideas about religion, and the meaning of life, were forming in India as well as in China. People had reached a stage when they wanted to know why they were on earth at all, whether there was a life after death, and why they should behave well, rather than badly.

The ancestors of the Hindus had lived in India since about 1500 B.C. They had arrived as invaders from the north-west, travelling from central Asia through Afghanistan to north India. They had destroyed a people belonging to a much earlier civilization, based on the Indus Valley. They regarded themselves as better than the original inhabitants of India, many of whom still lived in villages and homesteads throughout the country, and this superiority gradually grew into the elaborate caste-system of the Hindus.

A caste was a group of people who all did the

Mencius

Mencius was a disciple of Confucius who carried on the teachings. This is one of his sayings: 'When Yi (a famous archer) taught people to shoot, he told them to pull the string on the bow its full length. The man who wants to cultivate himself must also develop himself to the full extent. A great carpenter teaches his apprentice to use squares and compasses. The man who wants to cultivate himself, must also have squares and compasses for his conduct.'

same traditional job, and who were linked together by marriage, and by custom. They were separated from people of other castes by strict rules, which forbade them even to eat with 'outsiders'. The top caste was that of the Brahmins or priests, and the lowest people of all had no caste – they were the 'untouchables'. In between were the warriors, merchants and farmers, servants and labourers. Nobody was allowed to marry outside his own caste; as a man was born, so he remained for the rest of his life.

By the sixth century B.C., Hinduism had developed into a very mixed religion. There were dozens of different gods and goddesses; there were legends of gods who were sometimes born as men; there were sacred cows; and there were cruel goddesses, whose mouths dripped blood. There was also a much more spiritual belief that the human soul, or Atman, could unite with the spirit of the universe, the Brahma. There are still so many different beliefs that Hinduism has been called 'the encyclopaedia of all religions'. Because of this wide variety of worship, Hindus are very tolerant of other religions.

Buddha (about 560–480 B.C.)

In northern India, near the Himalayas, around the middle of the sixth century B.C., there lived a Hindu king. In about 560 B.C., the king's wife bore him a son, who was called Siddhartha Gautama. One day, a holy man asked to see the child. The baby was carried to the holy man, and it put its feet on to his bowed head. The holy man immediately threw himself to the ground before the child, and when he saw this, the king did the same. The child's action was to them a sign that Siddhartha Gautama would become a religious teacher, greater than the holy man himself.

But the king wanted his son to become a great prince rather than a poor monk, so he asked the holy man, 'What shall my son see to make him retire from the world?' The holy man answered: 'The four signs—an old man, a sick man, a dead man, and a monk.'

So from that time onwards the king made sure that his son lived within the walls of the palace. The child was brought up in great luxury, and he never saw hunger, or sickness, or death. He grew up, married, and had a son of his own. Then one day, when he was 29 years old, he left the palace to see for himself what lay beyond its walls. And he saw 'the four signs'.

Now Hinduism taught that all people were tied to the Wheel of Life. When they died, they were born again, and so on for ever. The reward of a good life was a happy rebirth; and punish-

The Caste System

A Hindu tries hard throughout his life to gain 'merit' (spiritual credit) for himself so that his next life on earth will be better. This is the only way to belong to a higher caste. It is impossible for him to improve his present position, but good behaviour might be rewarded in his next reincarnation (rebirth). Voluntary work, such as sweeping the temple grounds, giving food to beggars and to priests, gains a man merit.

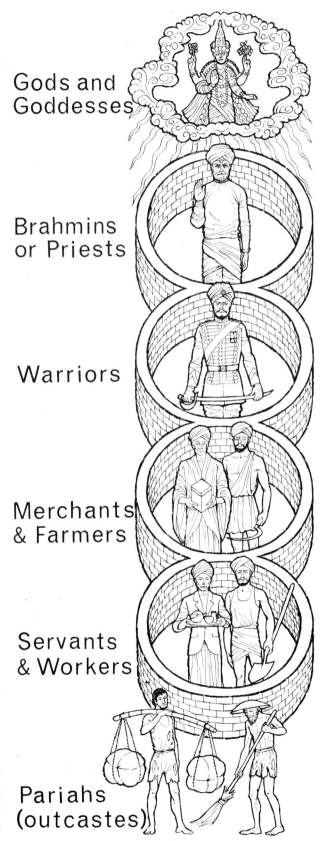

Gods and Goddesses

Brahmins or Priests

Warriors

Merchants & Farmers

Servants & Workers

Pariahs (outcastes)

ment for an evil life was to be born in a lower caste — or even as an animal or insect. If men had misfortunes, it meant that they had behaved badly in a previous life, but by effort and will-power they could deserve to be happier next time. Siddhartha Gautama saw that most of his fellow-countrymen lived miserable lives. There were so many poor and sick people. His pity and compassion for them was so great that he could no longer think of returning to the palace. He could not continue to enjoy such a life, now that he knew that youth and health led to disease, old age, and death. He left his family and his home, put on the yellow robes of a monk, and joined a group of holy men who wandered through the country teaching and thinking about religion. Gautama prayed and thought, and star-ved himself until he was as thin as they were. But still he did not find contentment. So he left the wandering monks and went to meditate by himself. For 49 days, the ancient writings tell us, he sat under a Bo tree, and at first he was tempted to return to his life of ease in the palace. But at the end of the 49 days he knew he had a message for the world. He was 'enlightened', (given spiritual understanding) and was from then on known as Buddha, 'the enlightened one'.

Buddha's way was neither the way of the rich in their palaces, nor the way of the starving holy men. He taught a 'middle way' between these two extremes. In his first sermon, preached to the monks he had once joined, he taught his Eight-fold Way. A man who followed the Eight-fold Way perfectly could become free of the Wheel of Life, and enter Nirvana, a state of union with the supreme spirit. Then he no longer had to be reborn to a life of suffering and disease.

'Where no thing is, where nothing is grasped, this is the Isle of No-Beyond, Nirvana I call it — the utter extinction of ageing and dying.'

Buddha did not believe that the ceremonies of the Hindu temples, and the worshipping of gods, were necessary or important. Indeed, there is no 'god' in the original Buddhism. It is a way of life, intended to give its followers eternal peace.

Buddha went about the country until he was 80 years old, preaching to his followers, and founding monasteries for the young men who wanted to study the Eight-fold Way. To follow Buddha, it was necessary to retire from the world completely. Buddhism changed after the Buddha's death, so that ordinary families could

Statue of Buddha
There are statues of the Buddha in all parts of the eastern world. Some show him standing, others sitting in the typi-cal cross-legged position shown above. Many of these statues are beautifully carved and coated with gold. Buddha's Eight-fold Way consisted of:

Right Knowledge	Right means of Livelihood
Right Intention	Right Effort
Right Speech	Right Mindfulness
Right Conduct	Right Concentration

also live their lives according to the Eight-fold Way, but without Buddha's other rules about men not marrying, and not working for money.

Missionaries carried the Way to China, Tibet, Ceylon, Burma, Java, Mongolia, Japan and Korea, and each of these countries changed the original teaching a little, so that it fitted in with their own ideas of how to live. The Chinese added Buddhism to Confucianism, and most of them followed both Ways.

But it seems that none of these peoples liked to have only a 'Way'. They wanted a religion, with temples and gods and goddesses. So by 200 B.C., there were statues of Buddha in Buddhist temples, and even a whole host of 'Bodhisattvas' or saints, who were worshipped as disciples of Buddha. They worshipped the Ami-tabha Buddha, a kind and merciful god who lived in the 'Pure Land' of heaven; and a goddess named Kuan Yin, who guided the good to ever-lasting life. So even the idea of Nirvana changed in these other countries. By 600 A.D., both Bud-dhism and Confucianism were very different from the teachings of their founders. In India itself, where Buddha had lived, his 'Way' grew so like Hinduism again that it has now almost died out.

GREECE & the NEAR EAST

B.C.
600

The FAR EAST

Greek city-states in
Italy and France

Hundreds of independent
states in China

Persians turn to Zoroastrianism

Excellent Chinese prose and poetry

Pythagoras' theorem..................

Democracy began in Athens...........
500

Confucius in China

Buddha in India

Battle of Marathon....................

Many Hindu writings composed

Parthenon built......................

Chinese calculated a
year of 365¼ days

Peloponnesian War began..............

Death of Socrates....................
400

Plato founded a school
called the Academy....................

Indians learnt to use iron
from Persia

Philip of Macedon invaded Greece

Chinese medicine very advanced

Alexander invaded Persia..............

Aristotle died........................

Ptolemies began to...................
rule Egypt
300

Chandragupta ruled all
North India

Seleucids powerful in Syria...........

Buddhism spread to
other countries;
Buddhist teachings
written down

China united

Archimedes invented a 'screw'
for lifting water to
a higher level........................
200

Buddhists started to
carve statues

57

Part III Greece and Rome

Chapter 8 The City States of Greece

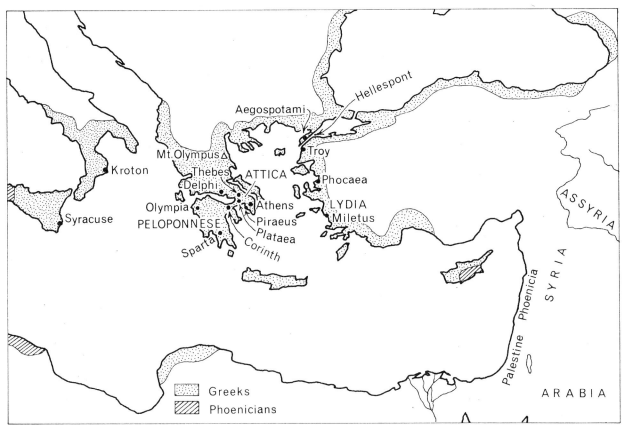

Greeks
Phoenicians

Let us now go westwards again to Europe, and see what was happening in the countries round the Aegean and Mediterranean Seas at the time of Confucius and Buddha. We have already seen how the Persians had enlarged their kingdom until by 520 B.C. they controlled a large part of Asia Minor. Read pages 34–37 again, and then look at the map above. You can see how the Persian empire looked across the sea towards the islands and bays of Greece. What sort of people lived on those tiny islands, separated from each other by the sea, and by craggy mountains? Even on the mainland, there were not

many fertile valleys, and after a few generations of cultivation, trees had become scarce, and so had grass. When the land could no longer support the population of Greece, small parties of people sailed away in little ships, to explore the lands to the east and west of their homeland.

Now there were Greek settlers on all the islands, and even on the coast of Asia Minor itself; there were Greeks on the shores of the Black Sea, and in present-day Italy and southern France. In all these places they built towns and set up their own governments. They took with them their customs and their legends, their skills and their traditions. They still thought of themselves as Greeks, even though their only connection with their homeland was through trade.

Greece, then, was not so much a nation, as a collection of city-states, each ruling itself, and each in turn rising to prosperity. Thebes*, Corinth, Miletus, Syracuse, Athens and Sparta were all at one time important centres, and the two we chiefly remember now are Athens and Sparta.

The emigration of Greeks to new colonies caused a lively trade to grow up, and soon the sea-faring states (and in particular Athens) were among the most important traders in the Mediterranean and even the Black Sea. They copied the new silver coins which the Lydians had invented, and with this new currency they bought goods to enrich their cities.

Athens, with its port at Piraeus, was a powerful state with a fine navy. Part of the population of Athens was always away at sea, carrying oil and wine to distant lands, and bringing to Athens the grain which she could not grow herself. The soil of Greece was more suited to growing olives and grapes than wheat, and people everywhere rely on a starchy food like wheat, or rice, or maize, for making their 'staple' diet of porridge or bread.

The Greeks and the Persians at War

Cyrus, king of Persia, fought a great battle with Croesus, King of Lydia, in Asia Minor. Now Croesus at that time was overlord of the Greek states in Asia, in an area that the Greeks called 'Ionia'. Croesus lost the battle, and his empire, including Ionia, was taken by the Persians. The Ionians hated their new masters, and they rebelled against them, which caused the Persians to punish them severely.

When the Athenians heard that their fellow-countrymen were being persecuted by the Persians, they sent ships across the sea, and then marched overland with the Ionians, and burnt the Persian city of Sardis. Cyrus's son, Darius I, was furious that such a small city-state as Athens should defy the might of Persia. His own people were all his slaves; they could be beheaded, or have their property taken from them, whenever he said the word. Now he was determined to force his rule on the Greeks too. He sent messengers to all the city-states, asking for tribute of earth and water, as a sign that they

*There are two towns called Thebes. The other one is in Upper Egypt.

Attic red-figured skyphos 490–480 B.C.
The Greeks made beautiful pottery jars to hold wine and olive oil for export. They were sometimes decorated with geometric designs, and sometimes with pictures of gods, people and animals. Whatever they did, the Greeks aimed to excel. The vase pictured above shows the Eleusinian goddesses, Demeter and Persephone.

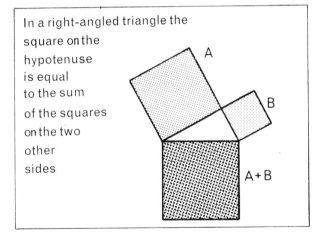

Pythagoras's Theorem
Every schoolboy or girl has heard of Pythagoras's theorem, illustrated here. Pythagoras lived in the sixth century B.C., and in about 530 he settled in Kroton, in southern Italy. He founded a brotherhood, which studied numbers, science, astronomy and music. Pythagoras believed that numbers were the purest of ideas, in which everything else could be expressed. His influence on the later Greeks was very great; it was not always a good influence, because they thought he was *totally* right, and did not develop his theories. Later generations of mathematicians were held back by this belief in the finished perfection of Pythagoras's ideas.

59

were willing to become Persia's allies. Many states hurriedly did as Darius asked, but it is said that the Athenians threw the messengers into a pit, and the Spartans pushed them down a well–telling them to collect their own earth and water!

Now there lived in Persia a man who had once been a leader in Athens. His name was Hippias, and he had been banished by the Athenians in 507 B.C. Hippias was an old man by this time (it was the year 490), but he still wanted to rule Athens. So he helped the Persian forces to find a good landing place, within easy reach of Athens, yet far enough away to be unguarded. On the map below you can see the route the Persians took.

When the Athenians heard that the Persians were landing at Marathon, a general named Miltiades ordered the young men to collect food for themselves, and march northwards to meet the enemy. If possible, he wanted to save Athens from being burnt and plundered as Eretria and Karystos had been. (See the map below.) They came to the plain of Marathon, and camped at the southern end, and here they were joined by men from the nearby small city of Plataea.

The Persians, as they began to line up in battle formation, with their best and strongest soldiers in the middle, suddenly saw an amazing sight: the little Athenian army was actually running straight towards them. The Persians thought the Greeks had gone mad, and they hastily got out their spears and shields and advanced to meet the running soldiers. Miltiades had put *his* strongest soldiers at the sides of the battle-line, and these men ran round the Persian army to left and right, and the Persians found themselves engaged in hand-to-hand fighting on all sides at

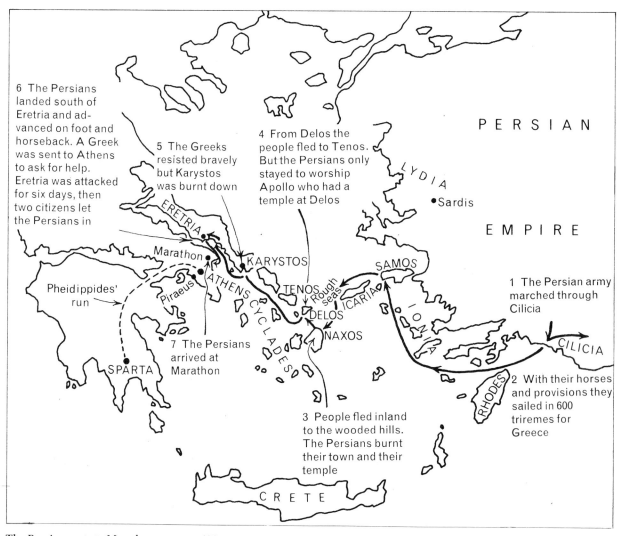

The Persian route to Marathon, summer 490 B.C.

once. By running towards the Persians, the Athenians had not allowed them time to let loose their usual deadly flight of arrows, and they were not nearly so good at fighting with swords. So the Persians panicked, and tried to retreat to their ships. But over 6000 of them were killed on the beaches or drowned in the sea. Herodotus, a Greek historian who recorded the Persian Wars, says that the Spartans were unable to join the Athenians until too late. Their lives were guided by the moon and the stars, and by custom they could not march until the moon was full.

After the horrible defeat at Marathon, the Persians sailed round to the Athenian port of Piraeus; but the Athenians, even though they were tired out by their hard fight on the beaches, had already returned there on foot, and were lined up on a hill overlooking the port. The Persian commander decided that one battle

against this determined people was enough, and he ordered his fleet to return home. Now all Greece was ready to defend the land from invasion by the Persian king. Ten years later, it was Sparta's turn to win glory in battle.

The Pass of Thermopylae

King Darius died, and his son Xerxes succeeded him. Xerxes was a cruel, vain man, who thought he could win any country for himself, so long as he had enough men. His soldiers, like those of Darius, came from all parts of his huge empire, and Herodotus says he even had Libyan and Ethiopian troops,

'... clothed in the skins of leopards and lions, and with long bows made of the stem of the palm-leaf ... They carried spears, the head of which was the sharpened horn of an antelope; and in addition they had knotted clubs. When

Bridging the Hellespont
The biggest problem for Xerxes was how to get his army across the Hellespont (see map on p. 58). He decided to build a bridge of boats across the water. Xerxes' first attempt failed, because a wind arose and blew the boats away. Herodotus says:
'Xerxes was full of wrath [anger], and straightway gave orders that the Hellespont should receive 300 lashes .... While the sea was thus punished by his orders, he likewise commanded that the overseers [foremen] of the work

should lose their heads.'
The second attempt succeeded. For each bridge his engineers tied over 400 boats together, with strong cables, and moored them with huge anchors. They laid planks across to form a road, and covered them with grass and brushwood. Then they built walls along each side, so that the horses and baggage animals could not see the water and be frightened. One bridge was used for the army; the other for the baggage animals and supplies. It took a whole week for the army to cross.

they went into battle they painted their bodies, half with chalk, half with vermilion [a brilliant red].'

This huge band of men, possibly about 300,000 altogether, with their horses and camels, their tents, baggage-animals, and food supplies, and their slaves carrying their armour, marched to fight the Greeks. It was the Athenians whom Xerxes especially wanted to punish; his army marched northwards through Thrace, and then followed the coastline towards Athens.

It was now August, 480 B.C., and the Olympic Games were being held. Nothing was allowed to stop the Games, so there was no proper Greek army ready to meet the Persians. In Sparta there was a religious festival, and so there also the main army could not move. But Leonidas, a king of Sparta, marched north in spite of the festival, with a picked band of soldiers called the 'Three Hundred' and many helots, or slaves. On the way other Greek soldiers joined this little band, and so the first people to meet the Persians were these few thousand men. Leonidas hoped that they would be able to hold the Persians in check until the Games and festival were over, to allow the other Greek armies time to come to their aid.

Leonidas picked a good place for his defence. Between the mountains and the sea there was a narrow pass called Thermopylae. Here the Phocians, in whose country it was, had built a wall to keep out raiders from the mountains. Leonidas and his men strengthened the wall, and waited in the pass for the Persians to arrive.

Xerxes, riding in a chariot behind the main army, was told that the pass ahead was blocked by Greeks. He decided to pitch camp, quite certain that the Greeks would run away when they saw how big his army was. He waited for five days. He laughed when he heard that the Spartans were practising gymnastic exercises, and combing their long hair. He was scornful when a Greek in his army told him this showed that the Spartans meant business; they always dressed their hair before a serious battle. Xerxes imagined that his men would deal with the Spartans in a few hours, and then he could march south to take the whole of Greece. On the sixth day, when it was clear that the Spartans would not run away, Xerxes ordered one of his army divisions to go forward and force their way through the Pass.

But Leonidas had chosen his battle-ground

The Olympic Games
Most of the city-states held yearly athletic meetings. There were also 'national' athletic meetings, in which Greeks from all over the country and the islands competed. The Olympic Games, held every four years, were the most famous. Everybody who could leave his work went to watch the athletes from his own town. During the Games, all quarrels and even wars were forgotten. The Greeks were completely absorbed in racing their horses and chariots, running, jumping, wrestling and throwing the discus. The winners were given a crown of olive leaves, and sometimes pottery jars of olive oil.

wisely. The Pass was so narrow that only a few of the enemy could approach at a time. Soon the entrance was piled high with enemy dead. When the Greeks wrote the history of this battle, they said that the Persian troops panicked, and would have run from the furiously fighting Spartans, but their officers were always ready with their long whips, and they desperately fought on. Xerxes now realized that the Spartans were tougher than he had thought. On the second day of the battle he sent in his own Persian guards, the Immortals[*], but even these experienced troops could not make the Spartans yield. Perhaps the Spartans might have managed to hold the Pass until help arrived, but for a Greek traitor. This man led some of the Persian troops by a mountain route, which came out to the south of Thermopylae. Someone ran and told Leonidas that he was going to be attacked from both sides at once, and he immediately commanded most of his forces to march southwards, to escape from the trap. He and his Three Hundred alone waited for the new attack.

[*]There were 1,000 Immortals. They were so named because if one man was killed, another immediately took his place.

As the Persians poured into the Pass from both sides, one by one the Greeks were killed. Leonidas was one of the first to die. The others fought to the bitter end, with broken spears, with stones and even with their bare hands, and they killed thousands of the invaders. But by nightfall there was not a single Spartan left alive, and the narrow Pass was choked with dead men. Xerxes marched towards Athens.

Meanwhile, in Athens, the leader Themistocles hastily sent all the women and children and old people out of the city, over the water to Salamis and Aegina. When Xerxes arrived, Athens was a town almost without people. But the Acropolis *, where the temples were, was guarded, and the priests and soldiers fought fiercely (but in vain) to save them from being burnt. While their town was blazing, Themistocles and the sailors were preparing their fleet five miles away at Piraeus.

Once he had won Athens, Xerxes turned his attention to Salamis. It was now autumn, and soon the weather would be too bad for fighting. The Persian navy sailed towards the island, and when the Greeks saw how many ships there were, many of them wanted to give up, and make peace with this mighty king who had such a vast army and navy. But Themistocles had already met the navy in battle once, while the Spartans were holding Thermopylae. His little

*See p. 70

ships had managed to do quite a lot of damage to the Persian fleet, and his men were eager to fight again. So Themistocles grouped his ships in the narrow channel between Athens and Salamis, and waited until they were surrounded by enemy ships. Xerxes also waited. He saw the Athenian navy caught, as he thought, like a mouse in the jaws of a cat. He ordered his throne to be brought on to the shore, so that he could sit and watch the cat close its teeth.

The Athenians attacked first. There were so many Persian ships that they got in each other's way. They were so large that the wind caught them and blew them so that their broad sides were facing the bows of the little Athenian ships. The Greeks used their own ships, which were armoured with battering-rams, to rip open the sides of the Persian warships. The Persians suffered terrible damage; Xerxes could hardly believe his eyes as the channel filled with wreckage.

The result was a complete victory for the Athenian navy, and Xerxes had to go home. Most of his army went with him, struggling back along roads that were now beginning to be covered with snow. In the spring, the Greeks really united to drive the Persians away for good, and they won two land battles on Greek soil. Xerxes never managed to conquer Greece, and in the end he gave up trying.

Greek Galley of 500 B.C.
Greek ships were narrow with shallow hulls (bodies) which allowed them to sail close to the rocky coastlines. If the winds were favourable they could be sailed from one island to the next, but in calm weather they were rowed by about 170 oarsmen. The oarsmen were arranged in three banks, probably on two levels. Ships with only two banks of oarsmen were called biremes, those with three rows — triremes (above).

Chapter 9 Athens and Sparta in the Fifth Century B.C.

After the Persian Wars were over, Athens entered its 'Golden Age'. The Athenians were very fond of debate, discussion and philosophy, and tried to understand man's place in the world. Also they tried to find out what the world was made of, what shape it was, and why it existed at all. One man said that all living things were based on water, another thought the material of life was a colourless liquid; and yet another said there were four basic elements*, earth, fire, air and water. A Greek scientist developed the first theory of atoms. They knew the earth was round (though many people did not believe this), they measured its size, and they even calculated its distance from the moon and the sun. Men called 'sophists' taught the young men how to think, and how to apply their brains to problems in mathematics, astronomy, medicine and philosophy — the love of wisdom. In the summer in Athens, men used to gather in the streets to talk about these matters, and to discuss geometry, or poetry, or the laws in their new government, which was called a 'democracy'.

Government by democracy was a new idea. It began in 507 B.C., when a leader called Cleisthenes 'took the people into partnership'. Democracy was a completely different way of government from anything the world had ever known before. We have already seen how in the earlier civilizations the king was the head of state, and the absolute ruler. In all these civilizations, from Egypt to China, it is often only the king whose name is now known to us. Greece was the first place in history in which ordinary common people were listened to, and whose names are remembered today. This is not only because the Greeks are nearer to us in time; the

A young Greek boy at school
The boy is being taught to read. On the right sits the pedagogue, an old slave who looks after the boy when at school.

Persians, and many other nations, were still ruled absolutely by a king, and we do not know very much about their common people's thoughts or ideas.

In Athens all adult males were automatically members of an Assembly, which voted for a Council to deal with day-to-day problems, and a Court to judge law cases. Nobody could seize power for himself, for once a year the Assembly was allowed to vote against anybody who seemed to have too much ambition. They wrote his name on a broken piece of pottery called an *ostrakon*, and if 6000 or more members of the Assembly voted against the same man, he was banished for ten years. After that, he could return and could claim his property once again.

Other states in Greece were ruled by kings called 'tyrants'. Our present word 'tyrant'

---

*Elements are the simplest parts into which something can be divided. Water is not really an element; it is made of two elements, hydrogen and oxygen. Nor, of course, are earth or fire or air.

means a bad, oppressive ruler, but Greek tyrants were not always bad. Some states were half-way to becoming democracies, and they were called 'oligarchies'. They were ruled by a few rich citizens. Athens itself had all these types of government at one time or another. (Hippias had been a tyrant of Athens.) The Athenians experimented with types of government just as they experimented with all other ideas.

A favourite Greek saying was 'Know thyself', and men were taught to think about their own motives, and to be honest with themselves. They were encouraged to strive for perfection, in their minds and in their bodies. Every male Athenian practised in the gymnasium every day, and they were scornful of those who would not strip naked and wrestle, or run, or throw the javelin.

Boys were taken to school by slaves called 'pedagogues'. Their teachers taught them to read, and to write with a pointed instrument called a stylus on a tablet covered with soft wax. They learnt to recite poetry, and to speak well in public. Music-masters taught them to play on the pipes or on the lute. The pedagogues, who sat and waited until the lessons were over, listened as well, and they sometimes became just as well-educated as their young masters.

The boys went home for their meals, which were prepared by their mothers and the household slaves. They ate simple dishes of goat's cheese, olives, honey and bread, and drank home-made wine. Their houses were built of sun-dried brick round a central courtyard. There was no proper water-supply, and the slaves were kept busy filling jars from springs and wells.

When they grew up, Athenian men were not often at home: they were too busy listening to the sophists, attending the Assembly or the gymnasium, or taking part in games and religious festivals. (There were so many slaves that there was no need for the freemen to work very hard.)

Beauty was all around the Athenians. On the highest part of Athens, the Acropolis, stood the Parthenon, a temple built to the goddess of Athens, Athena. Her statue inside was 40 feet high, and covered with gold. Round the Parthenon were other graceful temples with gleaming white columns and gabled (pointed) roofs. Athenians working in their fields and vineyards beyond the walls could see them shining in the sun.

Greek religion and their gods

Religion was a part of everyday living. It was the bond which held the scattered city-states together. The gods and goddesses were all thought of as having the same characteristics as ordinary men and women, but they had greater power and they lived forever. Their home was on Mount Olympus.

Each city-state had a sacred place, usually the highest part of the town, set aside for temples.

Zeus: ruled Mount Olympus as king of the gods and lord of the weather. The Olympic Games were held in his honour.

Pallas Athena: goddess who watched over all civilized life.

Apollo: worshipped at Delphi where as the god of prophecy, he had a famous oracle. He was the son of Zeus. He looked after musicians and archers and was a lover of truth.

Aphrodite: (pictured above) was the goddess of love and beauty.

Poseidon: god of the sea, was very important to sailors and fishermen. When he became angry he caused storms.

Dionysus: god of wine, could make people both happy and miserable. He brought the vine to Greece. His yearly festival was a public holiday when everyone enjoyed himself.

Pericles 490–429 B.C.

Pericles, one of the greatest statesmen of Athens, was a young boy during the Persian Wars. He was one of the people sent out of Athens to Salamis. When the wars were over, Pericles grew up in a city which was being rebuilt in every way. He was proud to be an Athenian. He very much approved of the Athenian sense of liberty, where a man was allowed to develop his own personality. He liked the way in which they were taught to be 'all-rounders', so that even the humblest citizens were able to play the lyre, recite poetry, act in plays, and take part in politics – as well as being first-class craftsmen by trade. Everybody did everything to the best of his ability. Pericles once said:

'Some people call the man who takes no part in public affairs unambitious. We Athenians call him useless.'

The only people who did not take part in the government were foreigners (often other Greeks), slaves, and women. Foreigners were tolerated,

Pericles

Play acting

The audience sat on stone seats in an outdoor theatre. The actors were on the stage in the middle. There was usually a chorus in these plays; it commented on the action, and told the audience the background of the story.

Actors wore masks to show what sort of part they were playing. The comedians wore smiling masks, and the players of tragedy wore masks with turned-down mouths. Today you may sometimes see these masks outside theatres: they are copied from old Greek masks.

People went to the theatre for the whole day. The plays were put on one after the other, and prizes were given for the ones people enjoyed most.

but were not allowed to vote; slaves had no rights at all; and although women were often the heroines of plays, and Athena was a much-respected goddess, in real life women were expected to keep in the background. Pericles himself said:

> 'The greatest glory of a woman is to be least talked about by men, whether they are praising or criticizing...'

The Theatre in Greece

In poetry and play-writing the Greeks had no equal. Every year the authors of plays competed to see whose play should be performed at the annual festival. Many of these plays still survive, and are sometimes performed today. They often tell stories that the Greeks knew well—stories about gods and goddesses, and the mortals they watched over. Many of them were tragedies, showing how men were really at the mercy of the gods, of their fellow-men, and even of their own thoughts and actions. The Greeks did not always want 'happy endings' for their plays. They knew that life was hard and people were often unhappy. People do not always have the fate they deserve. The Greeks were quite real-istic about this, and their ideas of right and wrong went far deeper than those of many people in civilized lands today.

But Greek theatre was not all tragic. There were gay comedies as well. The Greeks were able to laugh at themselves, and were never afraid of the truth, even if it was undignified

The Trojan Horse

The stories of the gods and heroes of old were written down by Homer in about 750 B.C. Most of the stories were tradi-tional tales, handed down for generations. Some of them are really faint memories of things that actually happened during the much earlier Mycenean civilization in Greece. The most famous story is about a ten-year war fought by the Greeks against Troy, a city near the Hellespont. The Greeks left a huge wooden horse outside the Trojan walls, and the townspeople dragged it into the town. That night a door opened in the body of the horse, and Greek soldiers climbed out and captured the town. Most of this story is legend; but we do know that Troy existed, and that it was destroyed. The Mycenean cities were over-run by less civilized Greek invaders from the north in about 1100 B.C. Refugees fled to the islands and to Athens. The Athenians were their descendants; the Spartans were the descendants of the invaders. By the time of Homer, only myths and legends of the Myceneans remained.

---

and made people look silly. So they watched plays which mocked the leaders of the Assembly, the sophists, the doctors, the high-born land-owners, and the ordinary workmen.

Everybody went to the theatre, and everybody argued about the plays afterwards, often far into the night. The writers of plays were greatly honoured, and a poet in fifth-century Athens was 'a light and winged and holy thing'.

Sparta

One state in Greece was entirely different from the rest. Sparta, to the west of Athens in the land called Peloponnesus, had two kings, and was ruled as a military state. The kings were more like generals, for they commanded the army, while the affairs of the kingdom were controlled by councillors. Leonidas, who died at Thermopylae, was a Spartan king.

Whereas Athens turned to the sea and kept a large navy, Sparta had no port, and the whole state was one large army. The Spartans lived and died as soldiers, and Spartan mothers used to tell their sons as they went into battle: 'Come back with your shield, or on it!' In other words, they must win or die.

This strange way of life was brought about because Sparta had even more slaves than the Athenians did. Early in their history the Spartans had conquered the neighbouring hill-peoples, and instead of allowing them to keep their own government, they enslaved the whole population. The slaves were known as 'helots'. The Spartans had to keep themselves armed and alert, because they were greatly outnumbered by the helots, and they were always afraid of rebellion. Sometimes groups of helots *did* try to revolt against their masters, but the Spartans had an efficient 'secret police' which usually managed to murder such plotters before they could act.

In order to keep Sparta like a military machine, the rulers banned all trade with foreigners, and even with other Greeks. Their houses were so bare that the beautiful foreign silks would have been out of place. They ate black bread and soup made of black beans, and ignored the more tasty olives and grapes eaten by the rest of the Greeks. Even the idea of coins was banned, so that no Spartan could buy from anybody in another state. Among themselves they used clumsy pieces of iron money, which were useless outside Sparta.

When a Spartan baby was born, its mother and father had to show it to a council of elders. Healthy babies were allowed to live, but weak babies were left out on the mountainsides to die. (Other Greek states also exposed weak children in this way.) When Spartan boys were seven years old, they were taken from their mothers, and joined the other young men in a barracks where they began their military training. They stayed there until they were grown up, and were not allowed to live in their own houses again until they were 30 years old.

Spartans were famous all over Greece for their skill in games and fighting, and also for their singing. When a young man was ready to fight for his country, he was given a suit of heavy

Spartan soldier
The Spartans were also known as 'Laconians'. They were famous for their dry, unemotional way of speaking. At Thermopylae they were told that the arrows of the Persians were so numerous that they would darken the sun. 'So much the better,' a Spartan replied, 'for we shall be able to fight in the shade.'

bronze armour, a red tunic, and a helmet decorated with dyed horsehair. The best and strongest soldiers formed the main bodyguard of Three Hundred—an honour which all Spartan men wished for. The Three Hundred were the envy of their companions, but even they had no freedom as we know it. Their whole lives were strictly disciplined, and even their wives were chosen for them, for they too had to be athletes, and strong enough to have healthy sons who would also become soldiers.

This military way of life, and their lack of beautiful temples or statues, made the Spartans totally different from the easy-going Athenians, with their love of perfection and their stress on fitness for its own sake. Yet both were Greek-speaking peoples, and as we have already seen, they sometimes united when an enemy threatened their lands.

Chapter 10 How Greek Fought Greek

As long as Athens remained a small self-contained city-state, all was well. But at the end of the Persian Wars, the Athenians formed an alliance with the Ionian city-states in Asia Minor. They made an agreement that these states should provide money or ships for a fleet that could protect all Greece from invasion. A politician named Aristides worked out how much money each state should give. The money was kept on the island of Delos, and the ships sailed off to join the Athenian fleet. From the name of the island, the federated states were known as the Delian League.

Unfortunately, after a time it was obvious that Athens was gaining more benefit from the League than any other state. The Athenians had now moved the money to Athens, and they were accused of using it to build the temples on the Acropolis. The other members of the League also objected because Athens was sending soldiers to live in their cities; they were removing the local politicians, and forcing the Ionians to obey Athenian laws. Altogether Athens was behaving as though the states of the Delian League were her own private empire.

Sparta was alarmed by this, because she was afraid that Athens would soon be the leader of the whole of Greece. It was certainly clear that by now Greece ought to have a united policy against Persia. But Sparta was not willing for that policy to be controlled by Athens. So, after Athens had threatened two of Sparta's allies, the Spartans decided that they must stop their rival. The long war that followed very much weakened the civilization Athens had built up. It also led, in the end, to the downfall of Sparta.

The war is called the Peloponnesian War after the Peloponnesian League, the group of states allied to Sparta. Most of them were in that part of Greece that is called the Peloponnesus.

Phoenicians trading
The main rivals to the Greek traders in the Mediterranean were the Phoenicians. These extremely successful merchant-seamen lived in towns on the eastern shores of the Mediterranean. Their ships carried embroidered linen sails, and were hung with purple and blue curtains. Purple dye (made from a kind of shell-fish) was their main export, but they also went from port to port buying and selling cargoes of horses, ivory and ebony (from Syria), tapestry and cloth (from Assyria); corn, honey and oil (from Palestine), and spices and gold (from Arabia). They sailed west and north, till they came to the tin-mines of Britain and Spain. Tin was in great demand in the Mediterranean countries, for mixing with copper to make bronze.

The Peloponnesian War 431–404 B.C.

The Greek city-states took sides in the war, and for 27 years Greek fought Greek. Every spring, when the snows had melted, the armies of Sparta, and the Athenian navy, set out to damage each other's lands. It was not a 'total war'; the ordinary life of Athens continued much as before, with poets and playwrights commenting on the political situation, and even making fun of the whole thing. But there were times when nobody could forget the horrors of war. When the Spartans marched far south into Attica, all the country people fled to Athens. The city was crowded with refugees, sleeping in the streets, in the markets, and even in the temples. It is not surprising that under these conditions food became short, and disease broke out. In the summer of 430, the plague was so bad that hundreds of Athenians died every day. Pericles himself caught it, and was so weakened that he died the following year.

Both sides were often cruel and merciless. The Athenians murdered all the men on an island that fought for Sparta, and took the women and children as slaves. When the people of the city

Reconstruction of Acropolis

of Syracuse in Sicily, who were allies of Sparta, captured an Athenian army, they put the prisoners to work in stone-quarries. Few of them survived, because the conditions were so terrible.

So the bitter quarrel went on. Sometimes city-states changed sides, sometimes even generals went over to the enemy. The end was complete defeat for the Athenians. King Agis of Sparta seized a small town only 14 miles from Athens, and was able to stop any help, or even food, from reaching the Athenians from the north. Worse news was to follow, for the Spartans made a treaty with Persia. They received money from a Persian prince and built their first navy. Now the Athenians were no longer masters of the sea. Under their leader Lysander, the Spartans surprised and captured an Athenian fleet, and sailed south towards Attica. They stopped grain ships reaching Athens from Ionia or the Black Sea. When the news of the naval disaster reached Athens, 'on that night, no man slept'. A few months later, Athens surrendered to the Spartans.

The 'Thirty Tyrants' and the fall of Sparta

The Spartans took away Athens' empire, tore down the city walls, and sailed away with her fleet. They set up a government of 30 men of their own choosing. Many Athenians were murdered, or had their property taken from them. The vine and olive orchards were nearly all destroyed, and these trees take many years to grow. Nobody had any money, and many slaves were therefore sold abroad so that people could buy food. In the year that followed, there was so much misrule in Athens that the people rose in protest. The Spartans had hoped to unite Greece under their leadership, but they did not know how to govern men who had always loved personal liberty. They themselves were too much like machines to rule wisely, and in only 35 years Athens was once again the spiritual centre of Greece.

One reason for the decline of Sparta was that suddenly the Spartans had money; the defeated states had to pay tribute to her. These people had never owned anything at all, and now they saw the advantage of wealth. Some became very rich, but they did not know how to deal with their money. Those who remained poor envied them, and there was great discontent in Sparta.

In the conquered states, the Spartan soldiers and politicians were hated and feared. They did nothing to bring the states back to prosperity, and soon there were rebellions all over Greece. Thebes in particular rose against the Spartans, and in 362 B.C. defeated them. Sparta had been held together by its military rule, and the new way of life caused the state to collapse.

A new kind of society now grew up in Greece. The army, the government, the theatre, and even the market-place began to be taken over by professionals. Soldiers were no longer recruited only in times of danger; there were now professional soldiers who were paid to fight. (When there were no wars in Greece, they sometimes went to Asia and fought for the Persians instead.) There were professional politicians in charge of state affairs. In the play-houses, people went to see a particular actor, rather than a particular play. (In the old days all the actors were amateurs, and the crowd did not know their names.) And there were now shops which sold bread and wove cloth, so that the housewives no longer had to give these jobs to slaves in their own homes. The city was becoming much more 'commercial', and in this new society people were more in-

a	A	b	B	g	Γ	d	Δ
alpha		beta		gamma		delta	
e	E	z	Z	e	H	th	Θ
epsilon		zeta		eta		theta	
i	I	c,k	K	l	Λ	m	M
iota		kappa		lambda		mu	
n	N	x	Ξ	o	O	p	Π
nu		xi		omicron		pi	
r,rh	P	s	Σ	t	T	y,u	Υ
rho		sigma		tau		upsilon	
ph	Φ	ch	X	ps	Ψ	o	Ω
phi		chi		psi		omega	

Writing

The Greeks took over the Phoenicians' way of writing, and they altered it to suit their own language. Our word *alphabet* comes from *alpha* and *beta*, the Greek names for A and B. The Greek for D is *delta*, from which we get our word delta, meaning a place where rivers join to make a triangle with the sea. (Look at the Nile Delta on p. 34.) We use some Greek letters as symbols in mathematics. The Greeks themselves still use the old alphabet.

clined to value money. Riches, and not mental and physical excellence, were now the new goal.

Socrates, 469–399 B.C.

But there were people who spoke against this worldly attitude, and the greatest critic was a philosopher named Socrates. He himself was a poor man, who had once been a stone-mason. But he left his job in order to find out about life, about himself, and about goodness. He was 66 years old when the wars with Sparta ended.

The way Socrates looked for goodness was by questioning everything, and thus making his friends (and himself) think more deeply than they had before. For instance, if someone said that loyalty was a good thing, Socrates would ask him questions like: 'What do we mean by loyalty? Is it *always* good? Is it a good thing to be loyal to a bad king? Does not a man have the right to his own opinion–and can he not therefore be *disloyal* in this situation?' And then the conversation would probably turn to whether a man could follow his own conscience, or whether he should obey his king, or his government, blindly.

Many of Socrates' listeners loved this kind of argument. It was different from the methods of the sophists, who just lectured to a silent audience. Socrates had a band of devoted followers, but he also made enemies. Politicians and other public men did not like to be beaten in argument by this old man, with his cloak in rags and with no sandals on his feet. It is a very human weakness that we all like to hold on to our beliefs, just because they are ours—even when they are shown to be wrong, or partly wrong. Some people did not realize that Socrates was genuinely searching for the truth, and not trying to trick them by clever argument.

Athens was only just beginning to restore order and confidence after the wars with Sparta, and the politicians felt that Socrates was destroying the beliefs and ideas that the city needed. It was the wrong time to make people uneasy about their ways of thinking, and unsure about their religion. Socrates, they felt, was a bad influence on the young men of the town. So they brought a charge against him of teaching young men to think and act wrongly, and of introducing strange gods.

At his trial, Socrates could have brought his wife and children to plead for him, but he did not. He could have asked to be exiled, and the request would probably have been granted. Instead he made a speech which only angered the Court. 'I am a sort of gadfly*,' he said, 'and the State is a great and noble horse which is slow to move, and requires to be stirred to life.' He told them they ought to give him free meals for the rest of his life, because they would never have anyone like him in their city again. Then he said perhaps they should fine him, and he named a tiny sum of money. But the majority of the citizens of Athens voted against him, and he was condemned to death by poison.

Socrates never wrote down his thoughts or conversations, but later his young friend Plato recorded everything he could remember. He shows Socrates to be an interesting and lively man, whose ideas are as true today as they were when he formulated them 2000 years ago.

Socrates

Socrates once said about a politician who was angry with him: 'Well, I don't suppose either of us knows anything beautiful or good, but I am better off than he is—for he knows nothing, and thinks that he knows; I neither know nor think that I know!'

The playwright Aristophanes wrote a comedy called 'The Clouds' in 423 B.C. It is about a simple man who has been ruined by his son's passion for chariot-racing. He takes his son to Socrates, in order that he may learn how to win his law-suits. In the play Socrates is paid to teach people how to win arguments by trickery. He did not teach for money in real life, neither did he cheat in argument. But unfortunately the Athenians believed in Aristophanes' view.

---

*Gadfly is a general name for various kinds of flies that bite animals.

Chapter 11 Alexander the Great

Now a completely new people became powerful in Greece. At the northern end of the Aegean Sea lay the country of Macedonia. The Macedonians were a mixed race, partly Greek but also partly descended from northern tribesmen. The Greeks thought of them as near-barbarians. In about 350 B.C., the Macedonians had a well-trained army, mainly of foot-soldiers armed with very long spears called pikes. They marched in a close formation called a phalanx, with their pikes pointing forwards towards the enemy, and their right arms protected by the next man's shield.

During the Persian Wars, Macedonia had fought *against* Greece, and the Greeks were very suspicious of this mixed race that lived so close to them. Philip, who was king of Macedon from 359–336 B.C. (50 years after the death of Socrates), was an ambitious man, determined to make his country powerful. He invaded Thrace, and seized for himself some rich gold mines. With his new wealth he provided Macedonia with an even bigger and better army. He invaded Thessaly, and marched far south into Greece.

Demosthenes, one of Athens' leaders, protested against this invasion, and said to the Athenians:

'See, Athenians, the height to which the fellow's insolence has soared: he makes noisy threats and talks big . . . he cannot rest content with what he has conquered: he is always taking in more, everywhere casting his net round us, while we sit idle and do nothing. When, Athenians, will you take the necessary action? What are you waiting for?'

But another Athenian named Isocrates wanted peace with the Macedonians. He appealed to Philip to unite Greece against the Persians. So Athens was divided into two parties, one for war and the other for peace.

The Macedonians invade Europe, Asia and Africa

Philip and his army marched right down to Boeotia, just north of Attica, and he defeated a mixed force of Athenians and Thebans. He was now in command of almost the whole of Greece, but before he could organize this new empire, he was murdered by his own palace officials.

Demosthenes was delighted to hear of Philip's death. He thought that the Macedonians would now go back to their own country, and that Philip's son Alexander was too young to be a nuisance. But Alexander was 20 and far from being a child. He had been taught by a remarkable Greek tutor named Aristotle. From him he learnt the ancient tales of Homer, and the traditions of the Greeks. Though only half-Greek himself, Alexander had great respect for Greek culture*, and saw himself as a descendant of the heroes of old. He immediately marched south to remind the Greeks that they were now part of *his* empire. Thebes rebelled, but the treatment the Thebans received from Alexander's army (6000 people were killed, and 8000 sold as slaves) horrified the other city-states. They decided that it was far safer to remain quiet under their new conqueror.

Then Alexander took a large army across the Hellespont into the Persian Empire. The King of Persia, whose name was Darius III, was lord of all the old countries of Assyria, Babylonia and Egypt, and he was very rich. Alexander, in spite of his Thracian gold mines, was comparatively poor. He was determined to win some of the wealth of Persia, and almost immediately he succeeded.

Darius's army was not nearly as well disciplined as Alexander's. His soldiers were mostly

---

*By culture we here mean a particular form of civilization and its characteristic products, intellectual, social, religious, artistic, etc.

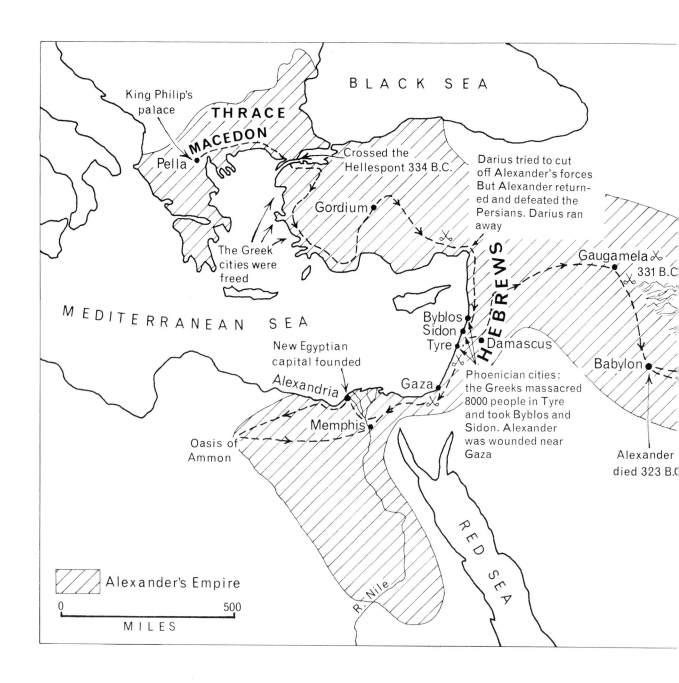

The following labels appear on the map:

BLACK SEA

King Philip's palace

THRACE
MACEDON

Pella

Crossed the Hellespont 334 B.C.

Gordium

Darius tried to cut off Alexander's forces But Alexander returned and defeated the Persians. Darius ran away

The Greek cities were freed

Gaugamela 331 B.C

MEDITERRANEAN SEA

HEBREWS

Byblos
Sidon
Tyre
Damascus

Babylon

New Egyptian capital founded

Alexandria

Gaza

Phoenician cities: the Greeks massacred 8000 people in Tyre and took Byblos and Sidon. Alexander was wounded near Gaza

Memphis

Alexander died 323 B.C

Oasis of Ammon

RED SEA

Alexander's Empire

0   500

MILES

R. Nile

mercenaries (hired soldiers), many of them from Greece. They were badly organized, and they had no personal loyalty to the king. They were quite likely to desert if they were not paid well. Darius's navy was not completely Persian either. Most of his ships and sailors were taken from the ports of Phoenicia and Ionia. Alexander quickly showed how superior his forces were: he defeated a Persian army soon after landing in Asia and then marched south to cut off the ports. He was so pleased with his victories that he sent home 300 suits of Persian armour, with the message:

'Alexander, son of Philip, and the Greeks (except the Spartans) have won these from the barbarians of Asia.'

After marching across Asia Minor, Alexander met a Persian army commanded by Darius himself, and again he defeated the Persians. Darius fled to the east, farther into Asia, while Alexander turned south into Syria where he captured the ancient Phoenician city of Tyre. Then he decided to cross the desert into North Africa. At the Nile delta he founded the town of Alexandria, and was proclaimed Pharaoh of Egypt. He was welcomed

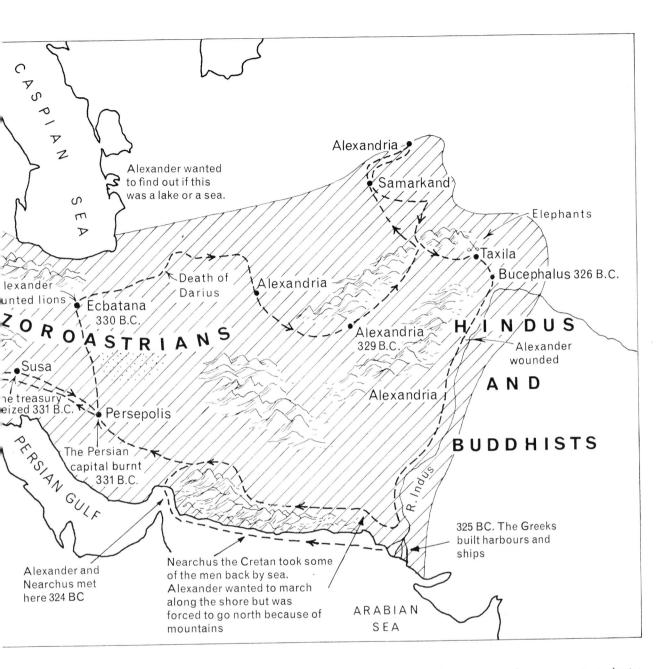

Alexander wanted to find out if this was a lake or a sea.

CASPIAN SEA

Alexander hunted lions

ZOROASTRIANS

Ecbatana 330 B.C.

Death of Darius

Alexandria

Alexandria 329 B.C.

HINDUS

Alexander wounded

Susa

the treasury seized 331 B.C.

PERSIAN GULF

Persepolis

The Persian capital burnt 331 B.C.

Alexandria

AND

Alexandria

BUDDHISTS

R. Indus

325 BC. The Greeks built harbours and ships

Alexandria

Samarkand

Elephants

Taxila

Bucephalus 326 B.C.

Alexander and Nearchus met here 324 BC

Nearchus the Cretan took some of the men back by sea. Alexander wanted to march along the shore but was forced to go north because of mountains

ARABIAN SEA

with rejoicing, for the Egyptians were tired of the harsh and brutal way in which the Persian satraps had treated them. But Alexander did not stay long in Egypt. He was afraid that the Persians in Asia might again seize the cities of Phoenicia and Ionia. He returned to fight once more with Darius.

At Gaugamela in Mesopotamia the Macedonians met the last and largest Persian army. The Persians now introduced into their army chariots with long knives fixed to the wheels. When the drivers whipped up the horses and

Gordium; Here Alexander was shown an ancient chariot lashed to a pole with a knot that an oracle had said could be untied only by the man who would one day rule all Asia. Alexander merely cut the knot in half with his sword.

Oasis of Ammon; Alexander went into the desert to consult a famous Egyptian oracle. (Oracles were supposed to forecast the future.)

Damascus; At this ancient city Alexander captured Darius's war chest containing all the money for paying his soldiers.

Alexandria; Five towns with this name are shown here. Only one is still called Alexandria.

Susa; Here the treasury was seized by Alexander while he was on his way from India.

rode straight at the enemy ranks, the knives cut the soldiers' legs and caused great damage. But this is a method which only succeeds when the enemy is not expecting it. Alexander's troops opened their ranks so that the chariots passed harmlessly through. Then it was a simple matter to kill the drivers and the horses before they could turn round and attack again. When Alexander led his horsemen against the centre of the Persian army, Darius again fled from the battle.

The Persian governor of Babylon surrendered to Alexander without a fight. At Susa, the Greeks seized Darius's treasure — all the money that had been collected to pay his army; and he burned the Persian capital, Persepolis.

The conqueror becomes a ruler

The Greeks had never thought of ruling an area larger than a city-state, so the making of a real Greek empire was something new. Alexander's victories caused him many problems. He could not leave his newly conquered cities completely unguarded; he must have a frontier that could be defended easily. Because his army was too small to hold so large an empire, he had to rule this vast area by the consent of the people, and not by terror; and Darius had to be found and captured. He was troubled by plots within his own army, and by dissatisfied Greeks who wanted to return home. It is astonishing that he succeeded so well in keeping his army together, and in solving most of the problems.

The first task was to find Darius. If he remained free, he might succeed in rallying the Persians again. So Alexander followed him day after day, and when he found him, Darius was already dying. One of his own noblemen who wanted to be king himself had stabbed Darius, but he, too, was soon killed. So now that there was no Persian king, Alexander made himself ruler.

Still he went on towards the east. His campaigns for the next few years were part conquests and part exploration. He built 16 new cities, all called Alexandria, where the streets were laid out in a grid-pattern (with roads crossing each other at right angles), and the buildings were Greek in style. (Most of these 'Alexandrias' are now called by different names.) Wherever he went he introduced Greek ideas, and built temples to Greek gods. Year after year the army marched with him. The men were often ill with dysentery and malaria, and they were afraid that they might never return home.

They were also upset because Alexander was giving favours to the Persians. Mazaeus, Persian governor of Babylon, still held his command under Alexander; and many times Alexander gave Persians posts that were senior to those held by Greeks. He encouraged his men to wear Persian clothing, and often wore it himself. He was trying to solve the problem of ruling by consent, by regarding the conquered Persians as friends rather than as an inferior, beaten race. He married two Asian wives, and he encouraged his men to marry local women.

But Alexander went too far in adopting Persian customs. In the old days, when a subject of the king of Persia wanted to speak to him, he had to lie full-length on the floor until he was told to rise up. Alexander now tried to make his men do the same. The Persians did not object, for they had always done so, but the Greeks were furious. They did not mind regarding Alexander as king of the Greeks — but he seemed to want to be treated as a god as well. In the end the Greeks won, and Alexander had to agree that they could stand in his presence.

Now the army crossed the mountains of Afghanistan and marched into India. There was a fierce battle with an Indian king named Porus, and even though the Indian army used elephants, which terrified the Greek horses (and probably the men too), the Greeks won.

Alexander wanted to press on eastwards, for, according to the geographers in his party, they were almost at the end of the world. They imagined that the earth was a flat plate, with a huge river called 'Ocean' running all round it. (Not all Greek scholars believed this — long before, there had been an idea that the world was round.) Alexander had even brought shipbuilders and sailors with him, so that they could sail on this Ocean. But the army was now too far from home. The soldiers heard rumours of deserts and jungles, and thousands more elephants between them and the sea, and they refused to go any further. Moreover, the monsoon had come, and the solid ground was now a mass of wet mud.

Alexander was furious with his army, and even said he would go on alone. But he consulted his oracle, and the signs were against such a journey. So reluctantly he turned back. When at last he reached Babylon again, he had been away ten years. In Persia there was now great confusion, and even though Alexander was exhausted from his wanderings, he could not rest. There were

quarrels to be settled, temples to be rebuilt, laws to be made, and the whole empire had to be organized. Alexander tried his utmost to persuade Greeks and Persians to live together in harmony and friendship. He decided to live in Babylon for a while. Babylon, which had once been so beautiful, was neglected and overgrown. The canals had been smashed by the Persians, and the surrounding country had gone back to swampy marshland. Slowly Alexander's workmen restored the buildings and drained the land.

Alexander's decision to live in this damp, mosquito-ridden city was fatal for him, and it lost the Greeks an empire. In June 323 B.C., when he was only 33 years old, he died in Babylon from malaria.

What happened afterwards

Alexander had no successor strong enough to carry on his work, and his great empire collapsed after he died. It was divided into six parts, each ruled by one of Alexander's generals. The two areas which flourished most were Syria and

Alexander's Army in Asia

The Issus mosaic at Pompeii shows the young Alexander (on the left) leading the charge against the Persian king, Darius, at Issus.

There were 35,000 foot-soldiers in Alexander's army and 5000 horsemen. The army also took with them siege towers on wheels, rams for breaking down town walls, catapults for hurling spears and stones, and materials for building bridges. Besides soldiers there were architects, builders, geographers, historians and biologists. Alexander sent specimens of new plants back to his old tutor, Aristotle.

Egypt. General Ptolemy became Pharaoh, and there were Pharaohs of the same name in Egypt for nearly 300 years. Syria was ruled by a family descended from General Seleucus, and were known as the Seleucids.

The Greek language, customs and culture lived on in many of the places Alexander conquered. The first Buddhist statues, imported into India from Afghanistan, are shown in Greek clothes and with Greek faces. The new towns had Greek architects, and their buildings were unmistakably Greek. Alexander had opened up a vast area of the world for Greek colonists, who continued to trade with the Mediterranean and Aegean countries. New farms in India, Turkestan and Persia grew wheat to sell in Greece and Italy; and for the first time the Mediterranean world was able to import citrus fruit, such as oranges and lemons; apricots, buffaloes, geese and cotton.

In Egypt, Alexandria became the new capital, and one of the most important cities in the world. Not far from the new marble palace of the Ptolemies, there was a famous university. Its scholars became known all over the European and Asian world: Euclid, who taught mathematics, Zenodorus, who produced the first Greek grammar; Erasistratus who studied medicine, and Eratosthenes the geographer. There were 700,000 books in the university library.

Silks from China, cotton goods from India, gold and silver from Persia, carpets from Turkey, and tin from Britain were all sold in the marketplace of Alexandria. But Alexandria was really the only town in Egypt which maintained a high standard of civilization. The Ptolemies did not always rule the country wisely, and in later years they turned it into a nationalized state. Landowners were compelled to till their land for the state, and were forbidden to work elsewhere. They received orders about what crops to grow, and how many animals to keep. They had to sell their produce to the state at fixed prices, and free competitive trading was forbidden by law. The people of Egypt became mere slaves in their own country, with their thoughts only on how they could survive another day. The glory of Egypt had at last departed.

Pharos

The Pharos of Alexandria was a lighthouse built in 284 B.C. by the first Ptolemy. It was 150 metres (480 feet) high and is one of the Seven Wonders of the Ancient World.

The other six wonders of the Ancient World are: (1) The pyramids of Giza, Egypt; (2) The Hanging Gardens of Semiramis, Babylon, Iraq; (3) The tomb of King Mausolus of Caria, Halicarnassus, Turkey; (4) The Temple of Diana, Ephesus, Turkey; (5) The Statue of Apollo, or Colossus of Rhodes; (6) The statue of Zeus, Olympia, Greece.

Chapter 12 The Rise of Rome

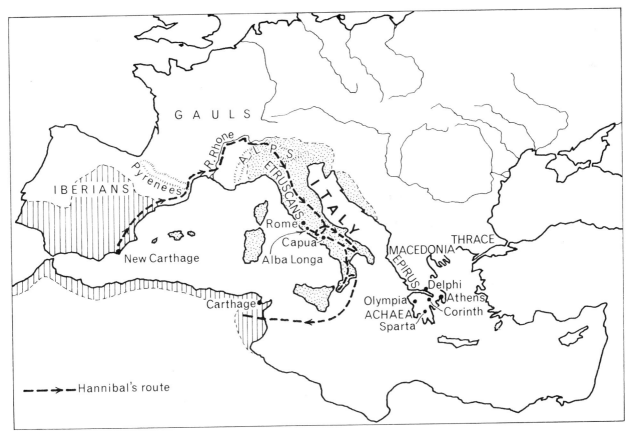

IBERIANS

GAULS

R. Rhone

Pyrenees

ALPS

ETRUSCANS

ITALY

Rome

Capua

Alba Longa

New Carthage

Carthage

MACEDONIA

THRACE

EPIRUS

Delphi

Athens

Corinth

Olympia

ACHAEA

Sparta

- - - ▶ —Hannibal's route

We have seen how the Greeks colonized the islands and the mainland round the 'toe' of Italy. But since all their trade was with the Greek islands and the Mediterranean ports, they did not disturb the other tribes who lived in the central and northern parts of present-day Italy.

The most advanced peoples of Italy at this time were the Etruscans, who had reached a high degree of civilization. They may have come originally from Lydia in Asia, and their art, their clothes, and their religion all show influence from the East. The Etruscans made statues of stone and bronze, painted pictures on their walls, and

built temples and tombs. They could read and write, and they traded with the Celts who lived north of the Alps.

Romulus and Remus

Besides the Etruscans there were many smaller tribes in Italy. There was one small community that was part of a group called 'Latins', and they lived near the river Tiber. Their chief town was called Rome, and we now know them as 'Romans'.

Much later in their history, the Romans invented legends about their origins. They said that in far-off times a prince of Troy named Aeneas

was ordered by the gods to lead his people westwards and found a new nation. Aeneas had many adventures on the way, but finally he arrived in Italy and joined forces with the Latins, who were already living there. His son founded a town called Alba Longa, and for several generations the descendants of Aeneas ruled central Italy.

Then, says the legend, a princess of the tribe gave birth to twins; the father of the boys was supposed to be the god Mars. The king demanded that the boys, who were called Romulus and Remus, should be left to die on the banks of the Tiber. There they were found by a she-wolf, who took them to her lair, and brought them up with her own cubs.

Later Romulus and Remus grew up in the care of a shepherd, and when they were men they became leaders of the tribe. Then there arose the question of which of them should be king. They decided to rely on heavenly help, and to search the sky for a sign. Remus looked up and saw six vultures, and immediately his friends said he

Dido and Aeneas

The Romans had a legend that Carthage was founded by a noble Phoenician lady named Dido. Aeneas landed at Carthage on his way to Italy, and fell in love with her. When he left Africa, she killed herself.

Carthage was certainly founded by the Phoenicians—but not until much later than the time of Aeneas—probably in about 800 B.C. The Romans called the Phoenicians 'Punici', so their wars against Carthage are known as the 'Punic Wars'.

should be king; but now Romulus saw 12 vultures, and *his* followers proclaimed *him* king. Then followed a long argument—'Romulus saw twice as many vultures!' 'Yes, but Remus saw the vultures first!'—and there was a battle in which Remus was killed. So Romulus ruled the city, and called it Rome. The date was now about 750 B.C. At the same time in Greece, Homer was writing down the tribal stories and legends, and the Olympic Games were held for the first time in 776 B.C. From about this date, Roman history ceases to be only legend, and becomes more reliable.

Rome becomes a Republic

The Romans began to form a city-state, gradually making their territory larger as they took over lands from their neighbours. From about 640 to 500 B.C., Rome seems to have been ruled by Etruscan kings, who taught the Romans their civilization. Rome began to look like a prosperous town, with temples, market-places and palaces. The Romans had a constitution, and an army recruited by the rich noblemen. They wore armour and carried shields and spears very like those of the Greeks.

But in time the Romans decided that they did not want to be ruled by Etruscans. King Tarquin, who was nicknamed 'the Proud', had expanded the state, and built new towns in outlying provinces. But he was not popular, and when he was away from Rome with his army, the people deposed, that is, dethroned him. They swore that never again should a king rule in Rome, and instead decided to have two magistrates who would hold office for a year only.

Rome had two kinds of citizens. The first group were called patricians. They were wealthy landowners, who had a vote in the Assembly, and who held all the high positions in the government and the courts. The rest of the people were called plebeians. They had no vote, and could not hold office. A plebeian was not allowed to marry a patrician, and so could never change his status—his position or rank. This inequality caused great trouble in the early days of the republic. Both classes had to pay taxes, and the plebeians forming the largest part of the army, they saw no reason why they should not have equal rights with the patricians. It was the army which finally changed the situation. On their return from a campaign, they organized a 'sit-down strike' outside Rome, and refused to return to battle. The patrician Assembly had to give in, and allow plebeians to send two (later ten) men called 'tribunes' to the Assembly. This was the beginning of greater power for plebeians and soon mixed marriages were allowed, and the plebeians even had their own Assembly.

Many of the patricians were dismayed at the way in which the lower-class citizens were gaining power. They believed that the rule of the country should be in the hands of the rich and well-born, who had time to become professional politicians. The struggle for power continued, the patricians losing ground all the time; in 289 B.C. the plebeians could even pass laws without asking permission from the Senate (the patricians' 'Upper House').

Pyrrhus

Meanwhile the armies of Rome were striking out in every direction, pushing the frontiers of the Roman Republic farther north, east and south. Rome was now the leading city of Italy, and all the other tribes, including the powerful Etruscans, had been subdued. The Greeks who lived in sea-ports in the south of Italy became alarmed, and they sent to Greece for help. An army arrived, led by a Greek called Pyrrhus. The Greeks managed to get hold of a number of war-elephants from India, and Pyrrhus brought some of them to Italy. At first they caused complete confusion among the Roman troops, but although Pyrrhus won two battles, and marched nearly as far as Rome, the Romans would not make peace. After fighting another, drawn, battle he had lost so many men that he went back to Greece, and the Greeks of southern Italy had to submit to Rome.

The Romans united Italy under their government by building roads throughout the country, and by seeing that all the various tribes obeyed

Pyrrhus

Pyrrhus was the king of a Greek state about 80 miles from Italy by sea. Although Pyrrhus won his battles in Italy, they had cost him so much in men and supplies that he returned home, saying, 'Another such victory and I am lost!' We use the term 'Pyrrhic victory' even now, to describe a contest won at too high a price.

81

the same Roman laws. Soon everybody was speaking the Roman language, Latin. Roman rule was not harsh, and the new roads brought great improvement in trade, so the conquered tribes settled down well, and there were few uprisings. The Romans used foreign soldiers in their armies, and this brought a sense of unity among the young men who fought side by side for a common purpose.

The Punic Wars

Across the water, on the North African shore, stood a busy port and town called Carthage. For centuries the people of Carthage had been among the most important traders and merchant-seamen of the western Mediterranean, and they even rounded Spain and sailed north to the barbarian islands of Britain. (There they exchanged cloth and wine for quantities of tin.) Their only trade rivals were the Greek colonists in Italy and France, but by 500 B.C. the Carthaginians had shown that they were the masters of the sea. Now these Carthaginians watched as Rome also began to trade by sea, and worse, to cross to Sicily, which the Carthaginians regarded as their own trading base. War broke out between the two powers.

The Romans had not yet built a proper fleet of ships, and so they were at a disadvantage. But one day they found a Carthaginian ship driven aground, on the shore, and they made 100 copies of it. They trained their soldiers to row by sitting them on wooden benches on the shore, but this makeshift training did not make very good sailors! The Carthaginians could easily win a sea-battle; so the Romans turned sea-battles into land-battles by equipping each ship with a *corvus*. This was a kind of bridge with an iron spike at the end, which they let down with a crash on to the deck of an enemy ship. The spike held the corvus in place, and armed Romans dashed across to fight hand-to-hand with the Carthaginians.

The Romans won the First Punic War, after the two navies had spent over 20 years chasing one another round Sicily and the toe of Italy. The Romans took the islands of Corsica, Sardinia, and Sicily.

Hannibal the Carthaginian

The Carthaginians tried to make an empire in Spain, and they built towns and trading posts all along the south coast. In the spring of 218 B.C., a Carthaginian leader named Hannibal went on the attack against Rome once more. He decided on a most daring plan; he would attack by land, from the north. He started from his Spanish port, New Carthage, with a large army; besides the Carthaginians themselves there were Iberians and Celts from Spain, and well-trained African troops, including tough Numidian horsemen. There were also thousands of baggage-animals, horses, mules and donkeys, and even 37 elephants with their Syrian or Indian riders. Elephants were no longer an unusual sight in the armies of Europe and Asia.

By the time Hannibal had crossed the Pyrenees mountains, his army had been reduced in numbers. Many men had been killed in battles with hostile tribesmen, some had been left behind because they were sick or wounded, and thousands had deserted. They had already marched for three months, and they were tired of the everlasting tramp in unfamiliar land. They had to beg, steal or fight for their food, or live off the charity of the herdsmen and cultivators whose homes and villages they passed on the way. It was growing late in the year, and the weather was turning colder. Hannibal had to use all his influence and charm to make his mixed army continue at all. Fortunately not all the tribes they met were unfriendly, and one tribe even gave them warm clothing and shoes and helped them to repair their weapons.

At last the ragged army reached the Alps— those immense mountains which stretch across the north of Italy, and in which there are peaks up to 14,000 or 15,000 feet high. This test of their courage and endurance was a greater ordeal than even Hannibal imagined it would be. Twice in the narrow passes between the mountains, wild tribesmen rushed at them to plunder their baggage. Mules and horses fell over the cliffs into the valleys below, and many of their precious bundles of food and clothing were lost. There was very little to eat in the high slopes, and men and animals alike starved. Most of the elephants died, and the hungry soldiers cut up their flesh and roasted it on their cooking fires.

By now their clothes and shoes were in rags, and they were dirty, hungry and exhausted. The wind tore at their bodies, and the rain and snow soaked them to the skin. Many were sick and had to be left to die. Then suddenly, the front of the army reached the top of the pass, and saw below the wide plain of north Italy. They had

been marching and fighting for five months, and at last their goal was in sight.

Hannibal made a speech to his men at the top of the pass, telling them that the worst was now over. But he was wrong. The way down was narrow and steep. The first men in the long line trod on soft snow, but by the time the last stragglers passed along that way, the snow had all been removed by the feet of other men, and they had to walk on slippery ice. But at last the survivors of that terrible journey were down in the plain, and after spending winter in camp, the long march south began.

The Second Punic War

The Romans heard of Hannibal's arrival, and they sent one of their consuls to stop the invader's advance. His name was Scipio, and he had just come from Spain, where he had missed Hannibal by only three days. (Hannibal was already safely across the Pyrenees.) The Roman legions were much more disciplined than the wild Celts whom Hannibal had been fighting in northern Spain and France. The Romans were confident of winning this battle, as they had won so many before. But they had never met a man like Hannibal. After a brief and bloody battle, Scipio had to retreat. His defeat was mainly due to the Numidian horsemen, who galloped quickly into

Hannibal's elephants

Nobody is certain whether Hannibal's elephants came from India or from Africa. When they were crossing the river Rhône, between the Pyrenees and the Alps, they built huge rafts for the elephants; fortunately, once they had stepped on to them, the elephants were too terrified to move. It must have been almost impossible to find enough food for them on the 1500 mile march to Italy. They slowed up the army in the Alps, because their drivers were continually having to find paths wide enough for them to walk on.

battle, armed with spears. They were away again before the Romans could harm them; and soon they were ready to attack in a completely different part of the battle-field.

This first victory encouraged the Carthaginians. They followed it with two more great battles, which they won by Hannibal's brilliant planning. In both cases the Roman army was led into an ambush; hidden Carthaginian troops attacked them suddenly and unexpectedly, and most of the dead on the field were Roman soldiers.

A strange situation now developed; the Romans did not want to have any more battles with the Carthaginians, because their losses had been

83

so large. So they had to allow Hannibal to stay in Italy, merely following his army about and occasionally capturing or killing small parties of men who left the main army in search of food. Hannibal took the city of Capua, which he made his headquarters, and he actually stayed in Italy with all his soldiers for 14 years.

During all this time there was only one more important battle. This was at Cannae when, it is said, 80,000 men were killed in one day. This is an astonishing figure; but with no medicines or pain-killing drugs, the fate of all badly wounded men was almost always death. Many begged their friends or their enemies to kill them, and so stop their agony. Both sides were horrified at the slaughter. The Roman army was almost completely destroyed and it was one of the worst defeats the Romans ever suffered.

But Hannibal never took Rome—it was too well built and guarded—and Rome would not make peace. His brother Hasdrubal tried to join him with a second army—using Hannibal's route over the Alps. But he was killed in north Italy by the Romans, and his head was cut off and sent to Hannibal's camp. Hannibal now knew that he would never conquer the Romans in their own land.

Another Roman army was commanded by Scipio's son, a military genius who came to be known later as Scipio Africanus. He went across the sea to Spain, and besieged all the Carthaginian towns there. He captured all of them except Cadiz. Then Scipio Africanus turned south, and landed in Africa near Hannibal's own capital, Carthage.

Hannibal had to leave Italy and go home to defend his country, and in a fierce battle he was finally defeated. Scipio had learnt his strategy from studying Hannibal's own methods. He had managed to persuade the Numidian prince to come over on to his side, and this time it was the Carthaginians who were plagued by the swift and deadly horsemen. When the Carthaginian elephants charged, the Romans were ready for them, and the Roman lines opened

Scipio Africanus

to let them harmlessly through, just as Darius's chariots had passed through Alexander's lines, 130 years before.

The Romans had won the Second Punic War. Hannibal escaped, and spent the rest of his life as a refugee in Asia. All the Carthaginian warships were set on fire, and her territories overseas given to Rome.

That is nearly the end of the story of the Carthaginians. They might have continued as a small trading nation, but the Romans could not forgive Carthage. They decided to wipe out the city completely. In 146 B.C., after a terrible siege, a Roman army destroyed Carthage. It is said that the Romans ploughed salt into all their lands, so that the survivors could never again till the soil of their homeland.

Chapter 13 The Roman Republic

If a Roman wanted to take public office, he first became a *quaestor*, or junior officer. He then became an *aedile*, and supervised public works, such as building, irrigation and tax-collecting; if he was a successful *aedile*, he might become a judge or *praetor*. Consuls, who were the two annually elected chief magistrates of Rome, were elected from among the *praetors*; and a man who had been made consul many times might become a *proconsul* or governor of a province – the top rung of the ladder.

The post of governor came into being when Rome started to claim other countries outside Italy as 'provinces'. Sicily, Sardinia, Corsica, parts of Spain and North Africa were ruled by Rome after the Punic Wars, and during the next 50 years the Romans conquered Syria, Palestine and Macedonia, and made them into Roman provinces as well. The *lingua franca* (common language) of the Roman world was not Latin but Greek. Many people in the new provinces had learnt Greek already, because of Alexander's conquests. Even the Romans themselves often spoke Greek – especially those living in the sea-ports of Italy, where they met Greek-speaking seamen. At first the Romans seemed to lack inspiration in their literature, art and architecture so they used Greek counterparts as models. They were a more serious minded people than the Greeks. Their art and literature both show this. They were down-to-earth and practical, and more concerned with day-to-day living than with philosophy and theory.

The Romans had got rid of their kings, and tried to rule their country as a republic, but this form of government never really worked successfully for them. There was too much difference between rich and poor people. Rich landowners bought up all the land and worked their large

Roman Army

The Roman army was divided into centuries, cohorts and legions. A century contained 100 men (sometimes only 80), six centuries made a cohort, and a legion had ten cohorts. The commander of a century was called a centurion.

In battle, a legion had three fighting lines. The front line went into battle first, there was a supporting line behind them, and in the rear a reserve line. The cavalry (horsemen) protected the left and right wings.

In the Greek phalanx, the whole army was fighting right from the start of the battle. The Roman idea of having a reserve line was an improvement, because these men were fresh and rested when their turn came to fight.

When they were not fighting, the legionaries had to drill, and march for miles with heavy packs on their backs. 'Their drills were bloodless battles; their battles bloody drills,' one writer said. If a legion mutinied or ran away from danger, every tenth man was killed.

farms with slave-labour. There were thousands of slaves in Italy now, brought in after the foreign wars. This meant that thousands of peasants were now landless and unemployed, and they flocked to Rome to look for work. In the town, businessmen built large blocks of flats to accommodate all these people. The houses were badly built, and sometimes they collapsed and killed dozens of families. Rome was very overcrowded, and a law was passed to stop carts and other wheeled vehicles from coming into the town during the daytime. So all the transporting of farm produce into the city had to be done by night. There was never a moment when the city was quiet.

The unemployed 'freemen' could not find work in the city, for the slaves were doing it all for no wages. The only way they could earn a living was to join the army.

In the old days the farmers provided soldiers from among their labourers for the army; wars were usually fought between planting the crops and harvesting them, so that the army could be disbanded in time for the men to go back to the land. But now that the soldiers depended on the army for their living, they were no longer eager to be released. So, although the army was disbanded after every campaign, most soldiers immediately signed on for another year's fighting, and retired into winter-quarters (lodgings) at the country's expense.

If there was no war, then there was nothing at all for the unemployed to do. A Roman historian said: 'The men who fight and die for Italy have nothing but air and light.... They are called the masters of the world, yet they have no clod (lump) of earth to call their own.' Various reformers tried to give land back to these people, and the country came to the brink of civil war because the landowners (many of whom were Senators) would not agree. The struggle was still between two classes of people, but the division was now slightly different. Because of earlier reforms, many people from families which were once plebeian, were now wealthy. The reforms had not really changed anything except the names of the two classes, for there was still an upper class (now called *optimares*), and the ordinary people (*populares*).

Besides the struggles between these two classes, there were rivalries between the Senators themselves. Sulla, one of the consuls for the year 88 B.C., was strong enough to make himself a dictator. He was cruel and merciless, and he

Togas
All Roman men wore togas made of woollen cloth, reaching the ankles. Senators wore a purple stripe on their togas, while an emperor might have a completely purple toga. Ordinary people were not allowed to wear purple clothes.

killed 6000 men who were the supporters of a Senator who had opposed him. They were executed just outside the Senate House while the members were in council. The Senators were shocked, but they could do nothing about it. Sulla told them to pay attention to his speech and not listen to the noise outside. 'Some naughty people,' he said, 'are being punished at my orders.' The Republic was no longer working properly, and though the Senate did not then know it, this form of government was about to end in Rome. But before it ended, there was a long civil war, and much Roman blood was shed.

Julius Caesar, 108–44 B.C.

Julius Caesar, one of the Romans most widely known about today, was born in about 108 B.C. He began his public career with the post of *quaestor* in Spain. And although this was a very junior appointment, it is said that he made his fortune while in office. He was a shrewd man, and ambitious. He realized that without spending money he could not rise to power, and he used his new fortune to bribe his way into high appointments. He paid for expensive gladiatorial* shows and chariot races, in order to win the support of the people. In 64 B.C. he was given the highest priestly rank in the land—the position known as *Pontifex Maximus*, the Chief Priest. The *Pontifex* was elected for life.

In 59 B.C. Caesar became a consul. He was heavily in debt, and he realized that he must somehow have financial support. He decided to join forces with two important men in the Senate, Pompey and Crassus. Pompey had led the army to war against the Syrians, and had made Palestine a province of Rome; Crassus was a rich land-owner. They were called the 'Triumvirate', the 'three-man-Government', and they held power even over the Senate.

The Gallic Wars

In 58 B.C. trouble broke out in Gaul. The Helvetii, a tribe who lived in western Switzerland, were constantly being attacked by German tribes from the north, and they decided to leave their homes and migrate westwards into present-day France. Caesar was now Governor of the provinces of Cisalpine Gaul and Illyricum (North Italy and the coast of modern Yugoslavia). He immediately marched into Gaul in order to stop the Helvetii from crossing the river Rhône; in the battle that followed thousands of the Helvetii were killed, and their provisions captured. It was a senseless war, because the Helvetii were not a threat to the Romans. Caesar probably fought in order to gain more money for himself, and more power and fame in Rome.

Before he went back to North Italy, Caesar joined forces with the local Gauls to stop the German tribes, living east of the river Rhine, from invading their country. The German king, Ariovistus, had already been officially titled 'king and friend of the Roman people', so the Romans

*Gladiators were men who fought with swords or other weapons against other gladiators or wild animals to entertain the Roman crowd in the 'circuses'.

Religion

Most of the Roman gods were adopted from the Greeks, but their names were changed. Zeus, king of the gods, became Jupiter*. Aphrodite became Venus and Poseidon, god of the sea, became Neptune. Dionysus, god of wine, was Bacchus to the Romans.

Besides these 'imported' gods, the Romans worshipped some much earlier gods of their own. Two especially important ones occupied a place in every home. They were the *lares* and *penates*, the household gods who looked after the family. The picture above shows members of a family making sacrifices to Lar. Most homes had a Larium where small sacrifices to Lar could be made to ensure the well-being and happiness of their family life.

*This is a case where the name has not been completely changed. Zeus became 'Deus Pater' or 'Father God' to the Romans, and that soon became Jupiter.

should not have made war on him. But Ariovistus foolishly led his army across the Rhine, knowing that Caesar would oppose him. He was utterly defeated by the Roman legions, and Caesar wrote: 'Two campaigns were thus finished in a single summer.'*

Up till now, there had been no thought of extending the Roman lands to the north. But during the years between 58 B.C. and 49 B.C., Caesar and his legions carried out what Caesar described as 'the conquest and pacification

*From *De Bello Gallico*, Caesar's campaign records.

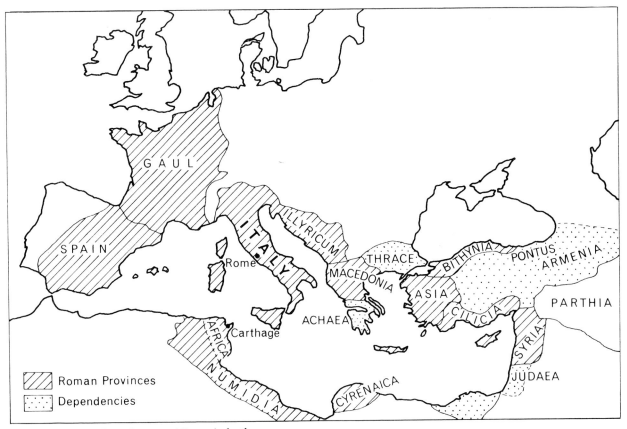

The Roman Republic at the time of Caesar's death.

of Gaul'. In fact his legions fought without pity against a brave and determined people, and because the Romans were better equipped and better disciplined, in those nine years they killed so many Gauls that it was impossible for the survivors to be anything else but 'peaceful'. Some tribes were almost completely wiped out defending their own homes.

The Gauls became so afraid of the Romans that they joined together to try to conquer the legions. One of the most confusing and bewildering things to them was Caesar's habit of doing the unexpected. When a Gallic king named Vercingetorix raised his flag as a signal of revolt, Caesar was over 100 miles away; yet he marched his legions day and night through snow, and reached Vercingetorix's capital long before the Gauls expected him. Caesar kept his legions alert and 'on their toes' by never telling them his plans in advance. He would suddenly order them to practise drill, or to march 20 miles in full armour just as they were settling down to a meal. They had to be prepared to go anywhere, at any time. No soldier was ever unfit through lack of exercise, even when he was far from the battle-line, or in winter-quarters. But though Caesar was strict, he was also just. His men were proud to be under his command. He called them 'comrades', and they knew that he would never make them bear sufferings and hardships that he himself could not endure.

By destroying so much of his enemies' land, and by killing all their soldiers, Caesar actually made the war more difficult for the Romans. For the other tribes became desperate, and this made them tougher and less likely to surrender. But even Vercingetorix was in the end forced to give in, because his people were starving in a besieged town called Alesia. They had even got to the point of considering eating the old people and the babies in the town, when Vercingetorix finally surrendered. Now Caesar held the whole of Gaul for Rome. In Rome itself, the delighted Senate declared a public thanksgiving that lasted for 20 days.

Meanwhile Crassus had been killed while at war in Asia, and the Triumvirate was broken up. Caesar and Pompey were now rivals for power rather than partners. During Caesar's absence, Pompey had become very powerful among the *optimares* who controlled the Senate. Caesar, however, was the idol of the *populares*. The Senate ordered Caesar to disband his army, but Caesar refused, and in 49 B.C. he marched south with his legions across the river Rubicon, into Italy. It was against the law to enter Italy with an army, and the Romans realized that Caesar meant to gain control of Rome by force. Pompey hurriedly left the city, and escaped with his legions to Greece.

Caesar was in many ways a rash man, and many times in his career he put himself and his men in great danger because of lack of planning. A modern historian has remarked that more than half of Caesar's campaigns were taken up with getting out of difficult situations that he should not have got into in the first place! It was only because he was so confident of his own powers, and was able to give confidence to his men, that they followed him at all.

The people of Rome expected Caesar to be as merciless as Sulla had been, and they trembled to think of the executions, and the seizing of property ahead. They had heard about Caesar's bloodthirsty methods in Gaul. But Caesar realized that a civil war (a war between the citizens of the same country), should be conducted differently, and he tried to win the people over to his side by mild and generous behaviour. But he knew that he would always be in danger while Pompey was alive, so he followed him with his army into Greece. Pompey was finally defeated at Pharsalus, in Thessaly, and he escaped, leaving behind most of his army. He went to Egypt and asked if he might live there.

Caesar in Egypt

In Egypt, Ptolemy XIV, the Pharaoh, was at war with his sister Cleopatra, who wanted the throne for herself. Ptolemy was afraid to let a Roman general into his country, so instead of receiving Pompey with friendship, he had him murdered. When Caesar arrived in pursuit of Pompey, he was handed his rival's embalmed* head.

Without realizing it, Ptolemy had brought great trouble for himself, for Caesar met and fell in love with Cleopatra, and took her side against the Pharaoh. Caesar stayed in Egypt for nearly a year, during which time Ptolemy was drowned in a battle when his barge capsized and sank on the river Nile. His warships were burnt by Caesar in Alexandria harbour, and his younger

*To embalm is to preserve a dead body from decaying.

Britain

In 55 B.C. and again the following year, Caesar took an army to Britain. The hostile islanders, many of them refugees from Gaul, fought fiercely against the legions. They used chariots to take them into battle, then the warriors leapt out and fought on foot. The charioteers took their vehicles away and had them ready to help in a quick retreat, or in moving the warriors to another part of the battle. Caesar did not have enough troops with him to conquer Britain. In the first century A.D. Romans invaded and conquered England and part of Scotland.

The picture above is a reconstruction of the barracks at a typical Roman fort in Britain in the first century A.D.

brother, Ptolemy XV, was made joint ruler with Cleopatra.

When at last Caesar returned to Rome, he was powerful enough to make himself dictator for ten years. But he did not stay long in Italy, for there were still many supporters of Pompey overseas, and he had to fight first in Libya and then in Spain before the civil war finally ended.

At last Caesar had achieved his aims—he was the sole ruler of Rome. He held the greatest feasts and gladiatorial shows that the city had ever known. In one day 400 lions were hunted to death in the arena, and two enormous armies of criminals and war captives were made to fight each other to the death, in order to excite and entertain the Roman people. Caesar even ordered that a great area of land should be flooded, so that a sham naval battle could be fought. Many of the citizens of Rome were thrilled by these extraordinary entertainments; others were horrified. There were four Triumphs in four days: to celebrate the victories in Gaul, Egypt, Syria and North Africa. Many chiefs and kings were led through Rome in chains, including Vercingetorix, who was publicly executed; and Cleopatra's sister Arsinoë, who was later released.

Caesar had his statue placed with the statues of the gods at the public games, inscribed 'to the unconquerable god'. He gave his friends new posts in the Senate; and since the *populares* had always been on his side, many of the new Senators were centurions, scribes, and even Gauls. He forbade the people to spend too much money on luxuries, while he himself wore purple garments and sat on a gold throne in the Senate House. He was king of Rome in all but name, and some of the Senators decided that he should actually be called 'King of Rome'. But two of the Senators, Cassius and Brutus, feared Caesar's power, and they knew that the other Senators would never vote against Caesar. So they plotted to kill Caesar before the Senate met to discuss the question of kingship.

The meeting was planned for the 15 March, 44 B.C. Caesar had already been warned by a fortune-teller to 'beware the Ides of March', but Brutus persuaded him to go to the meeting, even if only to dismiss the waiting Senators. On the steps of the Senate House, Caesar met the fortune-teller, and said to him scornfully, 'You see, the Ides of March have come', and the man replied, 'Yes, but they have not yet gone.' Less than an hour later, Caesar lay dead. As he sat listening to the Senators' petitions, a number of people pressed forward, took out hidden daggers, and stabbed him to death. Tradition has it that when Caesar saw that Brutus, whom he loved, was amongst the murderers, he cried out 'et tu, Brute?'* – 'You too, Brutus?' Shakespeare's play *Julius Caesar* dramatizes these events.

We still use some abbreviations from Latin in everyday English. For instance:

i.e.	id est	that is to say
p.m.	post meridiem	afternoon
A.D.	anno Domini	in the year of our Lord
etc.	et cetera	and the rest/others
p.s.	post scriptum	something that is 'written after'
N.B.	nota bene	'note well'
e.g.	exempli gratia	for (the sake of) example

Julius Caesar Act III, 1,7

Cleopatra and Mark Antony

Although the Ptolemies were Greeks and not Egyptians, they followed the customs of the old Egyptian Pharaohs. So Cleopatra had to marry her brother Ptolemy XIV. On his death, she married the younger brother, who became Ptolemy XV. Caesar married her in an Egyptian ceremony, and they had a son, Caesarion, who was later murdered in Rome. By this marriage the Egyptians recognized that a Roman dynasty had now taken over from the Greek one. After Caesar's death, Cleopatra married another Roman, Mark Antony, and they ruled together from Alexandria. But Octavian, later called Augustus, first emperor of Rome, defeated the Egyptian forces, and both Mark Antony and Cleopatra committed suicide. The coin above was made during the reign of Mark Antony and Cleopatra. It shows Cleopatra on one side, Mark Antony on the other.

The Julian Calendar

Julius Caesar reformed the calendar and named the seventh month 'July' after his own name. The Roman mosaic above depicts July and August. September, October, November and December originally meant 7th, 8th, 9th and 10th month, after the Latin words *septem, octo, novem,* and *decem.* When Caesar re-arranged the months they kept their names but are now the 9th, 10th, 11th and 12th months of the year. The 'Ides' fell on the 13th or 15th, the 'Nones' on the 5th or 7th of each month. The Julian calendar was in use until A.D. 1582.

Chapter 14 The Roman Empire

Julius Caesar's successor was his great-nephew, Octavian. Octavian had complete power in Rome, and called himself 'Augustus' or 'supreme'. Although he refused to be crowned, or accept any other title, he was in fact the first Roman emperor, and his reign began 300 years of peace in the Empire (though there were short uprisings from time to time). We call this the time of the *pax romana* or 'Roman peace'.

One of Augustus's first acts was to build a temple to his predecessor Julius Caesar, which encouraged the people to think of Caesar as a martyr, and a god. From this time onwards the emperors were all, in varying degrees, worshipped as gods, and their portraits appeared on the standards which the legions took into battle. Soon there were priests for the new emperor-worship, and people in the provinces who did not bow down before the emperor's shrine were severely punished. So although the 'provincials' (people who lived in the provinces) were free to worship their own gods, there was now a worship which was shared by all the people of the empire. The Roman gods, except for Jupiter and the *lares* and *penates*, were almost completely replaced by the new living god-emperor.

Augustus was not a vain man, and he probably did not for a moment believe that he was really divine. But he recognized that Rome, and the newly-conquered countries, needed a symbol that all the widely different peoples could look up to. It was no longer possible for this vast Empire to be ruled by a succession of yearly consuls, all of whom had different ideas about how to govern. Augustus kept the Senate, and let it make laws. But he himself had the real power.

Augustus was not at all like an Asian ruler— he did not need rich clothes, splendid palaces, and daily banquets to hold the respect of the

Virgil

The poet Virgil lived during the reign of Augustus. His greatest work is the *Aeneid*, a poem in 12 books, telling of the founding of the Latin race by Aeneas the Trojan. Aeneas tells the story of his wanderings to Dido in Carthage (see p. 68). At one point in his magical journey, Aeneas goes down to the Underworld and meets future heroes. One of these is Augustus, whom he calls 'the leader often promised, Augustus Caesar of divine descent; he shall establish a golden age in the countryside once ruled by Saturn.'

Virgil's books were so popular that they were used in schools even in his own lifetime.

people. In fact he wore only home-spun togas and leather sandals, and ate quite simple meals. He was always ready to hear the requests of his people, and he allowed residents of all Italy to become citizens of Rome. He kept in touch with the Empire by appointing 30 governors, each with his own province. He built roads and aqueducts*, temples and circuses in the provinces, and encouraged the provincials to live as the citizens of Rome did.

Had Augustus called himself king, and tried to get rid of the Senate, he would probably have been assassinated as Julius Caesar had been. But he cleverly combined dictatorship with rule by the Senate, and everybody was satisfied. He took on a difficult job, and handled it well and firmly. His last words were: 'Have I played my part in the comedy of life creditably enough?' Later generations agreed that he had, and spoke of him as the best emperor that had ever ruled over them. He had managed to stop the constant quarrels in Rome, and he prepared the way for the great *pax romana* in Europe, Asia and North Africa.

The Pax Romana

During the next 300 years, not all the emperors were as keen to 'play their part' as carefully and conscientiously as Augustus had. But in spite of this the Empire grew, and the conquered territories settled down, mainly because of excellent government in the provinces. Even Gaul, which had suffered so much from Julius Caesar's armies, began to flourish again in a new way, as people built new towns and villages on the Roman plan. Men from the provinces were sometimes called up into the Roman army as auxiliaries ('helping' troops), and they marched and fought with the legions as non-citizen units. The auxiliaries could become Roman citizens, with a grant of land, after 25 years' service, and many of them were happy to do so.

The Empire was now greater than the individual emperors. A Roman general once told the Gauls that they should bear the rule of a bad emperor in much the same way as they endured years of flood or drought; there were sure to be better times ahead, Roman law, and the ability of Roman officials, kept the Empire in peace in spite of troubles in Rome itself. Two of the best-known 'bad' (possibly even mad) emperors were Caligula and Nero. Caligula is said to have given his horse a marble stall and purple blankets, and made it a consul; and he forced rich men to leave their money to the state. Nero killed his own mother and his half-brother. During his reign Rome was burnt in an accidental fire, and rumour said that Nero had lit the fire himself, and had stood watching the flames, while playing

*Aqueducts are channels carrying water, usually *over* the land or across valleys, by being built on arches.

a lyre, a small kind of harp. After the fire Nero blamed the Christians for starting it, and he ordered them to be torn to pieces by lions in the arena where the gladiatorial shows were held. During A.D. 68 and 69, there were four emperors in Rome, one after the other. Two of them were murdered, and the third committed suicide. The fourth was Vespasian, one of the great emperors, who managed to put an end to the civil unrest.

Even the successful and 'good' emperors allowed a great deal of cruelty to go on in the Empire. The games and gladiatorial contests, where thousands of men were tortured and killed each year to entertain the Roman crowds, were often attended by the emperors themselves. It is not surprising that the Roman soldiers who were so used to seeing bloody entertainments in the arenas at home, were often brutal to their prisoners. But this was an age of cruelty, and their enemies, the Gauls, the Britons, and the German tribes, were just as cruel themselves. The remarkable thing is that after a battle, the conquerors and the conquered lived side by side at peace, working for the good of the community as a whole. Perhaps the gladiatorial shows and chariot-races, which were now held in all the major towns of the Empire, were a way of 'letting off steam' in times of peace. The Roman settlers in these towns had no feeling of superiority over the native inhabitants; Roman citizens married native wives, and they and their children lived in Roman-built towns under Roman law. This mixing up of peoples was the Roman strength; they could never have kept their Empire for so long if they had not allowed the conquered peoples to be equal under the law. Instead of feeling inferior and bitter, the provincials gradually acquired a new pride in themselves and their settled way of life.

Britain

By the second century A.D., the northern limit of the Empire was the great wall built by the emperor Hadrian across the width of Britain. On the wall, legionaries from Gaul and Spain, Britain itself, Syria and Italy, kept watch for attacks from Caledonia as Scotland was then called. Britain had been left alone for nearly 100 years after Julius Caesar's visits. Then, under the emperor Claudius, the legions sailed once again across the English Channel and marched inland, building roads and bridges, temples and towns. Some of the British tribes were friendly, others

hostile. The Britons in Wales fought fiercely in their mountain fortresses and strongholds; the people of Caledonia were never subdued. The Iceni, a tribe living in present-day Norfolk, revolted, and led by their queen Boudicca (or Boadicea), they marched south and burnt three new Roman-British towns, killing all the inhabitants with great ferocity. We have a description of this wild British queen, written by a Roman historian:

'She was very tall, in appearance terrifying, in the glance of her eye most fierce, and her voice was harsh. A great mass of the tawniest (yellow-brown) hair fell to her hips. Around her neck she wore a large golden necklace; and she wore a tunic of many colours over which a thick cloak was fastened with a brooch.'

She rode a war-chariot into battle; when she was at last defeated she poisoned herself.

For 40 years three Roman legions were kept busy in Britain, building forts, checking raiders, and putting down rebellions. And after the invasion was over, Britain, from Hadrian's Wall to the south coast, enjoyed Roman peace and prosperity. The Roman Governor of Britain was considered a great man, second only to the Governor of Syria.

Hadrian's Wall

Hadrian built a great wall from the river Tyne to the Solway, in order to help the legions defend Roman Britain against the northern tribes. Parts of the wall still exist today. It was over 112 kilometres (70 miles) long, protected by a ditch and a mud ramp. There were forts all along the wall, and on the southern side small markets grew up, with shops and taverns where the local people sold their goods to the soldiers stationed in the forts. Along the top of the wall, sentries walked to and fro between their own fort and the next, always on the lookout for the painted barbarians of the mountains. Amongst these were the Picts.

The trade routes of the Empire

In the east, most of Alexander's empire fell to the Romans. They built forts to guard their boundaries, and stationed soldiers from other parts of the Empire to control the new provinces. Although travelling was still a very slow business, soldiers and administrators often served hundreds of miles from their home towns. For the first time the ordinary common people began to see for themselves how other countries managed their affairs. Whole families left Italy and settled in 'colonies' in other parts of the Roman world. The emperors themselves often went to the provinces to review the troops; Claudius visited Britain, and Vespasian knew it well; and Trajan, an emperor whose birthplace was Spain, visited Alexander's palace in Babylon.

The Romans were not the only travellers: teachers and doctors, artists and sculptors, left their homes in Syria and Turkey, Greece and North Africa, and went to practise their skills in the flourishing towns of Italy. There was a great exchange of peoples, and there was also an increase in trade. Tin, gold, sheepskins and corn came from Britain by sea, and on the backs of donkeys along the straight Roman roads: camels and donkeys plodded day after day along the old Persian highways, bringing silks and precious stones from China and India, silver, crystal (a very clear kind of quartz) and salt from northern Asia, and corn from Russia. The Romans even bought spices which had been grown in Ceylon, but they did not go there themselves.

All the time the Romans had to be careful not to take too much from the provinces. They needed corn to feed the people of Rome, but if they went on demanding it even in time of famine, trouble followed.

On the Sea of Marmora, just south-west of the Black Sea, Byzantium grew in importance because of its central position for trade between east and west. There were so many trading ships sailing across the Black Sea that soon pirates became common, and the Romans had to keep a fleet of 40 ships to protect their cargo boats.

The ruins of Pompeii

In A.D. 79, the volcano Vesuvius (in the background of the picture) erupted and lava and ash completely buried two Roman cities. A Roman writer named Pliny watched the eruption from far off. He said it looked like 'a pine tree, for it shot up a great height . . . into several branches.' The eruption continued for three days, during which stones and ash were hurled across the countryside.

One of the buried cities, Pompeii, has been dug up by archaeologists, and beneath the layers of ash and lava were found buildings, furniture, and even fossilized remains of people and animals. Pompeii was a wealthy city, and most of the inhabitants could read and write. From the remains that have been uncovered we can see how a typical Roman city was organized. (The other city was Herculaneum.)

North Africa and Egypt

Trade with North Africa was even more important to Rome than trade with the east. The whole coast of North Africa was settled by farmers, whose corn crops went to feed the rest of the Empire. Egypt provided a great deal of the income of Rome, and the Roman emperors always took care to manage the country well. Every year corn and gold left Egypt for Italy by ship; these rich imports of gold meant that the townspeople of Rome did not have to pay high taxes; and in some reigns they were actually given free food and lodging, while the slaves did all the work.

In Egypt, Alexandria was still a great centre of learning, and as in other parts of the Empire, many of the inhabitants spoke Greek. There was a large Jewish population there, and they carried on a flourishing trade with the east. They used a caravan route from the Nile Valley to the Red Sea, to bring to Alexandria the silks and spices of China and India.

In Rome, and in the other cities of Italy, builders imported African marble, and painted African scenes on their walls. The Romans were fascinated by the tales of strange animals and dark-skinned people, which they heard from those who had travelled to Roman towns in Algeria, Libya and Egypt.* It was an exciting time for those with enquiring minds. There were so many new things to see and to learn about. The provincial people, whose culture had already been influenced by the Greeks, gained from their contacts with the rest of the world. Phi-

*Such towns as Tiddis, Leptis Magna and Alexandria.

Trajan's Column
Trajan, the first non-Italian emperor, built a new Forum in Rome in about A.D. 100. As architect, he chose a Greek who lived in Damascus, in the Roman province of Syria. The Forum held shops and offices, and two libraries, one for Greek books, and the other for Latin books. On a column between the two libraries, a spiral frieze (an ornamental band) was carved with scenes from Trajan's campaigns in Dacia, north of the Danube.

losophers and historians, mathematicians and astronomers went to the university at Alexandria; among them were some of the greatest thinkers the world has known. Scholars exchanged ideas, and built up a great library so that those who followed them might carry on where they had left off. Some of the ideas and theories of these men, living during the *pax romana*, were not improved upon until recent times.

Many provincials were now allowed to apply for Roman citizenship, and some even became emperors. Trajan and Hadrian, both excellent emperors, were Spaniards, and Septimius Severus was an African from Leptis Magna. There was a great feeling of unity in the Empire, and even the Greeks said, 'An attack on Rome is an attack on us.' The great genius of the Romans was that they were able to govern so many different countries, yet allow each one to keep its own customs, language and religion. Cyrus of Persia and Alexander of Macedonia had tried to do this too, but they did not have the thousands of quiet, efficient, able administrators that the Romans had, nor their ability to blend together the conqueror and the conquered.

Chapter 15 Life in the Empire

The Roman and Greek characters were quite different. A Roman preferred action, while to a Greek the most important thing was thinking. The Greeks regarded the Romans as barbarians when they first met them, because when the Romans conquered a civilized city, they destroyed the works of art—merely because they did not recognize that they were beautiful. The Romans, on the other hand, thought the Greeks were pleasure-loving and idle, and could not understand their liking for talk and discussion. One Roman consul told a group of Sophists that if they came to his court-house, he would settle their arguments for them: he did not understand that most of their discussions were about things that can have *no* final answer!

All Romans knew something of the laws of their country, and a lawyer was highly respected. In the days of the Empire he received fees for his services, but during the Republic he had to rely on presents from his clients, the people who used his services. A wrongdoer was granted a public trial, and his lawyer helped him to prepare his speech of defence. The accuser also had a lawyer as an adviser. There was no such thing as having 'the state' as the accuser as we do today for criminal trials; all lawsuits* were entered into by private persons, the one accusing the other—even for crimes like murder. Trials were often won by the lawyer who made the best speeches, and a man could become famous for the way in which he was able to win a trial.

Although the Romans seem to us now to have had little imagination, they were trustworthy and honest, law-abiding and just. The provincials respected them, and learnt to live by their laws.

A Roman family was ruled by the father. He had complete control over his sons until they

Roman dress

In the privacy of his own home, a Roman 'freeman' felt more comfortable without his toga, and appeared in the tunic, which normally he wore underneath. But if he went into the street so dressed, he was likely to be mistaken for a workman or even a slave, who is pictured above.

A Roman freeman's wife also wore a tunic, as in the picture, and a belted gown reaching down to the ankles. When she went out she wore a hood. Both men and women wore sandals tied with leather laces in the house, and stronger leather shoes out of doors. Peasants and slaves were either barefooted or wore clogs or sandals in the street. The Roman freemen disapproved of a man who wore sandals in the street, or a woman who was not dressed in the latest fashion.

---

* To take action against somebody in a court of law is 'to sue'; an action in a court of law is a lawsuit.

were 16 years old, and over his daughters until they married. All the decisions were made by him, although his wife was allowed to own property, and to have some influence over the upbringing of her children. The parents, if they were well off, would almost certainly find a Greek tutor for their children, and would encourage them to read and write in Greek as well as Latin. The girls as well as the boys learnt to read and write, and to know something of history, geography, mathematics and astronomy. They studied law, and learnt long passages from the law books by heart. The Greeks, you remember, used to get together over a meal to discuss philosophy, poetry, or religion. The Roman idea of good conversation was less intellectual and more gossipy, or more practical: they were inclined to talk scandal, or argue about the qualities of a new consul, or exchange the latest news of an uprising in Jerusalem. They could not see the point in endless discussion about abstract theoretical things.

Educated Romans often went to Greece and to Egypt as tourists, and they marvelled at the Parthenon and the pyramids, just as modern tourists do. By the time of Augustus, the pyramids were already nearly 3000 years old. The Ptolemy Pharaohs had restored many of the old temples, and they too attracted Roman travellers. We even know the names of some of these tourists, for they carved them on the temple walls!

All the big towns of the Empire, Londinium, Caesaraugusta, Lutetia, Byzantium, Neapolis, Tingis*, and many many others—copied the pattern of Rome. Wealthy Roman citizens, whether they were by birth British, or Celts from Gaul, or Syrians or Libyans, built houses just like those in Rome, with floors decorated with mosaics (pictures made with small coloured stones), courtyards with fountains, and wall recesses for the *lares* and *penates*. They ate, where possible, the same kinds of food, and they drank wine imported from the vineyards of Gaul and Italy. Their common culture became a common bond.

In Rome itself, in some periods it was said that the rich got sick from eating, and the poor from not eating. Certainly the rich ate huge meals with great enjoyment. They often invited friends in for the evening meal, which was the main time for eating. They lay on long couches

*On a modern map these towns are called London, Saragossa, Paris, Istanbul, Naples and Tangier.

Roman writing

By the time of the Republic, the letters of the alphabet had become almost the same as the capital letters we use today. We call the alphabet used in this book 'Roman'. The Latin inscription above, carved on stone, is part of a commemoration to a priest called Claudius Sossianus Severianus.

For ordinary writing, the Romans used wooden tablets coated with wax, on which they scratched the words with a pointed metal 'stylus'. When writing documents, letters or books, they used either papyrus or parchment made from sheepskin. Books were often written on one long sheet of papyrus, then rolled up: but sometimes they were cut and the pages sewn or stuck together, rather like modern books. They wrote with goose-feather pens and black ink. There were bookshops in the Forum where slaves sat all day copying popular books for sale.

I	III	V	VII	IX	XI	XXX
1	3	5	7	9	11	30

L	XC	C	D	M
50	90	100	500	1000

Roman numerals

Even now we sometimes use these Roman numerals to number chapters in a book, or the hours on a clock face, or as dates on a monument. The Romans had no nought, and without it, modern mathematics is not possible.

In the Roman system, if you wrote a lower number before a higher one, such as X before C—XC, the result was 'one hundred *minus* ten', or 90. The date '1977' would be written like this: MCMLXXVII

round the dining table, while slaves served them large helpings of eggs and fish, the small squirrel-like animals called dormice cooked in honey, poultry and small roasted birds, game and fruit. The poor in the cities were lucky to get a ration of bread and a handful of olives, washed down with a cup of sour wine. To stop them from rioting, and to keep them fed and occupied, some emperors allowed them free bread and put on free circus-shows. The upper classes were always afraid that the discontent of the unemployed, living in their smelly, unventilated and crowded apartment houses, would cause them to rise against the rich and bring civil war again to Rome.

Every year there were feast days on which everybody, rich and poor alike, stopped work and joined in the general rejoicing. In December, all Romans celebrated the Saturnalia, feast of the god Saturn, at which people gave each other presents, and a mock-king was crowned as ruler of the feast. The slaves had the day free, and their masters waited on them at dinner. On other feast days there were public games and circuses, and chariot races.

Home of a wealthy Roman

A Roman house in a wealthy district was built as two squares joined together. One square was called the 'atrium' and the other the 'peristyle'. The atrium was the place where the gentleman of the house had his offices, and perhaps a library. In the centre of the atrium was an unroofed space, within which there was a pool called the 'impluvium'. Small dark bedrooms opened off the atrium. There were no outside windows; in towns, shops were often built against the walls of a rich man's house.

The Roman family spent much of their time in the peristyle where, as you can see in the picture, there was a central garden surrounded by columns with statues, fountains and birdbaths. The dining-room and more bedrooms opened off the peristyle.

The builders of the Empire

All over the Empire, the Romans built roads. They were so well constructed, that many of them are still used today. They were built, where possible, completely straight. Where there were rivers, the Roman engineers built bridges or fords; where a hill crossed the route, they built tunnels, or cut away the banks. Each road had foundations about five feet deep, and they were made with whatever long-lasting materials were at hand. Usually there were heavy rocks for the foundations, then earth and rubble—broken bricks and stone. Near the towns, the top layer of the roads was made of stone blocks. (The word 'street' comes from the Latin for 'paved road'.) Elsewhere the surface might be gravel, flint, or even a type of cement. There was a drain at each side of the road, and kerbstones edging the road stopped the surface from sliding into the ditches. There were milestones along the way, usually marked with the name of the emperor during whose rule the road had been built. The legions marched along these roads, often with straggling lines of prisoners; baggage animals were led along them, and carts piled with trade goods rattled by from one end of the Empire to the other.

As well as roads, the Romans built aqueducts to carry water to the towns from the nearest river. The aqueducts were built as a series of arches, with a water-channel at the top. They had a continuous gradual downward slope towards the town, so that the water flowed at a steady rate all the time.

The Romans loved to bathe in public baths, and everywhere they went they constructed these huge buildings. They went to the baths to talk to their friends, as well as to clean themselves. There were rooms in which they could exercise with weights, or oil their bodies with scented oil or have them rubbed and massaged by slaves; there were hot baths, steam baths, cold showers, and changing rooms. The water was heated by a furnace, and the heat was also spread by pipes under the floor of the baths. Wealthy Romans often had private baths in their houses, and heated their rooms by hot air circulated underneath the floors. Some of the public baths were built of a type of cement, which was poured over a huge wooden framework.

Roman road—the Via Appia at Rome

A Greek once wrote admiringly of the Romans: 'You have measured out the world, bridged rivers, cut roads through mountains, filled the wastelands with staging posts . . . . Be all the gods and their children called upon to grant that this Empire and this city flourish for ever . . . .'

As time went by, it no longer mattered that 'citizens of Rome' had never actually been to the parent city. Even the emperors themselves did not always live there, but divided their time

Roman baths at Bath, in S.W. England

99

between the various towns in the provinces. Septimius Severus, the emperor from Leptis Magna, was born in North Africa, but died at York in northern England, in A.D. 211. Most of his advisers came from Asia and Africa, and he allowed foreign languages to be used instead of Latin in official Roman papers.

To a Roman citizen living when the Empire was at its height, it must have seemed that the world would go on forever in the same way. But over in the north-east, across the mountains and plains of Asia, vast numbers of men, whom the Romans called 'barbarians,' were slowly moving westwards. In the years to come, the Empire had increasing trouble with these nomadic tribes.

Commodus, who was emperor from A.D. 180–192, was more interested in gladiatorial shows and circuses than in defending the Danube frontier. In Rome itself at this time, half the population lived on free food and had free entertainment, while most of the other half were slaves. The Romans at home could not see that they must work to keep their Empire; they were fed at public expense—what more could they want? But Rome was using more money than it earned, and this situation could not last. When Commodus tried to increase taxation in his provinces, there were revolts and riots. He was finally killed by one of his own guards, and for the next 100 years the army had real control, and elected their own emperors. Civil wars between rival generals were common, and the Huns, Goths and Visigoths took advantage of these troubles to invade the borders of the Empire.

The last emperor to rule from Rome was Constantine. His mother was British, and he was born in York. His army marched into Italy from Britain and Gaul, and defeated other claimants to the throne. It is said that on his way to Rome he saw a vision in the sky—a cross, with the words HOC SIGNO VINCE—'by this sign, conquer'. Whatever the truth of this, he did make Christianity (the religion whose symbol is the cross) the official state religion of the Roman Empire.

Constantine could see that there was no point in maintaining Rome as the capital of the Empire.

He himself lived at Nicomedia, a port on the Sea of Marmora, and in A.D. 330 he transferred the administrative capital to Byzantium, one of Alexander the Great's cities. The name of the city was changed to Constantinople. (It is now Istanbul.)

Constantinople was then much more 'central' than Rome. It was truly the meeting point of east and west. It had long been a place where merchants exchanged their goods, and it was built in an ideal position, on a thin strip of land jutting into the sea. It had a good climate, and there was plenty of good farming land nearby. Here Constantine could build afresh the old spirit of discipline and training that had once made Rome itself great. The old capital became no more than a provincial town, though for a time there was an 'emperor of the West' who lived there.

But the attacks of the barbarian peoples from the east increased in strength. Most of these peoples belonged to the German tribes of the Franks, Goths, Saxons and Vandals. The legions fought valiantly to hold the Empire's long frontiers. For over 200 years they had succeeded, often after hard fighting, in defeating the invaders, but at last, in A.D. 407, the barbarians crossed the river Rhine into the Empire, plundering and destroying as they went, and this time they were too strong for the legions to drive them out. The Roman frontier had been broken for ever. Other tribes followed, and soon all of western Europe—Britain, Gaul, Spain, North Africa and even Italy—was lost to the Empire.

Constantine had been wise to move his capital; and Constantinople remained a centre of civilization long after the barbarians had overrun the western half of the Roman Empire. The period that followed is known as 'the Dark Ages'. But here and there, some of the wisdom and knowledge gained by the Greeks and Romans was remembered. Most of the people who kept the old learning alive were Christians, living in small monasteries as far apart as Ireland and Syria, Iceland and Ethiopia. On the remnants of the old civilizations, the world was to build new nations with new ideas and ideals.

Part IV Christianity and Islam
Chapter 16 Jesus of Nazareth

Palestine, on the eastern shores of the Mediterranean, was only a small part of the Roman Empire, but it was a very troublesome part. The Jews of Palestine did not like Roman rule. They already had to pay taxes to their own Temple, and now the Romans were demanding still more taxes to help pay for the administration of the Empire. Worse still, the Romans said that the Jews should worship the statue of their emperor.

Most of the other Roman provinces did not mind adding the Roman emperor to their long list of gods; but the Jews, who only had one God, Yahweh, objected strongly. They said they could not obey, because of their first and second Commandments (see page 38). And what was more, the earthly leader of the Jews, they said, was the High Priest of Jerusalem, not the emperor of a foreign power. There was a great deal of unrest in Palestine, and many uprisings, which the Romans repeatedly stopped by armed force.

In this troubled country, there was born a boy who was named Jesus. He was the son of Mary, a Jewish girl married to a carpenter of Nazareth, called Joseph. Joseph was said to be a descendant of King David. The story of Jesus is written down in the four Gospels, which are part of the New Testament in the Bible. Two of the Gospels start with the story of Jesus's birth. They tell how Joseph and Mary his wife travelled to Bethlehem, to take part in a census, or counting of people, ordered by the Romans. The little town was so crowded that there was no room for them to lodge at any inn, and they had to sleep in a stable. During this time, Jesus was born.

We do not know much about the childhood of Jesus. But St Luke tells us how his parents took him to Jerusalem when he was about 12 years old, for the Feast of the Passover. As Joseph and Mary were returning home, they missed Jesus, and had to go back to look for him. They found

John the Baptist
Although Palestine belonged to the Roman province of Syria, part of it (Galilee) was actually ruled for Rome by a king named Herod, who was half-Jewish.

Herod was allowed to have power in his part of Palestine as long as it was obedient to Rome, so he was eager to keep the peace. His own wealth and position depended on it. He saw how popular John the Baptist was, and he became afraid that the fiery preacher might lead the people to defy Rome. So he had him imprisoned and beheaded.

him in the Temple, listening spellbound to the priests' words. During this early part of his life, he surely must have learnt all he could about the Jewish faith, and thought about God, and man's relationship to God.

Jesus had a cousin named John, who was almost the same age as he was. When they were both about 30 years old, John was already a well-known holy man in Palestine. There were many wandering preachers in those days, and they often lived as John did, wearing camel-hair cloaks and eating wild berries and honey. John impressed the people of Palestine by his teaching, and crowds gathered round him when he started to baptize people in the river Jordan. They waded into the river, and John poured water on to their heads, as a sign that they repented for their sins, and would try to do better in future. John was known as 'the Baptist' because of his method of bringing people to repentance.

One day Jesus went to the river to be baptized by John. St Matthew says that when Jesus came out of the river, the Spirit of God came down from heaven like a dove, and a voice said, 'This is my beloved Son, in whom I am well pleased.'

Jesus helped John to baptize the people for several months, then he began a new kind of teaching. With a group of disciples he went about the land of Galilee talking to people about God as their Father, and healing the sick. Thousands of people followed him, and believed that he was the Messiah—that is, a leader for whom they had been waiting for generations. ('Messiah' means 'the Lord's Anointed one'. The word 'Christ' comes from the Greek word for 'Messiah'.)

The popular Jewish idea of a Messiah was of a man who would rid them of the Romans, and lead the Jews to glory by creating a splendid new kingdom. Obviously, to defeat the might of Rome, such a Messiah would have to be a strong and clever general, and he would need far more soldiers than little Palestine could produce. But in any case, Jesus was not at all like this. He did not believe in defying Rome. He taught that people should make peace with God the Father in their own hearts, and not bother so much about the irritations of everyday living. His Kingdom was 'not of this world'. It was within each person's own self, if he only cared to look for it.

Jesus was a most compassionate man, for he pitied the distress of others and desired to help them. He told people that God was a God of love, not of vengeance, as some of the old Jewish tales of God had made Him out to be. In almost every story in the Gospels, we read of the mercy and love of God. People began to feel that they could be happy and 'blessed' without being rich, or well-born.

Jesus healed many people in a way which is beyond our knowledge: for instance, people who had such diseases as a crippled hand, a twisted back, leprosy, fits and madness, are said by the Gospel-writers to have been cured by a touch of his hand. On one occasion Jesus even restored

The Gospel writers

'Gospel' originally meant 'good news'. Many people during the two centuries following Jesus's death wrote down the good news contained in his teaching; of these writings, four are part of the New Testament of the Bible.

St Mark was the first Gospel-writer of the four, and he probably wrote his book in Rome, having heard the story from Jesus's disciple, Peter. St Matthew added more incidents to Mark's writings, and his Gospel is fuller and more detailed. St Luke was probably a Gentile, and a healer. He seems to have used some stories that Mark and Matthew did not know about. St Luke's Gospel may have been told to the writer by John, one of Jesus's disciples, when he was a very old man.

The Gospel of St John was once supposed to have been written by this same John, the disciple. But some modern scholars think that this is doubtful. It was written later than the other three Gospels.

The illustration is of a painting from a seventeenth century Ethiopian manuscript of St Luke and St John.

a man to life. We know that he did not do these things 'for show', because he told his patients that they should be quiet about how they were healed; he said it was their own faith that led to their cure. God had restored their health because of their faith in Jesus.

Much of Jesus's teaching was by parable — that is, by means of a story which taught a lesson. This was a popular Jewish way of teaching, but Jesus went further than most Jewish preachers. He did not believe that people should merely 'follow the Law' by keeping the rules about what they could eat, or by doing no work on the Sabbath (Saturday). Many Jews thought that by offering the right sacrifices, and praying at the right times, and giving money to the poor, they were doing God's will. Jesus thought these acts were meaningless unless they were sincerely carried out. A poor fisherman might easily please God more than a rich priest who prayed all day. There are many instances in the Gospels where Jesus said things which surprised the crowd because they were fresh and new. He did not attempt to change Jewish laws and traditions: only to interpret them in a new and more joyous way. He laid particular stress on the following two precepts:

Love the Lord your God with all your heart, with all your soul, with all your mind, and with all your strength;

Love your neighbour as yourself.

Jesus did not deliberately start a new religion. He was only concerned with making the Jewish faith more alive. But his teachings did in fact lead to the religion we now call Christianity.

The priests were furious because Jesus criticized them, and because he allowed people to do things which *they* thought were against Jewish religious law. They tried to trap him by asking him difficult questions about whether it was lawful to pay tribute to the emperor of Rome; or whether his disciples should rub ears of corn together to make flour on the Sabbath. (They called this 'work'.) Jesus's replies were always calm and reasonable; the priests could not make him say anything that was irreverent to God, or even disloyal to Rome.

Jesus spent three years teaching the people in this way. Peter, one of the disciples, was the first to say that they thought Jesus must be the Messiah they were all looking for. The priests also waited for a Messiah, but they were outraged when they realized that Jesus might claim this title. They felt that their power

Judas betraying Christ in the Garden of Gethsemane
Judas was one of the twelve disciples of Jesus. We do not know why he betrayed Jesus. The Gospels say he received 30 pieces of silver for this action, but this amount would not seem enough to betray his master if it were just for greed. Perhaps this was only part-payment. After Jesus's death, Judas hanged himself, probably in remorse.

The Jewish Passover Feast
The Feast of the Passover was held every year at a special time; all male Jews were required to travel to Jerusalem for the ceremonies. There were ritual animal sacrifices in the Temple, and at the end of the day groups of people ate a meal together. The feast was held in memory of an event which occurred when the Israelites were slaves in Egypt: they saved themselves from death by smearing lambs' blood on their house doors. According to the Old Testament of the Bible, the Angel of Death then 'passed over' these houses.

Jews were not allowed to eat bread made with yeast during the Passover. This was in memory of their flight from Egypt, when there was no time to bake proper bread.

was threatened by this carpenter's son, and they easily persuaded the Roman procurator, Pontius Pilate, that Jesus's popularity might lead to a revolt. (A procurator was rather like a Provincial Commissioner.) Pilate knew that if the Jews had a popular leader who claimed to be the Messiah, the result might well be a bloody war. This he wanted to avoid – and so did the priests, and so did Herod. Jesus's mission was completely misunderstood by all these people, for he also passionately wanted peace – the peace of God in men's hearts as well as peace in Palestine, and peace in all the world.

This total misunderstanding led to great tragedy. Only three years after he began his teaching, Jesus rode into Jerusalem on a donkey, for the Feast of the Passover, and the people waved palm branches as he went by. Later, he went into a garden called Gethsemane to pray. Jesus knew the authorities were against him, and that he did not have long to live. Judas, one of his own disciples, but a traitor, led armed guards to him, and kissed him on the cheek, so as to point him out to the soldiers. Jesus was led away for trial before the Jewish court. We do not know all the details of this trial, but after it was over the priests gave Jesus back to the Romans, saying that he had called himself the King of the Jews. The Romans killed Jesus by the method they used for non-Roman citizens – crucifixion. But in spite of this horrible and degrading death, Jesus was not forgotten. His words and ideas live on today, kept alive by Christians all over the world. The early Christians found passages in the Jewish holy books to support their belief that Jesus, 'of the House of David', was the Messiah for whom they had been waiting. Many prophecies in the Old Testament seemed to fit in with events in the life of Jesus.

Christians everywhere celebrate two great festivals, Christmas, in honour of Jesus's birth, and Easter. On the Friday before Easter Sunday, they commemorate his death on the cross, and on the following Sunday (Easter Day), his miraculous resurrection, or rising again, from the dead. It is told in the Gospels that after three days Jesus's tomb was found empty, and for several weeks afterwards he was seen by many people. They say he walked and talked and ate with them, and then, St Luke wrote,

'And it came to pass, while He blessed them, He was parted from them, and carried up into heaven.'

The Early Christians

Jesus had often talked about a 'second coming', when he would return and establish an everlasting kingdom of peace. The disciples thought this would occur in their lifetime, and after Jesus's death many of them went out to preach this to the people. Some of his followers gave away all their goods, as Jesus had told them to, and lived a wandering life of poverty. In the Acts of the Apostles (in the New Testament of the Bible), we read how later missionaries left Palestine and preached about Jesus to the 'Gentiles' – that is, to non-Jews. They had great success among Greek-speaking peoples who believed in the idea of 'One God', but who could not become Jews because they did not want to follow the whole of the Jewish religious law. We have seen how Jesus had wanted to improve the old Jewish faith for the *Jews*; but it was the non-Jews who were more readily converted, that is, changed their beliefs, after his death. The Christian religion in the end became a completely Gentile faith.

The first Christians in Rome were persecuted and hated, because they were misunderstood. The Romans were generally tolerant of other people's religions: there is no record of any other

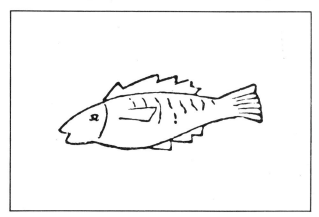

The sign of the fish
Early Christians were like a kind of universal club. They celebrated their own feasts (the 'Last Supper' instead of the Passover, for instance), and they tried to act according to their new faith. This was never easy, for almost everywhere they went, they were surrounded by Roman citizens, who worshipped many different gods.

The Christians had a sign by which they could recognize other Christians. It was a rough drawing of a fish. The Greek for 'fish' is 'ichthus', and the letters I CH TH U S could also stand for the initial letters of the Greek words for 'Jesus Christ, God, Son and Saviour'. The sign of the cross, now the universal Christian symbol, was not used in the early days of Christianity.

religious belief being forbidden. But, like the Jews, Christians refused to recognize the Roman emperor as a god, and so they were persecuted officially for this reason. And because of the persecution, they met in secret; the secret meetings led to all sorts of tales of sinful practices, and the Roman people thought they were plotting against the state.

Jesus had shown that even the poorest people, slaves, and even women — all of whom were kept out of many religions — could become Christians, and so many of the Roman Christians were very humble people. Hundreds of them were killed because of their faith, and some endured terrible deaths in the Roman arenas to provide entertainment for the crowd. But even this helped Christianity to spread, for the Roman spectators were very impressed by the Christians' courage as they stood facing the charging lions. They felt that a religion that inspired such bravery, even in women and children, must be worth following. Soon even some of the emperors agreed to allow people to follow this new religion, and it spread throughout the Empire. Antioch in Syria, Alexandria, and Rome itself, became the three great Christian centres of the world.

The Christian Church is organized

The four Gospels were written in Greek, so that all these different Christian communities might read the words of Jesus, and it was only later, in about A.D. 200, that Latin began to be used in churches. By then the Christians had developed an organization in which there were local churches headed by bishops. The bishops were under the authority of an archbishop, and by A.D. 700 all acknowledged the Bishop of Rome (the Pope or Father) as Head of the whole Church.

For a time the Christians at Constantinople (now capital of the eastern Roman Empire) also acknowledged the Pope in Rome, but quarrels broke out between east and west, and then eastern and western Christianity developed separately. The split led to the Churches we now call Roman Catholic on the one hand; and Greek and Russian Orthodox on the other.

Wherever they went, the new Christian missionaries of the west tried to win people to their religion by persuasion. In England, for instance, an early Christian writer says:

'The heathen temples of these people need not be destroyed, only the idols which are to be found in them . . . . If the temples are well

Peter and John healing the lame man outside the Temple
Jesus said to his disciple Peter; 'You are Peter, the Rock; and on this rock I will build my church.' [Peter comes from the Greek word *petros*, meaning rock.] After Jesus's death Peter carried on his work in Palestine. The priests forbade him to continue preaching in the name of Jesus; but after being punished by them, Peter continued to lead the new church. He taught the Gentiles in Asia Minor, and then went to Rome where it is believed he was crucified.

built, it is a good idea to detach them from the service of the devil, and to adapt them for the worship of the true God.'

The old pagan festivals were changed bit by bit, until they became Christian ceremonies. (Christmas took the place of the old Roman 'Saturnalia', and other new year festivals; Easter was once a spring festival to celebrate the return of the corn.) The same Christian writer says that teaching Christianity was like climbing a mountain; nobody would run to the top, but would advance slowly, step by step.

After the collapse of the western Roman Empire, in some remote places there were only a few Christians left, and they retired to monasteries and guarded the precious manuscripts which recorded their faith. In other parts, the 'barbarian' invaders of the Roman Empire had already been converted to Christianity themselves, and there grew up Christian kingdoms in which rough warriors tried to follow the ideas of the peace-loving Jesus.

Chapter 17 Christianity Spreads

The 'barbarian' invaders of Europe soon settled down in their new homes. There grew up many new kingdoms, some of which were converted to Christianity. Before they heard of this new religion, some of the peoples of Europe had believed in all kinds of 'nature' gods. None of their beliefs could explain what happened after death, and they were attracted by a religion which taught about a future heaven. One warlord in England persuaded his king to adopt Christianity by saying, 'Sometimes on a cold winter's night a bird flies through a window of the hall, into the warmth and light. It pauses a moment, then flies out again through a second window. Our life is like that. For a moment we are in the light and warmth. Then we return to

Charlemagne's Empire
Some time after Charlemagne's death in A.D. 814 Northmen from Scandinavia settled on the southern shore of the English Channel where they were called Normans. Later, in 1066, they crossed the Channel and conquered England.

the cold darkness. Let us find out more about the darkness, and turn it also into light!'

The Emperor Charlemagne, King of the Franks, A.D. 768–814
The most important kingdom of northern Europe was that of the Franks, in part of what is now called France and Western Germany. The Franks were converted to Christianity when

their king, Clovis, married the daughter of the king of a neighbouring Christian country, Burgundy. Clovis ruled the Franks from A.D. 482 to 511.

With Christianity went a desire to keep alive the old traditions of learning. The earliest known manuscript, written by hand and with beautiful decorated capital letters, comes from this period in France. As early as 591 the history of the Franks was written down by a monk named Gregory of Tours.

By this time, Muslim armies had started to cross from Arabia into Europe and Asia, conquering fresh territory for themselves 'in the name of Allah'. We shall hear more about their new religion, Islam, in Chapter 18. It was largely because of the great rivalry between the two religions, that the Christian countries of Europe flourished at all. For they had to unite in peace for their own protection, rather than conduct endless wars among themselves. In 751 the Pope in Rome was offered help by the Franks, and in return the king of the Franks, Pepin the Short, was given the title 'Father of the Romans'.

Pepin's son received even higher honours. He was called Charles the Great, or Charlemagne. He was crowned king of the Franks in 768, and from then onwards he spent his reign in improving the standard of civilization, and defending his borders against pagan tribesmen in the east, and Muslim Arabs in the south. He was so successful that by the end of his reign his empire extended over most of western Europe.

Pope Leo III was impressed by Charlemagne's strength. The eastern and western Christian churches had split apart by this time, and the Pope did not feel obliged to recognize the Roman emperor in Constantinople as his 'overlord'. (In any case, the Roman 'emperor' was now a woman!) So in 800 he invited Charlemagne to Rome, and he crowned him Holy Roman Emperor of the West on Christmas Day. Charlemagne was now recognized as the worldly ruler, while the Pope was the religious ruler, of most of western Europe.

Charlemagne himself was illiterate, but he knew the value of written works, and he had books read aloud to him. He tried to improve his people's education, and he brought learned scholars from monasteries all over Europe, including even the British Isles, to teach and advise. The language of the Franks was a kind of Latin; and since the monks who came to teach

Charlemagne

In the picture above Charlemagne, seated on the horse, watches over while a bishop baptizes some captured Saxons. The reluctant Saxons received baptism into the Christian faith under pain of death.

in France had learnt to speak Latin in their monasteries, they could already partly understand the Franks.

Christianity spread rapidly, though Charlemagne's methods of spreading it were scarcely Christian. He is said to have killed thousands of Saxons because they would not accept the new rules, one of which said:

'Any unbaptized Saxon who attempts to hide himself among his own people and refuses to accept baptism shall be put to death.'

No wonder Saxony soon became a Christian country!

But Charlemagne was quite sincere in his beliefs: his empire was built upon a religious foundation, and he probably felt that it would be dangerous to have a pagan kingdom within it.

The main towns of the empire grew up round great cathedrals, churches and abbeys. Hundreds of people served the Church, either as priests, or as monks, lay-brothers*, teachers and scribes.

The land around the Cathedral towns was tilled by farmers and labourers. In order to improve the traditional methods of agriculture, Frankish scribes studied old Roman books about farming. The farmers improved their grain crops and their dairy herds, their sheep and their vegetables, all of which they sold in the markets of the Cathedral towns.

Similar developments were taking place across the English Channel in Britain. There King Alfred made laws based on the ancient Hebrew laws of Moses. He was a learned man, and himself translated the book of songs in the Bible called the Psalms, and the prayer Jesus taught his followers which is called the Lord's Prayer, for use in his churches. But Britain was still a country divided into small kingdoms, without central government, and it did not develop as rapidly as France and Germany had done under Charlemagne.

Two hundred years after this time, the people living in one of the little kingdoms that had once been part of Charlemagne's empire, crossed the English Channel and conquered England. These people were called Normans (from 'Northmen'—they had originally come from Scandinavia). Their complete conquest of England is important, not only to English history, but to the history of all Europe. The Normans brought with them their own entirely different way of living, and new attitudes to law, religion and government. It is because of their arrival in Britain (and not because of the earlier Roman occupation) that so many words in the English language sound like Latin words—and in fact have Latin 'roots'.

After the Norman Conquest, England began once again to be conscious of the rest of Europe, and to imitate it. Her long period of isolation from the continent, which started when the Roman legions left at the beginning of the fifth century, was now over.

*People who lived in, or worked for, religious houses, but who had not themselves taken the religious vows.

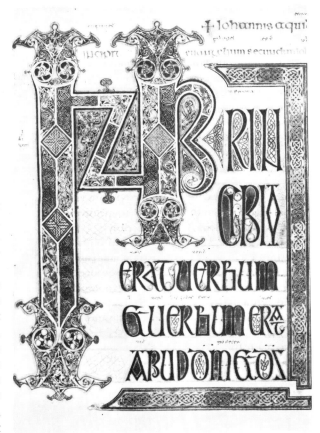

Manuscripts
An 'illuminated' [coloured and decorated] manuscript of the 8th century was a very elaborate affair. Scribes, often monks, used to sit day after day making copies for the church libraries and decorating the pages with fine brushwork in gold, red and blue. The manuscript above was written about A.D. 700 by the monks of Lindisfarne Abbey in the north of England. They wrote all the gospels in this beautiful illuminated style. The page above is the first page of the Gospel of St John.

The monks in their monasteries
We have seen how in India, Buddha preached a way of life that could really only be followed by people who went into monasteries and turned their backs on worldly things. Jesus's teaching had been different. He had shown ordinary people, men, women and children, how they could live better lives in their own homes, and while working at their old, familiar jobs.

But certain people in the early days of Christianity thought that the only way to be better men and women was to retire to a quiet place away from the towns and villages, and live alone in a cave or a hut. These people were called 'hermits'. They spent their time praying, and they only barely kept themselves alive with a little food and water. This kind of life was only suited to a very few. There were plenty of other people who wanted to follow Jesus's teachings, and who did not want to live such hard lives, entirely alone.

In the early years of the fourth century, a man named Pachomius gathered together a number of young men who wanted to pray and fast (eat very little), and he built a monastery for them on an island in the river Nile. There they worked on the land, made their own furniture, wove baskets and cloth, tanned leather, and studied the Gospels. Pachomius drew up a list of Rules for his monks, and they were used as the basis of all future monastic Orders (or communities).

The idea of monasteries spread. In 480 there was born in Italy a boy named Benedict. His parents were wealthy, but Benedict did not care for a life of ease. When he was only 15 years old he became a hermit, but later he decided to found a monastery of his own at Monte Cassino. Here the monks had to live in poverty, owning nothing. Their beds were hard, and they had only two gowns, called 'habits', a thin black one for summer and a fur-lined one for winter. Because of the colour of their gowns, they were known as the Black Monks. Each monk had a handkerchief, a pair of shoes, a needle, a knife and a pen. That was all. Their food—peas and beans, with bread and perhaps a little fish, poultry, or eggs—was shared out equally, and they ate in a communal dining-room.

The Benedictine 'Rule'

Benedict believed that to be idle was bad for a man, so almost every hour of the day was filled with work or prayer. The monks got up at 1.30 a.m. for two church services, known as Matins and Lauds. They stayed in the monastery church when Lauds was over, until the next 'Office' (service) of the day, Prime, which was at about 6 a.m. At about 8 a.m. there was an assembly, at which the head of the monastery, the Abbot, addressed the monks, and they heard the notices for the day.

Now the physical work began: some monks went off into the gardens and farms, others to the craft workshops, and those who were good at writing copied the Scriptures and decorated the pages with brightly coloured drawings. Two hours later they all returned to the church for the Sung Mass, after which came a welcome

St Jerome

In A.D. 382 a Christian scholar named Jerome collected together the existing Latin translations of the Gospels, and revised them to form a new version, approved by the Pope in Rome.

Jerome was a Hebrew scholar, and later he translated the Old Testament from Hebrew into Latin. The Latin Bible thus produced is known as the 'Vulgate'. This word comes from the Latin word meaning 'to make common'; the new Bible was so called because now the ordinary people of Rome could read it.

Benedictine monk

break for dinner—often the only meal of the day.

The rest of the day was divided between more work, two more church services, and a drink or sometimes a very light supper before bed. Even if they went to sleep immediately, the monks only had time for about 5 hours' rest before the next day began. All this was demanded by Benedict's Rule, which was based on that of Pachomius. It seems a hard Rule to us now, but Benedict did not mean his monks to be treated harshly. No man, he said, should push himself beyond endurance.

Bells were rung many times a day to tell the monks when to go to church, or to meals, or into the fields. And it was because of the need for accurate time-keeping in monasteries, that the mechanical clock developed. The first big clocks were set in church towers (see p. 128).

Many Benedictine monasteries were founded, first in Italy, and later in France and England. In all of them the Abbot was the representative of God—and as such his word was law. As the number of monks grew, the Abbots sent some of them off to lesser monasteries called Priories, ruled by a Prior. The Prior in turn was under the direction of the Abbot.

Strangers who arrived at the monastery for food and shelter were the monks' only contact with the outside world. It was their duty to feed and shelter travellers, for Jesus himself had said, 'I was a stranger, and ye took me in.' So 'to all guests fitting honour shall be shown, but most of all to servants of the faith, and to pilgrims'. The monastery became a place of refuge for the very poor people, who went every day to receive food or clothing.

Wealthier people sometimes sent their sons to be educated by the monks, and in time regular schools were established, where boys learnt to read and write in Latin. Because the monks used Latin all day themselves, they did not—and could not—teach anyone to read in the language of his own country. All the books were written in Latin, and so the old language of the Romans became a common bond between educated people all over Europe. It was not until the fifteenth and sixteenth centuries that people began to think seriously about translating their holy books into local languages. When that time came, it caused sweeping changes in Europe—as we shall see later.

By working hard on their land and in their workshops, and by selling their products in the

The Christian Kingdoms of Nubia
Nubia was converted to Christianity in the sixth century when a monk named Julian was sent to Africa by the Emperor Justinian of Constantinople. The Nubians built churches and decorated them with murals in the Byzantine style like the one of Saint Anna above, from the cathedral at Faras. They wrote inscriptions and books in their own language, and in Greek. Most of the writings have now been lost. Nubia and Ethiopia were the two great North African states that accepted the eastern form of Christianity.

Robin Hood
Robin Hood, the legendary figure who robbed the rich and gave money to the poor, was a great enemy of the rich Abbots and priests. We do not know when he lived exactly, probably between 1100 and 1300. As he was an outlaw (someone living 'outside the law') he lived, in hiding, in Sherwood Forest with his band of men.

markets, the monks often made a great deal of money; they could not keep it for themselves, so the monastery itself benefited. The Abbots received gifts from the king and from rich noblemen, and in time Benedict's hard Rule became softer. Many monastery churches began to contain beautiful paintings and gold and silver ornaments, set with jewels. The Abbots often did not follow the Rule at all—they lived in separate houses and ate rich meals. Sometimes a rich noble, or even the king, might be given hospitality (received as a guest) by the Abbot, and on these occasions the Abbot's kitchens provided an enormous feast for hundreds of people. Even the monks themselves lived less strictly, for the monasteries employed servants to do the humble cleaning and cooking and gardening jobs. In some monasteries there were more servants than there were monks.

Other Orders of monks were founded in an attempt to bring back the old strict discipline; among these were the Cistercians, or White Monks, who were not allowed to have servants. Instead they had two kinds of monks, those who attended all the services, and uneducated lay-brothers who did all the manual work. The White Monks had no ornaments in their churches, and they would not accept gifts. But in time even the White Monks grew rich—by selling wool abroad—and began to live less simply. It seems that it was almost impossible for the monasteries to remain poor and 'unworldly' for long.

The hard work of the monks and the good organization of the community were bound to increase their wealth.

Religious houses for women

Women also sometimes took vows of poverty, chastity (living unmarried and pure) and obedience. Religious houses for women (called nunneries) had been in existence since Benedict's time. As a rule the nunneries did not become as wealthy as the monasteries, because the nuns did not grow crops for sale or farm in the same way as the monks did. They spent most of their time caring for the poor, healing the sick, and embroidering tapestries and altar-cloths for the churches. Many of the nuns went into the nunnery because nobody had married them. In those days people thought that an unmarried girl was unable to look after herself, and would be better off as a nun. So many of the nuns were there not because they believed in a life of prayer and meditation, but because they had no choice.

The Bayeaux Tapestry
One of the earliest tapestries we know about is called the Bayeaux Tapestry. It may have been made by nuns at Bayeaux in France, but we are not certain. The Tapestry is 69 metres (230 feet) long, embroidered in coloured wools. It tells the story of the Norman's conquest of England. In the part shown below the Normans have just crossed the English Channel to invade England. The writing at the top is in Latin, and it says: 'and [they] came to Pevensey'. Pevensey is a bay near Hastings on the English coast, where the battle was fought.

St Francis of Assisi, 1182–1226

At the very end of the twelfth century – 700 years after Benedict founded his Black Monks – there came the idea of monks actually leaving their monasteries and going out to preach to the people. The first wandering monks were called Grey Friars, and they were founded by an Italian named Francis. He is now known as St Francis of Assisi.

Francis had an intense love of nature, and great gentleness. Later many legends grew up about how he talked to birds and animals, and how they came to him without fear. He called them names like 'brother Wolf' and 'sister Lark'. His self-denial and his goodness won Francis many followers, and in 1209 the Pope gave him permission to work among the poor, with 12 disciples, just as Jesus had done. Their headquarters was a little chapel and a group of huts near Assisi in Italy, but most of their time was spent wandering throughout the country, in grey peasants' dress, working in the fields in return for their food and lodging. In 1212 Francis started an Order of nuns, who also wore grey habits.

The number of Grey Friars grew, and in time the Pope wanted them to come under some form of discipline, in monasteries, like those of the Benedictines and Cistercians. A huge monastery and church were built at Assisi, and Francis was asked to become the first Abbot. But he refused, because he had been against the formal organization of his disciples. He had all along wanted them to live simply and do good to other people, not spend most of the day praying and working to increase the wealth of a monastery. So he resigned, and went off to pray and fast on Mt Alverno in the Apennine mountains.

The Grey Friars, or Franciscans, later became the largest of all the monastic communities, and they were famous as teachers of religion and law. Most of their recruits were poor men, and in turn they looked after the poor.

In Europe today you can see hundreds of ruins of monasteries. They are often huge buildings covering several acres of land. You can see where the large church stood, and the walled garden or 'cloister' where the monks walked in silence; the 'refectory', where the monks ate, and the 'dormitory' where they slept. On the plan you can also see the store rooms, the kitchens, the guest rooms, and the infirmary or hospital where the sick and old monks were

St Francis, meditating

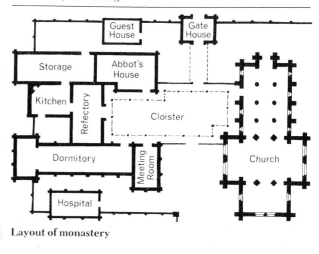

Layout of monastery

nursed with every care.

The monasteries served as centres to which people could bring their troubles, and their sick folk to be cured. The villagers were allowed to go to some of the church services, and they could appeal to the monks for food and clothing if they were destitute, that is, if they had none of the necessities of life. The monasteries were centres of learning and hard work, setting an example for the poor people of the district. As a result of the monks' hard work on the farms, agriculture all over Europe greatly improved; and because of their devotion to learning, and to creating great libraries of hand-made books, the desire for education spread.

Chapter 18 The Way of Allah

The Middle East in the Seventh Century

South of Palestine, in Arabia, there is a town called Mecca. Five hundred years after Jesus preached in Jerusalem, Mecca was a busy market town, and every day camel caravans entered and left the city carrying trade goods. The caravans travelled along well-worn roads between Egypt and the south of Arabia, or north-east to the trading towns of Asia. The merchants who met in the market place at Mecca were of all nations and all religions. Jews and Christians mingled with the pagan Arabs, and exchanged stories about their own countries and about their lives.

The three main powers of Europe and Asia in the seventh century A.D. were the Western Christians, the Eastern Christians, and the countries that made up the Persian Empire. The Eastern Christian Empire based on Constantinople we call Byzantium, after the old name of the town. For years the Byzantines had been hostile to the Persians, and often there was open war between them. This weakened both countries, and provided a great opportunity for the entry of a completely new force in the world—the followers of the Prophet Muhammad.

Sometimes, too, they talked about their religions.

In Mecca, in about 570, there was born a boy

named Muhammad. He belonged to the Quraysh tribe which controlled the city of Mecca. As he grew up, Muhammad became very interested in religion. The community in which he grew up believed in many different gods, all of whom had idols or statues for worship in the centre of Mecca. But Muhammad also liked to listen to foreigners talking about their own gods. At that time Jews and Arab Christians often visited Mecca, and he heard them speak of one God, not many. He listened to their stories of the old prophets, and he found that he agreed with their teaching. During his early life, when he was poor and later when he became a wealthy merchant, he spent his leisure hours apart from his friends, thinking about God.

One night, when Muhammad was about 40 years old, he suddenly saw a vision of the angel Gabriel, who, as he later said, 'came to me while I was asleep, with a cloth of brocade, on which was some writing.' The angel said to him, 'Read!' and Muhammad, frightened, replied, 'I cannot read it.' Three times the angel said, 'Read!' and then he said,

'Read in the name of the Lord your creator who has created man from a clot of blood. Read, your Lord is the most bountiful, who taught by means of the pen, taught man what he did not know.'

Muhammad was very disturbed by this dream, and told his wife Khadija what he had heard. She at once took him to see an old cousin of hers, Waraqa, who was a scholar of the Christian and Jewish holy books. He said that the angel was certainly the same messenger who had visited the ancient Jewish prophets. He persuaded Muhammad that he had been chosen to be a prophet of God.

So Muhammad began to preach about the One God, whom he called Allah. At first hardly anybody listened to him, and his only followers were Khadija, his adopted son Zaid, his cousin Ali, and his closest friends. But slowly his teachings spread, until the elders of his tribe began to be alarmed.

The Arabs had a sacred place in Mecca called the Ka'ba, which is still there today. The Ka'ba is a huge black windowless stone building, with a small black meteorite sunk into its side. Every year the tribes of Arabia came from all parts of the land to worship their gods at the Ka'ba, and to put offerings in front of the idols that surrounded it. Muhammad now said that the idols

Koran
Muhammad's words were written down by scribes, and after his death the various versions were collected and 'edited' to form the Holy Koran, used by Muslims all over the world today. They believe that the words are those of Allah, spoken through his prophet Muhammad.

should be broken and Allah alone worshipped. The pilgrims who came every year to the Ka'ba were a great source of income to Mecca, and the elders and merchants of the Quraysh tribe feared that Muhammad's new religion would ruin their trade, so, in an attempt to stop him preaching, they refused to buy from or sell goods to any of Muhammad's followers. Muhammad urged his followers to emigrate to the Christian country of Ethiopia, and many of them did so. He himself remained with his family in Mecca.

In the year 622, Muhammad too decided to leave Mecca, and go 280 miles through the desert to a city called Yathrib. Muhammad had many friends there, who, whenever they came on pilgrimage to Mecca, listened to his words and believed him. Muhammad left Mecca just in time, for that very night some of the Quraysh had plotted to kill him.

Yathrib was quite different from dry and dusty Mecca. It was an oasis in the desert, surrounded by palm trees and green grass. The inhabitants grew their own food, and there was plenty of grazing for their animals. In this green city there was no jealousy from rich merchants, and Muhammad was listened to with much greater sympathy.

The new teaching

Muhammad did not claim to be founding a new religion. He said only that he was following the religion of Abraham, the prophet who had first declared the idea of One God to the Hebrews. Muhammad claimed that the Jews had spoilt their religion by adding to it teachings that Abraham never intended them to have. Moses and Jesus, he said, had been appointed by God to purify the Hebrew religion, and bring back simplicity and truth. But the Christians he had met, Muhammad said, were once again leaving God's path. He, Muhammad, had been sent to help men return to the right way of life. He called the religion 'Al-Islam' — submission. Those who followed Islam (Muslims) submitted themselves entirely to Allah.

Muhammad emphasized that it was not enough to follow a religion in name only: it was necessary to live a good life. In the Koran it is written:

'Whoever believeth in Allah and the Last Day and doeth right, surely their reward is with their Lord . . .'

Hundreds of people in Yathrib were con-verted to the new faith, and they acknowledged Muhammad as their leader. They even changed the name of their city to Medina, which means The City — *the* city of the Prophet. Up till now all the Arabs had been fiercely tribal. They fought and died for their own tribes; no man would ever kill his own kinsman, and when a man was killed by someone from another tribe, his death was quickly avenged.

But in Medina the Muslims formed a close group, regardless of tribe. They no longer recognized the old tribal loyalties, for they believed that their loyalty should first be given to Allah and their fellow Muslims. When war broke out between the Muslims and their former comrades and kinsmen from Mecca, men even killed their brothers and cousins in the name of Allah. To many of the Arabs this was displeasing, so in the Koran we read:

'Warfare is decreed for you, though it is hate-

Prayer-mat
Muslims had no altars in their mosques, no images or pictures of God and no priests. All a man had to do to achieve communion [spiritual communication] with Allah was turn towards Mecca five times each day and pray.

Muslims were supposed to kneel on clean ground to pray and so there arose the custom whereby each man or each family owned a special prayer-mat or carpet. In the picture below a family is gathered on a prayer-mat to worship in the open desert.

ful for you; but it may happen that you hate a thing which is good for you, and it may happen that you love a thing which is bad for you. Allah knows, and you do not know.'

A few years later the Muslims were strong enough to march on Mecca, but there was little opposition and Muhammad returned to his own city without a fight. When the Muslims had thrown out all the idols surrounding the Ka'ba, Muhammad told the people to come and swear loyalty to him, and obedience to Allah. From that time onwards, pilgrims came to Mecca to worship one God only – Allah.

Now that they could no longer worship other gods at the Ka'ba, many Arab tribes were quite content to worship Allah, and become Muslims. Others were more defiant, and these the new Muslim army went out to fight.

When the Arab armies conquered a tribe, or later, a foreign town, they asked the inhabitants to become Muslims, by repeating the sentence, 'There is no God but Allah; Muhammad is his Messenger.' If they were prepared to swear this, their taxation was lighter. But the early Muslims realized that it was not possible for Christians and Jews to say these words, and for the most part they were tolerant of the "People of the Book", for Muslims, Christians and Jews all believed that the Old Testament of the Bible was the word of God.

One of the strictest rules was that no Muslim should kill another Muslim. The Muslim soldiers fought against any people who stopped them from spreading Islam. More Arab tribes joined them, and soon they were fighting on the frontiers of the Persian and Byzantine Empires. A war against unbelievers outside Arabia was called a *jihad* or 'holy war'.

The Holy Wars
Muhammad died in 632, and was succeeded by Abu Bakr, one of the very first converts to Islam. Abu Bakr was known as the 'Caliph' or 'successor', and this became the title for the leader of Islam. Abu Bakr and the two Caliphs who followed him continued the holy wars with such success that within ten years the Muslims had conquered much of Persia and the Byzantine Empire. The Caliph was now the leader of a huge empire.

Once the Arab armies had moved out of Arabia, they had to camp in hostile territory. There were raids on the new Arab borders, and these troubles

Ka'ba
Thousands of Muslims go each year to Mecca to perform the *hadj* or pilgrimage. Once pilgrims either walked the whole way, or joined camel caravans to visit the Holy City. Nowadays many of them travel by 'plane.

The five 'Pillars of the Faith' of Islam
The Koran laid down these five special 'commandments':

A Muslim must have faith in Allah and Muhammad as His prophet.
He must pray five times a day.
He must give alms to the poor.
He must fast every year for a month, at the season called Ramadan. (Eating only after sunset.)
He must go, if possible, on the pilgrimage to Mecca.

led the Muslim armies to invade even more territory, and so to extend the empire still further. In 639 the horsemen of Arabia turned westward towards the Nile, and began the conquest of Egypt and Libya.

The peoples that submitted to the Arab armies with their new religion, had the choice of either becoming Muslims, or else paying higher taxes for the Muslim soldiers to protect them. It is amazing that the early Caliphs managed to keep their empire together so well, for they had few soldiers actually living in the 'enemy' countries. At first the new empire was bound only by religion, and government and organization came later.

When that time did come, each new state was governed by a ruler of its own—who owed allegiance, that is loyalty and help, to the Caliph, but who occasionally behaved as though he himself were the only head of Islam, even calling himself 'Caliph' as well. These different rulers passed their titles on to their sons, and so although they were not kings in the old sense, we speak of the ruling families as 'dynasties'.

Now the Muslim empire was formed of a group of separate countries, each with a ruler who owed allegiance to the spiritual head of Islam.

Harun ar-Rashid, 786–809

In Mesopotamia, where the Sumerians, the Persians, and the Greeks had once ruled, there came to power a dynasty of Islamic rulers known as the Abbasids. Under these rulers, and particularly under the Caliph Harun ar-Rashid, Mesopotamia developed into a settled civilized country. The Arab conquerers were now rich with the revenue taken from captured cities, from the taxes that their new subjects had to pay, and from their own economic development. With their new wealth they built magnificent cities at Bokhara, Samarkand and Baghdad, where their colleges, schools, and hospitals were some of the best in the world.

Harun ar-Rashid himself lived in Baghdad, which was then the most civilized city of all. In the narrow streets shops sold beautiful jewels, pearls, gold ornaments and rich silks. There was great luxury in the houses, and women were encouraged to make themselves beautiful. To Harun's court came poets and musicians and story-tellers.

Scholars in Baghdad University collected the old Greek books and translated them into Arabic. Now they were able to build upon the learning of the Greeks, and add to it new ideas of their own. They made surveys and maps of the world from facts collected from geographers and travellers who visited the whole of the Muslim lands from India to Spain. They sent traders to the Far East, and set up small trading stations in China and Ceylon, in India, and on the coast of East Africa. Northern Europe was completely cut off from trade with these countries, and could not import gold, or spices, or silks. Charlemagne, who ruled northern France at the time when Harun ar-Rashid was Caliph at Baghdad, had to have coins made of silver, because he could not get enough gold.

Samarra minaret
The Muslims built mosques as places of worship, and one or more towers were built at the corners of the central courtyard. At each hour of prayer, the *muezzin* [a mosque official] climbed the minaret and called the Faithful to prayer. The Arabs studied the large buildings of the various countries they conquered. This minaret at Samarra in Iraq, is shaped like an old Babylonian ziggurat.

Islamic design
Because Islam forbids pictures of people, Muslim artists decorated buildings with words beautifully drawn, and within a definite framework, such as a circle, or a square. They also used words to decorate plates and bowls, as this example from Turkey shows.

Chapter 19 The Muslims reach Europe

Meanwhile other Muslim armies had carried their religion northwards into Spain and France, which alarmed the Pope in Italy, and his friends the Franks. Fortunately for the Christian kingdoms, the leader of the Franks was an able commander named Charles Martel ('the Hammer').* He led his forces out to meet the advancing Muslim army, and he defeated them at the battle of Poitiers in 732. But the Muslims stayed in southern Spain, and for five hundred years the two religious groups lived side by side. Although there were minor wars between them from time to time, in fact the Christians and Muslims tolerated each other, and it was not uncommon for Christians to serve in a Muslim army.

Abd ar-Rahman III, 912–61

The city of Cordova (modern Córdoba) lies on the river Guadalquivir, in the province of Spain we now call Andalusia, but which in the tenth century was part of the much larger Muslim country of 'Al-Andalus'. By the time the great ruler of the Umayyad dynasty in Spain, Abd ar-Rahman III came to power, Muslim ideas of wealth and splendour had spread from Baghdad to Andalus, and Cordova was the great centre of world learning. (Baghdad was no longer so important.)

The Caliphs of Cordova were learned men themselves, and they wished their people to be as well-educated as possible. So they built hundreds of primary schools where both boys and girls could learn to read and write in Arabic, to do arithmetic, and to learn the Koran by heart. When they had finished at the primary school they went on to higher schools and to university, where they studied the Greek translations that had reached them from Baghdad. At home, every educated man had a library of hand-written

*He was the grandfather of Charlemagne.

The Mosque at Cordova (interior)
In Spain, Jews and Christians were often the craftsmen for their Muslim masters, and they adapted their own artistic styles to suit the new buildings, the new kinds of clothes, and the new fashions in jewellery and weapons. Cordova was retaken by Christian Spaniards in 1236, and the mosque became a cathedral.

books, often chosen for the beauty of the writing alone.

The university also gave courses in medicine. Abd ar-Rahman's own doctor was a Jew named Ibn Shaprut (even non-Muslims in Cordova had Arabic-sounding names; 'ibn' means 'son of'). He was thought to be so wise that the Christian kings of Leon and Navarre, living in the north of Spain, 'borrowed' him from Abd ar-Rahman when a member of the royal family was sick.

Cordova had half-a-million inhabitants, and was one of the largest cities in the world at the time – far larger than any of the Christian cathedral towns of western Europe. It was clean and well-lit, and like Baghdad in days gone by, contained shops which sold beautiful luxury goods from the East. Cordova was particularly famous for leatherwork, which the Christians (who imported it) called 'Cordovan leather'. In time any leather-worker was known as a 'cordovaner', or 'cordwainer'.

Muslim rule in Spain was tolerant and useful. But during the centuries after Abd ar-Rahman's rule, the Christians of the north became stronger and tried hard to recover the land they had lost to the Muslims. Gradually they pushed the Muslims further and further south, until by 1300 only the province of Granada was left of the once large land of Andalus.

Muslim science

Ptolemy, the Greek scientist, had written a series of 13 books in which (among other things) he catalogued over 1000 stars, stated the distance between the earth and the sun, discussed eclipses, the movements of the planets, and the formation of the Milky Way. He thought that the earth was a sphere, and the centre of the Universe – with all the planets (*and* the sun) moving round it. In 827 Muslim scholars prepared the first translation of these books, which they called the Almagest (see picture on p. 123). Later, the Almagest was translated into Latin (in 1175), and the *Christian* countries began to use Ptolemy's work. As we shall see later, this led to a completely new theory of the way in which the solar system works.

In mathematics the Muslim countries were far ahead of Christian Europe, for they took over from the Indians the idea of having a *nought*. Up till now the peoples of the world had added numbers on counting-frames, but they had no symbol to show when a column was empty. The

Numerals
The Arabic numerals used in Baghdad and later in Spain look rather like the numbers we use today. The zero was represented by a dot, which was called *sunya* by the Hindus.

A practical reason why Christian merchants preferred the Roman system was that they thought they would be cheated by the Arabic notation. Muslim merchants could change 15 to 150 by merely adding a dot, whereas in Roman numerals XV (15) looked quite different from CL (150).

Indians used a dot for nought, or zero, and they called it *sunya*, meaning 'empty'.

This new symbol changed ideas about mathematics completely. Arithmetic became easier (the Romans had had great difficulty in multiplying, say, CXVIII by MDLV!), and with the nought there was the possibility of advanced mathematics – which in turn affected physics. Without the nought, much of algebra could never have developed; logarithms would be impossible, and the whole of our present-day science and engineering would never have come into being.

The Muslims were great borrowers. Besides taking over the zero from India, and astronomy from the Greeks, they learnt how to make paper from the Chinese. This meant that their books were much less heavy than the old parchment* rolls, and a library could hold more books, arranged upright on shelves. Most people in the Muslim 'empire' now spoke Arabic, just as their ancestors (who happened to be part of the Greek or Roman Empires) used to speak Greek or Latin as a *lingua franca* which bound the civilized world together.

The Christian kingdoms envied the Muslim 'caliphates' for their learning and wealth; but they could not imitate them because they said they were 'unbelievers'. For a long time they

*Parchment is the skin of a sheep or calf dried and made suitable for writing on.

did not even copy the zero in arithmetic, because they thought that it was a Muslim invention, and therefore somehow wrong. Mistrust and suspicion, added to jealousy, led to a final split between the peoples of the two religions.

A merchant goes to the East

The split into two 'rival' groups meant that it was now very difficult for Christian traders to go to the east by land, through Muslim territories. But even so, some merchants *did* manage to do so. One outstanding merchant-traveller was Marco Polo. He was the son of a merchant named Niccolo Polo, who had for many years dealt with other merchant-travellers from the east. Niccolo and his brother Maffeo made a lot of money by selling precious stones, silks and spices, in the markets of Venice.

Marco Polo was born in about 1254, and when he was 15 years old, he accompanied his uncle and his father on a great journey to the east.

Maffeo and Niccolo had travelled to Constantinople, and there they met a party of men who had been all the way overland to China, a land with a powerful king whom they called Kublai Khan. This king, they said, was wealthier than any other king in the world, and had a country larger than any of the countries of Europe. He was neither a Christian nor a Muslim, so they thought it would be a magnificent thing if they could convert him to Christianity. They returned to Venice to assemble a party of priests, but unfortunately for them, they could not persuade the Pope to send more than two men, and these soon turned back, for the journey was too hard for them.

But young Marco was more courageous. He carried on with the party, and the three Venetians stayed for many years in the country of Kublai Khan. They called this country 'Cathay', and this is the name by which China was known to Europeans for many years. The Polos became rich men, and the Khan was pleased to have them in his kingdom. Marco was sent by Kublai Khan to many other eastern countries, including India, Ceylon, Burma, Japan and Java. On his return to the court at Peking, he amused the Khan with tales of his travels.

Finally the Polos returned to Europe. It is said that they amazed the townspeople of Venice by appearing in their fine eastern clothes. After so many years in the east, they were probably the only clothes they possessed.

Christian kingdoms in the Middle Ages

The 'Middle Ages' in Europe was the time when the different countries settled down, mostly as small kingdoms under the type of government we know as the 'feudal system'. Every king (or in some countries, duke) had under him a group of lords and knights owing allegiance to him, the lords were owners of large amounts of land, which was farmed for them by peasants. Besides working for his lord, each peasant had his own strip of land, which he cultivated for his own needs, and the whole village shared a common field for grazing their animals.

At this time the rule of the king was supreme. In times of war, each lord had to collect together horsemen and foot-soldiers from among his tenants, to fight for the king; when there was no war, the knights practised fighting on horseback, archery (shooting with bows and arrows), and learnt an elaborate code of 'chivalry' – that is, correct and courteous behaviour.

Having chivalrous knights in armour was very romantic, and very necessary in times of war, but in peace time the knights had nothing very much to do, and they often quarrelled among themselves. Various European rulers went to war with each other, usually over the possession of territory. If you look at a modern map of Europe, you will see that Italy, Spain and France all have good natural boundaries of seas and mountains. In the Middle Ages all three countries were divided up into small kingdoms, which could change possession overnight when a king died, or – as often happened – when a duke's lands were given away as part of the dowry* of a princess.

The Crusades

In the tenth and eleventh centuries the Muslim dynasties in Europe and Asia were in trouble, for a hitherto comparatively unknown people called Turks swept across from the east and captured some of the Muslim cities of Asia. The Turks were also Muslims. They took the holy places of Palestine and they made war on the Byzantine Empire, threatening the Christian stronghold of Constantinople. In 1095 the Byzantine emperor appealed to the Pope in Rome for help, and the Pope decided it was

*A dowry is the money, land or other possessions a woman brings to her husband on marriage. In some countries it is called 'bride price'.

Painting of farming in the Middle Ages

The painters of the Middle Ages liked to paint pictures of their friends and neighbours at work in the fields, as this old illustration shows. Sometimes they painted a whole series of pictures showing the farming activities for each month in turn. The picture above was painted in the 10th century, for the month of August.

indeed time to help the eastern Christians. He thought he might perhaps be able to reunite the two branches of Christian faith by recapturing Jerusalem — and he could certainly give employment to the quarrelling knights and kings of Europe.

So the Pope preached a crusade — a war of religion — against the Turks (known then as 'Saracens'), and thousands of knights and foot-soldiers answered his call. Three armies set out from France, and another from Italy, and they marched right across Europe to Constantinople where the Byzantine emperor helped them to cross over the Sea of Marmara to meet the Turks in Asia Minor. After a lot of hard fighting and long thirsty marches they reached Jerusalem and captured it in 1099, three years after they left their homes.

Most of the crusaders went back to Europe, but some stayed to live in the new Christian kingdom of Jerusalem. As there were not many of them to guard their conquests, the crusaders fortified the cities of the Holy Land and built several castles of great strength. The idea of fighting for religious reasons became widespread in Europe, and during the next 170 years Christians organized six more crusades against the Muslims. But the success of the first crusade was not repeated and most of these crusades were failures. Gradually the Muslims became stronger, and in 1187 Saladin, the sultan of Egypt, recaptured Jerusalem.

Knights

The knights wore chainmail which gave them very good protection and allowed plenty of movement. Over their armour they wore cloth tunics with their own personal markings embroidered on them. They carried shields painted with the same design. The soldiers could thus recognize their own knights in battle, and keep near them.

121

Baibars, Sultan of Egypt, 1260–77

One of the crusaders' most deadly enemies was another sultan of Egypt, known as Baibars. He was a huge man, very energetic and able, a great athlete, and a devout Muslim. He was determined to rid the Middle East of the Christians from the west and the new Mongol invaders from the east. He was very successful against both these enemies, and by the time he died in 1277, most of the crusaders' castles and towns had been retaken.

The Christian countries of Byzantium, Sicily, and two kingdoms of northern Spain were anxious to remain friendly with so powerful a man, and the king of France even sent messengers to greet him. But he was unwilling to stop the war before all the former Muslim lands had been regained and the crusaders had returned to their own countries.

Some of the knights and soldiers from Europe had joined the crusades for religious reasons; others because they enjoyed fighting, or because they were criminals who dared not stay in their own countries. In those days all soldiers hoped to add to their pay by looting the towns they captured; and they thought that all the lands of the east were wealthy and prosperous. They expected rich rewards from loot, and also from making important prisoners pay ransom. In fact the opportunities for 'getting rich quick' were not so great as they thought; and determined rulers like Baibars showed them that they could not expect to recapture Jerusalem without a hard fight. The Christian countries gained hardly any territory in the east, and in 1453 the whole of the Christian world suffered a great blow when the Turks at last captured Constantinople.

Saladin

Saleh al-din, or Saladin, sultan of Egypt, is famous for his wars against the crusaders during the reign of England's King Richard the Lion-Heart. His own courtesy greatly impressed the crusaders, and the fine behaviour of many of the Muslim leaders led to new ideas of chivalry in Europe. It is said that when King Richard's horse was killed in battle, Saladin sent him a horse of his own, and forbade his men to fight until Richard had mounted it.

Cairo

Cairo, in the Middle Ages, was one of the great cities of the world. It was a city built within walls, in which were magnificently carved gates, one of which could be used only by the sultan. Inside the walls the houses had overhanging windows, and balconies, overlooking narrow twisted streets. The houses were generally built round courtyards with fountains and gardens. The family lived upstairs; the women were separated from the men, and they rarely went outside the houses.

The overhanging windows did not have glass in them. Instead they had a criss-cross pattern of carved wood, which let in air but kept out the fierce rays of the sun.

The photograph on the right shows buildings dating back to the Middle Ages which are still to be seen in Cairo today.

122

Chapter 20 Islam in Africa

In the seventh century A.D., some Muslims had already settled in Morocco, in North Africa. They spread the teaching of the Prophet, and traded with the neighbouring tribes. From Morocco, explorers and travellers marched south through the deserts with their camels, until they came to a town called Sijilmasa, where they traded their copper and cotton, tools and swords, and their strong Arab horses for gold, ivory and slaves.

The gold trade of Sijilmasa was very old. The gold itself came from an African kingdom far to the south, situated round the forested banks of the river Niger. This kingdom, which was called Ghana*, had probably been in existence from the fifth or sixth century, but long before that time, Berbers from North Africa were trading with the south for gold to sell to the Carthaginians and Romans.

The Ghanaians did not dig the gold themselves, for the mines lay in a country called Wangara, which was inhabited by a different tribe. These more primitive Africans used to leave gold nuggets and gold dust on the border of their country, and the Ghanaians exchanged it for salt. No word was spoken in this kind of bargaining: if the people of Wangara thought there was not enough salt put out beside their gold, then they removed the gold. If they agreed to the 'price', then they took the salt and the Ghanaians were free to remove the gold. This silent trading was very old in Africa, and was the method used by the Phoenicians and Carthaginians, when they wanted to exchange goods with Africans whose language they could not speak.

Salt was a very valuable commodity to the

Islamic Navigation
The Arabs translated Ptolemy's Greek star-maps in the ninth century A.D. The picture above is a drawing of the constellation [group of stars] *Bootes* (the herdsman) from an early Islamic manuscript of the Almagest. The Arabs used these star-maps in their navigation of the Indian Ocean and the Far East.

miners of the south. It is impossible to work—or even to live for very long—if you do not have enough salt in your body, and the Ghanaians and the workers of Wangara had no natural salt in their lands. But plenty of salt was taken every year to the markets of Sijilmasa from a place in the desert called Taghaza. So, for centuries, year after year, merchants left Ghana and travelled along recognized trade-routes northwards to Sijilmasa, where they exchanged their gold, ivory and slaves in the market-place for salt. And with the caravans, there gradually came to West Africa the faith and customs of Islam.

*This is not the same country as today's Ghana. It occupied about the same geographical position as present-day Mali.

The Almoravids

In north-west Africa, at the beginning of the eleventh century, a holy man named Ibn Yasin preached to his followers a very strict kind of Islam. He said that Muslims everywhere had become too soft, and were no longer following the ways of their founder, Muhammad, who, although not poor, had always lived very simply. Ibn Yasin was a good preacher, and he soon collected a huge following of tribesmen who were prepared to join in a *jihad* against the settlements of the desert. The followers of Ibn Yasin were called 'Almoravids'.

This horde of about 30,000 warriors, most of them foot-soldiers, attacked and took Sijilmasa, and then marched north and conquered some of the civilized cities of Morocco. Ibn Yasin died in Morocco, and after his death the army split into two halves, one part going north into Spain, where they said they would help the Andalusian caliphs to defeat the Christian kings of the north. In fact they took over the caliph's power, and in the fighting, many beautiful Muslim cities, including Cordova, were destroyed, and thousands of magnificent books were burnt.

The other half of the Almoravid army went south towards Ghana. In 1054 they had reached Andoghast, a town which paid tribute to Ghana, and the soldiers killed most of the inhabitants. The Ghanaian king, in his capital at Kumbi, hurriedly collected an army, and for a time he successfully kept the Almoravids at bay. But the fierce tribesmen of the north could not be kept out for ever, and in 1076 they destroyed Kumbi and the old kingdom of Ghana was permanently weakened.

Mali

But that was not the end of local power in West Africa. Other kingdoms grew prosperous, and were ruled by Muslim kings. South-west of the old kingdom of Ghana, also on the river Niger, the kings of Mali became the new leaders in the gold trade with North Africa. In about 1300, a Muslim writer named Ibn Khaldun said of the people of Mali:

'All the nations of the Sudan* stood in awe of them, and the merchants of North Africa travelled to their country.'

*The Sudan in the Middle Ages included a much larger area of North and West Africa than it does now. Many place-names now refer to slightly different geographical areas. Mali (or Melle) was in the western part of present-day Mali.

Benin

Benin, on the west coast of Africa, was a kingdom noted for its beautiful bronze statues as the one above of a hunter. The craftsmen of Benin passed on their skill from generation to generation. The king, or Oba, of Benin was a mighty ruler who had to be obeyed in all things. His young men hunted leopards, lions and elephants as training for their duties as soldiers.

Goods in Benin were exchanged for cowrie shells, and according to this account from a sixteenth-century English trader, food was plentiful:

'They would bring our men earthen pots . . . full of honey and honeycombs for a hundred shells. They would also bring great store of oranges and plantains which grow upon a tree, and are very like a cucumber but very pleasant in eating.'

The greatest of the rulers of Mali was called Mansa Musa, and he ruled from his capital city, Niami, from about 1307 to 1332. It was said that his empire was so large that it took four months to walk from the western boundary to the east, and the same length of time to go from north to south. This must have been an exaggeration, but Mansa Musa undoubtedly ruled over a very large area. His great fame in Europe and Asia came about because he went on a pilgrimage to Mecca. In 1324 he set out from Niami with an enormous camel caravan, carrying gold and ivory, and followed by courtiers, warriors, servants and slaves. El-Omari, a fourteenth-century writer, said:

'Twelve thousand young slaves dressed in

tunics of brocade and silk of Yemen carried his personal belongings.'

The caravan reached Cairo, a great city of learning and wealth. To impress such a city was not easy, but Mansa Musa managed to do so by his great generosity. He gave away so much gold (80 to 100 camel-loads, it is said) that for years afterwards the market-price for gold was much lower than usual. El-Omari visited Cairo 12 years after Mansa Musa's visit, to find that the Egyptians were still talking about this great king.

When he had performed the pilgrimage to Mecca, Mansa Musa returned to his own country with Arab scholars and teachers, and an architect from Andalus who built the king new mosques and palaces of brick (instead of the usual clay) at his cities of Timbuktu and Jenne. These two towns became centres of learning in much the same way as Baghdad, Cordova and Cairo had

done. The university of Timbuktu still existed and was respected until the end of the sixteenth century, when invaders from Morocco destroyed the books and the buildings. But even then, Timbuktu lived on in legend, and right up to the nineteenth century, European travellers expected to find a rich and learned city there.

So the Muslim religion spread, first throughout Arabia, then to the east as far as India, to Spain and Morocco in the west, to Ghana via the ancient trade-routes, and (as we shall later see) to the coast of East Africa. Everywhere where Muslims settled, they built beautiful towns which carried on a profitable trade. They kept alive the old learning of Greece and Rome, at a time when Europe was in ignorance. But their long mastery was nearly over. Soon the European nations emerged from 'the Middle Ages', and with new-found energy provided the world's next centres of learning, of culture and expansion.

The extent of the Arab Empire – 1000 AD

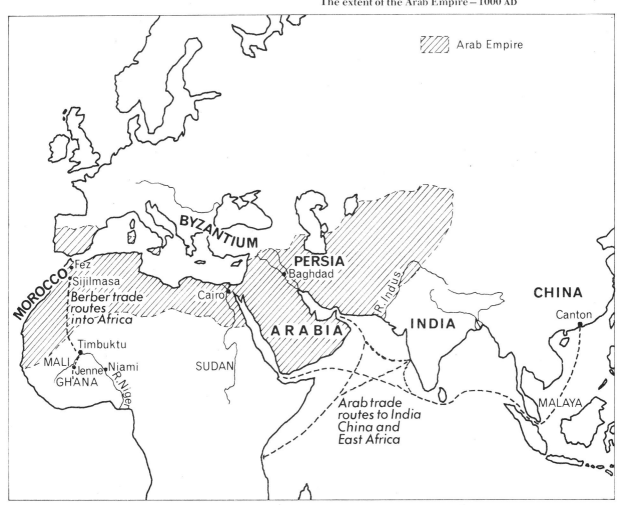

125

Part V Renaissance and Reformation

Chapter 21 The Old Learning Rediscovered

During the Middle Ages, Christian countries were divided up between different rulers, but they all had one thing in common. Everybody, king, knights and common people alike, obeyed the Church. Christianity was not a matter of opinion; it was a complete way of life, and nobody questioned it. Hell and the devil were very real, and people believed that for most of them, this life was an unpleasant prelude to an even worse future. Belief in the devil led to belief in witchcraft, and many people thought that all bad things like disease, or earthquakes, or crop-failure, were due to the influence of witches. Superstition, instead of scientific knowledge, led to a Europe that was not at all active mentally. Blind acceptance of superstitious explanations does not lead to new discoveries, or mental freedom.

But slowly things began to change; and the change first started in the birth-place of the Roman Empire—Italy. Italy was now divided up into a number of city-states, each ruled by a

'Witches' being ducked
People accused of witchcraft were often ducked in the local pond. The 'ducking stool' consisted of a chair with a metal strap across the front to hold the victim in. It was attached to a hoist which lowered the stool into the water.

For very bad offences the accused was ducked many times.

duke or a prince. Rome itself was ruled by the Pope, who was of course also the head of all Christendom. These states were constantly at war with one another, and with other dukedoms and kingdoms in France and Spain. Sometimes parts of Italy belonged either to French or to Spanish rulers. People began therefore to ask themselves whom they could look up to. If the authority of the king, or the duke, can be so easily removed, what about the authority of the Church? The bishops and the other clergymen were supposed to be superior to other people. Was this really so? Was this authority not just as 'artificial' as the leadership of a king?

Books become cheaper

At the same time as people were beginning to question 'authority', someone invented movable type for printing. We think that the inventor was a man named Johann Gutenberg, who lived in Germany from about 1398 to 1468. This is how the new printing worked: many 'mirror-images'* of each letter of the alphabet were carved on little blocks of wood, so that the letters could be joined together to make words. In this new movable type, printers could put any letter into any position they liked. It takes a long time to put together all the letters that make up a page of type, but when it is done they can be locked together in a frame, and hundreds of pages can be printed from them. When the whole book is finished, the type can be used again and again for other books.

The earliest piece of Gutenberg's printing we know of is an astronomical calendar, printed in 1447. He also printed a Bible (the Latin 'Vulgate' or 'common' Bible of St Jerome) and several shorter books. He personally did not grow rich from his new trade, but the idea spread rapidly throughout Europe, and 50 years later there were thousands of printing presses, mainly producing religious books and histories. There was great opposition from manuscript copiers, but they could not compete with the low prices of printed books, and soon they were only employed by rich men who preferred to buy a well-illustrated hand-written book (however expensive) to a mass-produced one.

The ordinary people of Europe began to buy books, and at last education became available for the less-wealthy people. It is difficult to imagine today, when we have well-stocked bookshops and libraries in every town, how exciting it must have been to own a book, and with what care it must have been handled. A man with a whole shelf of books was no longer dependent on other people's learning, but could read for himself, and whet his appetite for more. Young lads, who had perhaps grown up thinking they would be farmers, or cordwainers, or masons, or carpenters, as their fathers and grandfathers had been, now apprenticed themselves to printers, paper-makers, book-binders and type-makers.

Some printers issued copies of the classics —

*The type letters have to be 'mirror-images' — right side to the left, left side to the right — in order to come out right way round when the frame is turned over for printing.

Here foloweth The lyf of Saynt Jeromine And first of his name

Jeromme is sayd of Jhera that is hooly / And of nemus / that is to saye a woody / And soo Jheromme is as moche to saye as an hooly woody

William Caxton, printer
At first printers copied the old hand-drawn letters, to make a printed page look as much like a manuscript as possible. Here is an example, written in English, by the printer William Caxton, in 1483. It tells of St. Jerome.

Later, printers copied the simpler Roman letters, which are still used today. Germany, however, kept the old 'Gothic' letters right up to this century. This is what a printed line in an early twentieth century German book looked like. Compare it with Caxton's page above:

Ich sage hinfort nicht, daß ihr Knechte seid, denn

that is, the writings of Romans like Cicero, Julius Caesar and Virgil and of Greeks like Plutarch and Homer. Only a very small part of the works of these authors had been preserved in Italy, but there were many more in the Greek city of Constantinople. Scholars from Constantinople found plenty of willing pupils in Italy, and when Constantinople fell to the Turks in 1453, hundreds of other Greek-speaking scholars joined those already in Italy, and brought with them some of the old manuscripts.

All these books were eagerly read by all literate people, and so began the movement known as the Renaissance or 'rebirth' of learning. There was tremendous interest in finding out about how people lived in the past. Scholars tried to see how ancient Greek ideas fitted in with the teaching of Jesus. At last people once again began to think for themselves, instead of believing what the priests and the nobles told them, and their new thinking slowly changed Europe completely. The questions they asked led to new discoveries in mathematics, science and astronomy; and their new critical way of looking at the Church led to the Reformation and the Counter-Reformation, about which we shall be talking in the next two chapters.

During the fourteenth, fifteenth and sixteenth centuries the modern world was born. Instead of regarding people with new ideas as magicians, or devils, or even just plain mad, people began to respect them as scientists and philosophers — even if they did not agree with them. And when at last men and women emerged from a frightening world of superstition, they had new dignity and self-respect: they could look forward to the future with faith and hope.

The world of Copernicus and Galileo

We have seen how the Arabs improved navigation by studying the old Greek star-maps. But the Greeks, following Ptolemy, had thought that the whole Universe moved round the Earth. The Christian Church liked this idea, because it seemed to point to the importance of man, the most intelligent creature on Earth. God had created man 'in his own image', and he had created the Universe as a sort of background to his chief creation.

But Renaissance astronomers, looking at the stars year after year, could see that Ptolemy's system was incorrect. The planets did not behave as he had shown in his diagrams. Some of the astronomers began to think that perhaps the Earth was not the centre of the Universe after all.

One of the earliest astronomers to suggest that the Earth might be revolving round the sun was the Greek Aristarchus, about 250 B.C. In the middle of the fifteenth century A.D., Nikolaus Krebs tried to convince people of the same idea. But it was another Nikolaus who finally suc-

Old playing cards
Printing began when the Chinese carved wooden blocks, pressed them on to an inked pad, and then on to a piece of paper — rather like the rubber-stamps used in offices today. The idea eventually spread to Europe, and wooden blocks were used for printing playing cards, and Bible pictures. The playing card above is French, early sixteenth century.

Fourteenth century iron clock
Early mechanical clocks were large and driven by weights. This clock was made by blacksmiths in the fourteenth century for Wells Cathedral. Clocks were a great improvement on sundials, because they went on telling the time — even on cloudy days and at night. Time began to be important after the sun had set. The word 'clock' comes from the French word *cloche*, meaning bell.

(Above) These massive stones, positioned to outline a longship, have stood for centuries marking the scene of a Viking grave.

(Below) Detail from the Bayeux Tapestry showing Norman foot soldiers attacking the English. The Tapestry, dating from about 1066, is believed to have been commissioned by Bishop Odo of Bayeux to commemorate the Norman victory at the battle of Hastings.

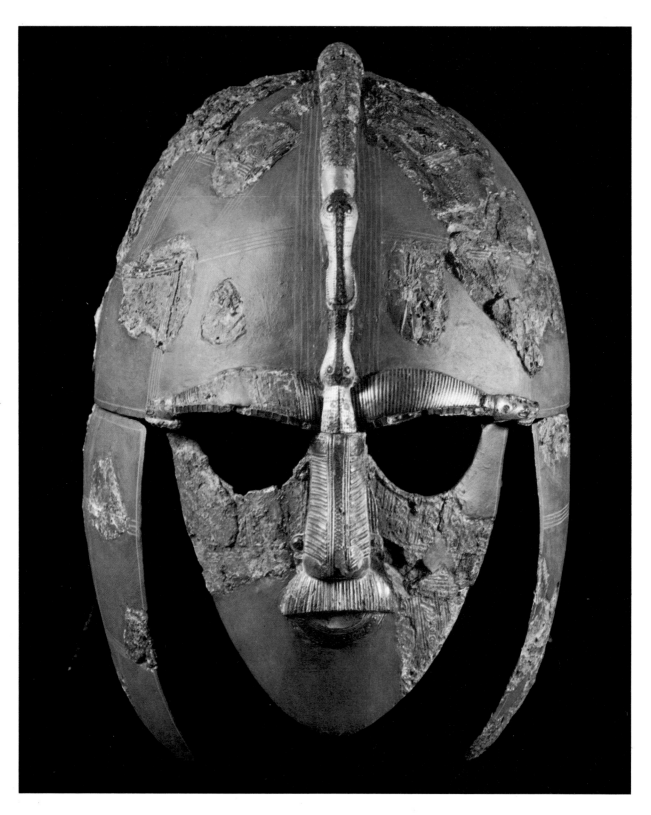

In 1939 at Sutton Hoo, Suffolk, a mound was excavated which contained a great treasure hoard, probably a memorial to some renowned warrior. Amongst the objects found were gold buckles and clasps, a sword, a purse filled with gold coins and this magnificent helmet which is now to be found in the British Museum, London.

Stained glass window, dating from the late twelfth century, in Strasbourg Cathedral. It depicts Charlemagne, King of the Franks and Emperor of the Western Empire. He enlarged the Frankish kingdom so that it extended from the shores of the Atlantic to the Elbe river in eastern Germany.

Fifteenth century portrait of Lorenzo from the Riccardo Medici Chapel in Florence. The work is attributed to Benozzo Gozzoli and shows Lorenzo sumptuously attired on horseback; it is a beautiful example of Renaissance Art.

ceeded in spreading this theory, and then only after his own death. He was a Polish priest called Koppernigk—better known to us as Copernicus. He published a book shortly before he died in 1543, describing the solar system, and showing that the Earth was a planet of the sun.

Copernicus's work was carried on by a great scientist named Galileo, who in 1610, with the help of a home-made telescope, saw that the planet Jupiter had moons or satellites of its own. He immediately realized that this could be thought of as a little model of the Copernican idea of the solar system. He also found that Venus passed through regular patterns, called phases, which clearly proved that the planet must be revolving round the sun, inside the Earth's own orbit. He wrote to the prince of Florence:

'I am filled with infinite astonishment and also infinite gratitude to God that it has pleased Him to make me alone the first observer of such wonderful things, which have been hidden in all past centuries.'

But Galileo experienced the opposition of the Church. He sent his critics telescopes, so that they might see the moons of Jupiter for themselves. But these unscientific people refused even to look through the telescopes.

Galileo was so sure of his discoveries that he resolved to publish them, whatever the consequences, and fortunately many of his writings survived. But he himself was condemned by the Church, and kept confined to his house until he died in 1642. He was bitterly scornful of this childish attitude, and he wrote:

'I believe that there is no greater hatred in the whole world, than the hatred of the ignorant for knowledge.'

Michelangelo, 1475–1564

One of the outstanding things about the Renaissance in Italy was the new interest in sculpture, in architecture, and in painting. Artists were in great demand by the rulers of the Italian cities, who wanted new buildings built and decorated— sometimes to their own honour and glory. So good painters found that they were engaged by noblemen to paint pictures on the walls of churches, and to carve huge statues to stand in the squares of the cities.

One of these painters and sculptors was Michelangelo, some of whose paintings still exist. In his choice of subjects he followed

Galileo demonstrating his telescope to the Doge of Venice in 1609

In Copernicus's system, the planets, which included the Earth, move round the sun. We now know that there are countless systems like our own in the Universe, in which each star is a sun, and many millions must have their own planets.

Later, Galileo, with the help of his telescope, proved that Venus, the brightest 'star' in the sky, shone with reflected light from the sun, and was not a ball of fire as everybody thought. All planets shine only with reflected light. The spacemen who landed on the Moon saw our own Earth shining in this way.

the more traditional artists of earlier times, whose themes were almost always religious. But he succeeded in making these themes more alive, and more 'natural'. He was a wonderful artist, and even in old age he practised pencil and chalk drawing. He was what we call a perfectionist, a man who was never satisfied with what he had done but was always seeking for the possibility of improvement.

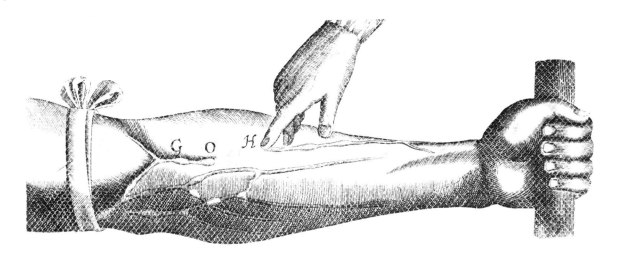

Leonardo da Vinci, 1452–1519

But great though Michelangelo was, there was one other man from Florence who was perhaps greater — one of the real geniuses of the world for all time. His name was Leonardo da Vinci. Besides being a brilliant artist, Leonardo was also keenly interested in science, and had an extraordinarily inventive brain. He wanted to know how things worked, and he complained that he could not paint properly unless he had first mastered the laws of science. He personally dissected, that is, cut up, dead bodies and discovered how the muscles worked, and where they lay. He examined the heart, found out its purpose, and he almost discovered how blood circulates round the body. Dozens of his drawings have survived, and even today, when we know so much more about anatomy (the structure of the body), we are amazed at Leonardo's knowledge.

Remember that in the fifteenth century, schoolboys did not learn science at school at all, so people had no idea of chemistry, or physics, or even biology. Leonardo, on his own, found out that air was not just one gas: he said that there were two, and that without one of them men would not be able to breathe. We now know that there are in fact more than two, but it is true that without one of them (oxygen) people would die. Another 'guess' was that sound travels in waves, which we know to be true.

These studies led Leonardo to an interest in the development of machinery, and if he had known about a fuel such as petrol, there is little doubt that mechanical devices would have been invented nearly 400 years earlier than they were.

Leonardo became the chief engineer to a

Circulation of the Blood

William Harvey was a doctor and teacher of anatomy. He encouraged his students to dissect bodies of humans and animals, rather than rely on book-learning. In 1628 he published an article on the circulation of the blood. The picture above is an illustration from the article, showing the blood vessels of the fore-arm. This Englishman's discovery helped doctors and surgeons understand more about the human body.

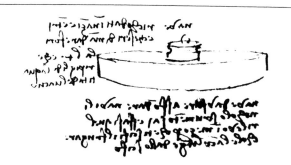

Leonardo da Vinci's submarine

Leonardo told nobody about the submarine he designed because of 'the evil nature of men who would practise assassination at the bottom of the sea by breaking ships in their lowest parts'. This is exactly what happened when submarines were invented 400 years later.

prince of Italy named Cesare Borgia, and he travelled all over the country advising him on how to build fortresses and canals. Although he hated the wars that tore Italy apart, his interest in machinery led him to draw diagrams for many new types of weapons, including a kind of armoured tank on four wheels, a helicopter, and a submarine! His inventions were later regarded just as being odd, and nobody bothered to follow them up. The principles he thought out could not be put to use because the world had not yet advanced far enough in its technical skill. It is only now that we realize how forward-looking Leonardo was.

Machiavelli, 1469–1527

Machiavelli, a leading politician of Florence, was always looking for new ways in which to bring together the Italian states. In his later years, he wrote: 'Because there is only one Master in heaven, there ought to be only one master on earth.' He knew there could be no lasting peace in Italy while the cities quarrelled among themselves, and they could not keep the French and Spaniards out if they did not have a united army. He was a great admirer of the old Roman system, whereby one man was the ruler, or dictator, of the whole empire. He wanted to see one man made dictator of Italy. He did not care much how this dream came about, and for this reason he has always been thought of as a schemer, cruel and ruthless (pitiless). He thought Cesare Borgia might be his ideal ruler, and he wrote a book called *The Prince* showing how such a man could rule by being firm, but without pity and without a conscience. Although Cesare Borgia fitted this description, he was not strong enough to become Machiavelli's ideal 'dictator'.

Machiavelli was the first Christian politician to study politics as a science. (Ibn Khaldun had done something of the same sort in the Muslim world.) He looked upon the history of the world as a great road along which mankind was travelling—not always in the right direction, but with some sort of purpose. Human beings, he thought, remained much the same throughout the centuries, but circumstances forced them to behave differently. In the Middle Ages, they had not used their talents to the full, whereas in the ancient world they had built splendid civilizations through their loyalty to a great leader. Machiavelli wanted to change the circumstances under which his fellow-Italians lived, and to create conditions where a new civilization might flourish.

Portrait of Machiavelli
Machiavelli wrote: 'Although a prince can sometimes afford to be virtuous, flattery, deceit and even murder are often necessary if the prince is to stay in power.' But Machiavelli himself was not a cruel man, and he did not mean that violent methods were necessarily good.

The new merchants

There were great opportunities for businessmen to grow rich during the Renaissance, and often whole families rose to power in the politics of their city because of their great wealth and standing. These families often used their money to 'buy' positions in the government, and even to influence the cardinals* in their choice of a Pope.

Only a few families controlled the banking system, the wool and weaving trades, and the shipping. It was these families who had the money and the leisure to employ artists like Michelangelo and Leonardo da Vinci. They lived on huge family estates, with great libraries and collections of statues in the grounds. They built churches and universities, hospitals and schools.

The spread of education helped the spirit of enquiry to grow. One result was a great discussion that went on all over Europe, in palaces and churches, in private houses and in taverns, about the Church and its place in the world.

*A cardinal is a Prince of the Church, a member of the Pope's Council or Sacred College which elects the Pope.

Chapter 22 A Split in the Christian Church

Right from ancient Egyptian and Sumerian days, the only people who really knew the 'secrets' of religion were the priests and the scribes. The laity, or common people, were told what they should believe, and they were often punished if they did not obey. So an important effect of the new printing presses was that ordinary men and women could learn the knowledge of the priests.

The translation of the Bible

Gutenberg's Bible was the Latin version, and could not be read by anyone who was not highly educated. In Switzerland in 1516, a great scholar named Desiderius Erasmus collected together several Greek translations of the New Testament, and produced a new Greek version. But again, this could be read by very few people. New translations were needed in the common languages of the people of Europe.

As early as 1388, a man named John Wycliffe had produced an English Bible, translated from St Jerome's Vulgate. But the clergy were not willing to allow the laity to read the Scriptures, and the English version was forbidden to be read in church until 1530. Between 1525 and 1535 William Tyndale used Greek and Hebrew sources to make other translations into English. He said:

> 'I would have women read the Gospels and the Epistles (letters) of St Paul: I would have the ploughman and the craftsman sing them at their work; I would have the traveller recite them to forget the weariness of his journey.'

This is exactly what happened all over Europe, for the Bible was now translated freely in every country. At first Bibles were scarce, and they were chained to reading desks in churches, but the printers worked night and day to produce copies which ordinary men and women could own and read in their own homes.

The Bible in English
This is the first page of the Old Testament translated from the original Hebrew into English by William Tyndale. It was printed in 1530.

Criticism begins

For hundreds of years, Christian kings and princes in Germany, in Spain, in France and in England all had to pay tribute to the Pope. Many people in these countries resented the fact that their money went out of their own country to Rome, and they suspected that it paid for the Pope's earthly glory rather than for the Church. One man, on reading a New Testament in his own language, found that there was 'little about the Pope, but much about Christ'—and that Jesus had not lived in a palace, surrounded by luxury. Even in Italy people began to criticize the Pope because he was more like a worldly prince than a religious leader, but owing to the politics of the various city-states, it was not wise to criticize too much; after all, the Pope's armies were strong enough to invade any city that disagreed with his religious policy. But outside Italy, criticism grew until it reached a great climax.

Martin Luther, 1483–1546

The person who really started the 'Reformation' of the Christian Church was a monk named Martin Luther. He was born in Saxony, part of the country governed by the Holy Roman Emperor, which included present-day Germany, Austria, Belgium and the Netherlands.

Luther was a devout man, but he was filled with great doubts about himself, and about God's purpose for the world. His father had wanted him to be a lawyer, but he decided instead to go into a monastery to try to solve the problems which troubled him. Later he wrote:

> 'If ever a monk got to heaven by his monkery, I would have got there. All my brothers in the monastery will testify that had I gone on with it I would have killed myself with prayers, reading and other works.'

But Luther did not believe that 'monkery' was the solution for him, and he left the monastery to go and teach in a university at Wittenberg, on the river Elbe. While he was there, he was chosen to accompany a friar to Rome.

But Luther was bitterly disappointed with what he found in the centre of Christianity. Rome was not the devout place he had imagined. The Pope was dressed in magnificent robes, and on ceremonial occasions wore a huge, glittering crown. The cardinals had enormous palaces with dozens of servants, and the common people were full of gossip about the worldly way in

John Huss

In Bohemia [now a part of Czechoslovakia], a reformer named John Huss (1369–1415) preached against sham miracles, and the wealth of the priests. His bishop forbade him to continue preaching, and his writings were taken away to be studied for 'heresy' [any teaching not approved by the Church]. But he continued to preach and write against what he thought was wrong in the church. In 1415 he was told to retract and say publicly that he had been wrong, and when he refused he was burnt to death. The new ideas that Huss introduced into Europe led to the 'conversion' of a young monk named Martin Luther.

which churchmen lived. There had been Popes, they said, who had children of their own, although they were not supposed to marry; cardinals were sometimes chosen because they could pay more than anyone else for the privilege; even small boys were made bishops, and what was worse, they were made bishops of many different places, not just one. (All these stories were true: one man had 11 bishoprics and was the abbot of nine abbeys—and he had first become bishop at the age of three!) Naturally not all the bishops and cardinals bought their positions, and not all were interested in worldly wealth, but there were enough such cases for gossip to be widespread.

But above all these things, Luther was horrified by the way in which the Church collected money by selling indulgences. In the old days, Christians who had sinned did penance—that is, they punished themselves for it, perhaps by going on a pilgrimage; or they performed some act of self-denial to make up for their sin. Now a man could buy an 'indulgence', that is, he merely had to pay money in order to keep his conscience quiet or avoid the punishment that awaited him after death. Anyone truly penitent Luther said, would welcome punishment, and would not expect to get off lightly.

When the people of Wittenberg flocked to buy indulgences from a monk named John Tetzel, Luther's anger really exploded. John Tetzel's indulgences promised forgiveness to a man's dead relatives as well as to himself. This was really taking advantage of the feelings of poor and ignorant men, for even if they might risk purgatory for themselves, how could they bear to allow a dead father, or wife, or child, to suffer, when their release could be bought with money? 'Those who say that a soul flies to heaven when a coin tinkles in the collection-box are preaching an invention of man.' So thought Luther, and he wrote down his angry protests in a pamphlet known as the '95 theses' (or arguments) and he nailed it to the door of the parish church, where everybody going to the morning service on All Saints' Day could read it.

The year was now 1517. Luther's protests might not have got any further, but for the printing press. His theses were published, and they circulated all over Europe. He gained thousands of followers, who also believed that the Christian Church ought to be reformed. In later pamphlets, he attacked the Pope's authority, and suggested that reform should come not from the clergy themselves, but from the laity. He wanted the church services to be made simpler, and he said that the clergy were not after all superior to other people, 'for all believers are priests'.

Pope Leo X and the cardinals were furious that this young man, the son of a poor miner, should attack them in this way. The Pope ordered that his books should be condemned, and that he should be excommunicated. This meant that he was no longer a member of the Church, could not go to services, or be pardoned for his sins. People believed that to be excommunicated meant being cut off from God's mercy for ever.

In 1521 Luther was called to the town of Worms to a kind of trial, presided over by the Emperor Charles V, and there he was declared an outlaw. The emperor said: 'A single monk who disagrees with what all Christianity has said for a thousand years must be wrong!'

The St Bartholomew Massacre
In France the Protestants were called 'Huguenots'. They were persecuted by the French Catholics, and many emigrated to other parts of Europe (and later, to South Africa). Among the early refugees was John Calvin, who went to Geneva, in southern Switzerland.

The French Huguenots built churches and worshipped in their own way, but they were in great danger from a special court that was created in order to suppress them. In 1572 the French king's mother, Catherine de Medici (she was an Italian) persuaded her son to kill all the Huguenots in Paris. On St Bartholomew's night, in a surprise attack, thousands of Huguenots were massacred in the streets. It took many hundreds of years for the two branches of Christianity to live together in peace, and even now there are sometimes outbreaks of violence between them. A recent example is in Ireland.

But the priests who attended the 'Diet of Worms'* as the trial was called, did not realize how far Luther's ideas had spread. Other monks were following his example. Some started to conduct church services in German, not in Latin. Others stopped the practice of confession.† Some monks and nuns married. It was too late for reform by the Churchmen themselves. The common men were also taking up the fight, and there was now no means of stopping the break-up of the Church.

In 1555, at the 'Peace of Augsburg', a legal council declared that every city should be able to choose whether it would remain in the Catholic Church in its old form, or join the new

Martin Luther at the Diet of Worms
Charles V, Holy Roman Emperor (1519–58) was a devout Catholic. He did his best to reform the Church from inside. Had he succeeded, Luther would not have had so much cause for his fiery preaching. The split in the Church led to quarrels among the princes of Germany and Charles's empire broke up. Charles retired to a monastery in Spain when he was 56. Above Martin Luther states his beliefs to Charles, at Worms.

Church (called Protestant, because its members 'protested' against the Pope's authority).

Luther had probably not intended to break the Christian Church into two halves in this way. Even some of his early supporters thought he had gone too far. Erasmus, who had been just as indignant as Luther about the sale of indulgences, at the great wealth of the priests, and about worshipping relics, could not agree with his extreme view. 'I laid a hen's egg,' he once said, 'but Luther hatched a bird of quite a different kind.'

*A Diet was a kind of Parliament; and in German, 'Worms' is pronounced 'Vorms'.

†The Church demanded that people should go regularly to confession, to confess their sins to a priest who had the power to forgive them in the name of God.

135

John Calvin, 1509–64

In Geneva, during the first half of the sixteenth century, there was a stern and strict young preacher named John Calvin who also disagreed with the old Church but strongly denied that he had been influenced by Luther. He said that God had spoken to him before he had ever heard of the fiery monk from Wittenberg. But Calvin's views on religion were as strong as Luther's, and having broken away from the Church of Rome, he himself supported a religious code which was indeed much harsher than any that Luther had advised.

Calvin not only rejected the pleasure-loving clergy of Rome—he also stopped the citizens of Geneva from singing and dancing, from gambling and drinking. He set up a Council in Geneva, in which a number of 'pastors' and 'elders' (senior laymen) looked after the moral welfare of the citizens. They had power to inspect people's houses and to order them to repair or construct drainage, and also to find out about their private lives—and if necessary, to expel from the city any who were not obeying the rules. Even school textbooks were chosen for the teachers, so that children should grow

John Calvin

John Calvin presides over a meeting of the Council of Geneva in 1549.

up thinking 'in the right way'. So, in spite of the great scholars of the Renaissance and Reformation, freedom of speech and freedom of action were still not the natural right of most of the peoples of Europe. Under the Peace of Augsburg, a *city* might decide its religious beliefs, but an individual could not. This acceptance of 'majority religion' by a state or by a city led to a great deal of cruelty in the following century.

Calvinism spreads to Scotland

Calvin's strict rule was taught to a great number of young men in his Geneva Academy, or school for priests; and they later went out to other parts of the world to spread the new form of Protestant Christianity. One of Calvin's followers was a preacher named John Knox, who introduced a stern Protestant faith into the kingdom of Scotland; it was very soon accepted by the whole country. England, south of the border, also became Protestant, but for a different reason. The person who brought this about was not a preacher, but the king himself.

The Church of England

In England, Henry VIII used the split in the Church for political ends. His wife, Catherine of Aragon, to whom he had been married for 18 years, had had many children, but only one, a girl, had lived. It was important that the king should have a male heir, for England had already had many years of wars about who should rule.

Henry asked the Pope for a divorce, but the Pope took so long to grant it that Henry became impatient. He decided to do without the Pope's consent. There were many people in the country who had read Luther's works and who sympathized with reforming the Church. Henry talked to them, and he even appointed a Protestant sympathizer named Thomas Cranmer as Archbishop of Canterbury. Cranmer showed his thanks by declaring that Henry's marriage had never been legal, and by allowing him to marry instead a girl named Anne Bullen (or Boleyn).

The Pope was furious when he heard the news; he excommunicated Cranmer, the bishops who had assisted him, and finally Henry himself. But Henry was no longer worried. He had decided to take over his country's Church and to make himself its head. Every bishop in the country had to sign a paper saying that Henry's marriage to Anne was lawful, and very few refused, although by signing it they were really agreeing that the Pope need not be obeyed.

The following year, Henry appointed an ambitious politician named Thomas Cromwell to look into the affairs of the Church. Cromwell sent officers to every monastery in the country, to find out how well or badly they were being run. Now, many of the great Benedictine and Cistercian monasteries were not being managed well at all. The old strict Rule was not being obeyed, the gardens were neglected, and the abbots were growing prosperous on all the goods they collected from their benefactors, and from the farmers who worked their farm-land.

Cromwell organized the dissolution of the monasteries—their closure and sometimes destruction. From 1535 to 1540, all the monks and nuns of England were sent away from the homes they had lived in for years, and even the wandering friars who preached in the streets were ordered to find other employment.

The land that had belonged to the monasteries went to the king, who later sold it to wealthy merchants. They in turn sold much of it—at a profit—to sheep-farmers, for by now the wool

Thomas Cromwell

trade was very important in England. In only a few years, and with very little opposition, England changed from being a Catholic country, owing allegiance to the Pope, into a Protestant country with the king as the Church's leader. The Anglican Church that resulted from Henry's and England's legal need for a male heir was different from other Protestant Churches, because it did not stem directly from Luther's or Calvin's teachings. (Later, in England, there were people who said that the Anglican Church was still too like the Church of Rome, and there were further splits.) But in spite of the fact that Henry broke away from the Pope for political rather than religious reasons, many people in England were obviously ready for some sort of reform in the Church. Public opinion favoured the change, especially in the cities and the country near London.

Chapter 23 The Catholic Reformation

To the followers of the Pope, the new branch of Christianity was a terrible and dangerous heresy. A threat of excommunication by the Pope was effective only if the person threatened believed in the Pope's power. But if he was not a devout Catholic, and looked to his king, or to a Protestant leader for his religious guidance, then the threat was meaningless. The Catholic Church at last realized that it should think out its policy, and try to resist the new movement.

Heresy

The Christian Church had always tried to stop people having opinions that were different from the 'official' ones. People who questioned the Church's teaching were called 'heretics'. They were accused of the sin of heresy.

In the early days of Christianity a heretic could have his property taken from him, and he could be banished from his own country. An early Christian writer, St John Chrysostom, said, 'To put a heretic to death would be to introduce upon earth an inexpiable (unpardonable) crime.' But by the time of the Reformation, many heretics *had* been put to death, usually by being burnt alive. The Pope sent Dominican friars about the country to find people suspected of heresy. The friars were called 'Inquisitors' (investigators), and they came to be greatly feared. A man accused by the Inquisitors of heresy could be put into prison merely on suspicion. If he accused other 'heretics' he might escape with his life. But if he defied the Inquisition, then he could be tortured, imprisoned for life, or handed over to the 'secular arm' for execution. (The secular arm was the ordinary 'police force' of the country. Secular means concerned with worldly, not religious, matters.)

The Inquisition was worse in Spain than anywhere else. Just as Henry VIII had taken over

Joan of Arc
In the early fifteenth century, Jeanne d'Arc, or Joan of Arc, a French girl, believed that angels spoke to her, and told her to lead the French forces against the English army. She was captured by the people of Burgundy in France, and sold to the English, who tried her for heresy. She would not deny hearing 'voices', and she said that she obeyed the direct voice of God rather than the Church. For this she was found guilty and burnt in 1431.

138

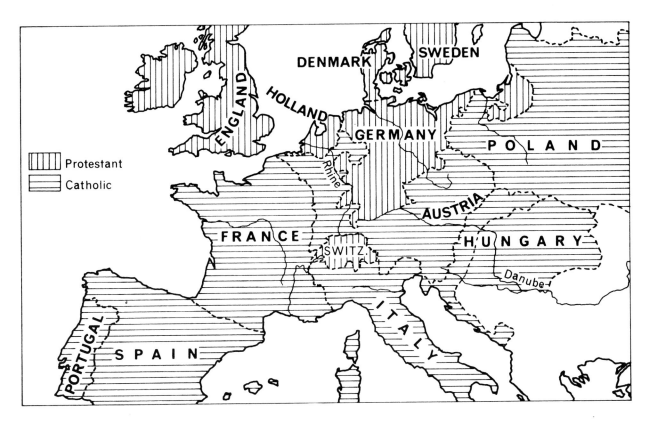

Protestant
Catholic

the Pope's power for his own purposes, so now King Ferdinand and Queen Isabella of Spain took over the idea of Inquisitors to keep Spain a Catholic country, and to get rid of the last remaining Muslims in Granada. There had been great friendliness between the two religious groups in the past, but now people were encouraged to give information against Muslims and even Jews. Their lands were seized by the King and Queen, and as both Jews and Muslims were often good business men, the Crown became very wealthy. The chief Inquisitor*, a cruel monk named Torquemada, even accused bishops of heresy and had them imprisoned.

Now, although the king and queen acquired great estates as a result of the persecutions, business in Spain decreased, because rich men could be reduced in a single day to poverty. Everybody wanted immediate payment instead of allowing credit, for who knew if the man who owed you money would ever be able to pay it? Tomorrow he might be in jail, and his wife and children left to live as best they might, turned out of their homes and without any way of earning

*His function was that of official investigator. He was in fact, Inquisitor General, director of the court of Inquisition in Spain.

The division between Catholic and Protestant Countries in the seventeenth century
In some countries, such as Ireland and Germany, the decision of the rulers was not always accepted, this lead to religious wars.

Jewish moneylender
Jews were regarded as 'different' from other people, because they kept to their own communities and they had different customs and beliefs. People who are different in these ways are often regarded with suspicion and even hated by those among whom they live. The Jews have had more than their fair share of hatred throughout their long history.

139

a living. If it had not been for a new source of wealth from new lands in the west (Chapter 30), Spain might very quickly have become bankrupt.

The Jesuits

To try to reform people by threats and torture is never very effective. The Catholic Church, now opposed by the Protestant Churches, began to try to reform itself from within. This movement is known as the 'Counter-Reformation'. In only a few years there was a completely new spirit in Rome. The Pope was elected once more for his holiness, and not for any worldly reason, and the cardinals were sincere, honest men who encouraged education as a means of spreading religion. The clergy took their lead from Rome, and once again led humble and sober lives; and scholars began to research into early Christian history.

In order to spread the new religious ideals, Ignatius Loyola, a Spaniard, wrote a book of 'Spiritual Exercises'. The book was a guide to men's meditations and thoughts about God. His main theme was, 'We must serve God as if everything depended upon ourselves; but we must pray as if all depended upon God.'

Loyola was a monk, and a university teacher. In 1534 he and a small group of friends met together in a French church, and vowed that they would take up the ideals of the early Christians. They would live on the charity of others, owning no property, and having no fixed homes. Above all, they would teach other people, convert the 'heathen', and try to go on a pilgrimage to Jerusalem.

This little band of men (only about seven or eight of them at first) walked all the way to Rome, and had an audience (a formal interview) with Pope Paul III. This Pope was one of the first to return to the old spiritual ideals of the Christian Church, and he welcomed Loyola and gave him money to continue his work. Loyola formed the 'Society of Jesus', and in a short time he had gathered many followers. In later years they

Ignatius Loyola

Universities

Until the time of the Reformation, European universities were mainly run by the Church. They taught Latin, Greek, mathematics and philosophy. When the students successfully completed their course of learning they obtained a doctor's or master's degree, which meant they were qualified to teach in a university if they wished.

were known as 'Jesuits', and they penetrated almost every country in the world. They spread the new Catholic ideas, and they founded schools and colleges in order to combat Protestantism. Their schools were so well run and became so famous for their learning that wealthy parents had no hesitation in sending their sons to the Jesuits. In particular they tried to build good schools in Protestant countries such as Germany, so that they could educate priests to replace those who had become Lutherans.

The Council of Trent

Charles V, the Holy Roman Emperor, was one of the first people in authority to be concerned about the wrong practices in the Church. He urged the Pope to call together a council to discuss ways and means of setting things right. The result of his concern was the Council of Trent, which met many times over a period of several years to set down the beliefs of Catholics, and to end the differences of opinion of Catholics in different countries. The council was not a complete success, because there were always more Italians in the sessions than there were representatives of any other country, and so they could out-vote the rest. But the Jesuits sent their best scholars of all nationalities, and the council did strengthen the power of the Catholic Church in Europe.

Neither the Catholics nor the Protestants were very sure of themselves, and for this reason both sides were often intolerant. Bitter quarrels broke out between scholars and between churchmen, and hundreds of good people on both sides were executed for no other reason than that they believed in the 'wrong' kind of Christianity. The religious quarrels of the sixteenth and seventeenth centuries led to the various European countries competing in other things as well. Catholic and Protestant countries were rivals in the search for new lands, and in opening new markets with the East, and with the newly-discovered America—as we shall see in the following chapters.

The Arts

During the fifteenth, sixteenth and seventeenth centuries, Europeans became more conscious of a need for using their brains as well as their hands. People wrote books, painted pictures, learnt about medicine, astronomy, history and geography. And just as *everybody* in ancient

William Shakespeare
The greatest English poet and playwright of the age was William Shakespeare. His works include historical plays about the kings of former times; tragedies about the downfall of great men; and comedies which are sometimes like fairy stories. Shakespeare's players acted in the Globe Theatre, London; this had a circular stage which allowed the audience to sit all around the actors.

Greece went to plays, talked politics, took part in athletic exercises, and played a musical instrument; so now, after the Renaissance, all educated people could sing, write verse, ride horses, and appreciate beautiful buildings, parks and gardens. They learnt foreign languages, read Latin, danced and practised fencing. They were aware of the current events of their time, and they took a great interest in the achievements of their fellow-countrymen.

These last few chapters have been about the things people *thought* about, and how they broadened their knowledge by using their brains; in the next section we shall see how these same centuries also produced explorers, adventurers and people willing to endure pain and great discomfort for the sake of an ideal.

Part VI Exploration and Conquest
Chapter 24 Looking beyond the Sea

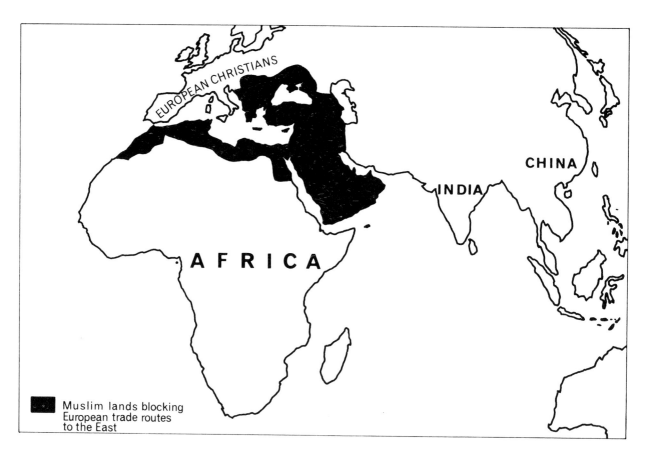

Muslim lands blocking
European trade routes
to the East

By the time of the Reformation, the great Muslim conquests were over. After that, battles between Christians and Muslims were less important to the history of the world. Lands sometimes changed hands, but in general, Muslim and Christian countries left each other alone.

There was a block of Muslim countries around the Mediterranean Sea (see map), which cut off Christian Europe from the countries of the East. The two main Christian ports of Venice and Genoa grew rich by buying goods from Muslim traders, and selling them to their northern neighbours.

For the most part, Muslims and Christians did not meet at all. But in various ways Christian countries were reminded of what they were missing by being separated by the Muslim block from Africa and the lands of the East.

The first real contact with another way of life came with the Crusades, one important result of which was that those Europeans who returned from the East brought with them new ideas of comfort and luxury. They had seen the palaces of Constantinople and Damascus, and enjoyed the hospitality of Eastern nobles. They also brought back new foods, and new ideas of how to flavour food with pepper and other spices. The demand for these Eastern goods increased, and money poured into Muslim lands to pay for them. The European knights and soldiers all learned new and less harsh ways of life. A prosperous and ambitious middle class of traders and merchants began to realize its own strength and importance. They were no longer content to be servants (almost slaves) of the wealthy. They wanted more rights and privileges. They became more independent than they had ever been before and more likely to seek adventure. The 'spirit of enquiry' of the Renaissance encouraged people to read for themselves the old Greek books about astronomy and geography. Old maps were brought out and studied. An increase in trade with other countries led to better boat-building. As seamen sailed farther and farther from home, so the shipbuilders tried to build ships to meet the greater risks of long voyages.

The second way in which the two cultures met was when Christians went on pilgrimages to the East. This was one way in which the well-to-do citizens took a holiday. They made their way down to southern Italy or Venice, and sailed across the Mediterranean to Palestine, the land in which Jesus had lived. When they returned to Europe they entertained their friends with tales of the strange things they had seen in Palestine and Syria, Egypt and Arabia. Just like modern tourists they brought back presents — silks imported from India and China, Persian carpets, spices, and carved ivory. Damascus, in Syria, was now the most important trading centre in the Middle East, and if they could afford it, travellers to Syria could buy all the luxuries they wanted.

The third sort of people who visited Muslim lands were perhaps the most adventurous of all. These were the merchants who travelled long distances on foot and on horseback, to find the *sources* of the wealth of cities like Damascus. One outstanding example of a merchant-traveller was Marco Polo, but there were many others. When Marco Polo finally returned to Europe, he wrote down all he could remember of the lands of the East, and so excited the interest — and the greed — of those who read his book that soon the governments of Europe were eager for their merchants to visit and trade with these lands.

So interest in the East developed in all the countries of Europe. But along with this interest,

Kublai Khan

Kublai Khan, the emperor of China in Marco Polo's time, was not Chinese. He came from Mongolia in the north, and he led an invasion of Mongols into China and overran it. The Mongols were expert horsemen, and no ordinary foot-soldiers could withstand them. In the far-off west, they had already invaded and conquered much of what is now Russia and Poland.

Kublai Khan made himself the emperor of the whole of China, and built his capital at Peking. In spite of the warlike manner in which he had gained the throne, he ruled wisely, and soon China was again famous for its art, poetry and peaceful ways. The Khan built beautiful palaces and gardens, and encouraged his people to unite and live together in harmony. He brought religious leaders and teachers to his capital, because he thought they would have a civilizing influence on the country.

there was a spirit of rivalry. Kings by now were becoming powerful, and there was competition between the new nation-states. In time the new split between Catholics and Protestants made the rivalry stronger. Each country wished to profit as much as possible from the trade with the East and to exclude others from it. It was important therefore to get through the Muslim barrier and reach the 'treasure-countries'.

But it was almost impossible for any expedition to go through Muslim territory. A few merchants were allowed to do so, but they had to pay so much in customs duties and taxes that their goods were very expensive to buy in Europe. The Christian countries saw this as good money getting into the hands of 'unbelievers'. If there was no way through by land, then the countries of Europe had to find a way round by sea. And the first European country to have any clear ideas on the solution to this problem was Portugal.

Henry the Navigator, 1394–1460

Henry the Navigator was a prince of Portugal. He had a great interest in exploration, and in anything to do with ships, though, in spite of his nickname, he was not himself a sailor. When he was a young man, Henry went to fight the Muslims at a place called Ceuta in North Africa. While he was there he saw the arrival of caravans from the centre of Africa, caravans which had come all the way from the towns of Songhai and Timbuktu, south of the Sahara. He realized that a country as small as Portugal could not possibly capture this trade from the Muslims; but was there any reason why they could not sail round the coast of Africa, and find another route to the gold-mines? With this idea in mind, Henry spent all his time consulting old maps, talking to sailors and adventurers, and encouraging his inventors to improve the existing compasses and other aids to navigation. Henry's first objects were to find Africa's gold and to convert Muslims and heathens to Christianity.

Soon, as a result of this one man's interest and imagination, the ship-builders and sail-makers, the traders and craftsmen of Portugal, were talking about the possibilities of voyages and trade-routes to new, and as yet undiscovered countries.

The reasons for exploration were all in existence: the desire to convert or to overcome the Muslims; the knowledge that there were rich cities in the East; and the lure of gold in Africa. Before long the exploration began.

The Way South

One of the questions that faced the Portuguese was, 'How safe is it to sail southwards round Africa?' Ptolemy, the map-maker of the Greeks, had said that it was impossible to live in the tropics, and many legends had grown up about how men turned black, or were shrivelled up like a leaf in a fire, when they crossed the Equator. In a world full of superstition, fear of the unknown was very great. But if Henry the

Henry the Navigator

Prester John

The legend was that Prester John (probably 'Priest John') was a powerful Christian king whose kingdom was somewhere in Africa, or Asia, or India—nobody quite knew where. He was said to be successfully keeping the Muslims out of his kingdom, so the Portuguese felt that he would be a powerful ally. Everywhere they went, they asked for news of Prester John. None of the inhabitants of Africa or India knew whom they were talking about, but they tried to be helpful. Many Portuguese, and many converted Africans, were sent inland on hopeless searches for the legendary king.

Navigator's dreams were to be fulfilled, these old theories had to be put to the test.

Year by year small, fast sailing-ships called caravels made their way down the west coast of Africa, first calling in for supplies at their newly-colonized Cape Verde Islands. Each expedition tried to push a little further southward, always asking for news of Prester John, and looking for new kingdoms with which they could trade.

In 1482 a sea-captain called Diogo Cão anchored in the waters of the river Congo, having successfully crossed the Equator without bursting into flames, or even noticeably changing colour! He left four Franciscan monks at an African village, with orders to look for the ruler of the Congo kingdom, and to discover whether this large river led to Prester John's country. He then returned home to Lisbon, with several Africans whom he had taken as hostages* for the safety of his Franciscans. These Africans were trained by the Portuguese in Lisbon so that they could act as interpreters and guides when Diogo Cão returned to the river Congo. Five years later the Africans were home again. Together with Cão and his sailors, they paddled up the river to the king's town, which was the capital of a large state. The Franciscans were well and happy. The king waited for his guests, seated on his wood-and-ivory stool, and surrounded by his councillors and advisors. Altogether it looked as though the Portuguese and Congolese would be able to bring each other considerable benefits. Trade in ivory, gold and slaves started almost straight away—a trade which was eventually to lead to the downfall of the kingdom of Congo. Later we shall see why this was so.

Overland to Calicut

Meanwhile, another Portuguese explorer was travelling overland to try to find out all he could about the west coast of India and the spice trade. His name was Pero de Covilhã†, and he went through Arabia disguised as a merchant. He joined a party of Arab merchants, without arousing suspicion (a remarkable feat), and so passed through all the dangers of the route in company with people who had been there before. He reached India, and set to work to discover all he could about the Muslim trade between India

*A hostage was a prisoner held as a guarantee of good behaviour by the people from whom he was taken.
†Also spelt Covilhão and Covilhan.

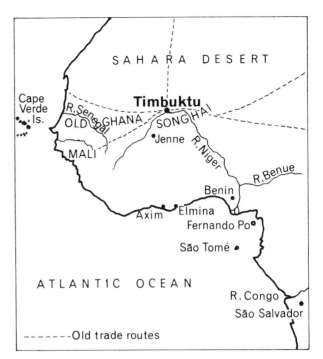

The West Coast of Africa
There had already been in Africa more splendid towns and palaces than those of the Congo Kingdom. Between the rivers Senegal and Niger, the kingdoms of Ghana, Mali and Songhai had grown rich by trading with the people of North Africa. Their trade routes through the desert were centuries old, and the fame of their kings had spread to Europe.

When the Muslim king of Mali went on a pilgrimage to Mecca in 1324, he took an enormous amount of gold with him. Dealers had to drop the price of gold because it was now so plentiful. A fourteenth century writer said: 'Twelve thousand young slaves dressed in tunics of brocade and silk of Yemen carried his personal belongings.' This king, whose name was Mansa Musa, returned to his own country with Arab scholars and teachers and schools in Timbuktu and Jenne became famous for their learning. The scholars taught history, religion and law.

These facts were forgotten in later centuries, and the European explorers of the nineteenth century talked of 'darkest Africa', and expected to find only savages there.

and East Africa. He saw horses from Arabia being taken ashore at Goa, and at Calicut the gold and ivory from East Africa being unloaded. The boats used by the traders were small and frail, sewn together with strips of coconut palm, and with no nails at all. They had triangular sails, and looked much less seaworthy than the vessels of Covilhã's home country.

Covilhã had an opportunity to find out for himself how well these little dhows could sail across the Indian Ocean; he paid for a passage in one of them, and went to Sofala, in south-eastern Africa.

145

(See map on p. 147) He was the first European to see any part of this coast, and he heard enough of the local gossip to convince him that there was a way round the southern tip of Africa. Once Portuguese ships could reach Sofala, he knew that they could easily continue across the Indian Ocean to the rich lands of India and China.

The trading dhow unloaded its cargo of cotton cloth, porcelain (china) plates, wheat and beads at the East African ports, and then sailed northwards to the Red Sea. Covilhã got off the boat here, and made his way overland to Cairo. Then he decided to go to Ethiopia to look for Prester John. Twenty years afterwards, when a delegation arrived from Portugal to visit the emperor of Ethiopia, they found him still there, with an Ethiopian wife. Pero da Covilhã left no account of his adventures, which is a great pity, but before he left Cairo, he had sent back letters to King John II of Portugal, describing the pepper, clove and cinnamon trades. This information encouraged the king to go on trying to find a way round Africa to the Indian Ocean, and in 1487 he sent the navigator Bartholomew Diaz with instructions to continue down the coast until he found the southern end of Africa.

The voyage of Bartholomew Diaz
It is difficult for us now to know exactly how Bartholomew Diaz's crew fared on this journey, for all the reports and maps were kept strictly secret by the Portuguese of the time, and they have since been lost. The Portuguese did not want other nations to find out what they were doing. By Portuguese law passing on maps or information about trade-routes was an offence punishable by death.

Bartholomew Diaz's little 'lateen rigged' (triangular-sailed) ship was blown away from the course his pilot had set, and the sailors knew that they were much farther west than they wanted to be—but they didn't know *how* much farther. When the wind dropped, they sailed eastward again, and were astonished at not reaching land. In great fear, they turned the boat towards the north, discovered land, and to their amazement realized that they had found the route round Africa. They were in the area we now call Mossel Bay.

Diaz was delighted to find that they had achieved their purpose, and was eager to go on towards the north and up the new coastline. But his men panicked and refused to go any farther. They were now in an unknown sea, and who knew what dangers they might have to face? They had very little fresh water, and food was scarce. They did not know whether they would meet friends or enemies, and they were not armed for battle. Bartholomew Diaz was finally persuaded that he had gone far enough. So they returned, and saw for the first time the harbour we now know as Table Bay. Diaz called the southern tip of Africa 'The Cape of Storms', because he was unlucky enough to arrive there in bad weather. His king renamed it 'The Cape of Good Hope', because now it seemed that there was a promise of new and exciting voyages.

Map showing voyage of Bartholomew Diaz, in 1487–8, during which he reached the Cape of Good Hope

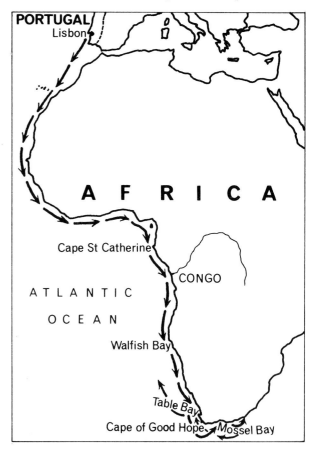

146

Chapter 25 The Land of Zenj

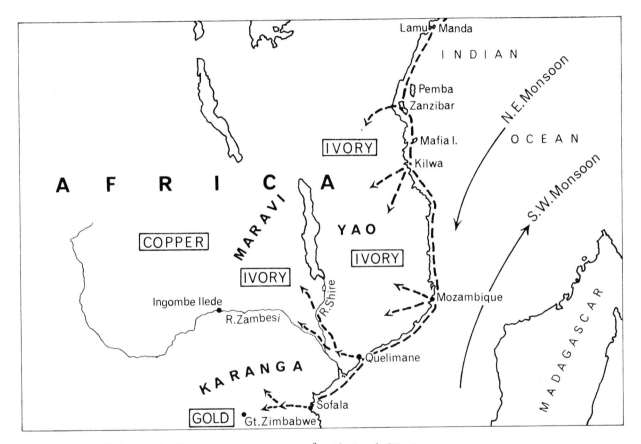

In the days of the early Portuguese voyages of discovery, East Africa was already well-known to the Muslims from south Arabia (and others who had settled on the west coast of India) as the 'land of Zenj'. (It is also sometimes spelt 'Zinj' or 'Zanj'.)

From about the ninth or tenth centuries, traders from Arabia had made small settlements along the east coast of Africa. Then, probably about the thirteenth century, a number of Muslims from towns in Somalia, north of present-day Kenya, emigrated to these settlements, and built new towns of their own. They cultivated

The Land of Zenj

The people of the coast traded with the interior along several different trade routes. In the north, the Maravi (Malawi) traded ivory with Arabs who travelled up the Shire River. Ingombe Ilede was once a flourishing trading town where Arab merchants bought ivory. The ivory was carried to the coast by African men, some of whom were probably sold as slaves at the end of the journey.

Further south, Arabs exchanged their cloth, beads and knives for gold from the country of Monomatapa.

crops, kept livestock (domestic animals), and fished in the cool waters inside the coral reefs which protect the harbours and inlets of the coast.

There was frequent intermarriage between the Arabs and the Africans of the coast, and they started to create a new kind of culture, which was a mixture of the Arab and African ways of life, yet different from both. These people became the rulers of the towns, and the wealthy merchants. The rest of the population were Africans, most of whom were probably not converted to Islam. They kept to their own customs, and did not copy the richer people very much.

Most of the settlements were built on islands, as protection against raids from inland tribes. There was no need to fortify the islands against attacks from the sea; until the fifteenth century all incoming ships had been friendly trading dhows. The main settlements are shown on the map on p. 147.

An early traveller from Morocco named Ibn Battuta, visited Kilwa in 1331. This is what he wrote about it:

'Kilwa is one of the most beautiful and well-constructed towns in the world. The whole of it is elegantly built. The roofs are built with mangrove poles. There is very much rain.'

About 250 years later, the Portuguese also praised Kilwa, although by that time it was not such a prosperous town as it had formerly been. This is the Portuguese description:

'There is an island hard by the mainland which is called Kilwa, in which is a Moorish (Muslim) town with many fair houses of stone and mortar, with many windows after our fashion, very well arranged in streets, with many flat roofs. The doors are of wood, well carved, with excellent carpentry. Around it are streams and orchards with many channels of sweet water.'

The towns on the coast were loosely connected, with a common language and religion, but with no common allegiance to any one sultan (ruler) or nation. The people had little to disturb them. Craftsmen wove cloth, carved wood, built stone or wooden houses and mosques, and made jewellery and ornaments. The weather was good, there was enough rain for the crops, the sea was full of fish, and the coconut palms gave food, drink, matting and roofing. There was no need to work very hard in order to be fed and clothed on a tropical coast. Perhaps because of this, and because a hot moist climate does not make people very energetic, the Muslims of the coast made no attempt to build towns inland. They were a sea-board people, more interested in their

Coins
The sultans of Kilwa minted tiny coins from the thirteenth to the sixteenth centuries. The coins bear the name of the sultan, and sometimes also a prayer to Allah for the sultan's prosperity. Today archaeologists can learn about the history of the East African coast from coins found in ruins and near the sites of old 'Zenj' towns. There were 569 coins in this pot, found on Mafia Island in 1964.

trade with India and Arabia than with the tribes in their own continent.

Already in Ibn Battuta's time, the Zenj towns lived on the trade which Covilhã later reported to the king of Portugal. In exchange for African gold, ivory, tortoiseshell and rhino-horn, they received iron weapons and tools, Islamic pottery, silk and cotton goods, and glass from Arabia and India. These goods were carried to and from the East African coast in the same kind of tiny dhows that have been sailing across these waters ever since. The wealth of the towns, with their shining buildings, well laid out streets, stone mosques and palaces, all came from this trade, and particularly from the trade in gold and ivory from the interior.

The main route by which the gold came was along the great river Zambezi, and southwards to the port of Sofala. The sultans of Kilwa were powerful enough to rule over Sofala, and take most of the profits of the gold trade for themselves. The country from which the gold came was ruled by a king called by the Portuguese, Monomotapa, and his people were the Karanga. Their descendants still live in present-day Rhodesia. ('Monomotapa' was the Portuguese way of pronouncing 'Mwinemutapa', which

means 'the plunderer'. It was a praise-name given to him by his own people because of his great conquests.)

The ordinary coast-people's contact with the outside world was limited to the news they got from the crews of sailing dhows, which arrived on their shores between December and April; the dhows stayed on the coast until the north-east monsoon blew, and the sailors returned to India during April and May. The crews brought news from the Spice Islands (the East Indies), from India, and even from China. They brought no news from Christian Europe, so the coming of the Europeans was an unexpected shock.

Strangers in the Indian Ocean

Ten years after Bartholomew Diaz's voyage, three little sailing ships made their way round the Cape of Good Hope and sailed northwards, looking for new countries, Prester John, and opportunities for trade. The Portuguese — though they did not know it, or in any way intend it — were about to put an end to the prosperity of the East Coast of Africa.

The leader of the expedition was Vasco da Gama, a soldier and mariner, now about 37 years old. His navigator was the real hero of this voyage. He had sailed on a course that took them far away from the west coast of Africa, and by doing so he had avoided the worst of the contrary winds. During the ten years that had passed since Bartholomew Diaz rounded the Cape, ships' designs had been slightly altered, and ships' instruments had been improved. But they were still very inadequate for such danger-

Trade with the Far East
The dhows came to the coast towns of the Zenj between the months of December and April. With them they brought news from the East and the goods and wares for which they had traded ivory.

The square-rigged carrack
The square-rigged carrack was adopted by Vasco da Gama as an improvement on the caravel as used by Bartholomew Diaz. The caravel carried two lateen (triangular) sails and one small square sail. It sailed well in shallow water and could anchor very close to the shore. The carrack, fitted with up to five square-rigged sails was more suited to the open seas.

ous journeys, and the crew relied completely on the skill and knowledge of their navigators.

This little group of ships arrived at Mozambique in March 1498, and saw in the bay a line of canoes and four large trading dhows. The dhows were a surprise to them, and so indeed was the sultan himself, who later came to greet them with full ceremony. Vasco da Gama's men were amazed at the prosperity of Mozambique. This created a difficult situation for the

Portuguese, because the only presents they had in their ships were things like beads, bells, and cheap cloth. And here were the inhabitants of Mozambique, unloading beautiful silks, cottons and porcelain from the dhows of India and Arabia! However, the citizens of Mozambique treated their visitors with courtesy and kindness, and the Portuguese ate their fill of oranges and limes, and also coconuts, which were something new to them. The sick men began to recover, and everyone's spirits rose at the sight of the riches of Mozambique.

For explorers searching for the Christian kingdom of Prester John, it was a disappointment to find that the inhabitants spoke Arabic, and were Muslims. They kept their own religion secret, and for a while the islanders thought they were Muslim Turks. Trouble started when they discovered their mistake, and the Portuguese left in a hurry, taking with them two pilots who knew the coast well.

Northwards along the coast they went, missing Kilwa because the winds blew them past the harbour. But even so, the dhows from Mozambique sailed faster than the Portuguese fleet, and their crews warned the inhabitants of the more northerly coastal towns that they were about to have Christian visitors. This is what an Arab historian, writing in about 1520, had to say about the Portuguese arrival:

'After a few days there came word that the ships had passed Kilwa and had gone on to Mafia. The lord of Mafia rejoiced, for he thought they (the Portuguese) were good and honest men. But those who knew the truth confirmed that they were corrupt and dishonest persons who had only come to spy out the land in order to seize it. And they determined to cut the anchors of their ships so that they should drift ashore and be wrecked by the Muslims.'

Each side was quick to suspect the other of treachery because of their different religious beliefs, and in view of what happened later, the Muslims were quite right to do so. The Mombasa islanders were cautious about accepting the Portuguese as friends, though they allowed them to have fruit, meat and water. But the news from Mozambique had its effect, and the islanders did try to set the ships adrift. A Portuguese account says:

'Those who swam to the *Berrio* began to cut the cable. The men on watch thought at first

Vasco da Gama

that they were tunny fish, but when they perceived their mistake they shouted to the other vessels. The other swimmers had already got hold of the rigging (the ropes of the sails) of the mizzen-mast[*]. Seeing themselves discovered, they silently slipped down and fled. These and other wicked tricks were practised upon us by these dogs, but Our Lord did not allow them to succeed because they were unbelievers.'

The same author did not seem to think it at all 'wicked' that the Portuguese had that same day poured boiling oil on the skin of two Arabs, to make them confess any treachery against them.

Malindi had also had news of the visitors. But here the Portuguese received a better welcome, for the sultan of Malindi was an old enemy of the sultan of Mombasa, and he must have said to himself, 'The enemy of my enemy is my friend.' Only a few Portuguese sailors were allowed

[*] The mizzen-mast is the mast nearest to the back of a three-masted ship.

150

on shore, and Vasco da Gama himself refused to meet the sultan anywhere except out at sea. But in spite of this lack of trust, the people of Malindi were completely friendly to the Portuguese. They gave them a pilot to assist the navigator on the journey to India, and a quantity of square water containers, such as they used on their own dhows. Then with many friendly farewells, they watched the strange European ships sail away with the monsoon winds.

The Portuguese reach India

The merchants of Arabia and the Malabar coast of India were the people who every year received the ivory and gold, tortoiseshell and rhino-horn, from the ports of East Africa. In Calicut, the chief trading port, Arab merchants made contact with others all the way round the coast of India, as far as the Spice Islands and even China. Trading ships from these Far Eastern ports reached India, and there the goods were either sold inland, or sent across the Indian Ocean to pay for more African gold. The Indian traders were busy men, for they had a great continent to deal with. The rulers of the many Indian states liked to have rich silks from China, and jewellery made from the gold of Sofala.

The 'zamorin' or king of Calicut was a Hindu, but the traders were Muslims. There was great tolerance in India for different religious beliefs; but the Muslims there became just as unfriendly towards Christian traders as their kinsfolk everywhere else.

Vasco da Gama's men arrived in Calicut on 21 May 1498. The traders were accustomed to foreign trading ships, and sold the Portuguese some pepper and cinnamon. But there was something about this expedition that the Arabs did not like. It looked as though the newcomers wanted to take their trade from them, rather than use them as trading partners. The zamorin was anxious; the prosperity of his city depended upon trade, yet he knew that if he granted the Portuguese trading-rights, his Arab traders would be angry. On the other hand, the Portuguese ships were all well armed with guns, which they might easily decide to use on his city.

In the end he asked the Portuguese for customs' duty, and when they refused to pay it he imprisoned some of the ships' crew. Vasco da Gama immediately captured some Indian citizens, and kept them as hostages till his crew members were returned.

The Padrão at Malindi
Everywhere they went the Portuguese put up stone pillars or *padrãos*. The padrão at Malindi has been cased with coral rock, but part of the original pillar may still be inside. The cross is made of stone from Lisbon, so it is probably the original one.

The sailors who went ashore spoke of Malindi enthusiastically. The well-laid out streets were lined with large houses, each having a wooden verandah. The rulers wore Arab dress, and there were also some Gujerati traders living there. The town remained loyal to Portugal for 100 years.

Today Malindi is just a small fishing village, with a row of 'tourist' hotels along the beach. Nearby is the old Arab town of Gedi, which, although in ruins, gives a good idea of the sort of stone buildings in which the coastal peoples used to live.

The Portuguese were obviously not welcome, but this did not discourage them. Vasco da Gama returned to Portugal to report to King John, and within a year a second expedition was on its way. The zamorin was going to have many worries in the future.

Chapter 26 The New World in the West

During the time that they had been pushing south along the west coast of Africa, the Portuguese were so concerned with their new 'factories' (trading stations) there, that Christopher Columbus, the greatest explorer of his time, could not get them to listen to him. He had an entirely different plan: he wanted to sail westward, and get to the Spice Islands and China (he called it Cathay) by sailing straight across the Atlantic Ocean.

We now know that this was impossible, because the continent of America lies between Europe and China; but Columbus and a few others had come to the conclusion that China was only about 3,500 miles away. They imagined the world to be smaller than it really is — the true distance from Portugal to China is more than three times as great as Columbus supposed. Only a few highly educated men believed the old Greek geographers, whose ideas of distance had been more exact.

Disappointed that Portugal would not give him ships, Columbus went to Spain to try his luck with King Ferdinand and Queen Isabella. They received him kindly, but at first were unwilling to finance his venture. Their wars against the Muslims of Granada (southern Spain) were to them more important, and paying their troops had used up a great deal of public money. But finally the Spaniards took Granada and, in 1492, five years before Vasco da Gama rounded Africa, Columbus set sail. The Spanish king and queen had provided him with three ships, because they at last realized that Portugal was already ahead of them, and that they had better hurry up and discover new trade outlets of their own. Portugal would resist any Spanish attempt to sail round 'their' land; the Spaniards could therefore only hope that there was indeed another route to the Spice Islands and Cathay,

as this mariner Christopher Columbus said.

For two months the three Spanish ships sailed west, seeing no land at all. Columbus sailed in the largest ship, the *Santa Maria*. They ran into an area now called the Sargasso Sea, where for days the sea was completely calm, and the sails hung idly without picking up a breath of wind. Nowadays ships set a course which avoids the Sargasso Sea, because besides being windless, it is full of floating weeds. Columbus thought the sea-weed meant that they were near land. But almost anything encouraged him to think they had nearly reached Cathay. He saw birds, a whale and flying-fish, and each time he assured the sailors that land must be only a short distance away. He even tasted the water and told them that it seemed to him to be 'less salty'!

Land, when they found it, was not part of a great continent; it was the island of San Salvador. The explorers gave thanks to God for their safe arrival, and began to look for fresh water and fruit. There were no palaces or even large buildings on the island — only small palm-thatched huts — and Columbus reluctantly had to admit that this was not Marco Polo's Cathay. But perhaps, he thought, it was a part of India? The natives had long, straight hair, so this was certainly a possibility. Columbus regarded it as a fact. He called the natives 'Indians' and they have been called 'Indians' or 'West Indians' ever since.

When they had explored the island, they set off again to find Cathay and the Khan. But at island after island they found only poor villagers, and although some of them wore gold ornaments, earrings and bracelets, there did not seem to be any evidence of a great civilization. This is how Columbus described the islanders:

'They are very well built, with very handsome

bodies and thin faces. Their hair is coarse, almost like the hair of a horse's tail, and short. They wear their hair down over their eyebrows, except for a few strands behind, which they wear long and never cut. Some of them are painted black... and some of them are painted white, and some red, and some in any colour that they find. Some of them paint their faces, some their whole bodies, some only the eyes, and some only the nose.... They are all generally fairly tall, good-looking and well proportioned.'

Columbus kept on trying to make the Indians understand that he wanted to find the Khan and gold, and they always pointed out to sea to some other place far over the horizon. At each new island a little ceremony was held, whereby it was formally taken over by Columbus on behalf of the king and queen of Spain.

The men were always glad to get ashore, and to eat their fill of the strange new plants they came across; the sweet potatoes and pineapples they found particularly delicious, and they took samples of them back to Spain. There was wild cotton, with which the natives wove cloth, and with which each made for himself a hanging bed which they called a 'hamac'. (We have now changed the spelling to 'hammock'.) Before this time, sailors had always slept on the bare decks of their ships. Now they copied the Indians' hammocks to make a dry (and rat-free) bed above the level of the dirty and often wet deck.

But the king and queen of Spain could hardly be expected to regard a few fruits and vegetables or a bed made of some kind of netting as great treasure—they wanted news of gold and silver and precious stones, and to make the journey seem worthwhile, Columbus's men collected all the gold they could find.

Then came disaster: on a reef off their new 'possession', Española, the *Santa Maria* was wrecked. Fortunately nobody was drowned, and the now homeless men built a fort on the island, using the ship's timbers. Columbus decided to keep the fort as a permanent colony, so that later voyagers would have a place to buy food. He asked for volunteers to start the colony, and 39 men decided to stay. The rest, including Columbus, returned to Seville in the other two ships, taking with them some of the Indians, samples of gold, and spices, weapons, cotton and parrots. After a terrible voyage, with raging storms almost tearing the little boats to pieces,

Christopher Columbus, bearing the Spanish flag, sets foot on the New World.

An Indian *hamac*

they arrived home. Columbus was given a grand welcome, and immediately became famous. Spain was in the 'exploration-race' at last, and at any time might discover the land of Cathay. To keep peace between Portugal and Spain, the Pope drew a line across the map of the world (see map on page 155), giving Portugal the non-Christian lands in one half and those in the other to Spain. But later, when other countries wanted to sail ships to explore lands across the oceans, they were angry that the Pope had reserved the new discoveries for the Portuguese and Spaniards, especially as the Pope who made the ruling was himself a Spaniard.

Columbus made three more voyages to the West Indies, but he had more disappointments than encouragements. The greatest disappointment of all was that he never reached Cathay. The colonists on Española were all dead when he returned, but he persevered and started other settlements. He proposed to send home each year as much gold as the settlers could find, and spices and slaves. The Spanish king and queen were not much in favour of having 'Indian' slaves, but the gold was a different matter.

By now, the ships' crews were getting tired of exploring islands that all seemed alike to them. They became greedy for gold, and they got into fights with the Indians. There were no game animals and not enough wild fruit to provide them all with fresh food, and the Indians did

The West Indies in the sixteenth century
The peoples of these islands were Arawaks and Caribs. The Caribs have given their name to the Caribbean Sea. Some of the islands now have different names from the ones the Spaniards gave them. Can you say which are different, and what the present names are?

not see why they should continually give away food from their own stocks. So the sailors started to steal. From now onwards the Indians were suspicious of the white men, and not at all willing to let them have everything they asked for.

Columbus was often sick on his later voyages, and had a lot of trouble with his eyes. His old enthusiasm died. He even landed on the coast of mainland South America, and took it for granted that this was just another island. Even when he reached a mighty river (the Orinoco) he did not realize the truth—although such a great river could never have been found on an island. Columbus was getting old and tired. Spain was disappointed by his inability to produce large quantities of gold, and he no longer received a royal welcome when he returned from a voyage. He died poor and unrewarded in 1506.

History has been kinder to him. We now realize that his discoveries, even though he never reached China or India, were to lead to a future expansion far greater than that pioneered by the Portuguese explorers. His navigation was as perfect as it could be with the instruments in his ship. Time after time he set off for a particular place, and accurately arrived there. His achievement

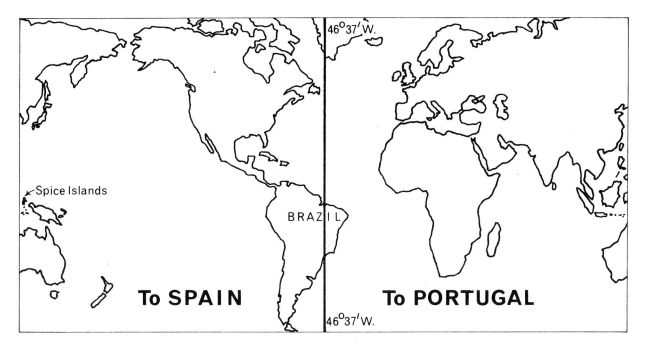

To SPAIN

To PORTUGAL

The world as divided by the Pope in 1494, showing which areas belonged to the Spaniards and which to the Portuguese.

was far more remarkable than the later one of da Gama. He had no local pilots to help him, and there were no known trade-routes.

Columbus's strength of character was such that he could persuade his men to continue even when they were dying of scurvy, and nearly mad with starvation, and terrified by hurricanes and of imaginary sea-monsters. As a sailor and navigator Columbus had no equal: as an administrator he was not so clever, and his settlements were not a success.

Vasco Nunez de Balboa

Even though Columbus was no longer honoured by Spain, the Spaniards did not hesitate to follow up his discoveries. They had a bigger country and more men than Portugal, and they sent fleet after fleet out to the west, using Columbus's charts and profiting from his experience.

Seven years after Columbus's death, a soldier named Vasco Nunez de Balboa was led by Indians across the narrow strip of land that separates the Atlantic and Pacific Oceans. The mystery was solved: Balboa saw that this new country could not be in Asia at all. Asia must lie even further away, across another great sea. He himself was standing on a narrow neck of land that might perhaps join two huge unexplored land masses. In full armour, holding the flag of Spain aloft, Balboa performed the now-familiar ceremony of claiming the land for Spain.

Into the new sea

It was now clear that there was no way of getting a ship from one ocean to another without a passage through or round the new continent. Ferdinand Magellan was the first to discover the passage round the south of South America, and by using this route, one of his ships even managed to sail all the way round the world.

Magellan was a Portuguese sea-captain, who had earlier followed Vasco da Gama's route to Calicut; and then went farther, round Ceylon, and even to the 'Spice Islands'. He had been dismissed from the Portuguese service for trading with the Muslims. So, like Columbus, he went to the Spanish king, and asked if the king would help him to find a westward way to the Spice Islands. The king was pleased to have a commander who already knew so much about the Portuguese possessions, and he gladly agreed. You can follow Magellan's voyage by reading the notes on the map on page 157.

Sailing through the Straits was a frightening experience, and one which not many later explorers dared to repeat. But at last they were through, and Magellan's fleet sailed out into a blue, calm ocean. It was Magellan who named the sea 'Pacific', though later voyagers discovered that it was not always as peaceful as the name suggested. Once in the new ocean, Magellan's little fleet sailed for 98 days before they reached any land—in spite of having the south-easterly trade winds to help them. Magellan had no idea that the Pacific would be so vast. The winds took him on a course that missed the islands of the South Seas, where he might have stopped to refresh the crew. He had to forbid his men to talk about the dangers that lay ahead, and they became even more silent and sullen as the food rotted and the water became undrinkable. By the time they sighted land, they were in a terrible state, living on stinking water, crumbs of biscuit mixed with maggots and rat-dirt, sawdust, and even leather soaked in sea-water. Any sailor who caught a rat could sell it to one of his starving mates for half-a-crown—an enormous sum to those men. Nearly everyone suffered from scurvy, and their gums were so swollen that they covered their teeth.

They disembarked at last on one of the Philippine Islands, and there a quarrel broke out with the islanders. That was the end of the journey for Magellan: he and 40 of his crew were killed, and many others wounded. The survivors had more trials to face before they reached Spain again by way of India and South Africa. The whole journey lasted three years, and only about 20 men out of the original 270 arrived home. The rest had died of disease and starvation, in fights, or as prisoners of the Portuguese in the Spice Islands. These 20 men were the first people ever to sail right round the world.

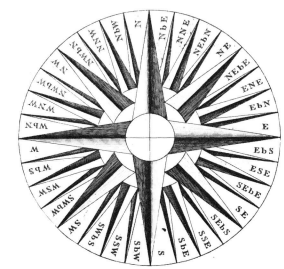

Old engraving showing the 32 points of a compass

Above: cross-staff   *Below:* astrolabe

Aids to Navigation

The compass contains a magnetized steel needle which always points to the *magnetic north*. There are 32 points (positions) marked on a compass and from it the sailors could tell which way they were going but not how far they had gone.

The cross-staff: the shorter piece of wood of the cross-staff could be moved up and down the main bar, which was marked like a ruler. The user pushed the cross-piece along the bar until it covered the distance between the horizon and the sun. He could then work out the *latitude* (the distance north or south of the equator) from the measurement recorded on the bar. He would know from this how *far* he had gone, provided he was travelling in a north-south direction.

The astrolabe also calculated the latitude. The calculations were taken from the positions of the stars, or heavenly bodies. It was more accurate than the cross-staff. At this time there was no way of finding the *longitude* (distance in degrees east or west of a fixed point of the earth's surface). This was because mechanical clocks for use on ships had not been invented.

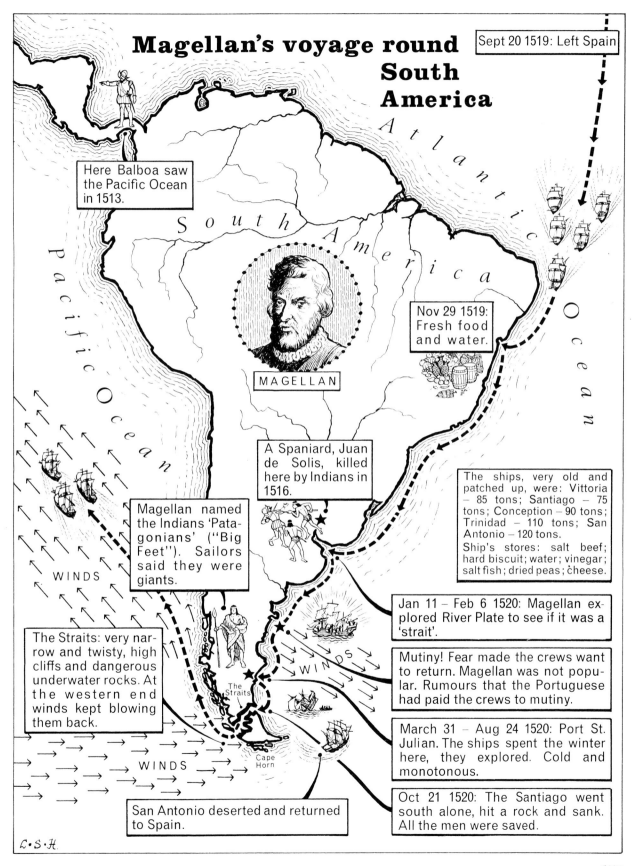

Magellan's voyage round South America

Sept 20 1519: Left Spain

Here Balboa saw the Pacific Ocean in 1513.

Nov 29 1519: Fresh food and water.

MAGELLAN

A Spaniard, Juan de Solis, killed here by Indians in 1516.

Magellan named the Indians 'Patagonians' ("Big Feet"). Sailors said they were giants.

WINDS

The Straits: very narrow and twisty, high cliffs and dangerous underwater rocks. At the western end winds kept blowing them back.

WINDS

The Straits

Cape Horn

San Antonio deserted and returned to Spain.

The ships, very old and patched up, were: Vittoria – 85 tons; Santiago – 75 tons; Conception – 90 tons; Trinidad – 110 tons; San Antonio – 120 tons.
Ship's stores: salt beef; hard biscuit; water; vinegar; salt fish; dried peas; cheese.

Jan 11 – Feb 6 1520: Magellan explored River Plate to see if it was a 'strait'.

Mutiny! Fear made the crews want to return. Magellan was not popular. Rumours that the Portuguese had paid the crews to mutiny.

March 31 – Aug 24 1520: Port St. Julian. The ships spent the winter here, they explored. Cold and monotonous.

Oct 21 1520: The Santiago went south alone, hit a rock and sank. All the men were saved.

WINDS

L·S·H

157

Chapter 27 The Portuguese Empire in the East

News of Columbus's discoveries reached Portugal, and the king, in his capital city, Lisbon, was now determined to open the Indian Ocean to his trading ships. He sent one expedition after another to subdue the coasts of East Africa and India. He gave his ships' captains instructions to secure trading profits and to win the people to Christianity. If they could not do this by persuasion, then they were to use force.

Almeida uses force

In 1505, a sea-captain named Francisco d'Almeida went to East Africa to make sure that the sultans paid their tribute to Portugal, and to build forts to strengthen the Portuguese position in the Ocean. He reached Kilwa with 22 ships and 1500 men, and, because it had not paid any tribute for two years, he fired the ships' guns at the town and then set it on fire. He built a small fort, and left 150 people, including a commander, a governor, priests and clerks, to keep the town in order.

Almeida went on to Mombasa. There he found a very different situation. A Portuguese who had deserted to the other side sent the defiant message: 'Tell the Admiral he will not find, as he did in Kilwa, a lot of chickens waiting to have their necks wrung, but 20,000 men.' The islanders had brought in extra bowmen from the mainland when they heard that the Portuguese had returned, and they all defended the island bravely. But even such tough opposition did not stop the invaders for long—Mombasa fell, and soon the whole coast had to obey the new masters.

The sultans were dismayed to find that they could not just ignore their uninvited guests. The Portuguese took all the wealth they could find, and even forced the East African towns to pay heavy tribute for the privilege of being left in peace. Many times the sultans tried to defy

A sixteenth-century drawing of Mombasa

them, but the results were always bad, or even disastrous, for the townspeople. Portuguese ships entered their harbours and bombarded ordinary houses with the ships' cannons; armed men invaded the narrow streets, and although the inhabitants defended their property and their lives with showers of arrows and stones from the rooftops, in the end they always had to give in. Then there always would come the most dreadful weapon of all—fire. The price the Arabs and Africans had to pay for their 'disobedience' was the total destruction of their homes, their coconut palms and their crops—by burning.

The Portuguese administered East Africa from two towns; Malindi (later Mombasa) in the north, and Mozambique in the south. In both towns there were forts to protect the Portuguese from their enemies—enemies who might come at them from the local mainland, or from across the sea. Mombasa's Fort Jesus (see p. 169), designed by an Italian architect, still overlooks the narrow stretch of water between the island and the mainland. It was not completely safe however; Arabs from the Persian Gulf captured it twice in later years and flew their red flag over the battlements. Once the Arab victory followed a long siege, during which the Portuguese defenders starved and died by the hundreds from disease.

The fort at Mozambique also saw some bitter fighting, not between Arabs and Portuguese, but between the Portuguese and newcomers to the coast—the Dutch. The Mozambique fort always suffered from lack of proper care and repair; its Captains were too busy enriching themselves by sending trading expeditions up the Zambezi to the lands of the Monomotapa.

The worst restriction for the Arabs in East Africa was that they were not allowed to trade without Portuguese licences. The Portuguese now knew exactly how much profit was made on the trading journeys, and they seized as much of it as they could. In time their greed and lack of foresight led to their own downfall. They had been told by their king to 'secure trading profits', and for a time they had done so. Had they allowed the East African towns to continue to earn a good living by trade, the Portuguese themselves would have been able to stay in the area longer. But the local people were naturally not interested in trading if they could not profit from it themselves.

In 1600, only 100 years after the Portuguese first landed on the East African coast, a Franciscan friar wrote about Mombasa:

'The inhabitants are Moors, who, although formerly rich, now live in utter poverty— their most usual occupation is that of making mats, baskets, and straw hats so perfectly finished that the Portuguese bring them out to wear on feast days.'

Although individual Portuguese traders or soldiers must have learnt a little Swahili, Portuguese documents about East Africa do not mention the language at all; the majority were only interested in trade and they did not realize that to trade with people you have to try to understand them; and to understand someone, you must first try to learn his language.

Great Zimbabwe

The ruins of Great Zimbabwe are very interesting. They date back to the early Middle Ages and were probably built by Bantu tribes. A Portuguese writer, Joao de Barros said about the gold-bearing country of the Monomotapa:

'The mines are the most ancient known in the country, and they are all in the plain, in the midst of which is a square fortress of masonry (stonework) within and without, built of stones of marvellous size, and there appears to be no mortar joining them. . . . The natives of the country call all these buildings "zimbabwe".'

India

After Francisco d'Almeida had sacked Kilwa and Mombasa, and left some soldiers to hold these towns for the Portuguese, he sailed on to India. He built a fort and a house for himself at Cochin, and became the first 'Viceroy* of India', though in fact he only ruled over a few Indian coastal towns.

In these towns the traders were very alarmed when they saw that the Portuguese meant to stay permanently. There was so much to lose that they looked for allies to help them drive the Portuguese away. At the other end of their trade routes, the Egyptians, Turks and Arabs were also anxious not to lose their profits — and farther north, the Venetians became worried.

Venice had for centuries been the great market-place for Muslim and eastern goods, which were sold to the more northerly European countries. The Venetians had to try to stop the Portuguese taking Chinese and Indian luxury goods back to Portugal, and creating a new 'market-place' there. In haste the Venetians helped the Egyptians to build a fleet of 12 ships in the Red Sea. This fleet sailed out into the Indian Ocean to do battle with the Portuguese, and at Diu they joined the tiny fleet of the zamorin † of Calicut. They learnt that the Portuguese were not to be driven away so easily. The Portuguese carracks sank the Turkish ships, which would take much time and money to replace. Almeida's sailors had won the first round for Portugal; they now had mastery of the Indian Ocean. Almeida wrote to King Manuel, 'As long as you are powerful at sea, you will hold India.'

Albuquerque becomes Viceroy

Almeida's successor was a man named Afonso d'Albuquerque. He wanted Portugal to be much more than just 'powerful at sea'. His aim was to build more new trading-posts on the Indian coast, and to strengthen the Portuguese position on land all round the Indian Ocean. Goa — which Albuquerque seized — became the centre of trade in the eastern ocean, and the capital of the Portuguese empire in the East. Albuquerque

---

*A viceroy is a man appointed by a king to rule an overseas territory for him. Columbus was called 'Admiral of the Ocean, Viceroy and Governor of the Indies'.

†Zamorin was the title used for the sovereign of Calicut.

Portuguese ships in the sixteenth century
Portuguese ships stood higher in the water than Venetian ones. This meant that the Portuguese could fire down on their enemies, and so had advantage over them.

There was no timber in Arabia for ship-building, so the people of Ormuz (on the Persian Gulf) could not even put one or two pirate ships into the Indian Ocean without much preparation and spending a lot of money. Later the Turks built long, low, narrow, oar and sail driven ships, called galleys, in the Red Sea with materials that had to be carried across the isthmus of Suez on camels and donkeys. But still the Portuguese ships were better, and had more guns.

In the sixteenth-century illustration above you can see the sailors navigating the ship, using an astrolabe and a cross-staff.

---

himself lived there, and from Goa ruled over his scattered empire. His Captains* at Malindi and Mozambique took orders from him, and not from Lisbon, and he built and kept in touch with forts in Ceylon, Malacca, the east coast of India, and even China.

Albuquerque was both a great sailor and a great administrator; he laid the foundations of the empire well. Had there been others like him, the Portuguese might have lasted longer in the East. But the men sent to Goa as viceroys after Albuquerque were often harsh and ruthless. It took a long time for news to reach Goa from the distant forts: East Africa, for instance, was completely cut off for half the year, when the

---

*The Captains of Malindi and Mozambique were governors — they were not necessarily 'sea-captains'.

Eighteenth century English painting of Bristol docks and quay. During this period Bristol was an important trading port and a hub of activity. The work now hangs in the Bristol City Art Gallery.

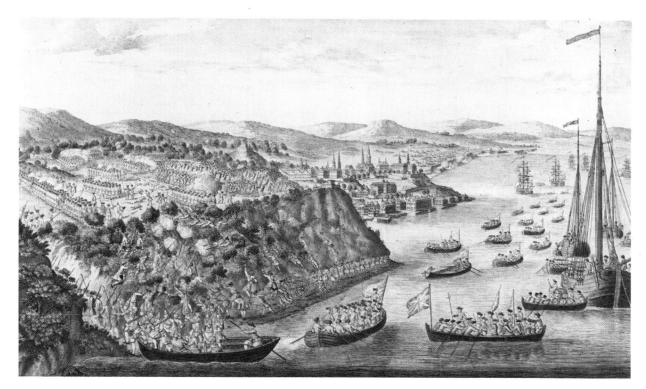

(Above) The taking of Quebec 13th September, 1759. 'Showing the manner of debarking the English, of the resolute scrambling of light infantry upon rocky precipices to dislodge the captain's post which defended a small entrenched path through which the troops were to pass'.

(Below) Painting showing the meeting of Lee and Jackson before the battle of Chancellorsville during the American Civil War. The attack cut the Northern army almost in two, but the Confederate victory cost the life of Jackson, Lee's ablest general.

(Above) Washington, having first marched south, went east around Cornwallis' force. On 3rd January, 1777 he won a great victory at Princeton. Painting of the battle of Princeton by William Mercer. Historical Society of Pennsylvania.

(Below) Painting showing the dispersal of a native tribe by white immigrant settlers near Baines river, Australia.

Satirical Russian poster from the Russio-Japanese war. Disputes between the Japanese and the Russians in 1904 as to who should govern Manchuria, north China, led to the outbreak of war.

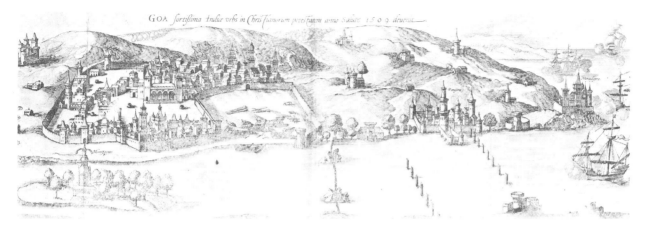

monsoon winds were blowing in the wrong direction. But in any case the Portuguese had no firm policy for their empire. They were interested in trading, but they did not see that it was necessary to be on friendly terms with the local people. Their trading-posts were like little islands, ignorant of the life around them. The native rulers were allowed to have power over their people, so long as they did as they were told, and produced the yearly tribute. If they refused, punishment was harsh and swift.

The trading-post in Ceylon

South of India is the beautiful island of Ceylon. The island was divided into seven tiny Buddhist kingdoms when Francisco d'Albuquerque, Afonso's son, first went there to build a fort. One of the kings granted him land at Colombo, on the west coast, but the whole time the Portuguese were in Ceylon, one kingdom after another tried to drive them away.

Ceylon was famous for its semi-precious stones, moonstones, sapphires and rubies, and for its cinnamon. The centre of the island is mountainous, and up in the hills lies the town of Kandy. Here the Buddhists kept a holy relic of Buddha—a tooth. The king of Kandy fought the Portuguese, who said they had carried off the sacred tooth, and burnt it at Goa. (The Sinhalese—they are the Buddhist inhabitants of Ceylon— denied this, and they still claim that the tooth is in the Buddhist temple at Kandy.)

In spite of this the Portuguese made a favourable impression in Ceylon on the whole. They successfully converted hundreds of humble fishermen and land-workers to Christianity. They intermarried with the local people, and— as in Goa—today there are many people living in Ceylon who have Portuguese names.

Goa

Goa traded with Persia and Ormuz, and each trading-ship brought cargoes of horses, dates, almonds and raisins. Albuquerque spent time and thought in building his capital. Goa even had equal privileges with Lisbon itself. The Catholic priests built churches, and a cathedral which is still used for worship today. In 1542 a famous Jesuit, St Francis Xavier, arrived in Goa to preach and baptize. Many people from other parts of the Portuguese empire in East Africa and the East were sent to Goa to be educated.

Although Goa is now part of India, it contains many traces of the centuries of Portuguese rule. Most Goans are Catholics and most have Portuguese surnames such as Ferrao, Gomes, Pereira, Fernandes and Almeida.

Malacca

Albuquerque wanted Portugal to control all the trade-routes of the Indian Ocean, but most ships from South-East Asia and China came through the Strait of Malacca where they paid tribute to the sultan. Malacca was a rich port which had for a long time been the capital of a powerful Malay empire. The sultan had a large army, but in 1511 Albuquerque arrived before the city with a fleet and, after hard fighting, captured it. Then he built a great fortress called 'A Famosa' (The Famous) to hold Malacca for Portugal.

The fort at Malacca provided a convenient base for further exploration. Albuquerque sent explorers south-westward and they built settlements in the Moluccas (the Spice Islands) and on the coast of China. As a trading centre, Malacca was more important than Goa, because it controlled the route to these new forts, and under the rule of the Portuguese it continued to grow and prosper. But as a place to live in, it was uncomfortable. The west coast has many mangrove swamps and it is very hot and wet. From October to February the soldiers and

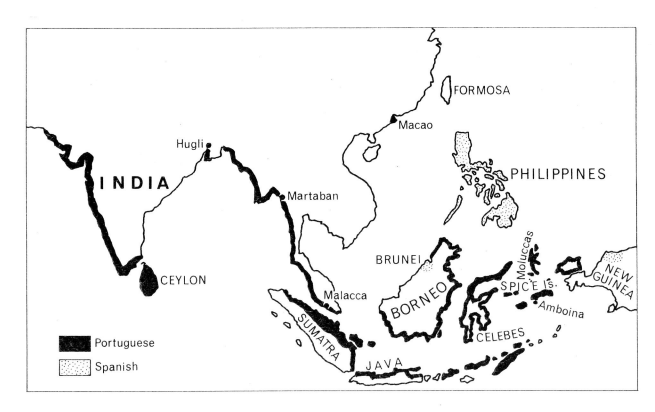

Portuguese possessions in the Far East, 1498–1580

civilians in the fort were cut off from their sea-routes by high seas and contrary winds. They could not go far inland because of thick tropical jungle, inhabited by wild animals, and by tribesmen armed with blow-pipes and poisonous darts. For the most part the soldiers stayed in their forts, which they had to defend from time to time against the attacks of the Malay sultan.

The Spice Islands and China

The islands of the Moluccas and several ports on the China coast were already carrying on a flourishing trade with the Persian Gulf when the Portuguese arrived. The Muslims had established themselves as the chief traders and rulers, and so once again there was a religious clash. The Portuguese built a fort at Amboina, but after Magellan's voyage, the Spaniards declared that *they* really owned these rich islands. Finally they allowed the Portuguese to buy them!

There was so much nutmeg, cloves and pepper in the Spice Islands, and so much cinnamon in Ceylon, that in spite of the long journeys and the expense of fitting ships and maintaining forts, the trade was very profitable. The Portuguese succeeded in taking over the Muslim trade in several Chinese ports, and in 1557 the Chinese officially allowed them to build a fort at Macao. This is the only port they still hold on the mainland; the rest of their Far Eastern possessions, apart from part of the island of Timor, have gradually been lost.

By 1550, the charts show that on their return journey, ships used to sail far north before turning westward, in order to take advantage of the north-eastern monsoon. Then the well-laden fleet sailed home to Lisbon. The Indian Ocean was now controlled by the Portuguese, for Albuquerque followed up the success of the battle of Diu by raiding the Muslim town of Ormuz on the Persian Gulf. He built a fort there, and left a garrison of men to guard the town. Now it was Lisbon, not Venice, that became the market-place for spices from the East.

Chapter 28 The Portuguese in the Atlantic

In the countries we now call Ghana and Nigeria, the Portuguese made contact with the local chiefs and kings. Most of the chiefs did not mind the Portuguese caravels trading with their people, but they were very unwilling to let the Portuguese build forts. One chief, named Caramansa, reluctantly agreed when the Portuguese leader, Diogo de Azambuja, persuaded him that the fort would make it easier to carry on trade. But misunderstandings arose because of language difficulties and lack of local knowledge; the Portuguese, not realizing what they were doing, took rocks to build their fort from a hill which Caramansa's people regarded as sacred. Caramansa was furious, and his warriors attacked the Portuguese. Then the fort had to be finished quickly for their protection, and it is not surprising that the Africans were suspicious of these foreigners, shut up inside their stone enclosure.

This Gold Coast fort, built in 1482, was named Elmina, meaning 'The Mine', because of its nearness to the gold mines. Smaller forts were maintained all along the coast, and the Portuguese imported and planted oranges and lemons from their own country, and rice from the East. Later they also brought new plants from America: guavas, pineapples, maize, tobacco and cassava. The news of their forts spread to the inland tribes, and the African chiefs sent messengers to see the strange white men. The Portuguese then sent messengers of their own to the interior, to find out where the gold came from. Though in most cases they did not succeed, they tried to persuade the Africans with gifts of cloth, beads, small bells, and glass to show them the mines. These were also the 'trade-goods' which they exchanged for gold, ivory and pepper.

One of the Portuguese forts was near the African state of Benin. This vigorous kingdom was

Elmina Fort

This is a sixteenth-century account of the preparations for building Elmina Fort:

> Once the building of the fort was decided upon, he [the king of Portugal] ordered the equipping of a fleet of 10 caravels and 2 barques ... to carry hewed stone, tiles and wood, as well as munitions and provisions for 600 men, one hundred of whom were craftsmen, and 500 soldiers.

friendly to the new arrivals, and trade flourished. Nobody in West Africa had much use for ivory or gold except as decoration, so there was plenty to spare for trade. The people of Benin were quite willing to exchange such things for the Portuguese trade-goods, which were a novelty to them. But after only about 50 years the trade changed on both sides. The Europeans wanted to buy men and women to re-sell as slaves; and the Africans wanted weapons, metal and alcohol. Then the peaceful and innocent trading days were over.

The Congo Kingdom

Forty years after Diogo Cão landed at the mouth of the river Congo, the Mani-Congo (king of the Congo country), whom the Portuguese called King Afonso I, was eager to Europeanize his kingdom, and he was pleased when his new European friends sent him missionaries, soldiers and traders. At first all went well. The king and his court dressed in European clothes, and were given Portuguese titles. The Portuguese aim was to set up a Christian kingdom in Africa. They were quite sincere in their desire for peace and good relations between the two countries. For one thing they would have a base from which to start looking for Prester John; and the Africans would receive European goods in exchange for the gold which they did not value very highly.

King Afonso did everything in his power to be a friend to the Portuguese, and to make the new alliance work. He wrote letter after letter to his 'royal brother' in Lisbon, asking for medical supplies, teachers, and a ship of his own. On his side, the Portuguese king wanted peaceful trade, but his servants in Africa were often concerned only to help themselves rather than to help either their own country or the Congo kingdom. Afonso refused to give up hope. He sent many of his young men off to be educated in Lisbon. Some of them, however, never got farther than São Tomé, an island off present-day Gabon. The Portuguese had made this island their chief port of call in the south, and all their ships went there rather than to the mouth of the Congo. So passengers and letters for Lisbon all had to be taken by boat to São Tomé first. The Portuguese had started to plant sugar-cane on São Tomé, and they did not have enough cheap labour to work the plantations: so when Afonso sent young men there, the Portuguese kept many of them as slaves.

One of the young men who *did* get farther than São Tomé, and who was eventually educated in Lisbon, was Afonso's son Henrique. He was trained to be a priest, and he even became the first African bishop, and was ordained* by the Pope himself in Rome. Henrique returned to the Congo kingdom, full of admiration for the European way of life, only to find that the Portuguese in his own country did not share his high ideals.

*To ordain means formally and ceremonially to give somebody the title and responsibilities of a priest or, in this case, of a bishop.

Portuguese soldier
This is how the bronze-workers of Benin saw the Portuguese soldiers. With guns ready to fire they were seen as a threatening force and not the peaceful traders that they were first thought to be.

By the end of his reign, in the 1540s, Afonso was cut off from Lisbon, because no ships came direct to his kingdom, and his letters remained unanswered. (Probably many of them never even left São Tomé.) The slave trade, which removed hundreds of young men and women from Congo and nearby Angola to São Tomé and the Americas, caused terrible hardship and havoc in West Africa. In 1526 Afonso wrote a very polite and friendly letter to King John III of Portugal, imploring him to stop the slave trade, which was ruining his country. But his letter was ignored. The slave trade got worse, and went on and on for the next 250 years, leaving a once prosperous land empty and poverty-stricken.

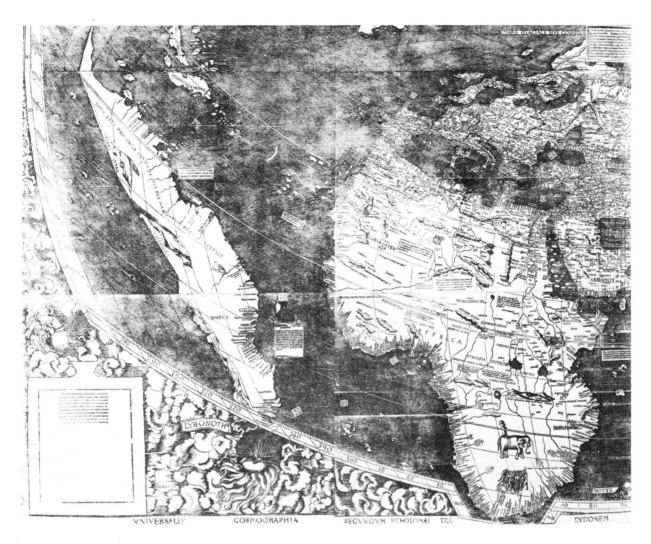

VNIVERSALIS   COSMOGRAPHIA   SECVNDVM PTHOLOMÆI TRA   DITIONEM

There were three main reasons why the West Africans did not benefit from their contact with the Portuguese.

Portuguese sailors were discovering and occupying too many overseas ports in proportion to the number of able administrators their small country could hope to appoint. Moreover, these administrators were often more interested in personal gain than in honest trading for their country.

The produce of the Spice Islands and later the produce of Brazil in South America, was more profitable than the gold or ivory of Africa. Consequently, if the Captain of the Spice Islands and the Mani-Congo both asked for doctors, or preachers, or a new ship, then the Spice Islands were supplied first.

Finally, Africa became more important as an exporter of men than of any other commodity. It was the slave trade which finally ruined the

America

In 1507 a German mapmaker named Martin Waldseemüller published a map of the New World, the southern part of which he called America, after Amerigo Vespucci. The name has stayed and it was soon to be used for the northern United States as well. Waldseemüller might more justly have called the new land 'Columbia' after the first mariner to set foot on its shores; without the inspiration and example of Columbus, Vespucci might never have sailed westward at all.

West African states.

The Portuguese discover Brazil

In 1500 a Portuguese sea-captain named Pedro Alvares Cabral set sail from Lisbon, and followed Vasco da Gama's route to the south. He was supposed to be on his way to India, but he sailed so far westward that he reached the mainland of South America. Some historians say that this was an accident, and he was blown farther west than he meant to go; others say that the Portuguese had

165

found out some of the Spanish secret information about the western Atlantic, and Cabral was *told* to look for a coastline in the west. Whichever story is true, Cabral certainly found himself in the country we now call Brazil. He landed, and laid claim to Brazil for Portugal. He sent one of his supply ships back to Portugal with news of this new land; then he sailed away again.

Cabral went back across the Atlantic and continued his journey to India, and Brazil's next visitor from Europe was an Italian named Amerigo Vespucci. Vespucci had become a Spanish citizen, and he had helped to prepare ships for Columbus's voyages. He picked up a great deal of information about navigation, and in 1499 he went to the West Indies as navigator in a Spanish ship. Like Columbus, he was convinced that the coast of America was a part of Asia: on his return to Spain he asked if he might take an expedition to look for Ceylon and India. The Spaniards were unwilling to give him permission, so he went to Portugal, where he was more fortunate. (Many mariners of this time went from country to country looking for someone who would finance them on their exploring journeys. Columbus and Magellan were not the only ones.)

On Vespucci's next voyage (paid for by the Portuguese), he explored a great deal of the coast of South America, and he saw the true nature of the newly-discovered land. This, he said, is not Asia. It is a different continent entirely, which 'it is proper to call a new world'.

Portugal at this time was more concerned with building up connections in the East, where the trade in silks, precious stones, pepper and spices was so profitable, than with exploring this new territory. Spain had almost finished *her* conquests in America before Portugal decided to find out more about Brazil. The unexplored area was enormous, and it had many great rivers, between which there were dense forests and high mountains. The Portuguese divided the vast land into 15 parts, each of which was to be governed by a Captain. As in East Africa and India, the Captains were favoured courtiers, and not pioneers or administrators. Only two of the 15 Captains were really successful in making their captaincies thrive. The first of these settlements was São Vicente, near present-day Santos, established by Martin Afonso de Souza. He built a port and from there went southwards, exploring and mapping the coast. The Captain of the second successful settlement was Duarte Coelho, a farmer who set up sugar-plantations, and started to export sugar to Europe. His captaincy was in present-day Pernambuco. Sugar and tobacco became the main Brazilian crops, and where they were well-managed, the plantations flourished.

The division of Brazil into captaincies was a mistake, because without any central control they all suffered from attacks by Indians*, and raids by French pirate ships. So in 1549 Tomé de Souza, a man who had had experience in India, arrived in Brazil to unite the captaincies into one country. He built a capital town at Salvador, and brought in new immigrants—people who were prepared to work hard and farm the land. Soon the country started to be self-supporting. Here, at last, the Portuguese had a settlers' colony, instead of a little 'factory' in an already-developed foreign land.

The search for labour

The country was too vast, and the number of immigrants too small, for the plantations to be worked without some other big labour force. The Portuguese started by enslaving Indians, and making them work on the plantations—and later in the mines—for long hours and small wages. The Indians were not used to such hard labour and they were often worked to death. Some fled to the new missionary settlements, which were always glad to receive converts. The missionaries did their best to protect the Indians from plantation owners, who began to look elsewhere for slaves.

Over on the other side of the Atlantic Ocean, their Portuguese fellow-countrymen in the Congo kingdom and in Angola were already shipping a few African slaves every year to Europe and the Middle East. On hearing that Brazil was short of manpower, they decided to transport African men and women to Brazil and sell them there. By 1600 Tomé de Souza's capital had a population of 2000 whites and about twice as many African and Indian slaves. The Spaniards, the British, the French and the Dutch all fitted out ships to carry the new human cargo, and did a tremendous trade in all the newly-colonized parts of America. The terrible sale of human beings became more profitable

---

* The natives of South America were also called 'Indians'— in fact the word meant almost the same as 'native' to the Portuguese. They have kept the name ever since. The 'Indians' in this chapter are all South American Indians.

and important to the European nations than the trade in gold and ivory.

Because there were people to convert in the interior of the country and perhaps because they could be more independent there, the Jesuit missionaries were not content to remain on the coast near the rich settlements. They penetrated far inland, and thousands of Indians came to work on the new mission plantations. Almost the first building in any Portuguese or Spanish town was a church. The converted Indians were treated with care and understanding by the missionaries, and taught to grow crops and raise cattle.

Many of the white immigrants to Brazil did not have the money to buy or run plantations in the rich sugar-growing districts, and they too went inland and started to farm there instead. But there were not enough Indians to work for them locally, and the African slaves who were now arriving were too expensive for them. So the white men organized themselves into armed gangs, known as *bandeirantes,* and raided villages and mission settlements for slaves. They were particularly eager to carry off converted Indians, for these had already been taught how to farm by the missionaries. As time passed the *bandeirantes* went even farther for slaves, and started to raid the neighbouring Spanish territories.

Over the next 200 years the Portuguese had to fight off attacks by other Europeans, the Dutch, the English and the French. The Dutch took possession of the north of Brazil for some time but were eventually expelled. To the south the Portuguese and Spaniards fought for possession of the territory that is now called Uruguay, which the Portuguese finally lost.

During this time many Portuguese settlers intermarried with Indians and with Africans and in time people did not say they were 'Portuguese' or 'Indian' or 'African' but were proud to proclaim that they were all Brazilians.

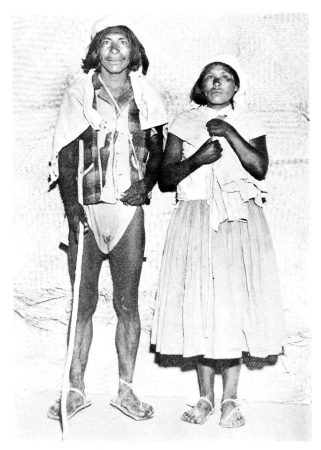

South American Indians
The consequences of the arrival of Europeans in America were terrible for the South American Indians. Before the 'civilizing' white men came, the Indians wore very little clothing (sometimes none at all). The missionaries taught them that it was 'not decent' to be naked. They made them wear cotton clothes. These clothes got wet in the torrential rains of South America; but they did not dry nearly so quickly as the Indians' naked bodies had done. Before long the Indians were dying in hundreds from chest diseases and other illness brought on by being chilled. They were sent down mines and used as slaves and many suffered and died from exhaustion because of this unfamiliar work. The white men, without knowing it, also brought diseases such as small-pox and measles which had a fatal effect on the Indians. These diseases had never been known in South America before.

Chapter 29 The Dutch rival the Portuguese

By the end of the sixteenth century, most of the European nations were sending ships to West Africa, and French and English ships were even reaching the Indian Ocean and the East. But the nation which at that time competed most successfully with the Portuguese was Holland.

The Dutch had made their country into a strong sea-going nation in a very short time. Until 1579 Holland had been part of the Netherlands states, which were under Spanish rule. But she had at last won her long war for independence from Spain. Now the Dutch entered the world scene—not as adventurers and discoverers, but as businessmen and traders.

Portugal brought spices and silks from the East, then by arrangement, Holland took them and distributed them to other European countries. Had Portugal been bigger and richer, she might have been able to buy the spices in the East *and* distribute them. As it was, the Portuguese sailors took all the risks, and the merchants of Antwerp made most of the profits. Holland soon became a very wealthy country.

But in 1580, when Spain and Portugal became united, Philip II, King of Spain, refused to let the Dutch enter Portuguese harbours. He hoped to destroy their trade and their prosperity. The Dutch however were not so easily defeated— they decided to make their own way to the Spice Islands. The Pope had divided the world between Spain and Portugal, but this did not worry the Protestant Dutch. The Portuguese had managed to keep the route secret for a full century by hiding their maps, and by spreading tales about the dangers on land and at sea. But the Dutch had no trouble in rounding the Cape, and in 1595 they quite easily found their way across the Indian Ocean.

From the beginning the Dutch had great success in the East. Their trade-goods were better than those of the Portuguese, and at first they were careful to make no enemies. By 1602, only seven years after their first voyage, they had taken a large part of the trade in the Spice Islands, in China, in Malaya and in Ceylon. They soon realized that the Portuguese empire was much weaker than anybody had thought. The Portuguese Captains were urgently warned to be on their guard, but it was too late. One by one their forts fell to the Dutch—often with the help of the local people. In 1641, after a long siege, the Dutch captured Malacca. It had been the richest port between India and China, but its great days were now over; the Dutch neglected it and soon Malacca became small and unimportant.

The only trading-posts left to the Portuguese were Goa, Diu and Daman in India; Macao in China, and part of Timor. The East had never brought them as much wealth as they had hoped; and King John IV of Portugal once cried: 'I wish to God that I could rid myself honourably of the East Indies.'

The Dutch East India Company

In 1602 the Dutch government formed the East India Company. This company owned all the ships trading with the East Indies; no merchant was now allowed to trade on his own account, or to form a rival company. In this way both profits and risks were shared by the whole country.

The East India Company was also partly the navy of Holland. The ships were all armed, and manned by soldiers as well as sailors, and they were quite ready to do battle with Spanish or Portuguese or English ships, and to fight or besiege enemy forts from the sea. The Company also administered the new possessions overseas. All the governors, traders, soldiers and lawyers were under the rule of the Company, and each new Dutch territory was self-governing.

The officials were paid high salaries, and forbidden to become businessmen themselves. This was a much stronger and far more efficient system than that of the Portuguese, whose whole Eastern empire was governed from Goa, and whose officials were allowed to make money from private trade.

Fort Jesus, Mombasa
This was the main fort of the Portuguese on the East Coast of Africa, built in 1593. The Dutch never attacked it—probably because it was the strongest Portuguese fort on the coast —and the Portuguese stayed in Mombasa for another 100 years.

The Dutch and the King of Kandy
Although the Portuguese had had great success in converting the coastal fishermen and farmers in Ceylon, they had one great enemy there. Up in the hills lived the fierce King Rajasinga of Kandy. King Rajasinga hated the Portuguese, and he sent an army to help the Dutch to remove them from the island. The Portuguese governor of the time was an arrogant and cruel man. It is said that he 'would hang up the people by their heels, and split them down the middle.... Lesser malefactors (wrongdoers) he was merciful to, cutting off only their right hands.' This man swore to treat the Dutch in the same way, but the Dutch were too clever for him. Behind their army they placed a row of cannons: when the Portuguese thought they had pressed the soldiers back, they found themselves right on top of the cannons—which the Dutch then fired.

The Dutch besieged all the east coast ports of Ceylon in 1607, and the west coast ports soon after, but it took over 50 years for them to take the whole country from the Portuguese.

Jan Pieters Coen and the Moluccas
Coen was the able governor who first started to create a Dutch empire in the East. He was a hard man, who believed in using force to get what he wanted.

The Dutch needed a place where the produce from the Spice Islands, from Ceylon, India, China and Japan could be collected and stored. Ships went back to Holland only twice a year, in December and February, but the local trading-ships visited the various ports of the empire more often. Coen found an ideal place for a central 'store-house'. It was a port on the island of Java, which belonged to the sultan of a kingdom called Mataran. Coen seized the town, and renamed it Batavia.

Soon settlers went out to live there, in newly-built stone houses with fine furnishings. They built forts, churches, offices and roads. The law in all the new towns was Roman-Dutch law, the same as in Holland. With their excellent business sense, the Dutch soon created a very prosperous empire.

Trade monopoly

Coen was supposed to follow instructions from Holland; but of course it took about 18 months for replies to his requests to arrive in Batavia. This meant that he was really in control in the East. Any unwelcome instructions from home could always be quietly forgotten!

The people of the Spice Islands thought they would be better off under the Dutch, but they were mistaken. They were forced to sign a treaty which gave the Dutch the monopoly (sole control) of the spice trade. This meant that the Dutch could buy the spices very cheaply, because nobody else was allowed to buy them. So the people of the Moluccas found that they were now poorer than they had been under the Portuguese. Their own imports—rice, sago and cotton—had been brought to them in Japanese ships, but now the Dutch themselves were the only people officially allowed to bring goods to the Spice Islands. They bought cotton and silk from the west coast of India, and rice from China and Japan, and exchanged these goods for spices. Similarly the pepper from the east coast of India was used for trade with the Persians (who had retaken Ormuz from the Portuguese). In this way the Dutch avoided having to bring all their trade goods from Europe (see map opposite).

On the whole the Dutch monopoly was very profitable but they were continually having to fight off ships of other nations, and keep a watch for pirates and smugglers. On the coasts of India, moreover, there was often much resistance from the local zamorins and sultans.

The Dutch land at the Cape

Before crossing the Indian Ocean on their way to the East, the Dutch ships needed somewhere to obtain fresh water and food, and a place where their sick men could recover. (The number of deaths at sea, from scurvy, dysentery and fever was always very high indeed.) The Portuguese used Mozambique and the East African towns for this purpose, and for a long time the Dutch also tried to gain a foothold there. But the Portuguese managed to keep them out of Mozambique. This had a far-reaching effect on the history of Africa, for the Dutch decided instead to build a landing-place at the Cape of Good Hope.

In 1652 Jan van Riebeeck and a small party of tough Dutchmen landed at the Cape, and built a small settlement there. They had no intention of looking for gold, or of trading in ivory and

Dutch ship
The Dutch were determined that they should be the only European traders in Africa and Asia. They built sturdy ships and engaged tough sea-captains.

slaves—they merely wanted to plant vegetables and raise cattle, so that their trading-ships could take fresh supplies on board.

The settlement was not very successful at first, for the Cape is not an ideal place for a port of call. There are terrible storms at sea in this area at some seasons of the year, and a lot of rich Dutch cargoes went to the bottom because of shipwrecks. But in calm weather the sailors enjoyed a brief rest in their seven-month long journey to Batavia. Later, the port became well established, and ships of all nationalities called there, so the Dutch merchants did a good trade by selling vegetables and meat to their rivals.

Soon pioneers started to 'trek'* far inland to find more good farming country. Slaves were imported from Madagascar, Mozambique and Malaya, and their descendants still live in South Africa today. Later, the more northerly African tribes were also made to work for the Dutch. The system of 'white supremacy' (European rule over Africans) in southern Africa was already beginning. Van Riebeeck's original small settlement became a Dutch colony, and from it grew what was eventually called the Union (now the Republic) of South Africa. The Dutch language, in the course of time, changed in both pronunciation and grammar, and today we know it as Afrikaans. The Dutch word for farmer—Boer— became the word for all South African Dutchmen.

*Trek—this word came from Dutch South Africa and meant to make a journey by ox wagon.

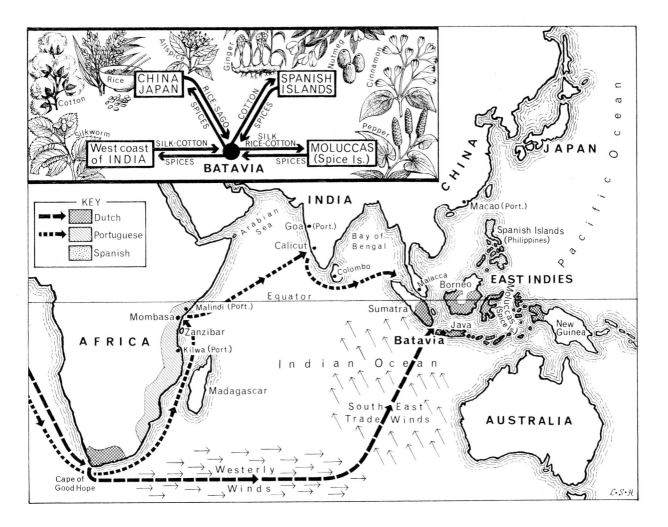

Religion in the Dutch Empire

The Portuguese had sent thousands of priests to the East and to West Africa; the Dutch sent hardly any. Dutch priests were called *predikants*, and they were helped by lay-preachers—often people of quite poor education, who simply read parts of the Bible aloud to others, and sometimes taught in schools. They did not have a great deal of success in converting the native peoples. Those who had already been converted by the Portuguese were specially stubborn. The Catholic faith, with its ceremonies, was much nearer certain Eastern faiths, and some of the people of the East took to it easily. The *predikants'* religion seemed colourless by comparison. The Dutch were tolerant of all the Eastern religions, and they allowed worship in the temples and mosques to continue. But they would not allow Catholic churches to hold services because Holland had suffered many years of oppressive rule by Catholic Spain.

West Africa

'Gold is your god!' the West Africans said to the Dutch traders. They could see that these new arrivals were not even going to try to improve the African states. They just wanted money. In 1595 a regular trade in gold and ivory started, and soon forts were being built all along the coast. The Portuguese had to accept the existence of two Dutch forts, Fort Mouri and Fort Butri, one on each side of their own fort at Elmina. Worse still, the Dutch sold weapons to the African tribes, so that they could fight the Portuguese. But the Portuguese did not give in without a struggle. They managed to keep Elmina until 1637, when, after several attacks, the Dutch seized the fort for themselves.

The Dutch forts were all better defended than the Portuguese ones had been, and ships of other nationalities were unable to drive their occupants away. The English, Danes, Swedes, Germans and French were all now sending ships to trade

171

with 'the Guinea Coast' and some of them even built forts of their own. The Dutch fort of St Antony at Axim was specially built near inland gold mines, which the Dutch worked themselves.

But most of the forts were doing an increasing amount of business in slaves. There was so much profit in the slave trade that all the nations trading with West Africa were trying to find chiefs who would sell them their prisoners – and sometimes even their own countrymen. Those nations which had forts were obviously better off, because they could keep the slaves locked up until they had enough to fill a slave ship. The people of Angola, Congo, Dahomey, and the Gold Coast all went in fear of the slave traders, both African and European, who would seize anybody they could find, and sell them overseas at a profit. In return the chiefs received firearms and alcohol. This terrible trade, which reached its height in the eighteenth century, turned the once peaceful African villages into half-deserted ruins, whose inhabitants were full of hate and suspicion. The governments of Europe were to blame for letting the trade go on – for years they all 'turned a blind eye'.

Dreams of an empire in the West
In 1630, a Dutch nobleman named Count John Maurice of Nassau-Siegen*, embarked at Amsterdam for the long voyage across the Atlantic Ocean to Pernambuco. Six years had passed since the Dutch first tried to take a part of Brazil from the Portuguese. Now they had seized Pernambuco, and Count Maurice was on his way to take up the post of governor.

The Count had a very clear idea of how he wanted to govern Pernambuco. In the first place he proposed to make peace with the Portuguese, and work side by side with them. He argued that there was room for everybody in South America, and that the best way to benefit both Holland and Brazil was by tolerance.

Unfortunately for Count Maurice, the governors of the Dutch East India Company were more interested in making quick profits. They refused to support the far-seeing Count, and in 1644 he resigned and left the colony. Soon afterwards, the Dutch left Brazil altogether.

New Amsterdam
But Brazil was not the only territory in the West

to be claimed by the Dutch. They had several ports in the West Indies, and during the seventeenth century, many Dutch Protestants left their homes to settle in the promising lands of North America. Another company, the Dutch West India Company, was formed to look after their interests.

In 1607, an Englishman named Henry Hudson was employed by the Dutch 'for to discover a passage by the North Pole to China'. Instead, he discovered what later became the site of New York. Other explorers had missed this very favourable landing-place, because of the dense forests on Long Island, which hid the mouth of the river. Henry Hudson stepped ashore in red ceremonial dress with gold trimmings; the North American Indians remembered his arrival for scores of years, and could describe his magnificent clothes in detail. The Dutch made a settlement here, and· called it New Amsterdam.

Governor Peter Stuyvesant of New Amsterdam ruled his people strictly and under his leadership the colony grew. But unfortunately his religion was a very narrow kind of Protestantism, and he disapproved strongly even of other Protestants. The Quakers and Lutherans in particular, who had left their homes in Holland because they were not allowed to worship freely, found that life in the New World was even harder. There was a good deal of discontent, and the local town councillors fought Stuyvesant's decisions.

During his governorship, the Indians began to realize that the Europeans would soon take away all their land. It was not only the Dutch: settlers from England, France and Spain were also pouring into North America. Three times Stuyvesant had to take out his hastily recruited troops to fight against Indian warriors. Often lonely farms were raided, and the farmers and their families brutally killed by the Indians. There was cruelty on both sides, and sometimes the Dutch burnt whole villages. Stuyvesant tried to stop the Dutch from selling guns and alcohol to the Indians, because he argued – quite rightly – that this was just asking for trouble. Because of these upsets, New Amsterdam never became a properly settled community. In 1664 an English fleet landed troops in the mouth of the river, and the captain claimed the island in the

---

*The island of Mauritius had been named after him in 1598.

172

name of King Charles II of England. Stuyvesant had had no warning of the English approach, and he had to hand over the town. It now became known as New York.

New Amsterdam
A view of New Amsterdam at the beginning of the Dutch settlement.

Holland

In Holland, the people had never been so prosperous. The housewives baked meats and puddings with the new spices, the dressmakers and tailors were busy turning the silks and cottons of the East into rich clothes. With new foods, and with beer and wine to accompany them, the wealthy merchants and landowners lived easy lives. After meals, the men brought out their clay pipes and smoked the new weed called tobacco, brought to Europe from America. The making of pipes became a very large industry.

The Dutch had money to spare for luxuries, especially for works of art, with which they decorated their houses. Many houses, whether in Holland or in far-off Batavia, had beautiful pictures of indoor and outdoor scenes on the walls, and huge portraits of the master and mistress of the house.

Peter Stuyvesant, Governor of New Amsterdam

173

Chapter 30 The Thirst for Gold

The Portuguese had discovered that the South American Indians of Brazil were not very advanced culturally, or politically. The Spaniards, exploring to the north and west of Brazil, found a very different state of affairs.

They landed on the coast of Yucatán, and there found that instead of naked savages, the inhabitants were civilized people living in stone houses and wearing woven clothing. If that had been all the Spaniards noticed, they might have gone away again. But everywhere they looked they saw gold; gold ornaments, gold bracelets and necklaces, and gold coins for money. Yet the people of Yucatán were not in fact as rich as they had been once, and even more wealthy people, called Aztecs, were living in their own small kingdom in Mexico. When the Spanish general Hernando Cortez heard about these people, he set off at once to find the Aztecs.

'We Spaniards suffer from a disease that only gold can cure,' Cortez is supposed to have said. And he sent a message to King Montezuma of the Aztecs, asking for a meeting. In return, Montezuma sent so many rich and costly presents to Cortez, that the Spaniards' 'disease' grew worse. They had to have the riches of Montezuma's golden city, Tenochtitlán, for themselves.

Cortez and his small army started off from Vera Cruz (which Cortez had founded) in 1519. The journey was long and mountainous, and often the army had to fight its way through groups of hostile Indians shooting arrows from the dense jungle trees. But they also had to cross lands belonging to a tribe called the Tlaxcatec, and this turned out to be fortunate for the Spaniards: the Tlaxcatec were unwilling subjects of Montezuma, and they were quite prepared to see him overthrown, so their warriors joined the Spanish army.

South and Central America

This mixed force struggled through jungles and over high steep mountain passes, and then suddenly, while they were still many miles away, they saw the glittering city of Tenochtitlán.

'We didn't know what to say, or whether it was real, with all the cities on the land and in the lake, the causeway with bridges one after the other, and before us the great city of Mexico.'

So wrote Bernal Diaz, the official diary-keeper of Hernando Cortez. They crossed the causeway and the bridges, and as they entered the city, a strange thing happened. The Aztecs welcomed them with great joy, and even seemed prepared to worship them. Montezuma and his priests had decided that the Spaniards were their gods, returned to earth in human form. By tradition, the feathered serpent-god Quetzalcoatl was supposed to return in this way together with a race of white 'supermen'. The return of Quetzalcoatl was to be the end of the Aztec kingdom, and the beginning of the Aztec 'heaven'. Tragically, Cortez' arrival certainly meant the end of the Aztec kingdom, but no heaven was put in its place. Montezuma was persuaded to recognize the king of Spain as his overlord and to hand over vast quantities of gold as tribute. Efforts to persuade him to become a Christian were not successful.

Meanwhile, Cortez had to leave the capital and return to Vera Cruz, where fighting had broken out. When he reached Tenochtitlán again, he found that his soldiers had been misbehaving, and were being besieged in a palace which Montezuma had set aside for their use and in which the Spaniards held Montezuma as a hostage. The Aztecs were in an angry mood. Cortez furiously ordered Montezuma to stop his people from attacking the Spaniards, and Montezuma, who only wanted peace, appeared on the palace wall and began to speak to the Aztecs who were attacking it. Then someone threw a stone at the king, inflicting a wound from which he later died. There was no longer any hope of a peaceful occupation of the city. The Spaniards had to fight every inch of the way back over the causeway to escape the fury of the Aztecs.

Two years later Cortez, with a new army, defeated 200,000 Aztecs and captured the city. As before, the Aztecs were terrified of his horses, and of the cannons and metal weapons of the invaders. Iron was unknown to them and their light weapons were quite inadequate; after a bloody fight the power and glory of the Aztec kingdom disappeared for ever. The priceless gold and silver treasures of Tenochtitlán were simply melted down and the metal shipped to Spain in blocks instead of in the form of beautiful ornaments.

Aztecs
Montezuma was ruler over a great many of the tribes of Mexico. His priests were very knowledgeable people, and gifted in astronomy and mathematics. Their religion demanded human sacrifice, and every year thousands of people were killed by having their hearts cut out from their bodies.

The Incas
Far to the south, on the west coast of South America, another American Indian tribe had become famous and great. The Incas of Peru had conquered much of the mountainous country to the east of them, and had built a magnificent capital city at Cuzco, 3466 metres (11,370 feet) above sea-level. The Inca kingdom was a difficult one to administer, because it was so vast, and because the highland peoples were completely different from the lowland peoples — yet all were one kingdom. Their clothes and their houses and even their food had to be different, because of the great differences in climate. On the coast, sun-dried mud houses with thatched roofs were adequate: in the cold hills, the people developed a way of building stone houses and palaces and temples, that even survived earthquakes. The stones were fitted together so exactly that no mortar was needed to keep them in place.

The Incas worshipped a sun-god, whose representative on earth was their ruler, the Sapa Inca. The Sapa Inca (or Sole Inca) and his queen ruled a people who worked together like bees in a hive: each man knew his job, and contributed to the good of the community. All farm produce was collected and stored in communal granaries and storehouses, to be given out in equal shares. Even the children, and the old people, had their jobs and their rewards.

Every male member of the tribe, and of the tribes that paid tribute to the Sapa Inca, had to do a period of military service. He put on the padded tunic, and wooden helmet covered with bronze, and was taught to use spears, pikes, axes and clubs. Iron was unknown to the Incas as it was to the Aztecs, and the weapons were tipped with bronze. The army was fed from special store-houses, which were used by the rest of the population only in an emergency.

Everyday food for all the Incas consisted of maize, millet, potatoes, sweet peppers, bananas and mangoes. Sometimes runners from the coast brought fish to Cuzco, wrapped in seaweed to keep it fresh. Occasionally the people ate the meat of a llama, or killed one of the little guinea-pigs that they raised for food.

Between the towns and the villages there was a well-developed system of roads. Parts of the mountain roads were paved and stepped where necessary; the coast roads were made of clay and protected by walls to keep them from being covered by sand. The llama-drivers, and the king's messengers, used these roads frequently. There is a great deal of difference in the amount of oxygen for breathing, and in temperature, between the coast of Peru and Cuzco. In the mountains, the water is so cold that it has to be warmed before it can be drunk comfortably. A coast-dweller who travelled the whole way might feel ill and faint at Cuzco; and a city-dweller from the mountains would feel most uncomfortable in the heat of the coast. So the country's messengers used to work in relays. One messenger ran from the coast perhaps ten miles to a village where another messenger took over from him. *He* travelled to the next staging-post, and a third messenger carried on. So each man remained at the altitude best suited to him.

The men in iron arrive

Just before the Spaniards arrived in Peru, an event had occurred which completely disorganized the Incas. For the first time, on the death of a Sapa Inca, there were two people who claimed the throne. They were half-brothers, both sons of the Sapa Inca. The son with the greater claim was killed by his brother Atahualpa. This was the ruler who now had to fight the new threat to Inca power—the Spaniards.

Francisco Pizarro, Spanish governor of New Castile, first heard about the wealth and glory of the Incas when he was in the lands bordering the Gulf of Mexico. Eager to see this land for himself, he took a small force of men and horses, and sailed down the west coast to an Inca port called Tumbez. Like the Aztecs, the Incas far from resisting the strangers, gave them food served on gold plates, wine in gold cups, and gifts of gold ornaments. This, Pizarro thought, was the city of gold he had heard about. So he was astonished to hear the inhabitants of Tumbez talk of a much richer city called Cuzco, high up in the mountains. There, they said, the temple of the sun-god was covered with sheets of gold, and all the people wore gold and silver as a matter of course.

Pizarro did not have the equipment to take an expedition into the Andes, so he returned to Spain to collect men, horses and supplies. Two years later, in 1532, he made the exhausting and dangerous journey through steaming jungles and over freezing mountains. Pizarro at this time was nearly 60 years old, and he was attempting a journey which killed many of his young followers. The dangers from Indian arrows, from disease, hunger and cold were so great that most of his men were only persuaded to go on by the promise of gold.

At last they reached Caxamalca (Cajamarca) where Atahualpa had camped; he and his courtiers came to meet Pizarro in the large central square of the city. Pizarro's party came into the square with their daggers well concealed. Armed soldiers were hidden all round the square. The Incas were unarmed. This, they thought, was to be a friendly ceremonial meeting. But when Pizarro told Atahualpa he must accept the Spanish king as his lord, and give up the sun-god for the Catholic religion, the Sapa Inca angrily refused. Pizarro shouted to his men and they seized Atahualpa and massacred his followers. Pizarro agreed to let Atahualpa free on payment of a roomful of gold. But even when this colossal amount of gold had been paid, Pizarro still did not keep his part of the bargain. He found an excuse for trying the Sapa Inca and had him executed.

The death of Atahualpa marked the end of the Inca kingdom, although the Spaniards tried to keep some of the former organization going for another century. They introduced horses and cattle, pigs and sheep, and grew vines, wheat and olives on the slopes of the mountains.

But they demanded too much tribute from the people, and the ordinary peasants became little more than slaves. The upper classes mixed freely with the Spaniards, and there was a good deal of intermarriage. Here, as in Brazil, a mixed breed of 'mestizos' came into being.

The Mayas

The people whom Cortez had first met in Yucatán had once been even more highly civilized than the Aztecs. Their weaving, pottery-making, stone-carving (without iron tools) and building were as great as anything produced by the ancient Egyptians. They were completely cut off from the rest of the world, yet quite independently, and without copying any other peoples, they managed to build observatories, and to study the stars so well that their astronomy was even more accurate than that of the Greeks.

They built pyramids and temples, many of which still stand today. They had a highly organized religion, which included human sacrifice. In their ancient cities, priests wearing jaguar-skin tunics, elaborate feathered headdresses and many colourful ornaments, interpreted the Maya calendar to the people. They predicted eclipses, and (like the Egyptian priests) controlled the all-important crop-planting. But unlike Egypt, the land of the Mayas had no river, and their towns grew up near deep natural wells.

By the time the Spaniard, Francisco de Montejo, arrived with an army in 1540, the Maya civilization was declining. Catholic churches were built in new Spanish towns, and the Mayas were needed as an endless supply of cheap labour. They worked in the fields, and in the mines. But their gold was taken, and added to the gold from Mexico and Peru. Spain became richer as the 'conquistadores' (conquerers) took possession by force of the wealth of civilizations that were older and in some ways finer than their own.

Naturally, having found three such rich kingdoms in Central and South America, the Spaniards thought that there must be others. They sent many expeditions to the Gulf of Mexico, and explored both the east and the west coast of North America. Inland, they sent parties of men right across the continent, from Florida to California. From Cuzco, men went north, south and east, in search of more wealth. They now had a legend to drive them on—a story told by the Indians that somewhere there was a man dressed all in gold. They called him 'El Dorado',

Quipus
As well as carrying verbal messages, Inca messengers carried a rod on which were tied a number of coloured knotted strings. This was called a *quipu*. Each string and each knot could be changed to alter the meaning. They could be used to record history, keep accounts, or work out measurements for buildings. People who knew the language of the *quipus* could 'talk' to each other even if they belonged to a different tribe and otherwise spoke another language.

the golden one. He was as imaginary as Prester John, and the search for him cost the Spaniards hundreds of lives. Many of them died of hunger and cold; many more become prisoners of the Indians.

Pizarro's brother was lucky to return from a terrible march through thick jungle and mosquito-filled swamps. On their arrival in Quito in 1542, his men were 'clothed in skins, on foot, without shoes, worn out and so thin that they scarcely knew each other'. It is amazing that so much exploration was achieved in conditions like these. It was the greedy desire for gold that forced the Spaniards on, but they never again found a rich civilization to spoil and plunder.

Meanwhile, colonists were building new towns on the ruins of Cuzco and Tenochtitlán. Catholic churches replaced the pyramid temples, and palaces decorated in the Spanish style took the place of the plain buildings in which the Sapa Inca and Montezuma had lived. Explorers like Cortez and Columbus died poor; the administrators who followed them often became very wealthy in their new homes.

Chapter 31   England joins the Exploration Race

The English first heard about Columbus's voyages from a Venetian sailor named John Cabot, who arrived in England about 1484. The king of England, Henry VII, decided to send Cabot westward on an expedition of his own. Cabot set sail from Bristol in 1497 in a ship called the *Matthew*, reached what is now called Cape Breton Island, and discovered the rich fishing grounds of Newfoundland. But he did not bring home any gold or spices, and he did not find Cathay, so the king's interest died.

After Cabot's voyages, the English made no really important voyages of discovery westwards for 50 years. While Spain and Portugal were conquering their 'new worlds', the English remained at home. Henry VII's son, Henry VIII, was too busy with English affairs to bother with explorers; and his daughter Mary, who succeeded him, was a Catholic, who married King Philip II of Spain. So during *her* reign the English were allies of Spain. But after Queen Mary's death, her half-sister Elizabeth (a Protestant) came to the throne. Queen Elizabeth I is one of the most famous English monarchs, and under her rule, many important English voyages of exploration took place. It is impossible to tell the story of all these adventures, and we can do no more than mention a few of the outstanding Elizabethans.

By this time, of course, it was common knowledge that America was a new world between Europe and Asia, and many explorers now looked for a northern route to the East. Sir Hugh Willoughby tried to find a passage to India by sailing northwards round Russia. He failed, and was frozen to death in the bitterly cold northern seas. On the same voyage, his friend Richard Chancellor, separated from Willoughby by bad weather also sailed north round Norway, and discovered the White Sea. He then travelled overland to Moscow, and had dinner with the tsar of

Queen Elizabeth I

Russia. On his return he described his experiences in Russia, and the customs of the Russians. He was particularly interested in the ladies, who painted and powdered their faces in such a fashion that he said they resembled millers' wives, 'for they look as though they were beaten about the face with a bag of meal, but their eyebrows they colour as black as jet'.

The result of Chancellor's journey was that England and Russia began to trade with each other, and the Muscovy Company was formed. For a time the English concentrated on trading with Russia, and also in defying the Portuguese by trading with the Muslims of North Africa (which they called 'Barbary'), and the Levant (countries on the east coast of the Mediterranean). Richard Hakluyt, who wrote down the stories of many Elizabethan sailors and explorers, says:

'The Portugals were much offended with this our new trade into Barbary . . . and gave out that if they took us in these parts, they would treat us as their mortal enemies.'

The English in Africa

Attempts by the English to sail down the West Coast of Africa were timid at first, partly because the Portuguese were their 'mortal enemies'. (They would much rather have found a north-west or north-east passage to the East for themselves.) But gradually the English sea-captains learnt to avoid Portuguese patrol ships, and sometimes they even managed to find Portuguese navigators who were willing to lead them past the forts, and into deserted harbours. They traded with Africans for ivory and gold, and one of these early traders, John Lok, observed:

'Whoever would deal with them must behave civilly, for they will not traffic (trade) if they be ill-used.'

The trade in 'pepper and elephants' teeth, oil of palm, cloth made of cotton wool very curiously woven, and cloth made of the bark of palm trees' was sufficiently profitable for the English to start yet another trading company. This company, founded in 1618, was called The Company of Adventurers of London trading into Africa. The Company built forts of its own on the West Coast, and agreed to supply 30,000 slaves every year to the West Indies.

But before the formation of this Company, 'gentlemen adventurers' working on their own had already begun to trade in slaves. The first Englishman to do so was John Hawkins, a member of a famous ship-building family in Plymouth. There was no demand for slaves in England, so he took them across the Atlantic and sold them to the Spaniards. The Spanish settlements in the West Indies had been forbidden to trade with the English, but the slave-traders in the Caribbean were so eager to have slaves that they secretly bought John Hawkins's cargo.

The English in the Indian Ocean

The first voyages round the Cape to the East brought many disasters and deaths. The English did not have the Dutch captains' excellent maps to help them, and they had to make their own charts from their own experience.

Early explorers sailed up the East African coast as far as the Comoro Islands and Zanzibar, where they were received cautiously. The East Africans did not know what to make of a second European power in their harbours, and the Portuguese forbade foreign ships to enter East African ports after an incident off Pemba. This is what happened: a member of the crew of a

East Indiamen
The ships of the East India Company, known as 'East Indiamen', were a little larger than the early exploring ships. Men still suffered from scurvy and ships had to call in at islands constantly in order to take fresh water, vegetables and fruit on board. Otherwise they lived on mouldy biscuits and maggot-ridden salt meat. Rats and cockroaches swarmed all over the ships and were even eaten by the sailors in emergencies.

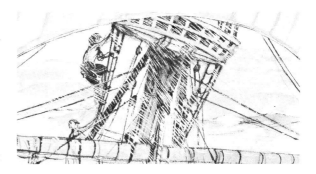

The seamen wore their ordinary clothes on board, usually without shoes or stockings. There was no waterproof clothing and during the monsoon rains, or in Atlantic storms, the sailors were hardly ever dry. Besides this, they suffered great discomfort from fleas and lice. It is not surprising that, on long voyages, the captain considered himself lucky if *only* one-fifth of his men died.

Because of the rich cargoes they carried, sailors had to be alert for pirate ships and ready to man the guns in a fight. There was also the danger of collisions with other ships; in foggy weather the seamen banged drums, rang bells and fired their muskets to warn other ships of their presence.

ship called *Ascension* went ashore to fill a water-barrel. For some reason he was seized and killed. The English captain immediately thought that this was the beginning of a Portuguese attack, so he quickly put to sea. Next day the *Ascension* captured three dhows, and took the crews on board. From an account of the disaster that followed, it seems that the African sailors drew their knives, probably in an attempt to escape. Whereupon all 30 of them were killed by the *Ascension's* crew. After that, English ships usually went straight across the Ocean to India, after stopping for water at the Cape of Good Hope.

In 1601 the English founded an East India Company of their own. This Company was first granted a monopoly of all trade for 15 years, then later King James I optimistically renewed it 'for ever'. By James's reign the Company was doing good business, and gentlemen in England were keen for their sons to join the 'East Indiamen' as apprentices. For the young apprentices it was an adventurous life, and on their return they had many exciting stories to tell, of pirates, fights with the Portuguese, storms at sea and shipwrecks. Trading ships reached Java, the Moluccas, and Surat in India. On all these expeditions, the English ships had to try to avoid both the Portuguese and the Dutch.

In 1623 the Dutch and English came to blows at Amboina, and many English merchants were killed. After that the English stayed away from the Spice Islands, and turned their attention more and more to India. Their new settlements in Bengal, Bombay and Madras became the foundation of their Indian Empire.

Gradually the Dutch and English recognized certain trading areas as Dutch and others as English, and local quarrels became less frequent. Their colonial ventures in the East now had firm roots.

Pirates in the Caribbean

The riches of Peru were taken by the Spaniards up the west coast of South America to Panama, then put on to mules and carried in long 'trains' across the narrow strip of land to the Atlantic coast. From there the treasure went to a Spanish island called San Juan de Ulua, opposite the settlement of Vera Cruz which Cortez had founded. Mexican gold was also sent to San Juan,

and once a year a huge Spanish treasure-fleet took this enormously rich cargo across the Atlantic Ocean to Spain.

One day the English captain John Hawkins arrived at San Juan, after his ships had been nearly battered to pieces by a storm just outside the Gulf of Mexico. He sailed boldly into the harbour, and asked permission to land and make all necessary repairs. The Spaniards agreed, and the sailors gratefully went ashore to find water and fresh food. Suddenly, without warning, the Spaniards attacked them. Many of the English sailors were killed and many more were captured. Hawkins escaped from San Juan de Ulua, and so did Francis Drake, then a young captain on board one of his ships. Drake was shocked by the treachery of the Spaniards and for the rest of his life he carried on a personal battle against them.

'The Dragon'

Drake's exploits around the 'Spanish Main' sound like a boys' adventure story. In 1572, after many voyages, he attacked the town of Nombre de Dios on the Isthmus of Panama, captured a treasure ship and returned safely to England. Queen Elizabeth had to pretend not to notice that one of her sea-captains was behaving like a pirate. She assured the Spanish ambassador in England that any sea-captain caught raiding Spanish ships or settlements would be punished. But at the same time she gave Drake money for his voyages, and received the best pieces of Spanish jewellery for herself!

Drake was a very skilful seaman, and an excellent organizer. He insisted that his officers and men shared the work equally, saying: 'I must have the gentleman to haul and draw (work) with the mariner, and the mariner with the gentleman.' He was strict with his men, but they all loved him and respected him. He made sure that all his sailors knew how to fight on land as well as sail their ships, and consequently did not crowd his ships with soldiers as the Spaniards did.

Drake's navigation was as good as that of any of the earlier explorers of the Atlantic and Pacific Oceans. In 1578 he followed Magellan's route through the Straits and out into the Pacific, with a small fleet of ships. Hakluyt wrote, 'The Strait of Magellan is the gate of entry into the treasure of both the East and the East Indies.'

Once through the Strait, a gale blew Drake's

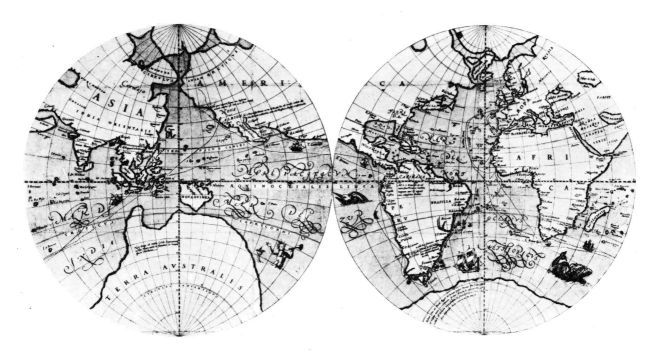

Sir Francis Drake's voyage round the world
This is a map of Drake's voyage around the world. It was printed about ten years after his return to England, in 1590.

ships southwards, away from the coast of South America, and for weeks he and his companions saw no land at all. Everyone believed that Tierra del Fuego was the *northern* tip of a huge new, unexplored continent called 'Terra Australis' on the maps of the time. But Drake's own ship, the *Golden Hind*, was blown so far south that Drake was able to say that the geographers were wrong. One ship in Drake's little fleet disappeared for ever, and another managed to struggle back to England through the Strait. But Drake battled against the wind and eventually returned to the western shores of South America.

Now came his chance for a really profitable piece of piracy. The Spaniards had built a fleet of ships at Panama, which they sailed up and down the Peruvian coast, and northwards to their new settlements in North America. Naturally they did not bother to keep a lookout for enemy ships, because there had never been any on this coast. So as they sailed northwards, the English sailors stopped in the Spanish harbours and raided the unsuspecting settlers. One man was sleeping out in the open, with several bars of silver beside him. The raiders managed to take away the silver without even waking him!

There was panic among the Spaniards when they realized that the dreaded Drake, whom they called the 'Terrible Dragon', was in the Pacific. All the ports were alerted, but they were not able to prevent the Dragon from his most successful piece of piracy. He captured a Spanish ship which was so full of treasure that the little English ships were unable to take it all on board. Then they sailed northwards, to see if they could find a northern passage home, but finding that the coastline turned westward, Drake decided to follow Magellan's example and sail west, right round the world.

In the Moluccas the English fleet added six tons of cloves to their already overloaded ships, and then continued their voyage round Africa and home to Plymouth. Unfortunately for Drake, this was the year (1580) in which Spain and Portugal united. Spain was thus the most powerful nation in Europe, and Queen Elizabeth dared not offend King Philip. She had therefore to pretend to be displeased when Drake sailed into harbour with many thousands of pounds worth of Spanish treasure. He was officially ignored by the Court, but in fact he became a hero to everyone. The queen herself relented, and in spite of Spanish disapproval, Francis Drake was knighted the following year, and he became Mayor of Plymouth.

The Spanish Armada

The Spaniards and the English finally came to open warfare in 1588. England had long been waiting for the Spanish fleet (which they called the Armada, or 'armed force'). As soon as the great crescent of ships was sighted, beacons (warning fires) were lit on hilltops to carry the news throughout the country.

The Spanish ships carried so many soldiers that they might themselves have been able to attempt an invasion. This is what the English expected and their ships, quicker and easier to handle than those of the Spaniards and Portuguese, kept between the Armada and the coast all the way up the English Channel. But in fact the king of Spain had ordered the Armada to sail to a position where it could help and protect an invasion of England by the army of the Duke of Parma from the Netherlands, then under Spanish rule. Neither the king nor the admiral knew how unprepared he was for such action.

The Spanish admiral, the Duke of Medina Sidonia, led his fleet up the English Channel, strictly obeying the orders he had received in Spain. The English captains had to prevent invasion but did not know where it might be attempted. When the Armada sailed in a close, crescent formation the English found it very difficult to attack and little damage had been done to it by the time it anchored off Calais. The Spanish admiral knew that was a bad place to stop but by now he needed water, food, cannon-balls and, above all, information about the Duke of Parma's plans. This was the English captains' opportunity. That night they deliberately set some supply-ships on fire, and let the wind blow them among the enemy fleet. Very little real

harm was done by these fire-ships, but the Spaniards scattered.

The crescent formation was broken at last when, next morning, they sailed up the east coast of England, trying to shake off the English ships, which for the first time were able to inflict serious hurt on some of the enemy vessels. Then came a wind that blew the Armada steadily north. The English followed as far as the coast of Scotland by which time it was clear that there would be no invasion. Storms, disease, starvation and lack of water afflicted the Spanish fleet as it went round the north of Scotland and south past Ireland where more ships were wrecked. Of the 130 ships that left Lisbon only 67 got back to Spain.

While the Spanish fleet was being blown towards Scotland, Queen Elizabeth went to Tilbury, near London, to review her troops. In the speech she made to them, she said:

'I know I have the body of a weak and feeble woman, but I have the heart of a king, and a king of England too, and think foul scorn that Parma or Spain, or any prince of Europe, should dare to invade the borders of my realm.'

The defeat of the Spaniards at sea was a turning-point in the history of Europe, and perhaps also of the world. Had Spain won, Spanish influence would have spread over far more of Europe, Asia and America. The enormous English-speaking areas of the world today might have spoken another language, and adopted another culture. As it was, the English, free from the danger of invasion, set out to increase their queen's realms, while Spain declined in importance.

182

Chapter 32 Settlers in North America

The Spaniards had established themselves firmly in Central America by 1533 and had conquered the Inca nation in South America. In northern North America, at about the same time, a French explorer named Jacques Cartier landed at the mouth of the river St Lawrence. The French were still trying to find a north-west passage to the Pacific, and they thought the St Lawrence mouth was the beginning of a Strait. Cartier sailed up the river as far as an island near Quebec, and there he encountered a tribe of friendly Indians. By signs he asked them the name of this place, and they replied 'Canada'. Cartier thought that this was their name for the whole country; it was in fact their word for a village.

The Indians also told Cartier about a rich country called Saguenay, where there was gold and precious stones. When he returned home and told King Francis I of France about Saguenay, the king thought that he was going to be the lord of another great empire like those of Peru or Mexico. He was very happy to supply Cartier with more ships and men, so that he could explore the river St Lawrence properly. Cartier went on two more expeditions, but he never found Saguenay. In fact, it did not exist. But he decided that the land near the river would be wonderful for settlement, and he turned his mind to trading with the Indians, and colonizing the new land. His main settlement was on the site of present-day Montreal.

Almost 50 years after Cartier's death, in 1603, the French sent their first governor to Canada. His name was Samuel de Champlain. He had already been on expeditions to the West Indies and South America, and he was the first person to suggest that a canal should be cut across the Isthmus of Panama. But that was all Spanish territory, and there was very little that a French-

man could do to make such a dream come true. He continued Cartier's work of exploring the St Lawrence, and tried to find a way past the many rapids and waterfalls on the river. He founded the city of Quebec, and started many other small settlements where fur-traders could buy and sell their goods. They bought all kinds of animal skins from the Indians, cured (preserved) them, and sold them to merchants who sailed up the river to their trading-stations. These settlements remained small; besides fur traders there were only fishermen and peasant-farmers living in them. At this stage, Champlain did not want settlers who would not contribute to the development of the settlements.

Champlain was a great believer in keeping friendly with the Indians, and they liked and trusted him. He found out a great deal about their way of life, and once he even joined a war-party of Indian braves (warriors) of the Algonquin tribe. Their enemies the Iroquois turned to the English for help, and so Europeans became involved in Indian quarrels.

Champlain's exploring trips took him far to the west, and he was the first white man to see Lakes Huron and Ontario. He must have heard about the other Great Lakes, but he seems to have been misled into thinking they were not lakes, but the sea. Still thinking of the possibility of a way by water to the Pacific, he sent an expedition to find this 'Sea of the West'. No way through was discovered, but this and other expeditions (many of them led by Jesuit missionaries) found out a tremendous amount about the geography of North America. They made contact with the Spaniards in Mexico, and with the English on the shores of Hudson Bay; while westwards they reached the Rocky Mountains. The first person to cross the North American continent was a Scottish fur trader named Alexander Mackenzie, very much later, in 1793. Long before this happened, the thoughts of Europeans were turning away from the idea of making easy money in America. The land was so fertile that newcomers now arrived to build themselves homes and to farm rather than to explore.

The 'Lost Colony'

One of the first Englishmen to become interested in colonizing North America was the famous Sir Walter Raleigh. He and the English geographer Richard Hakluyt together wrote a book that gave instructions on how to start a colony. The book also suggested that new settlements should be founded by the state, and not by private individuals. Unfortunately Raleigh's attempts to build colonies were complete failures, partly because the men chosen to make their homes in America were unsuitable for such a tough and thankless task. Raleigh himself did not lead any of the expeditions.

The only attempt which might have been successful was made when Raleigh sent out a party of men with their families under the leadership of a man named John White. White was to be 'Governor of the City of Ralegh* in Virginia'. His party landed at a place called Roanoke, where Raleigh had already sent 15 settlers with stores to last for two years. The new party could find no trace of these men, which was disheartening, because they had expected to find warm houses and food awaiting them at their journey's end. Whatever the fate of these fifteen men was, it was probably the same as that of White's little colony. When supplies ran short, White took their ship back to England, promising to return almost at once. He left behind 89 men, 17 women and 11 children, including his own daughter and her newborn baby, Virginia Dare. For various reasons White was unable to return for two years. When he got back he found that the 'City of Ralegh' was an empty, overgrown, deserted clearing in the forest.

The English at home were shocked to hear that all these settlers had vanished, and many later expeditions were asked to search for the inhabitants of the 'Lost Colony'. But no definite explanation of their disappearance was ever found, though years later there was an Indian

*Walter Raleigh spelt his name in many different ways. Nowadays we usually keep to the spelling 'Raleigh'.

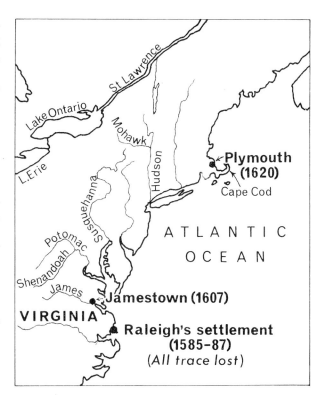

Early English settlements in North America, 1585–1620

story that all except seven of the settlers had been killed. The Indians of Roanoke were gentle people, whose main occupation was hunting and fishing: perhaps they grew tired of the Englishmen's demands for food. Or perhaps another more warlike tribe captured them. One of the seven said to have been saved was a 'young maid', who may possibly have been Virginia Dare. If so, she very likely lived for the rest of her life as an Indian 'squaw' in the tribe of her captors.

John Smith and Pocohontas

In spite of repeated failures to colonize the land named Virginia, the London merchants were still eager to try. So they formed the 'London Company in Virginia', and in 1606 they sent out a party of 105 colonists under the leadership of a young man named John Smith. Their settlement was called Jamestown, in honour of the new English king, James I.

But the Company was no better at choosing suitable colonists than Sir Walter Raleigh had been, and Smith had a hard time trying to keep them all alive. Sometimes Indians made surprise attacks, but Jamestown was on a peninsula, and easy to defend, so they did not do any lasting

John White's drawing of colonists landing in Virginia
John White was very interested in all he saw in the New World, and he made a collection of drawings of the people, plants and animals. He hoped that his pictures would attract more English settlers.

damage. More serious was the shortage of food. John Smith was the only member of the party who was successful in trading with the Indians for maize: other colonists tried, but they did not return. In winter they all had to live on whatever birds and animals they managed to kill.

When Jamestown became more settled, John Smith left to explore the river Chickahominy, and he then had an adventure for which he has always been remembered. He was captured by Indians, and to save himself he gave their leader a round ivory compass. The Indians had never seen such a thing before, and they watched with surprise as the delicate needle swung round under its protective glass. In his own account of the event, John Smith (who wrote about himself as 'he') said:

'Within an hour after, they tied him to a tree, and as many as could, stood about him prepared to shoot him, but the King* holding up the compass in his hand, they all laid down their bows and arrows, and in a triumphant manner led him to Orapaks, where he was after their manner kindly feasted, and well used.'

But that was not the end of the matter. The

*Early explorers often quite wrongly called minor chiefs and headmen 'King'; the 'Emperor' mentioned later was chief Powhatan.

Indian braves performed a war-dance round him, and then fed him with great quantities of venison (deer-meat) 'which made him think they would fat him to eat him'. Then for about three days they performed a ceremony which was designed to show them whether he wished them well or not. They tried to make him their leader for a raid on Jamestown, but he told them that they would never be able to resist the guns used by the settlers.

So at last he was taken to the chief of the tribe, Powhatan. And Powhatan's decision was that he should die. Two large stones were laid on the floor, and John Smith was stretched on the stones. Just as the braves were about to beat out his brains with their clubs, Powhatan's young daughter, Pocohontas, rushed forward and laid her own head on top of his. 'Whereat,' said John Smith, 'the Emperor was contented he should live.' After this lucky escape, John Smith was given land in exchange for 'two great guns and a grindstone', and he was allowed to return to Jamestown.

Meanwhile the colonists struggled along, battling all the while against hunger and disease. It was a losing battle, and in one short year after their arrival in America, there were only 38 people left. This was a dreadful death-rate, and

Jamestown would have failed completely had not a ship arrived bringing fresh stores, and 120 more settlers. They were under the leadership of Captain Newport. The London Company was not so interested in making the colony self-supporting as it was in making money: Captain Newport's instructions were to look for gold, to discover a passage to the Pacific, and to find 'the Lost Colony'. Smith tried to do all these things, as well as ensuring that sufficient corn was planted, and that the Indians were treated well. It was a superhuman task, and naturally he could not do all these things properly. The London Company was constantly telling him that they wanted more valuable cargoes sent back to England.

John Smith was an excellent choice for the job of starting a colony in Virginia. If only the Company had left him to do as he thought right, he would probably have succeeded. But the policy was directed in London, by men who had never been to America, and had no idea of the difficulties the colonists had to face. It was not until colonies became independent of European Companies that the colonization of America became really successful.

The Pilgrim Fathers

King James I of England was a strange man, and not very likeable. But he was king, and he had to be obeyed. He had been brought up as a strict Protestant, but was very intolerant of those who belonged to different branches of the Protestant faith. 'You will reform,' he shouted on one occasion, 'or I will harry you out of the land!'

One religious group who preferred to leave before they were harried out were called Separatists. They were a very extreme kind of Protestant, who thought that the Reformation did not return closely enough to a simple Christianity. The Separatists dressed very plainly, often in grey and white, and their lives were rather dull because they did not believe in dancing, or holiday fairs, or even merrymaking in private. They drank no wine, and wore no jewellery.

At first this group went to Holland, but later they decided to leave Europe altogether and become pioneers in a new country. The London merchants gave them a ship called the *Mayflower* so that they could go to Virginia. In 1620 they sailed from Plymouth in England but they missed Virginia, and instead landed at Cape Cod. They

Pocohontas, the chief's daughter, saves John Smith's life by laying her head on his

The Pilgrim Fathers arriving at Virginia

The *Mayflower* was shockingly overcrowded. Each passenger had to provide his own food and the cabins were very small. A whole family slept in bunks, one above the other, with scarcely room to turn around. Even though the Separatists lived simple lives at home, they were horrified by the conditions during their two months on board the *Mayflower*. William Bradford said of their arrival:

'Being thus past the vast ocean and a sea of troubles ... they now had no friends to welcome them nor inns to entertain or refresh their weather-beaten bodies ...'

186

called their first settlement Plymouth, and the new colony, New England. Many years later the people of the United States of America called them the 'Pilgrim Fathers'.

These devoted people did their best to start work on building houses and collecting food. They had very few stores left from the voyage, and winter was approaching. Their sufferings during that first winter were terrible, and by the time spring came, half of them were dead. But the rest of the little band persevered, and with a man called William Bradford as governor for the next 30 years, they gradually managed to create a colony. They caught herrings, cod and mackerel, and sold them to traders. They became excellent ship-builders, and used their ships to carry goods to England from other American colonies. Their cargoes consisted of fish, wood, tobacco, hemp, sugar and wheat.

William Penn

Farther south, another Christian religious group made its home in this country. They were the Quakers, and their leader was an Englishman called William Penn. Penn's father had lent a large sum of money to King Charles I, James I's son. The king readily agreed to repay Penn on his father's death, not with money, but with a grant of land in America. Penn wanted to call his land 'Sylvania', which means 'woodlands', and it was the king who persuaded him to add his own name; the new colony became Pennsylvania.

Penn sat down and wrote a 'Last Farewell to England' (in fact he returned many times), and then sailed from Deal on the south-east coast. The journey was a nightmare, because someone came on board already infected with smallpox. In such crowded surroundings, with little room to move, nobody could escape the disease, and by the time the ship reached the shores of America, one-third of the passengers had died.

But again, from a disastrous start grew a thriving colony. Within two years there were 300 houses in Pennsylvania, built in the new town called Philadelphia, which means 'brotherly love'. Pennsylvania turned out to be a very fertile land, particularly for grain-crops like wheat and barley. Each man worked his own land, and they did not rely entirely on slave-labour, as the Spanish and English planters of the southern part of America did. So whereas in the south there were a few very rich landowners and thousands of slaves, farther north there was a

William Penn trading with the Indians

less wealthy middle class with fewer very poor people.

Penn always paid the Indians well for any land he bought (unlike Peter Minuit, a Dutchman, who bought New Amsterdam for a few yards of cloth). In return he asked that they should sell their furs and skins only to Pennsylvanians, and not to 'the enemies of England'. All English settlers at this time considered that their colonies belonged to Britain and it was, of course, the British fleet that was expected to defend them from attack.

But in spite of Penn's justice and sense of fair dealing, he was not popular in England, and was once put on trial for suspected treason. He was found not guilty, but this and later accusations affected his health. But by the time he died in 1718, British colonization of America was firmly established.

By 1732 there were 13 British colonies, spread along the east coast of North America. These colonies had many quarrels among themselves, and there were terrible wars with the Indians, who were pushed farther and farther west. Although the colonists had not yet gone very far inland, it was now certain that the time would come when all the vast, beautiful and rich territory of North America would belong to the European settlers.

Chapter 33 Terra Australis

To finish the story of the Voyages of Exploration, the discovery of one more great territory must be mentioned—that of the continent of Australia. Although, as long ago as 1578, Francis Drake had proved that the southern tip of South America, Tierra del Fuego, was an island and not part of a new continent, explorers and geographers believed in the existence of a great southern continent, which they called 'Terra Australis', for another two whole centuries. They argued that since there was so much land north of the equator, there must be an equal area of land to the south of the equator as well. So far, they had only discovered a relatively small amount of land to the south, so they thought that Terra Australis must be a vast continent, balancing the whole of Europe and Asia.

Before 1700 explorers of various countries put in at ports in the South Seas, and thought that they had reached part of Terra Australis. The Spanish explorer Torres had passed through the Strait that bears his name in 1605. Dutch seamen followed: Arnhem to Arnhem Land in 1623, Carpenter to the Gulf of Carpentaria in 1628, Tasman (who also discovered New Zealand) to Tasmania in 1642. The first Englishman to arrive was Dampier, at Dampier Land, in 1688. But none of them thought Australia was worth colonizing and its exact size and shape remained uncertain. The first person to discover that New Zealand was two islands, and to chart the east coast of Australia, was another Englishman, Captain James Cook.

Captain Cook had sailed many times to North America, and he was a great seaman. He was very interested in scientific exploration, and on his voyages he took with him experts to study the plants and animals on the lands he discovered. He was the first sea-captain to provide fruit juice for his sailors, and so to end the dread-

A Remarkable Animal *found on one of the Hope Islands in* Captᵗⁿ Cook's *first Voyage*

Kangaroo
Captain Cook described a kangaroo in his journal in 1770:
> 'I saw this morning one of these animals. It was the full size of a greyhound and shaped like one, with a long tail which it carried like a greyhound. I should have taken it for a wild dog, but for its walking or running in which it jumped like a hare or a deer. Excepting the head and ears, which was something like a hare's, it bears no sort of resemblance to any European animal I ever saw.'

ed scurvy, and to insist that his ship was kept clean and that the sailors washed themselves and their clothes. Before his time many sailors died on any long voyage, but during three years at sea in hot and cold climates, out of the 112 men of the crew of his ship *Resolution* only one man died of disease.

Cook made three great voyages into the Pacific Ocean, twice sailing round the world. In the years 1769–70 he explored the coasts of New Zealand. On his second voyage he went farther south than any ship had been before, sailing among the icebergs of the Antarctic Ocean, and proved that there could be no great southern continent. He did not, of course, come in sight of the frozen continent of Antarctica. On his third voyage he tried to find a way round the north of North America but had to turn back because of the ice in the Arctic Ocean. Then he sailed south to the Pacific islands in which he was intensely interested, but in 1779 he was killed by a group of Hawaiians on the beach of their island.

Cook had claimed Australia for Britain, and the colonization of Australia began in 1788 when the British started to use a part of the east coast, called Botany Bay, as a prison settlement. Free settlers soon followed, and after 1797, when sheep were introduced from Europe, the new colony began to prosper.

The results of the voyages of discovery were varied and far-reaching on the peoples of Africa, America and Asia.

For Africa the consequences of White exploration were exploitation and misery. In East Africa and on the west coast of India, the Portuguese wrecked the traditional trade, and the once flourishing towns declined. In West Africa, metal knives, guns and gunpowder were handed over in exchange for gold and silver and ivory – goods of much more lasting value; and the time came when African chiefs were willing to sell their fellow-Africans into slavery. We have already seen the damage that the slave trade did to West Africa.

In North America, trade between Indians and Europeans gradually gave way to trade between white Americans and Europeans, as the Indians were pushed farther and farther westwards by settlers. In time the Indians lost their hunting grounds and their numbers steadily decreased. Today most of them live in reservations with

Captain Cook and his men receiving an offering in the Sandwich Islands

little to do. In return, they learnt European ways, but this must have seemed a poor exchange for their old free way of life.

In Asia, very little was changed. The Europeans were established in India, Ceylon, the Spice Islands and the Philippines, but in the country districts, life went on much as it had always done.

The ships calling at the South Sea Islands left behind metal pots and pans, nails and knives; and Captain Cook brought cattle, pigs, goats and hens, because there were no native domestic animals there. He also advised the British government to allow ships to call at the islands frequently, because he realized that once the islanders got used to European utensils and weapons, they would come to rely on them. Cook was very fond of the islanders, and was perhaps the first great explorer to care what happened to people of a different race and culture.

The Christian religion of the sixteenth and seventeenth centuries did not help men to understand cultures other than their own; for the priests taught that those who had never heard of Christianity were 'heathen', and therefore inferior. They must be brought to the true faith (by force if necessary). Because of this, nobody thought it immoral to rob the heathen of their land, or to exchange a handful of beads for a lump of gold. So the explorers put up flags and erected monuments, claiming their new discoveries for this or that European country. The claims of 'inferior' people already living there were ignored.

The new territorial discoveries and acquisitions had a profound and long-lasting effect upon European life. The repercussions of these early acts are still being felt and men are continually trying to find peaceful solutions to situations which were bred through the greed of their ancestors. In the beginning, however, only the advantages were appreciated.

Firstly, they enabled people to learn more about the geography of the world. Maps now included the newly-charted shores of America and Asia, and travellers' tales about foreign lands became more realistic. Gradually the fears about sea-monsters and queer half-human creatures grew less. Red Indians and Africans were taken to Europe, where men saw that these strangers were after all much the same as themselves.

Now that printing was making books cheaper, accounts of the adventures of sailors, explorers and colonists could be read by all literate people. Their world had suddenly grown larger and more interesting. King James I of England heard about America's talking parrots, and he asked to be given one. Other people with sons on the ships also had new pets from overseas.

Secondly, the discoveries made an enormous difference to the trading-pattern of Europe. Up till now, the main trading countries ringed the Mediterranean Sea. Now the main trading nations were those with coastlines facing the Atlantic Ocean: Portugal, Spain, Britain and Holland. (We have seen how Portuguese trade in the Indian Ocean took away Venice's monopoly of luxury goods from the East.) During the centuries that followed, hundreds of small trading ships sailed between Europe and America, or between Europe and the Far East.

Thirdly, gold and silver and precious stones arrived in such quantities (particularly from South America), that soon their value decreased. This meant that each gold or silver coin in a man's pocket would buy less. The rise in prices did not matter much to the merchants, because they had more money anyway. They became very important people, and the kings of Europe had to listen to their demands. They were the people who now financed the European countries, and even controlled other economies in foreign lands.

Some of these merchants began to deal in money itself, instead of in wool, or tea, or corn. They built Banks and Exchanges, lent money which had to be repaid with interest, and started the system whereby goods could be bought by cheques, promissory notes and bills of exchange, rather than by coins. Bank notes were also manufactured, in order to save people from having to carry large amounts of heavy coins about. The international financiers were so important that even kings were glad to allow their sons and daughters to marry into their families.

Fourthly, everybody got used to new customs. The merchant or courtier with his pipe and tobacco, the seamstress drinking her coffee, the child chewing a stick of sugar, the housewife preserving food with cinnamon, cloves and pepper—everybody's life was changed to some extent by the voyages.

The World in 1700

'An African Scene'

You can see how little the peoples of the world knew about each other by this eighteenth century picture drawn by a visitor to South Guinea. Other Europeans who saw the picture were meant to believe that it showed a typical 'foreign' scene. The animal in the bottom right hand corner, going into the trap, was named by the artist 'a tiger'.

When you see a locked room or a locked cupboard or a house that is all shut up, I expect you are curious to know what is inside. There is always something fascinating about things we know nothing about. The world in 1700 was rather like a row of locked houses. The people in one house knew nothing or very little about the people in the others. The people of Africa had never heard of Russia. The people of China knew little about Europe. The people of India did not realize that the natives of America were called 'Red Indians' by European travellers. We are now going to unlock those houses and see what was happening inside.

The Europeans *did* travel. Perhaps they were more curious than other people of that time.

Houses of the rich and the poor in Europe

Throughout the world there were rich people and poor people. In most countries the rich took advantage of the poor either by making them work for them as slaves or serfs or by taxing them heavily. This state of affairs was accepted in most lands because the people had never known anything different. But in eighteenth century Europe, the lower classes began to revolt against oppression. They demanded political equality and the opportunity to become as rich as their oppressors. These revolutions led to democracy and representative government—things which are common now, not only in western Europe, but in many countries of the world.

Certainly they wanted the products of distant countries, such as silk and spices, gold and ivory, and were better equipped with sea-going ships to fetch them. Whatever the reasons were, by 1700 many Europeans had travelled on voyages of exploration to other lands.

When the explorers returned home with their strange and exciting stories about unknown continents and peoples, others of their country-men set off to see these wonders for themselves. Traders sailed to Africa, Asia and the Americas and set up their own small bases on the coasts of these foreign lands. To North America and South Africa Europeans went, not just to trade, but to settle, hoping to find in a new land that freedom to live and worship as they pleased that was denied them in their own country. So, by 1700, the peoples of the world, who for thousands of years had lived in ignorance of each other, were beginning to meet.

But it was only a beginning. There were still barriers which kept people apart. Most of them were natural barriers. Climate and tropical diseases kept most foreigners from penetrating very far into Africa. High mountains and great expanses of sea cut India off from the rest of the world. Thick forests and empty plains hindered the advance of colonists into North America. Other barriers, however, were man made. As we shall see, the rulers of China and Japan deliberately cut off their countries from the rest of the world. They believed they could go on living in a 'closed' house. Events have shown they were badly mistaken.

One aspect of history which is to be discussed here, therefore, concerns how the different peoples of the world came to know each other. Another aspect is concerned with the rise and fall of empires. Ever since the time of the ancient Egyptians there have been empire builders in the world. The rise of empires is a natural part of human history. Just as strong men tend to dominate weaker men, so strong nations tend to conquer and control smaller nations. The distribution of territorial strength in 1700 clearly illustrates this trait.

In northern Europe and Asia the Russians had extended their rule over millions of peoples of various races. The Chinese emperor ruled over most of the rest of Asia. North and Central India were controlled by the Moguls. The Ottoman Turks claimed an empire which started in eastern Europe and included Asia Minor, Syria, Palestine, parts of Arabia, Egypt and most of North Africa. In Europe two branches of the same family, the Habsburgs, ruled the empires of Spain and Austria. Portugal, Spain, Britain, France and Holland, by setting up trading posts and colonies in distant parts of the world, had begun to build up overseas empires. In Central Africa the Rozwe, Lunda and Luba peoples had established empires stretching over thousands of square miles. Some of these empires were still increasing. Others had passed their peak and were to be destroyed as new empires rose to take their place.

As Europeans travelled abroad they took their ideas and culture with them. The nations of Europe, like most of the nations in the world, lived under the rule of kings or emperors who had almost unlimited power. But there were a few countries which had begun to move beyond this political stage. England had already had a revolution which had succeeded in limiting the power of the king and making parliament the real power in the land. Holland, too, had what we can call a 'constitutional monarchy'*. These changes were the result of feelings and beliefs about personal freedom and the rights of people to have a share in the government of their country. These ideas had not spread very far by 1700 but they were to spread to many countries in the next 200 years.

Something else which was only just beginning

The tower of the temple built at Zimbabwe, capital of the Rozwi empire.

in Europe in 1700 was industrialization. All over the world people led slow, simple lives. They grew their crops as they had been grown for centuries. They made cloth and tools using simple methods in their own homes. They travelled on foot, or on horseback or in carts and carriages pulled by horses, donkeys or oxen. Their main roads were little more than tracks. In 1700, in Europe, a few men knew about steam power. They began to use it for pumping water out of mines. From this first use of steam grew factories full of clanking machinery, railways, new methods of farming and a whole system of international trade.

Since 1700 enormous changes have come over the world. If a man who had lived years before 1700 could have returned to his own country in that year, he would have found very little that was new or surprising. If a man living in 1700 could return to his own land today he would probably not recognize the place.

---

*This means that the country is ruled by a king but that he governs according to laws made by the representatives of the people in parliament.

Part VII 1700-1914, An Age of Revolutions

Chapter 34 Population Explosion and Scientific Revolution

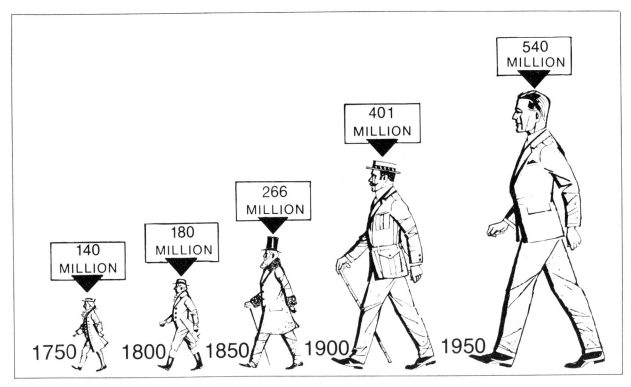

Population of Europe, 1750–1950

The most important thing that has happened in the world in the last 200 years is the growth of population. The figures above refer to Europe alone. In 1750 there were 140 million people on the continent of Europe. This number had been little changed for centuries. But from then on it began to increase rapidly. Now there are four times as many people in Europe as there were in 1750. This increase is so large and sudden that people have called it 'the population explosion'. What is true of Europe is true of other parts of the world also. Think what this population increase means: more mouths to feed, more minds to educate, more houses to be built, more jobs to be found, more land to be farmed.

Throughout the remainder of this book, the history of particular countries will be examined. First let us take a look at the world as a whole between 1700–1914. Many problems and developments were experienced by all countries and it is helpful for understanding the history of Russia, America, China, India, Africa and other lands if one has some idea of general world events to serve as a background.

Population

The first point to note about these years is the great increase in population which occurred. Before the eighteenth century large numbers of people died of disease and hunger. It was not unusual for only two or three children out of a family of twelve or fifteen to live beyond infancy. Men and women were considered *old* if they reached *40 or 50*. From about 1750 the death rate began to fall. That means: fewer children died, old people lived longer and fewer men and women died of disease.

There were many and various reasons for the fall in the death rate, but one of the most important was the development of man's knowledge of medical science and hygiene. In this chapter are discussed some of those major advances in medical knowledge. But first let us see what changes were taking place in the study of science at the beginning of our period.

As you have already seen, some of the world's ancient civilizations had made important scientific discoveries. The Egyptians, the Greeks, the Islamic empires, the Chinese, the Indians, all had made important contributions to man's knowledge of himself and his universe. Then, during the period called the Renaissance, Europe had taken the lead. Science, which had been mixed up with religion, superstition and witchcraft, appeared as a separate form of study. It also began to split up into different kinds of study: mathematics, astronomy, chemistry, physics, medicine, biology. But there was a common approach to all these sciences: instead of starting with their own beliefs about the universe and everything in it, scientists observed, experimented and *then* produced theories to explain what they had discovered. (This is known as the *empirical* approach and is basic to all science.) More and more gifted men made scientific study a full time activity and ever since about 1700 so many discoveries have been made about the universe that we talk about the Scientific Revolution.

Sir Isaac Newton

In 1700 the greatest living scientist was Sir Isaac Newton. He was, first and foremost, a mathematician, and he discovered some of the laws of mathematics. But he was also interested in astronomy and physics. One problem that puzzled him and all scientists was, 'What force or power holds the universe together? What makes the moon go round the earth, and the earth go round the sun?' One day, as he sat in his garden in the shade of an apple tree, a ripe fruit fell from the tree. It was, of course, the force of gravity at work, which men had known about for years. But it made Newton wonder whether it was not the same force that attracted the moon to the earth and the earth to the sun. After years of experiment and calculation, he proved that it was. Later

Newton's reflecting telescope

Sir Isaac Newton splitting light through a prism

Sir Isaac Newton (1642–1727) made a number of important scientific discoveries. One of the most important was the reflecting telescope. Ever since Galileo invented the simple telescope, astronomers had been gazing at the sky. But they found that many of the stars and planets appeared indistinct. Newton produced the telescope shown here, in which the light passed through carefully arranged lenses and was then reflected in a mirror. This made the objects seen through the telescope appear much clearer. While producing this telescope Newton made the important discovery that ordinary light is made up of several colours — the colours of the *spectrum*.

on he made important discoveries about the nature of light and the speed at which it travels.

Antoine Lavoisier

Antoine Lavoisier may be called the father of modern chemistry. He lived in France all his life and for many years worked as a tax collector (the government did not *pay* men to be scientists). In his spare time he carried out chemical experiments, always under the most careful conditions. He was very interested in the effect of heat on certain substances and reached the conclusion that chemical substances are made up of different *elements*. Thus he proved that both air and water contain the *elements* hydrogen and oxygen. This marked a completely new beginning for chemical science. Unfortunately, his talents were not appreciated by the French government. During the French Revolution (see below in this Part, Chapter 36) a jealous rival complained about Lavoisier. The great scientist was arrested, and— simply because he had been a tax collector before the revolution—he was executed. A friend said of Lavoisier's death, 'It took only a moment to cut off that head, and perhaps a century will not be enough to produce another one like it.'

John Dalton

John Dalton was born of poor parents in 1766. Soon after leaving school at the age of ten he became a schoolmaster and devoted many years to teaching children. But he was also a brilliant scientist and set up his own small laboratory. Working quietly and humbly in his spare time, he produced new theories of startling brilliance. His most important discovery was put forward in his Atomic Theory. This stated that all substances are made up of atoms and that the atom is the smallest piece of matter in the universe. Dalton was also the first man to discover and describe colour blindness (he was, himself, colour blind). Nowadays it is very important to test for colour blindness people wishing to go into certain jobs (e.g. airline pilots, ships' navigators, etc.). He lived very simply, earning money by giving private lessons in mathematics. If his country had not realized how important his work was, he would not have been able to continue with it. Fortunately for science he went on doing valuable experiments until he was an old man.

Antoine Lavoisier

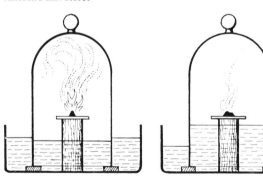

An experiment to show what air is made of

Antoine Lavoisier (1743–94) trained as a lawyer in his native France, but became greatly interested in chemistry and gave up law. He carried out chemical experiments in his spare time, always being very careful to check and weigh his chemicals. It was this carefulness which led him to make the first discoveries about the air we breathe. Scientists thought that whenever something burned it gave off a gas called *phlogiston*. If this was so, it would mean that what was left after burning would be lighter *and* that the air (containing phlogiston) would be heavier. Lavoisier tested this idea by burning some phosphorus inside a bell-jar over water. As the phosphorus burned, water was drawn up into the jar. After the experiment the substance left (phosphoric oxide) was *heavier* than the phosphorus. These facts proved that *something* had gone *out* of the air *into* the phosphorus. This *something* he called oxygen. Thus began the study of air, and what it is made of.

Michael Faraday

Wherever an electric light is switched on, electric factory equipment is set working, a telephone rings, or an electric kettle boils, men owe a debt to Michael Faraday. Young Michael was another poor boy who longed to become a scientist and whose wish came true. He worked in a bookshop until one day, when he was 21, someone gave him a ticket to a lecture to be given by Sir Humphrey Davy, one of the leading scientists of the day. Michael was deeply interested as the great man spoke and showed his experiments. So excited was young Faraday that he wrote to Sir Humphrey afterwards and asked him for a job. He was in luck. Davy was looking for an assistant and chose the keen young bookseller. From his new master Faraday learned all he could and by 1827 he was ready to take up his first important position.

He had been making his own experiments for many years and had become particularly interested in the relationship between magnetism and electricity. For a long time men had been able to make a bar of metal magnetic by passing an electric current round it. Faraday wanted to know if he could reverse this process and make electricity from magnetism. By September 1831 he thought he could see how this might be done. The next two months were spent in great activity. On 28 October 1831 Faraday produced a simple machine which could produce electricity from a magnet. This was the first electric dynamo, a machine which could give a continuous and reliable electric current. Today enormous dynamos, driven by water power (this is what hydro-electric schemes are for) can provide enough electricity to give power and light to large cities. Michael Faraday was the founder of the age of electricity.

Charles Darwin

Charles Darwin was the son of a doctor. He had a good education and his father planned that Charles would follow in his own profession. But Charles showed little interest in medicine and so it was decided that he should enter the Church. This also failed to appeal to the young man. In fact he did not seem to know what he wanted to do. He was very interested in nature and filled notebooks with his drawings of animals and plants. But there did not seem to be much future in that. Then in 1831 Darwin was asked to go on a journey in the survey ship *Beagle* to South America and the Pacific Islands. Charles was

John Dalton

Though John Dalton (1766–1844) was a great scientist who made vitally important discoveries in chemistry and physics, he lived simply and devoted himself to teaching young children and continuing with his experiments. Fortunately, other scientists realized Dalton's greatness and persuaded the British government to pay him to continue his research. He was loved and respected by many.

Michael Faraday

Michael Faraday (1791–1867) was another humble man of science. Despite the fact that he performed over 16,000 experiments and gave the world electricity, he could write, 'I am no discoverer, but simply one of a vast crowd of workers ... who in the providence of God are ... appointed to show forth His mercy ... in conferring fresh benefits on His people.'

delighted at the thought of travel, of seeing new lands and of being able to record new specimens in his notebooks. The expedition set off at the end of 1831.

As Darwin made his detailed notes of all that he saw in South America, he began to be particularly interested in how things develop. He studied rocks, to discover how hills, valleys, coral reefs and islands had been formed. This led him to an interest in fossils (the remains of animals and plants which may be millions of years old and which are found beneath the surface of the ground). He decided that all living things (which are divided into groups or *species*) had developed over millions of years from very simple forms. During those years some species had died out and others had survived. All these ideas were in his mind when the *Beagle* returned to England in 1836.

Darwin worked at his new theories for over 20 years. Then, in 1859, he published them in what has become one of the most important books of recent times, *The Origin of Species*. Poor Darwin! The book met with angry criticism—some from other scientists and some from Church leaders, who claimed that Darwin's theory went against the Bible's account of the creation of the world in six days. Some Christians were particularly angry about Darwin's suggestion that man had developed from a kind of monkey. Darwin refused to argue with the Church leaders. Like all scientists, Darwin believed that he was bound to examine the world around him and record what he discovered. Gradually other scientists accepted Darwin's theory. In time even Church leaders accepted that *The Origin of Species* was not an attack on the Bible. When Charles Darwin died in 1882, people realized how much he had added to human knowledge. He was buried in the great Westminster Abbey in London. In a nearby tomb was the body of Sir Isaac Newton, buried over 150 years earlier. A great deal had happened to the scientific world in those 150 years.

The discoveries and inventions of these and other scientists have completely changed the way millions of people live. They have made possible the growth of industry, improved farming, the study of human and animal diseases, the provision of new kinds of power. We started this chapter by mentioning the growth of population. The branch of science which had the greatest effect on population was medicine. Thanks to discoveries made between 1700 and 1914, diseases can be cured

H.M.S. Beagle

Cartoon of Charles Darwin
This picture of Charles Darwin draws him with the body of an ape because he suggested in his book *The Origin of Species* that man developed from a kind of monkey. Darwin developed his theory of evolution after his journey around the world in 1831 in the ship *Beagle*. He made notes of the people, animals, birds and plants of many different countries.

that used to kill people. In Europe a hundred years ago the *average* age at which people died was about 30. Today the average age of death is 70. That means that many more people live much longer. This is largely due to medical science.

The Control of Disease

Two hundred years ago one of the most terrible diseases known to man was smallpox. It was terrible because there was no cure for it. Almost every year it broke out in some part of the world. Most of the people who caught it died. Those who survived were marked for life with unpleasant scars. In 1782, a young English doctor, Edward Jenner, heard from a peasant girl that people who caught cowpox (a cattle disease) never caught smallpox. This idea had been rejected by other doctors as superstition, but Jenner took it seriously. He devoted many of the next 14 years to making careful experiments and notes on both diseases. At last he thought he had the answer. But did he dare to try it out? The risks were very great. Then, on 14 May 1796, a girl came to see him suffering from cowpox. Jenner felt that he *had* to take this opportunity. Some

children were playing outside his window. He called one of them in. After removing some fluid from one of the girl's sores, Jenner made a scratch on the boy's arm and put some of the fluid into the cut (this process is called vaccination). The boy, of course, had a mild attack of cowpox a few days later. Now came the dangerous part. On 1 July Jenner injected some smallpox fluid into the same boy—enough to give him a bad attack of the deadly disease. During the next few days Jenner waited anxious and impatient. Every day he examined the boy. After two weeks it was clear that he was *not* going to get smallpox. Edward Jenner had found a form of vaccination which prevented smallpox. As soon as he made his discovery known, doctors all over the world wrote to ask for supplies of vaccine.

The simple country doctor became famous and had to hire three secretaries to deal with his letters. When he died in 1823 he had seen the killer disease, smallpox, brought under control in Europe and the United States of America and vaccination beginning to be practised in India, the West Indies, Indonesia and parts of Africa. Today vaccination against smallpox is a basic

People in London queue for vaccinations a hundred years ago

medical service in most countries and people are not allowed to travel outside their own country before they are vaccinated. Fifty years later Jenner's work was followed up by another great man of medicine, Louis Pasteur of France. It was he who discovered that many diseases are caused by tiny creatures known as *microbes* which are in the air around us and are passed through the air from sufferers to healthy people. Pasteur realized that Jenner's discovery of vaccination might be applied to other diseases. Now whole populations can be protected against diseases that were once regarded as 'killers'.

Improvements in Surgery

If you go into the operating theatre of a modern hospital you will find the doctors and nurses dressed in clean overalls. You will see them put rubber gloves over their hands before starting work. You will notice that they wash their hands very carefully and that they wear masks over their mouths. The instruments they use are kept in special heated containers. All these precautions are to make sure that no dirt or microbes reach the patient during the operation. The patient, too, is washed and wrapped in clean clothes. When he is brought into the room on a trolley he is already asleep, because he has been

An early surgical operation
Operations before the mid-nineteenth century were terrible ordeals. The patient was wide awake (unless he fainted with pain). The tools were crude and often dirty. 80% of patients died during or after operations.

A surgical operation in the mid-nineteenth century after Morton's and Lister's discoveries
Here is a picture of surgeons performing an operation a hundred years ago. One keeps the patient asleep (using Morton's discovery) while the other one works. The machine on the little table is Lister's antiseptic spray, which keeps the air around the wound clean. The instruments also are kept clean.

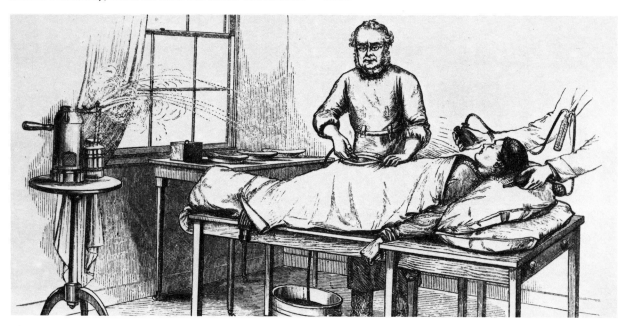

drugged. He does not wake up until the operation is all over. Surgical operations today are clean and safe. They save thousands of lives every year.

If you had watched an operation in, say, 1800, the scene would have been very different. The patient, very much awake, would be strapped to the table, the doctors standing around him in their everyday clothes. In fact, surgeons were very proud of their blood-stained, black coats and wore them everywhere. Because their patient was awake and would struggle, they had to work quickly and sometimes made mistakes. They never thought of washing their hands until *after* the operation — to remove the blood. They were very relieved — and even surprised — if their patient lived. For, even if a man survived the operation, he often died afterwards because dirt had got into the wound while the surgeons had been working.

William Morton and Joseph Lister

All this was changed by two men. William Morton was an American dentist. He knew that many people were unwilling to come to him with their bad teeth because they were afraid of the pain. After giving the problem a great deal of thought Morton discovered that, if he rubbed a liquid called ether on to a patient's gums, the patient could not feel the pain of a tooth being filled. But Morton was not satisfied. If ether could make *part* of the body 'go to sleep', could it do the same for the whole body? He decided he needed more training in pure medicine and became a medical student. When he watched a surgical operation for the first time he was horrified at the pain suffered by the patient. He went on in secret with experiments with ether, realizing that the results might be important for doctors as well as dentists. One day, Morton locked himself in his office, sat down in the dentist's chair and prepared to perform an experiment on himself — an experiment that could be dangerous. He soaked a handkerchief in ether and pressed it over his face. He immediately fell asleep. When he awoke eight minutes had passed. Morton was delighted. The very same day (30 September 1846) he used ether while removing a patient's bad tooth. A few days later the young dentist received permission from one of America's leading surgeons to try out his discovery during an operation. A very nervous William Morton arrived in the operating theatre on the appointed day. He had worked out a way of keeping the ether fumes flowing along a tube to the patient's face. With a crowd of medical students watching, the patient was put to sleep and felt no pain as Dr Warren operated on his neck. William Morton had removed pain from surgery.

Joseph Lister was a doctor who worked in a hospital in Scotland. He enjoyed his work, but found himself in disagreement with some of his colleagues. They believed that if a patient died after an operation it was because of something wrong with his body. Lister was convinced that fresh disease broke out because dirt got into the wound during the operation. His ideas were confirmed when he heard of Louis Pasteur's discovery of microbes, which carried disease through the air. Was there any way of killing microbes? This was what Lister asked himself. Then he heard of a new discovery called carbolic acid and decided to try it out. On 12 August 1865 he had to operate on a small boy who had been run over and who had a badly broken leg. This time Lister washed his hands and everything he used in carbolic acid. The boy recovered completely from the operation. Lister now went further and developed an instrument which sprayed the air around the wound with carbolic acid. His colleagues were unconvinced by Lister's 'new-fangled' ideas. But they had to take his ideas seriously when all his patients survived their operations and many of theirs did not. Soon doctors from all over Europe and the U.S.A. were visiting Joseph Lister and returning to their own countries to try out his discovery — with complete success. Long before his death, in 1912, Joseph Lister had become a famous and honoured doctor. He deserved his fame, for his discovery has saved millions of lives. Thanks to Lister surgical operations are now, not only painless, but safe.

In this chapter you have read about just *a few* of the men of science who lived between 1700 and 1914 and who helped to make the world a healthier, pleasanter and safer place. There were hundreds of others — some famous, others not so famous — who made their own contributions to human knowledge.

Now we must think about some other inventions and discoveries which changed farming and industry. We shall see that *they* were not all for the benefit of mankind.

Chapter 35 Industrial and Agrarian Revolutions

Small-scale industry before the factory age

Making thread and cloth in the early eighteenth century was a slow process. Most of the spinning was done by country women while their husbands were out in the fields. This picture shows spinning done in a poor farmer's cottage by his wife and daughter, while his old mother looks on. The thread was then sent to weavers who owned one or more large hand looms. Soon, however, men found how to use another source of power – water. They began to build textile mills or factories beside rivers and the water turned a large mill-wheel. This, in turn, worked machines which spun and stretched threads ready for weaving. These factories produced woollen, cotton or silk material, starting from the original fibre, and employed hundreds of people. But because they relied on water power they had to be built by rivers and this was a limitation. Not until steam power was applied to textile machinery did the factory age really begin. The picture opposite shows a textile factory of a later age. You can see that many people can work together in a small room, using the machinery to produce a very large quantity of material. Nowadays, all the work is done by machines, and one person can work hundreds of spinning frames or weaving machines.

A revolution is anything which makes great changes to the way people live. Nothing has changed the world more than the invention of machines and the discovery of new kinds of power. It is these developments that we call the Industrial Revolution. The Industrial Revolution began in Britain over two hundred years ago. By the middle of the nineteenth century it had spread to other European countries and the United States of America. By the early twentieth century Japan had joined the ranks of industrial nations. In the 1930s Soviet Russia became a powerful industrialized state. Today many nations in Africa, Asia and South America are experiencing *their* industrial revolutions.

A pumping engine in use at an English colliery

Steam Power

When water boils steam is driven off. If this steam is confined in a small space it develops a great pressure which may be strong enough to burst the container. Men had known about the power of steam for centuries. Over a hundred years before the birth of Christ a Greek inventor had used steam to operate a child's toy. But not until the end of the seventeenth century did anyone try to make serious use of steam power. In 1698, an Englishman by the name of Thomas Savery invented a steam-driven pump which would remove water from coal mines and enable the miners to work in greater safety. It was a start but Savery's engine had many faults. A great deal of the steam power was wasted and an enormous amount of coal was used to heat the water and provide the steam. Fourteen years later the steam pump was much improved by Thomas Newcomen and his 'atmospheric engine' (as he called it) was soon being used in mines in different parts of Britain.

But the *real* inventor of the steam engine was James Watt. He was a Scottish instrument maker. One day in 1763 he was asked to repair a model of Newcomen's engine. As he went about his work, Watt saw that, though the atmospheric engine was an improvement on Savery's pump, it still only used a fraction of the energy created by the steam. Watt gave much thought to the solving of this problem and, in 1769, produced an engine which worked better than anything so far invented and used less fuel. But Watt did not stop there. He continued to make improvements to his machine. Then, in 1781, with the help of Matthew Boulton, a businessman who provided him with money, James Watt adapted his steam

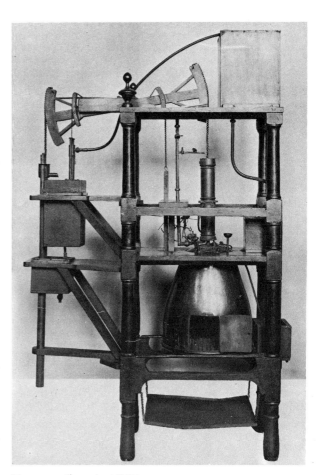
Newcomen's engine, 1717

engine so that it would turn a wheel or a shaft. *Now* steam power could be applied to any heavy piece of machinery.

The new steam engines were quickly made use of by the owners of textile factories. Cotton and woollen mills, which had before used water power, now changed to steam power. Now factories no longer needed to be beside rivers. Instead, new factories were built near the coalfields, so that fuel could be easily obtained for the steam engines. More and more factories and mills were built in the same areas and factory towns appeared. Each factory employed hundreds of people and so the owners hurriedly built houses for their workers. Thus industrial towns became crowded cities, where people lived and worked with the sound of rumbling, clattering machinery always in their ears and the smell of coal smoke always in their nostrils.

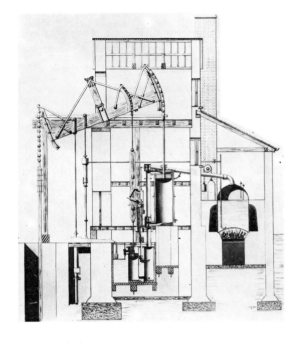

Boulton and Watt's pumping engine 1777. Right is a diagram of the sort of machine seen in use below for the Birmingham Canal Navigations. Watt settled in that city where the manufacture of steam engines was begun by the firm of Boulton and Watt. The former partner handled the business aspect and confidently left the inventive side to his colleague's genius.

Boulton and Watt's engine of 1788: above, a diagram of the engine seen in use below

Steam was used not only in factories; men found ways of making smaller steam engines that could be used to drive ships and locomotives.

Railways and Ships

No country can develop as an industrial nation if its transport system is poor. Large quantities of materials have to be taken to the factories and finished goods must be carried quickly and cheaply to the towns and harbours. In the early years of the Industrial Revolution the only way of carrying heavy goods over long distances seemed to be by water. In Britain, Europe and the U.S.A. men dug canals to link existing rivers and lakes so that cotton, iron, coal and other goods could be carried in long barges between the ports and the factory towns. Railway engines, like steam pumps, were first used in coal mines. They were used to carry the coal from the pit to the storage yards or the canals. But, by 1820, the possibilities of steam locomotives had been realized. In 1829 a competition was held in the north of England for the best railway engine suitable for goods and passenger transport. The prize was won by a locomotive called *Rocket* made by George Stephenson, which reached the astonishing speed (for those days) of 48 kilometres per hour. The railway age had arrived.

Now the world went mad about railways. The first railway in the U.S.A. was opened in 1831. Immediately more companies were founded to build railways which would 'open up' the western parts of North America (see Part IX, Chapter 40). Railways were built not only in the industrial nations. Europeans believed that this new form of transport would 'open up' to trade those parts of the world which were as yet largely unknown to white men. The following table shows the dates when the first railways were opened in various countries.

1829	Britain
1831	U.S.A.
1836	Canada
1837	Cuba
1838	Russia
1852	Egypt
1853	India
1855	Australia
1860	South Africa
1872	Japan
1875	China (destroyed almost immediately

The new versus the old

New methods of transport, like the train, were not accepted willingly by everyone. Owners of stage coaches tried to make their vehicles faster than the new railway trains. About 1850, most people in Europe and North America preferred to travel in coaches like the one shown above, but the new trains eventually proved more popular. Although they were smoky and noisy, they were more comfortable and faster and the limitations imposed by animal fatigue had been removed.

The *Rocket*, prize-winning engine designed by George Stephenson in 1829

205

on the orders of the Chinese government after
a man was killed by a train)

1877   Mexico
1879   Senegal
1898   Nigeria
1902   East Africa Protectorate (Kenya)

By the end of the nineteenth century there
were few countries in the world where railways
had not been introduced. They enabled the leading industrial nations to expand their trade very
rapidly. They enabled non-industrial regions to
be settled and developed quickly. They enabled
colonial powers to strengthen their control of
overseas territories and to take full advantage of
their resources.

The development of steam ships was slower,
but just as important. In the early years of the
nineteenth century, steamboats were built to be
used on rivers and canals. Many of them proved
to be very unpopular because the waves from
their paddles tore down the river banks. And
there were other problems. The engines and fuel
took up an enormous amount of space and so
made steamships unsuitable as cargo carriers.
Vibrations from engines and the paddles, which
were on either side of the ship, tended to loosen
the wooden planks of the ship's hull (or body).

The noise and smoke (and the fear of explosion)
made steamships unpopular with passengers.
But gradually shipbuilders overcame these problems. By 1840 steamships were sailing regularly
across the north Atlantic Ocean and around the
Mediterranean Sea.

In 1839 a centuries old shipbuilding tradition
was broken when the British East India Co.
bought its first *iron* ship. The opposition to this
new development was enormous. Ships had
always been made of wood, people argued. The
iron would rust away, they said. But as the years
went by the iron ships proved to be far more
suited to steam power than wooden ones. They
lasted longer and they gave less trouble. Later in
the century steel replaced iron as the best material for shipbuilding. A number of inventors tackled
the problem of engine space. In the 1850s side
paddles were replaced by the screw-propeller
which turned in the water at the back of the ship
and drove it forward. Engine improvements
continued until 1894 when Charles Parsons
demonstrated a launch driven by a steam machine
called a turbine. This was a much smaller engine
than anything yet produced and made better use
of the steam power developed in the boiler.
Parsons proved his new engine three years later
when his launch *Turbina* beat the fastest ships in
the British navy.

**New versus the old at sea: a clipper, and *The Great Western*,
a steamship designed by Isambard Kingdom Brunel.**
Sailing ships were improved to make them faster for long
journeys. The great *clippers* carried a large area of sail and
could travel very fast (the record was 584 kilometres in one
day) from China and India to Europe and the U.S.A. The
engines of the first steam ships took up much space that
might have been used for cargo. But as improvements were
made the new vessels were seen to be faster and more reliable
in all weathers. By the end of the nineteenth century there
were very few clippers in use.

Engineering

The Industrial Revolution created a new profession — engineering. Men had to design and build canals, ships and railways, bridges and better roads, factories and factory machines and, as time went by, large shops, office blocks and public buildings for the great new cities. The great engineering works of the nineteenth and early twentieth centuries would need a book all to themselves but there is one feat of engineering you should know about. Not only was it a great example of engineering; it has also changed the course of world history.

The Suez Canal

For centuries men had dreamed of linking the Indian Ocean and the Mediterranean Sea by means of a canal. Between the Mediterranean and the northern end of the Red Sea there lay a hundred and sixty kilometres of desert. This narrow strip of sand separated two of the world's great trading areas. Since no suitable overland route could be found for carrying cargo between East and West, ships travelling between Europe and the lands of India and the Far East had to make the long journey round Africa. Why had no one ever managed to build a canal? There had in fact been a canal link built by the ancient Egyptians. This joined the Red Sea and the Nile, but that had been blocked in the seventh century A.D. Engineers who thought about the problem of linking the Red Sea and the Mediterranean believed it was impossible because, they said, there was a difference in level between the two seas and water would flow rapidly along the canal.

In 1832 a man went to Egypt who was determined to achieve the impossible. He was Ferdinand de Lesseps and he was appointed French Vice-Consul. Throughout his time in Egypt he collected information about the Isthmus of Suez and began to work out how a canal could be built. But everyone laughed at his idea and it was not until 1854 that de Lesseps was able to make any progress. He persuaded Said Pasha, an old friend who had now become Viceroy of Egypt, to let him form a company which would build a canal. But it was one thing to form a company and quite another to persuade people to invest money in it. For five more years the scheme was held up by financial difficulties and arguments between the governments of France, Britain, Egypt and Turkey (the Sultan of Turkey was ruler of Egypt at that

Isambard Kingdom Brunel, an engineering genius

Saltash iron bridge

One of the greatest and certainly one of the strangest engineers of the nineteenth century was I. K. Brunel (1806–59). This small man had great imagination and enthusiasm. He designed many bridges for the new railway companies but his greatest was the iron bridge at Saltash. It was unusual in its time because of the large central spans and the engineering feat of sinking the support for the central pier 25 metres into the bed of the river.

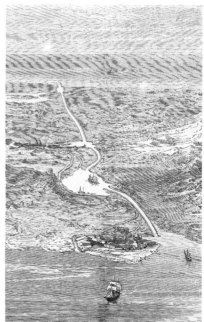

time). At last, in April 1859, work began. De Lesseps employed thousands of labourers from Egypt, Europe, Syria, Africa and Arabia. He brought steam-powered machines from France to help dig the canal and carry away the sand and rock. Had it not been for the machines, the work would have taken years longer than it did and would probably have proved impossible. But, thanks to steam power and the engineering genius of Ferdinand de Lesseps, the work was completed and, amidst great celebrations, the Suez Canal was opened by the Empress of France on 17 November 1869.

Immediately ships began to use the new route, which cut weeks off the old journey round the Cape. International trade developed even faster. European interest in Asia and in eastern Africa grew. The building of the Suez Canal encouraged the European search for colonies which took place in the closing years of the nineteenth century.

The Internal Combustion Engine
The nineteenth century was the age of steam power but before the century was over a new kind of power had been discovered which was to produce even more revolutionary changes in human life. The new discoveries had so far had little effect on road transport. Engineers had worked to improve many European roads. Inventors had produced a number of steam-driven

The Suez canal
The Suez canal provided a direct link between the European world and the Asian world. It joined the Red Sea to the Mediterranean Sea, running through dry, flat desert. On the right, you can see a 'bird's eye view' of the canal, and the left-hand picture shows men at work building the canal with huge steam-powered machines from France. Thousands of men were employed building the canal between 1859 and 1869.

Church's steam carriage

carriages but the size of the engines and the amount of fuel which had to be carried made them unsuitable for small vehicles. But while the horse and horse-drawn carriage remained the only means of travelling by road, other men were trying to make smaller engines and to find something other than steam to drive them. Then, in 1858 petroleum oil was discovered in the U.S.A. Immediately engineers were excited by this new fuel. It was in 1884 that a German, Gottlieb Daimler, produced the first *internal combustion engine* driven by petroleum (or petrol as we usually call it). Three years later he used his engine to drive the first motor car. Within twenty years the petrol engine was being used to drive cars, buses, lorries and aeroplanes.

Electricity

The other really great invention of the age was electric power. We have seen how Michael Faraday produced the first dynamo. By the end of the nineteenth century many European and American cities had electric light, electric trams and industries using electrical power.

Steam, petroleum oil, electricity—three new sources of power that made revolutionary changes to the way the world's people lived. More coal mines had to be dug to provide the fuel for steam engines. More iron and steel factories had to be built to provide the materials to build machines, railway engines, motor-cars, etc. Oil wells had to be drilled to provide petrol and oil for the new engines. This meant that the effects of the Industrial Revolution were felt all over the world. Europeans travelled to other countries to find oil, iron ore, cotton, copper and other raw materials. In this way people who had never heard of steam power and petrol engines found their lives changed by the Industrial Revolution.

Other effects of the Industrial Revolution

We have mentioned steam, electricity, engines, ships, iron, coal and steel, but we have said very little about people who lived during the Industrial Revolution. What was life like for the new factory workers? The simple answer is that life was very bad for them. As thousands of families came into the new towns from the countryside, the towns grew rapidly. Most of the houses were built quickly and badly by contractors only seeking a quick profit. They were overcrowded and without proper sanitation. Under these conditions diseases spread quickly and a serious

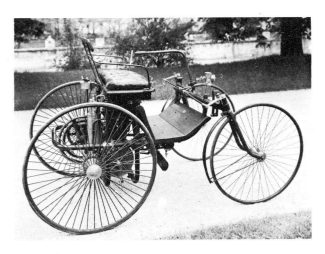

Daimler's first motor car
This was the first 'horseless carriage' (as the early motor cars were called). As you can see it was not a very comfortable vehicle. The wheels did not have rubber tyres and a journey by horseless carriage was very bumpy. Fortunately Daimler's motor car could not go faster than sixteen kilometres per hour.

A traffic jam in nineteenth century London
The towns in England quickly became overcrowded in the 1870s, as large numbers of families who could no longer find employment in the country moved to the towns.

epidemic might kill thousands of people in one town.

Conditions in the factories were no better. As well as the dirt and overcrowding (owners packed as many machines and workers as possible into their factories), there were the large, noisy and dangerous machines. There were no laws governing factory conditions (factory laws were gradually introduced during the nineteenth century) and it was quite common for workers to be seriously injured or even killed by getting caught in the machines. No law forced owners to put guards on dangerous machines or pay workmen for their injuries. Anybody unable to work simply lost his job – and that often meant that his family would starve. It was not only men who worked in the factories. Women and children were employed there also. They worked very long hours for very low wages, the factory owners being concerned only to make huge profits. This situation was particularly bad in Britain in the last century. It is worth noting that while many British politicians and businessmen were fighting hard against the African slave trade (see page 230), thousands of their fellow countrymen were enduring conditions even worse than those of the slaves. Of course, not all the factory workers were prepared to accept these conditions without protest. As we shall see in the next chapter, it was the European factory workers who supported important new movements such as trade unionism, socialism and communism.

Agrarian Revolution

All these changes taking place in the eighteenth and nineteenth centuries had their effect on farming. In 1700 most of the people of Europe lived by farming or working on other peoples farms. Farming methods had not changed for centuries. But the population increase meant that there were more people to be fed and so more food had to be grown. Farmers began to consider how their land could be worked more efficiently. So, by 1914 a *revolution* had occurred in farming just as one had occurred in industry, known as the Agrarian (or Land) Revolution. It brought about four major changes in the English way of life which will be considered individually.

Bigger Farms

First, there was the making of bigger farms. In the old days of the feudal system, every field was divided into strips and each peasant had his own

An industrial slum
Scenes like the one above are a grim warning to those countries which are experiencing their industrial revolution now.

210

strip to cultivate. This system was wasteful: it meant that several men had to work in each field; it meant that every man had to use the same methods and could not improve his farming; it meant that weeds from the strips of a bad farmer spread on to his neighbour's strips. The *enclosure movement* changed all this. Wealthy men bought up large areas of farmland and enclosed their new estates with hedges.

What did this mean for the old inhabitants of the land? Small farmers were bought out or forced off their land by the new men. Few of them could afford new farms because the price of land was rising. Some became hired labourers where before they had owned land. Some emigrated to the U.S.A., and the new colonies in Canada, South Africa (and later East Africa), Australia and New Zealand. Some moved to the towns to work in the new factories or to open their own small shops and businesses.

Things were much worse for the peasants. Whole villages were destroyed by estate owners seeking more farmland. While many families were given new homes and still employed by new farmers, there were many men who were no longer wanted. They had served the village in various ways—as shepherd, miller, blacksmith, etc. Now the village had gone, their work had gone too. The 'fortunate' villagers who were still employed were now completely dependent on the farmers. Before they had had their own strips of ploughland and a share of the village pasture. Their own crops and flocks had fed and clothed them. Now they had only their wages. Many peasants had also made money by weaving, spinning, basket-making and other home industries. As we have seen, the Industrial Revolution put a stop to these pastimes. So the farm labourers became poorer. In bad times, when the farmers were not making much money, the labourers' wages were reduced, or they were thrown out of work completely. It is not surprising therefore, that, during the nineteenth century, there was a large movement of people away from the countryside and into the dirty, crowded industrial towns—a movement of people seeking more money and a better life.

Improved Methods

Larger farms and the discoveries of some of the scientists made it possible for farmers to improve their methods. For the first time scientific stock (farm animal) breeding began as farmers tried

A planned working class housing estate
The picture on page 210 shows the bad condition in which many of Europe's industrial workers lived during the Industrial Revolution. As thousands of men moved with their families into the factory towns to find jobs, builders put up cheap houses for them to live in. The houses were small, crowded together, often with no running water or drainage. They soon became overcrowded, dirty hovels where disease spread rapidly. Such areas are known as *slums* and there are still many to be seen in cities of today. But a few employers cared very much about the living conditions of the workers, and built for them well-built, attractive houses, laid out with gardens and open spaces. Cadbury Brothers, the chocolate manufacturers, built the houses pictured above. Later generations of politicians began to plan the towns and built similar housing estates for working people.

Farm workers burning ricks of hay
In some areas, the bitterness and unhappiness of unemployed farm workers showed itself in violence and destruction.

211

to produce cows that would give more milk, cattle that would have more flesh on them, sheep that would yield more wool, and so on. In the nineteenth century the chemical scientists came to the aid of farmers by discovering fertilisers that would make crops grow better. Farmers' clubs were founded and farming magazines published so that landowners could exchange ideas about new methods. The whole farming industry began to change from the fairly simple occupation it was two hundred years ago into the highly complex profession it is today.

A horse-drawn plough used before the Agrarian Revolution

Machines

As time went by men realized that machines could be used in farming as well as industry. From the time of Jethro Tull's invention of the seed drill (1701) onwards, machines were introduced which did farm work efficiently and cut down the number of men needed on the farm. By 1914 steam-driven machines were in use for ploughing, threshing, harvesting, mowing and a variety of other jobs.

An early harvesting machine, the Johnson reaper and binder

Food Preservation

Farmers will only produce more food if they know they can sell it. For many years sale of farm produce was limited because it could not be preserved very long. Meat and vegetables begin to go bad very quickly if they are exposed to the air. In 1839 some American businessmen developed a canning process. They found that if food is heated, then stored in air-tight tins, it will last for years without going bad. It was also Americans who developed *refrigeration*. This means keeping food (especially meat) at very low temperatures and is another way of stopping food from going bad. By the end of the nineteenth century the U.S.A. was exporting large quantities of meat in special refrigerated containers. These two discoveries, canning and refrigeration, greatly encouraged all kinds of farming.

A modern Massey-Ferguson harvesting machine
The invention of farming machinery made ploughing and harvesting quicker and used less men on the land, thus freeing manpower for the new industries.

Chapter 36 Political Revolutions

The years 1700 to 1914 were an age of revolutions in science, industry and in agriculture. They were also years of political revolution. Like the other revolutions, this kind of revolution also began in Europe. In 1700 nearly all the countries of Europe were controlled by kings and emperors whose powers were almost unlimited. In most countries also a system of feudalism existed. Feudalism meant that the peasants were under the control of powerful nobles and landlords and had few rights of their own. The kings relied on the nobles for advice and support. The lower levels of society had no political representation. In this kind of political and social system there was little to prevent the kings and their ministers doing just what they wanted. But there were some countries, such as Britain and Holland, where the position of the rulers had been challenged and where the kings had been forced to give up some of their powers to the representatives of the people in parliament.

The English Civil War 1640–1649

During the Renaissance and Reformation of the sixteenth century many Englishmen had learned to think for themselves in a new way. They no longer accepted everything they were told by the Church and the government. The English middle classes, made up of farmers, merchants and gentlemen, were better educated than they had been in the past and they wanted more share in the running of the country. They were represented in the House of Commons, one of the two parts of the English Parliament, and the House of Commons was discussing more and more matters that had always previously been decided by the king and his ministers. As you can imagine, relations between king and parliament grew worse and worse.

Trouble really broke out soon after Charles I

The beheading of King Charles I of England
In 1649 the people of England, led by their members of parliament, executed their king. This happened after England had been divided by civil war for many years. (They claimed that Charles was a tyrant and a traitor to his country.) Among the acts they objected to were Charles's attempts to change the religion of England and to collect taxes without the consent of parliament. This was the first time in modern history that a people had risen against their ruler in defence of political freedom and parliamentary government. Kings and queens of England since that time have had far less power than Charles I. From England the new political ideas spread to Europe and North America where other revolutions occurred.

213

came to the throne in 1625. He claimed to rule by *divine right*. That means he believed that God had chosen him to rule England and that, therefore, anybody who opposed him (King Charles) was sinning against God. Charles began to collect taxes from the people without the consent of Parliament. Many people believed that he also wanted to make England a Roman Catholic country again (as it had been before the Reformation). In 1640 Parliament raised an army to fight the King and make him rule constitutionally (i.e. with and through Parliament). The country was divided between those who supported King Charles and those who supported Parliament. A country gentleman called Oliver Cromwell eventually became the leader of the parliamentary forces. Civil war raged on and off for the next eight years. There were struggles not only between the King and Parliament but also between Parliament and Cromwell's army (the Roundheads) and between the Roundheads and the Scots. In 1648 Cromwell and his followers were finally victorious. In January 1649 King Charles I was tried, found guilty of treason against the people, and executed. A republic was formed in England and a few years later Oliver Cromwell became its ruler under the title of Lord Protector.

The Republic lasted only eleven years; Cromwell never won the support of the majority of the English people. He believed that the country should be ruled by 'godly' men who would make the people live 'virtuous' lives. In Cromwell's opinion a 'virtuous' life involved not going to theatres and sports meetings, not enjoying music or dancing, having very few holidays and not even celebrating Christmas. It is not surprising that very few Englishmen accepted Cromwell's ideas about 'virtue' and 'godliness'. Most of the people who had supported Charles I could not accept the idea of England without a king and looked on Cromwell as a tyrant, who had no right to rule. Cromwell even had trouble from some of his own supporters. In any revolution there are always some revolutionaries who want to go farther than others. Cromwell found that he had to control the extremists on his own side. Some of them, called *Levellers*, wanted all Englishmen to have the vote. Cromwell knew that the result of this would be a parliament over which he had little control so he gave orders that the Levellers should be suppressed. (It was almost

Charles I on horseback

Oliver Cromwell

From this picture of King Charles I of England, you can form quite a good idea of the sort of man he was. He believed God had given him the heavy responsibility of ruling England. This made him determined to rule firmly. His enemies thought of him as stubborn and proud. He did not think of himself as an ordinary man. Even just before his death he could say, 'A subject and a sovereign are completely different things.' Oliver Cromwell, who led the opposition to Charles I, was an ordinary English farmer. He was not proud of himself or his position. When an artist arrived to paint his picture, Cromwell said to him, 'Paint my picture exactly like me, and do not flatter* me at all, but show all these wrinkles, pimples, warts, and everything as you see me, otherwise I will never pay a farthing for it.' You can see that the artist did as he was told.

---

*Portrait painters of those days used to leave out of their pictures or hide any marks or scars on the faces of the great men and women they painted.

another 300 years before the idea of 'one man, one vote' was fully accepted in Britain.) Oliver Cromwell became so unpopular that when he died in 1658 very few people were sorry. After his death disputes again broke out between Parliament and the army until at last, in 1660, the late king's son, who was in exile in Europe, was invited to return to England as King Charles II. Large crowds of happy and relieved Englishmen cheered him all the way along the road to London.

What had the Civil War achieved? Though Britain once more had a king his powers were greatly limited. He had to rule through parliament. He could make no laws and demand no taxes without the consent of parliament. Parliament could discuss all matters that affected the country. This meant that England now had a *constitutional monarchy.* Any king who, in future, might want to interfere with the rights of the English people would remember the fate of Charles I and would change his mind. But England was still not a democracy because only a minority of the people (the wealthy landowners) could elect members of parliament and have a say in the country's government.

Meanwhile things were even worse in some other European countries than they had been in England under Charles I. Feudalism had almost died out in England but on the Continent most of the peasants were completely dependent on landlords for whom they had to work and who had almost complete power over their lives. During the eighteenth century writers and philosophers began to write about political freedom and to demand that the ruling classes should give up some of their powers. Other men and women decided to make their protest in a different way. They left their countries and emigrated to North America to start a new life away from the oppression of bad governments.

Revolution in North America

Most of the North American colonies were owned by Britain, though France and Spain had territory there also. In the 'New World', as it was called, the settlers had a hard life, making farms out of rough ground, building their own houses, protecting themselves from Red Indians, bringing up their children in primitive surroundings. But at least they were free to plan their own lives and set up their own forms of local government. Or, at least,

Charles II arriving in England from exile
Many Englishmen went to welcome Charles II as their king when he arrived in England in 1660. Only eleven years before he had been forced to flee to Europe to save his life, and his father had been executed as a tyrant. But most English people detested the Republican government, and were delighted to have a king again.

Importation of wives for the Jamestown Settlers
On account of the lack of women in the colony. In 1620 ninety young women were induced to seek husbands and their fortunes in Virginia. The following spring sixty others landed at the settlement and became the wives of the pioneers.

215

they were *fairly* free. As you will see in Part IX the English colonists grew tired of having some of their affairs controlled from London and in 1776 they declared themselves independent of British rule. This led to a war between Britain and the North American colonists, which ended in 1783, when the British were forced to recognize the independence of the United States of America.

The French Revolution

The success of the American colonists inspired other freedom-lovers in Europe. It was only a few years later, in 1789, that the first great political revolt of modern times broke out. This was the French Revolution. For years France had suffered from bad government and the oppression of the poor by the rich. The peasants were under the complete feudal control of the landlords. Both they and the tradespeople were very heavily taxed. Central and local government was corrupt and inefficient. Much of the enormous amount of money paid in taxes never reached the treasury; it was stolen by dishonest officials. The Church was very rich and paid little tax. Most of its leaders were wealthy, well-fed men with large houses, many servants, carriages, horses and dogs for hunting. Few of them were devoted to religion. The rich aristocrats paid no taxes at all and lived in great luxury. They had almost complete control over the lower classes of society. If a man offended an aristocrat he might find himself awoken by soldiers in the middle of the night. The soldiers would be carrying a *lettre de cachet*—a 'sealed letter' from the king authorizing the poor man to be put in prison. Once in prison he might stay there for years—or until he died. Most of the king's ministers were from the aristocracy.

There *was* a parliament in France. It was called the States General and the middle classes were represented on it. But by 1789 the States General had not met for 175 years! It was the well-educated members of the middle classes — lawyers, teachers, doctors, etc.—who were most angry about the situation in France. They wanted to see their country better governed. They read books by men such as Voltaire and Rousseau, who criticized the government. They formed secret clubs to discuss political problems.

In 1789 the leaders of the middle classes had their chance to tell the government what they wanted. The King was heavily in debt. His

Rousseau

Voltaire

Two Frenchmen who did a great deal to spread new political ideas were J. J. Rousseau (1712–1778) and Voltaire (1694–1778). Rousseau said 'Man is born free, but is everywhere in chains' (bound by bad government and laws). He suggested new democratic forms of government in his great book *The Social Contract*. Voltaire attacked and made fun of kings, nobles and government officials in his books and plays. The ideas of these men spread rapidly among the educated classes and helped to bring about the French Revolution.

216

ministers realized that they could not obtain enough money to run the country without changing the taxation system to include the nobles and the Church leaders. They thought that the middle classes would gladly support such a change so they advised the King to call a meeting of the States General. So, the States General *did* meet. Immediately the representatives of the middle classes demanded an end to many things that were wrong in France. They demanded that the King should rule through a parliament which would meet regularly. The government began to consider these demands.

While the politicians talked the poor people of Paris acted. Poverty and hunger had already made them angry and desperate. Now, popular leaders stirred them to revolution by telling them that the government was collapsing and that the King would have to give the people what they wanted. On 14 July they attacked and captured the great royal prison, known as the Bastille. Similar revolts now occurred all over France. From this point onwards the moderate people, who wanted only to get rid of certain grievances and set up a constitutional monarchy, were overruled by the extremists and revolutionaries who wanted to destroy completely the old government and social system.

Unfortunately the revolutionaries found it easier to destroy the old France than to build a new France. They executed Louis XVI and some members of his family. They overthrew royal government. They killed thousands of members of noble families. They destroyed the power of the Church. But different revolutionary governments rose and fell while poverty, suffering and administrative confusion grew worse. Other countries, fearing that the revolution might spread, made war on France and the horrors of warfare were added to the people's sufferings. As the years went by real power passed into the hands of fewer and fewer people. By 1802 one man had become the real ruler of France. His name was Napoleon Bonaparte. In 1804 he named himself Emperor. Once more France was ruled by a royal dictator.

Had the revolution been a failure? It had not brought France democratic government. It *had* brought France years of bloodshed and suffering. It provided the opportunity for mob rule* and

*Extremists who have the support of violent crowds of people. The leaders of the larger and more moderate sections of the population find it difficult to stand up to such men.

The Storming of the Bastille
On 14 July 1789 the people of Paris attacked the royal prison known as the Bastille. After several hours of fighting they captured the great fortress. This event began the French Revolution. In France 14 July is still kept as a holiday.

The execution of Louis XVI
In 1793 the leaders of the revolution executed King Louis and other members of the royal family. They used the guillotine, which claimed thousands of lives during the worst days of the revolution, known as 'The Reign of Terror'.

217

violence. It involved France in foreign wars. But it did put an end to many old evils. It gave France a fairer system of taxation. It ended the privileges of the nobles and Church leaders. It ended feudalism. It gave the middle classes a greater share in the running of the country and this, in turn, encouraged trade and industry. It reformed the administration, made all men equal before the law and provided education and other social benefits for the people.

Napoleon Bonaparte

The men who planned the Revolution were idealists (i.e. they believed in 'ideals' or principles such as 'freedom', 'equality', 'brotherhood', 'justice'). Idealists do not usually make good leaders. That is why the various revolutionary governments between 1789 and 1802 collapsed and there were long periods of political chaos. It needed a strong and determined man like Napoleon to rule France firmly and give it good government. Napoleon Bonaparte was one of the greatest generals in the history of the world. He led French armies for nineteen years and lost very few battles during that time. No one was better than he at moving large armies quickly over long distances. He was quite pitiless. He was responsible for the deaths of millions of soldiers. At one time he left a defeated army in Egypt while he escaped home to France.

Napoleon did a great deal for France but he also nearly ruined the country. He established firm government. He reformed the law and the education system. But he did not give France what she most needed – peace. He continued the wars against other European states. Though he won many great victories he exhausted his country. So many French soldiers had died that Napoleon had to fight some of his last battles with boys of fourteen. In 1814 he was defeated. The countries he had conquered were given their freedom, a new king, Louis XVIII, was placed on the French throne and Napoleon himself was sent to exile on the tiny island of Elba, off the coast of Italy. In 1815 he escaped, raised another army and tried to regain control of France but he was defeated at the Battle of

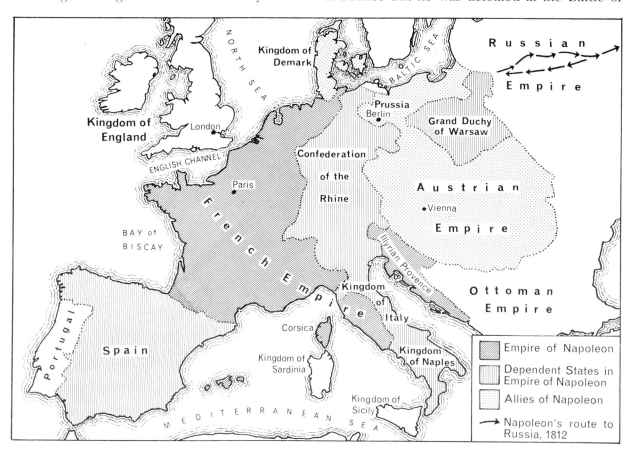

The French Empire under Napoleon

Waterloo. This time he was sent to the Atlantic island of St Helena far off the coast of West Africa. He died there in 1821.

Revolutions in Germany and Austria

Europe had not seen the end of revolutions. The ideals which had inspired the French revolutionaries were spreading to other lands. When the leading politicians met at Vienna, the capital of Austria, in 1814–15, to redraw the map of Europe, they tried to arrange things as they had been before Napoleon began his conquests. This meant that the German peoples were divided into nearly 40 small states, most of them under the control of Austria. Italy, too, was split into a number of small kingdoms and dukedoms and here also Austria had a great deal of influence. The large Austrian Empire contained people of many different races and nationalities. Nearly all the states of Europe were controlled by absolute monarchs (i.e. kings whose political power was unlimited) and still had some kind of feudal system.

Throughout Europe peasants, tradespeople, teachers, lawyers and many others who did not belong to the ruling classes were dissatisfied. They wanted the changes that had been made in France to be made in their own country. They wanted parliaments and representative government; they also wanted freedom from foreign control. Germans, Poles, Hungarians, Italians, Czechs — all wanted their own national states. Political clubs were formed, meetings and demonstrations were held, nationalist newspapers were printed in secret, and from time to time there were riots and disturbances. In 1830 and 1848 there were serious revolutions all over Europe. Though they were eventually suppressed by the authorities they did achieve a great deal. By the middle of the century feudalism had almost disappeared from Europe and many states had their own parliaments.

Bismarck and Germany

One reason why the European revolutions did not succeed completely was that they were organized by idealists. As in France, so in other

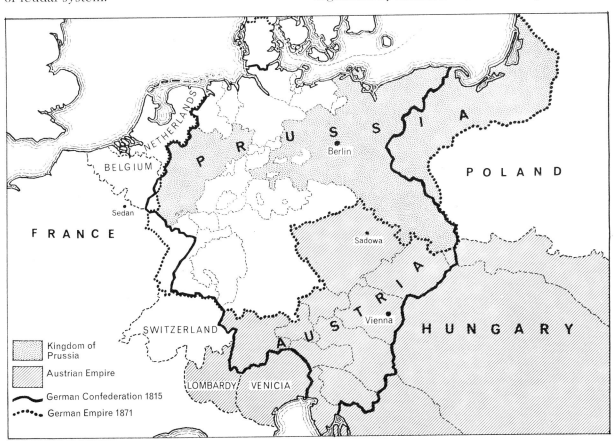

Germany, 1814–71

countries it took strong men to create independent, well-governed modern nations. The man who freed the German states from Austrian control and made them into one nation was Otto von Bismarck. He came from the German state of Prussia and was a keen nationalist. He hated Austria and wanted to see Germany united under Prussian leadership. He was not an idealist. He laughed at men who thought they could unite Germany by setting up parliaments and trying to get the states to agree to work together. He knew that only determined action and war — 'blood and iron', as he called it — would create a Germany free of Austrian control.

Bismarck as chief minister of Prussia spent years building up the best army in Europe. Also, he deliberately started wars which he knew would bring other German states to Prussia's aid. In 1866 at the Battle of Sadowa Prussia completely defeated an Austrian army. From that time onward the north German states were firmly united and Austrian control of Germany came to an end. But the states of southern Germany were still independent of Prussia. In 1870 Bismarck tricked France into declaring war on Prussia. He persuaded all the German states that the French wanted to conquer Germany. So they naturally sent troops to help Prussia. France was quickly defeated (the main battle was fought at Sedan) and in 1871 all the German states united to form the German Empire. As we shall see later, this empire was to be responsible for starting two world wars.

Otto von Bismarck, Prussian chief minister

The Unification of Italy
As a result of a revolution in 1848, Piedmont, one of the Italian states, broke free of Austrian influence. The king agreed to a liberal constitution being set up which included an elected parliament. From then on Piedmont, and particularly its Prime Minister, Cavour, worked to unite all the Italian states under a similar liberal constitution. Cavour had to struggle not only against Austria, which controlled Venetia and Lombardy, but also the Pope, who governed the Papal States, and the other Italian rulers, who were only kept in power by Austrian influence.

Cavour encouraged nationalist movements throughout Italy and also sought the help of other countries, such as France, Prussia and Britain. In 1859 France helped Piedmont in a war against Austria. As a result Lombardy was

The battle of Sedan in the Franco-Prussian war

220

conquered and four other states revolted against their rulers to ally themselves with Piedmont. In 1860 the Kingdom of the Two Sicilies revolted under the leadership of a fine soldier, Garibaldi. In the same year Cavour invaded the Papal States, all of which, except Rome, fell to Piedmontese forces. In 1866 Piedmont helped Prussia in her successful war with Austria and, as a result, Venetia was handed over to the new Italian nation. Now Italy was united and had an elected parliament, meeting in Turin, the capital of Piedmont. Only one thing was missing: Rome, the ancient capital city of the Italian people, was a separate state ruled by the Pope. It was protected by French troops. When France was weakened by the war with Prussia (1870–1) the soldiers were withdrawn and the Pope was forced to hand over his last remaining province to the Italian government.

These were only the more important political revolutions which took place during the nineteenth century. By 1900 most countries of Europe had a parliamentary system of government and their citizens of all classes had many if not all the same rights and privileges. But not all European countries were fully democratic. Democracy means that everyone, by electing members of parliament, has some say in the way the country is run. Democracy aims to create a society in which everyone has freedom and opportunity to improve his standard of living. In many European states the lower classes of society were not represented in parliament. Nineteenth century revolutions had mostly extended political power to the middle classes; especially the businessmen and traders (who are sometimes referred to as the *bourgeoisie*.)

Socialism

This is one reason why Socialism developed in the last quarter of the nineteenth century. It appealed to the under-privileged lower classes. Socialism goes farther than democracy. It says that democracy is not enough. In a democracy rich people will still be able to take unfair advantage of poor people. Socialists wanted to see industry, business and agriculture run, not by individuals, but by the government. This would mean that all workers were working for themselves, since all the profits of business, industry and farming could be spent on schools, medical services and other things for the people. As democracy developed it gradually destroyed

The unification of Italy

Garibaldi, Italian nationalist

221

At the hustings in early nineteenth century England
Political power in England in the early nineteenth century was still in the hands of the middle and upper classes. Only people who owned land could vote. There was no such thing as a secret ballot. The candidates for election stood on a platform called the 'hustings' and voting was by show of hands. As you can imagine, this system led to a great deal of bribery and violence, candidates paying or forcing men to vote for them. The secret ballot was introduced in Britain in 1872. Throughout the nineteenth century more and more people were allowed to vote, but full democracy took a long time to arrive. Only in 1931 did all the people over 21 years of age gain the right to vote. The picture above, from a humorous book of the time, makes fun of nineteenth century elections.

the political power of the wealthy. Socialism tried to break their economic power.

By 1914 Socialism had had little success in the western world (i.e. western Europe and North America). It was naturally resisted by businessmen, factory owners and farmers. But various forms of democracy were established in almost all the countries of Europe and North America. It was in countries like Russia and China where democracy had been rejected by the government, that Socialism gained ground. When the revolutions came in these countries it was not democracy that was established, but forms of Socialism.

The Spread of Political Ideas
As Europeans and Americans in the eighteenth and nineteenth centuries travelled abroad they

222

took their political ideas with them. Leaders of other states were interested to hear about the different kinds of government in foreign countries. The Japanese, who were anxious to modernize their country, deliberately abolished feudalism and introduced parliamentary government. When European nations invaded and colonized countries in Asia and Africa they exploited the land and people for their own profit and for many years allowed the local people no say in government. But, at the same time, they were teaching the conquered peoples western ideas—including ideas about parliamentary democracy. A hundred and fifty years after 1789, Indians, Kenyans, Nigerians and other colonial peoples were demanding the same political freedoms that the French had fought for in their revolution.

A Kenyan voter records his choice in a modern election
The elderly gentleman voting in this picture may well have been born before the British colonial government gained control of Kenya. In his lifetime, he has seen the change from tribal government, to colonial rule, to the introduction of democracy and Independence. Although Kenyan Africans fought against British rule, they learned from their colonial rulers western democratic ideas; for example, the ballot box seen here, a way of making voting secret.

Part VIII   European Conquest and Colonization
Chapter 37   The Old Colonial System

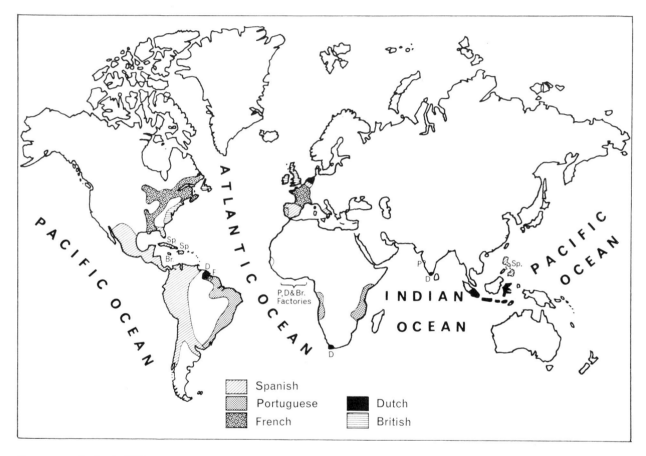

European colonies in 1700

The European voyages of discovery of the fifteenth, sixteenth and seventeenth centuries meant that once new lands had been discovered by explorers, enterprising groups of their countrymen could go out to settle—to farm, mine or trade.

Home governments and monarchs encouraged these emigrants to live in what became known as colonies; the reasons for this encouragement were both economic and territorial. The prime

motivation lay in a policy called mercantilism which functioned as the Old Colonial System.

At the time European kings believed that they could make their nations rich and powerful by trade. To do this they had to sell more goods to other countries than they bought (in other words, exports had to be worth more than imports). The difference in value between imports and exports would have to be made up with money (or gold and silver bars) and the country would therefore

This page

(Left) The shrine of the thunder god Shango as reproduced in the Museum of Mankind. Shango hurls his thunderbolts to earth, killing those who offend him. To prevent this, sacrifices are made to the god symbolized by prehistoric stone axeheads, which can be seen in the bowls. The leather bags at the top of the picture are part of the equipment of every priest of Shango.

(Above right) The Olduvai Gorge, formed by rivers cutting into a plateau surface of northern Tanzania, under wetter conditions. The main river and its tributaries have exposed rocks from the level of this bright red upper sandstone down to where, near the valley bottom, Dr and Mrs Leakey uncovered the remains of prehistoric Man.

Opposite page

(Above left) An example of Roman sculpture; a marble figure in the peristyle of the House of the Vettii, Pompeii, named after the two rich merchants who had it built.

(Above right) Colossal statues of Ramesses II, one of the great pharaoh's of Egypt's New Kingdom, flank the columns in the first court at Luxor.

(Below) The Via dell'Abbondanza was Pompeii's longest street, and at 9.2 metres it was wider than most. The stepping stones helped pedestrians to cross from one raised footpath to the other, and also to keep their feet dry.

(Overleaf) Maasai tribesmen, wearing simple red garments and carrying knobkerries and spears, reflect the wandering life of the huntsmen on the Kenya savannahs living little differently from their forefathers thousands of years ago.

(Right) A wooden drinking cup from which beer made from maize was drunk.

(Below) Here are the remains of the Inca city of Machu Picchu built some 500 years ago. It is situated between two mountain peaks on a saddle of land high above the Uru-bamba Valley in Peru. The town is divided by a *plaza* or central meeting place.

(Right) A totem pole and house of coastal Indians re-erected near the University of British Columbia, Vancouver.

(Below) A Canadian timber-built church from an early settlement in the St Lawrence Valley. Its style, derived from contemporary European architecture, is typical of the American north-east.

(Top left) Worship can take place anywhere. All a Moslem needs is a prayer mat. In large mosques there are three officials: a *muezzin* to call the people to prayer, an *imam* to lead the recital of prayers and a *khatib* to preach.

(Top right) Mosques like this one in Damascus, Syria, are richly ornamented. While there are no pictures or statues, or images of any sort, artists have covered the walls with beautiful mosaic designs and Arabic texts from the Qur'an. A niche called a *mihrab*, set in one wall, shows the direction of Mecca towards which the congregation must prostrate themselves during prayer.

(Below) *Id al fitr — the little feast* marks the end of the month-long fast of Ramadan. Before the feasting begins, a large congregation of men have put on fresh clothes and gathered to say their prayers outside a mosque in Northern Nigeria.

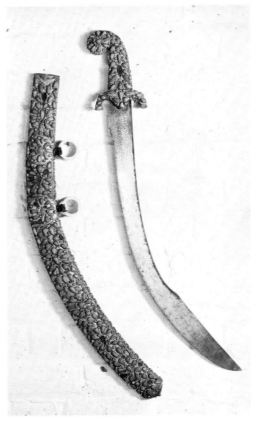

This page
(Top) The bar at the front of this Persian helmet can be let down to cover the face. Decoration is partly in gold.

(Bottom) Pieces of coral and coloured stones decorate the hilt and scabbard of this Egyptian sword.

(Overleaf) This manuscript now in the British Museum, depicts Persian warriors of 500 years ago. Some use matchlocks; others carry bows and arrows in cases fixed to their saddles. Other weapons include curved-bladed swords and round shields.

(Opposite) This is one of the huge statues made of brick-
work and covered with glazed tiles which guard the several
entrances through the galleries surrounding the Wat Phra
Keo, one of Thailand's royal temples.

(Above) The absolute serenity of Buddha; this figure lies in a
Ceylonese temple.

Opposite page
(Above) The surroundings to each Chinese tomb were designed very much as a small palace. This pavilion is in fact a
hall of sacrifice for the Emperor Yung-lo's tomb.

(Below) A bronze figure of a galloping or flying horse is
poised on the back of a swallow. It is from the Eastern Han
dynasty and was found in 1969 in a general's tomb in Kansu
Province.

Opposite page
(Above) Leading from the entrance of the valley containing the tombs of the Chinese emperors of the Ming Dynasty (A.D. 1368–1644) situated thirty miles from Peking, is the Spirit Way with its avenue of huge stone figures. There are 36: 24 animals and 12 humans; they face inwards, some to guard the dead emperor as he went by, others to scare away enemies and evil spirits.

(Below) The Theological College of the Mother of the Shah in Isfahan, Persia, was built at the expense of the mother of Shah Sultan Husein between A.D. 1706–14 as a training college for theological students.

This page
The Mosque of Shaikh Lutfullah, in Isfahan, completed in A.D. 1619. The exterior has magnificent tile-work and stalactite decoration, and the interior consists of one large, octagonal chamber with mosaic tiles of 'incredible richness'.

(Above Left) A Hindu temple in India. These are usually lavishly adorned with carved images which are frequently painted. Token offerings of food, money and prayers are made individually to the Brahmin priest. Some temples are dedicated to Vishnu, the Preserver, or Siva, the Destroyer, but all Hindu gods work as one with Brahman, the Eternal Power, controlling the universe.

(Below Left) Pilgrimages to holy places are undertaken by all castes. Benares, on the holy river Ganges, sees thousands of pilgrims every day, to cleanse and purify themselves. They bathe from the ghats or steps along its bank.

(Above) Castel del Monte, the massive Norman fortress in south-east Italy, built to overlook the fertile, but vulnerable coastal plains.

(Below) Here at Chipping Norton, in England, is one of the few remaining woollen mills — a worsted factory set in a dry valley, typical of the many which dissect the gentle dip-slope of the Cotswolds.

become rich. Let us take an example. Suppose Britain exported to Holland cotton, sugar and wool, worth £500,000. Suppose Britain imported from Holland wine, woollen cloth and spices, worth £250,000. Then Holland would have to pay Britain the difference (£250,000) in gold or silver. It was the object of mercantilism to accumulate gold in this way.

Mercantilism led to the Old Colonial System. Colonies were founded for two reasons. First of all they had to supply raw materials and goods to the mother country. From the East Indies the Dutch obtained spices. From East Africa the Portuguese carried ivory. In South America the Spaniards found gold and silver. In the West Indies British colonists grew sugar. There was great rivalry between the European nations to trade with foreign countries, so each colonial power tried to control very strictly the trade with its colonies. For example, in the seventeenth century the British parliament passed a number of Navigation Acts. These stated that all trade between England and her colonies must be carried on by English or colonial ships. The most valuable colonial products must not be taken to countries outside the British Empire.

The second reason for the foundation of colonies was that, as they developed, they would become important importers of goods. For instance the British government encouraged the development of colonies in North America not only so that Britain could obtain cotton, tobacco and other goods from them. The government realized that the colonists would need pots and pans, tools and guns, clothing and household goods. Since imports to the colonies were strictly controlled by the Navigation Acts, Britain would have a ready-made market in North America.

By 1700 the Old Colonial System was at its height. Although some of the colonial powers had already begun to sink because of competition with European rivals, Portugal, Spain, Holland, Britain and France all had valuable empires. Opposite is a map showing the more important overseas possessions of these countries.

The Americas

Because most of Europe's leading nations were looking for colonies there was much rivalry between them. This rivalry sometimes led to war. There were many examples of this in the Americas, the region that Europeans called the 'New World'. In the middle of the seventeenth century

---

African slaves working a sugar mill in the West Indies
Slavery and colonialism went together. As soon as Europeans realized the money that could be made from the production of sugar, rum and tobacco in the Americas they took over the land and brought slaves from West Africa to work on the plantations. Here you see negro slaves working a sugar mill.

England and Holland were at war. As a result of England's victory the Dutch lost their settlements on the North American coast. As you know, this made it possible for the British colonies of New York, New Jersey and Pennsylvania to be founded.

But the British possessions in the Americas were very small compared with those of other countries. Spain controlled Florida, Central America, Cuba and other West Indian islands as well as a large part of South America. Other settlements in the West Indies and along the coast of South America belonged to Holland, France and Britain. France also claimed a large inland territory in North America. This was known as New France and included the basins of (the areas drained by) the rivers Mississippi and St Lawrence and the regions around the Great Lakes (Canada).

There were two main reasons why this situation might lead to war. The first was trade. The produce of this whole region was very valuable in Europe. High prices were paid for sugar, cotton, molasses, tobacco, ginger and indigo. You may already know something of the extremely profitable 'triangular trade' between Europe, Africa and the Americas – a trade which included slaves on the terrible 'middle passage'. Many men made fortunes out of trade with the Americas and they all wanted to increase their profits. This led to battles between rival settlements, to piracy and to attempts to take over control of important areas.

These rivalries were sometimes partial causes of European wars. One of the reasons why Britain fought in the War of the Spanish Succession (1702–13) was her fear that France would gain control of Spain's overseas territories. At the end of the war Britain gained territory in Canada and the right to trade in slaves with Spain's West Indian settlements.

The Seven Years War, 1756–1763

The other cause of war was the conflict between French and British settlers in North America. The presence of French citizens in Canada and along the river Mississippi made it impossible for the British to settle farther inland. The French began to attack British settlements, sometimes with the aid of Red Indian warriors. In 1756 Britain and France went to war. There were several reasons for this but trade rivalry (mainly in North America and India) was one. The English

Prime Minister, William Pitt, was determined to make his country the world's leading colonial and naval power. Late in the war Spain joined in on the side of France but the two powers were unable to defeat Britain. After seven years of war a peace treaty was signed which gave the British almost all that Pitt had hoped for. The French left Canada, gave up important West Indian possessions to Britain and acknowledged British supremacy in India (you can read about the Seven Years War in India in Part XII). Spain yielded Florida to Britain.

The East Indies and Africa

The discovery of sea routes from Europe to the East had led in the fifteenth and sixteenth centuries to great rivalry between the Portuguese, Dutch, French and British for control of trade with the East Indies (known as the Spice Islands) and India. Ships of the different nations attacked each other at sea and there was a scramble for ownership of trading posts along the coasts of Africa and Asia and island bases in the Atlantic and Pacific Oceans. The Portuguese grew gradually weaker and only maintained colonies and factories on the east and west coasts of Africa, at Goa in India and Macao in China. The British and French fought for control of India and by 1763 the British had defeated their rivals.

The British did not find the Dutch so easy to defeat. By the middle of the seventeenth century the Dutch had made it quite clear that they intended to keep control of the valuable spice trade with the East Indies. They made their headquarters on the island of Java and set up bases on other islands and on the mainland. The British East India Company lost many ships in battles with the Dutch and at last decided not to try to set up trading posts farther east than India.

Wolfe at Quebec

One of the most famous events in the history of warfare took place during the Seven Years War. It was the capture of the French stronghold at Quebec by an English force under the leadership of General Wolfe. Several attempts to take the town had already failed when Wolfe decided on a bold and dangerous plan. He and his men were rowed at night to the foot of the cliffs near Quebec. These cliffs, known as the Heights of Abraham, were so steep that the French believed no one could climb them. But the English did climb them and were able to make a surprise attack on the French headquarters next day. During the battle both Wolfe and the French general, Montcalm, another fine soldier, were killed. The English captured Quebec and, in so doing, gained control of Canada.

In 1652 the Dutch established a small settlement at Cape Town on the southern tip of Africa. It was founded as a port of call for Dutch ships travelling to and from the East. But soon stories reached Holland about this warm, pleasant land which was healthy for Europeans and where familiar crops could be grown. More and more Dutchmen travelled to Cape Town and the settlement grew into a colony. As they moved farther and farther inland the Europeans found a fertile country occupied only by a few Bushmen or Hottentot hunters, whom they drove out, killed or enslaved. The Dutchmen (or Boers or Afrikaners, as they later called themselves) wanted to found large farms; every Boer aimed to build his farmhouse where he could not see the smoke from his neighbour's chimney. It is not surprising, therefore, that by the end of the eighteenth century Cape Town had grown into Cape Colony and covered thousands of square miles of southern Africa.

At the end of the eighteenth century Europe's nations were once more plunged into war as a result of the French Revolution and the activities of the French dictator, Napoleon Bonaparte. Because of this the colonial situation changed again. When Napoleon was defeated France lost still more territory (all island bases) to Britain while Holland was forced to give Cape Colony to the British. (Britain wanted Cape Colony to guard the sea route to India but another reason was provided by the increasing number of Englishmen who were settling in South Africa as farmers.)

By 1815, when the European wars ended and the continent began to enjoy half a century of peace, the colonial struggle between various European powers, which had lasted for over 300 years, was temporarily over. Britain had emerged as the leading colonial nation. She had colonies and trading posts right round the world and the centre of her overseas empire was India. By comparison the French, Dutch, Spanish and Portuguese empires were much smaller, though still valuable to their founder-nations.

Decline of the Old Colonial System
But the colonial system which existed in 1815

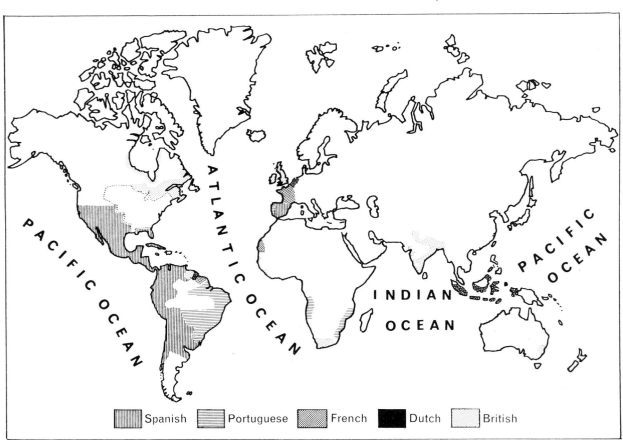

Spanish   Portuguese   French   Dutch   British

European colonies in 1815

was no longer the Old Colonial System. It is true that European governments continued to keep overseas colonies but some of those governments no longer thought about their colonies in the same way. They no longer believed that colonies existed only for the benefit of the mother country. Why was this? There were two main reasons. One was that a number of colonies had already begun to assert their own rights. The other reason was the new political ideas in Europe which we considered in Part VII.

Revolutions

In 1776 the thirteen North American colonies declared themselves independent of Britain (see Part III). Britain fought hard to keep control of this important part of her overseas empire but by 1783 she had to admit defeat. So the United States of America was born. Settlers in other parts of the world felt much the same way as the Americans. They felt love and respect for their old home countries but did not want to be controlled by them. At the beginning of the nineteenth century Spanish and Portuguese colonists in South America gained their independence.

Changing Political Ideas

You have already seen how new political and religious ideas led to revolutions and new forms of government in some European countries. These ideas also led to changes in the colonies. First there was the belief in political freedom. Settlers in the overseas colonies refused to be completely controlled from Europe. The American colonies set up their own assemblies, or governments, and when parliament in London refused to take any notice of them, they declared themselves independent. Similarly, settlers in Australia, South Africa, New Zealand and Canada demanded and gained an increasing amount of self-government. It was not only people in the colonies who felt like this: many Europeans believed that the colonists had a right to govern themselves. As you know, the Old Colonial System depended on the colonies being controlled by the mother country. The System could not work if the overseas territories became independent or semi-independent. In the mid-nineteenth century a famous British statesman suggested that Britain should get rid of some of her territories. He said: 'These wretched colonies will all be independent in a few years and they are millstones round our necks.' But this

Simon Bolivar

During the years of the Old Colonial System much of South America had been overrun by Spanish and Portuguese conquerors. At the beginning of the nineteenth century the peoples of South America began to revolt against colonial rule. The man who did more than anyone else to free his country was Simon Bolivar. He was a Spaniard, born in what is now Venezuela. In 1811 he began to fight for the independence of Spanish American colonies. In spite of frequent defeats he fought on, and in 1819 he overthrew Spanish rule in north-western South America. Afterwards he helped Panama and Peru gain their independence. By 1828 almost all of South and Central America, including the ex-Portuguese Colony of Brazil, was independent. Bolivar hoped to see the new republics join together in a federation rather like the United States of America. Though this was never achieved, Simon Bolivar is still remembered as *the Liberator of South America.*

independence was only for the European settlers. It did not include the Red Indians in America, the Aborigines in Australia, or the Bantu and Bushmen of South Africa.

The Anti-Slavery Movement

The second new idea which helped to kill the Old Colonial System was the idea that slavery and slave trading were wrong. Political thinkers argued that if some men were free, then *all* men must be free, whatever their race and colour. Some sections of the Christian Church, particul-

229

arly the Quakers and Methodists, began to teach that slavery was against the will of God. A number of wealthy Englishmen got together to take action against slavery and slave trading. The leaders of the group were Granville Sharp, William Wilberforce and Thomas Clarkson. In 1772 they fought a legal action in the English courts as a result of which slavery was declared illegal in England, but this did not stop British subjects trading in slaves to the colonies.

During the early years of the nineteenth century the leading nations of Europe all made slave trading illegal. Denmark was the first country to take action (slave trading in Danish colonies became illegal in 1802). In 1807 Britain made the slave trade illegal and by 1830 all former slave-trading nations had done the same. At the Congress of Vienna in 1815 the European states agreed to do all in their power to stop illegal slave trading. In fact most of the work was left to Britain, and British naval patrols sailed along the East and West coasts of Africa trying to capture ships carrying slaves.

For although the slave trade had become illegal, it still went on. The reason for this was that *slavery* itself had not been stopped in European colonies. Since slaves were still wanted and fetched a high price, traders continued to bring them from Africa to the plantations.

In 1823 the British Anti-Slavery Society was formed and the men who had fought against the slave trade now fought against slavery. Some of the newly-independent states of South and Central America abolished slavery during the 1820s. Britain ended slavery in her colonies in 1833. Gradually the other colonial powers did the same. Where slavery existed it was an important part of a country's economy. In many areas abolition met with angry opposition. In North America it led to civil war between the states supporting and the states opposing slavery (see Part III). In South Africa it led to wars between the Boer settlers and the British. Some colonial powers (e.g. Belgium and Portugal) continued to practise slavery in their African colonies but they called it by a different name in order to disguise it. The illegal slave trade continued until the very end of the nineteenth century. But gradually the two great evils of slavery and slave trading died out. Long before they did so the Old Colonial System which had depended largely on a good supply of slaves had come to an end.

A fashionable lady in the eighteenth century with her blackamore slave

Nearly all African slaves were bought by European traders for use on agricultural plantations in the Americas or on African coastal islands. But some were taken back to Europe. Here you see a rich English lady with her African slave — known as a 'blackamoor'. English ladies thought it amusing and fashionable to be attended by African boys. Yet slavery was not officially recognized in England where people were proud of their freedom. In 1772 the opponents of slavery took legal action against a man who had beaten his negro slave. This was a very important case because the judge, Lord Mansfield, decided that by English law when a slave sets foot in Britain, he immediately becomes free. From that moment there was no more slavery in Britain.

Chapter 38 A New Kind of Colonialism

By 1815 Britain and Russia were the only countries which still had large empires. In the following years both these powers gradually added to their colonial territory. Russia (see Part X) expanded eastwards and southwards into Asia and the Middle East. Britain took possession of a number of islands and coastal regions in and around the Pacific Ocean. The other European nations showed almost no interest in colonialism for over half a century. In 1830 France conquered Algeria but it was very many years before France added to her territory and began to form a large African empire. Between 1815 and 1870 the European nations were too concerned with their own affairs — political revolutions, industrial development, etc. — to spare much thought for the rest of the world.

The Second British Empire
Only one European country enjoyed both peace and wealth in the nineteenth century, Great Britain. As you know, Britain led the way in the industrial and agrarian revolutions and this led to a great increase in trade. British engineers could make railway engines and machines that men in other countries did not know how to make. British mills produced cloth which was better and cheaper than that made in other countries. It is not surprising that Britain became the world's leading trading nation. But not everyone in Britain shared in this wealth, as we have seen. There was a great deal of poverty and unemployment. Many men felt they had no chance of a decent life in Britain and began to wonder whether conditions would be better abroad.

It was the growth of trade and emigration which led to the founding of the second British empire. More than ever British merchants needed supplies of raw materials and markets for their goods. Settlers looked for areas where the climate and

'The White Man's Burden'
One of the reasons (or excuses) given by European nations for colonizing other countries was the responsibility of the white man to civilize the 'backward peoples' of the world. This responsibility was sometimes referred to as 'the white man's burden'. This cartoon shows what some American and European people thought of this idea. It shows figures representing the U.S.A., Britain, Germany and France being carried by colonial peoples. In reality the native populations were being exploited physically through slavery and financially through the removal of their lands' natural resources.

conditions would enable them to live comfortably and farm profitably. In the middle years of the century three colonial areas were developed: Canada, South Africa and Australasia (Australia and New Zealand).

231

Canada

By 1832 there were over 50,000 British men and women emigrating to Canada every year. The main problem in the colony was the unfriendly relations between British and French settlers (many Frenchmen had stayed on in Canada after the Seven Years' War). Another problem was that of representative government. Like the American colonists, the people of Canada began to complain that they were too strictly controlled by the government in London. These difficulties led to riots in 1837. An important moment of choice had come for the British government. Should it try to force the colonists to remain loyal to Britain and risk another war of independence? Or should it grant the Canadians' demand for representative government? If self-government were granted, would Canada drift away from Britain completely and become just like any other foreign nation?

The government decided to send a representative to Canada to study the situation carefully. They chose Lord Durham. Lord Durham went to Canada, returned, and made his report in 1839. The Durham Report is one of the most important documents in the long history of imperialism. It recommended a large degree of self-government for Canada and stated that Canadians should be free to develop for themselves the kind of government most suited to their needs. This worked so well that it was later applied in Australia, New Zealand, South Africa and other colonies. It meant that instead of the countries of the empire splitting up and becoming completely separate states, they became, in time, independent member states of the British Commonwealth of Nations. In 1867 Canada became a 'dominion'. That means that Canada still recognized the monarch of Britain as Head of State but was otherwise completely independent.

Australia

You will remember that Europeans knew very little about Australia. Captain James Cook explored the fertile eastern side of the continent between 1768 and 1771. Even then it was of little interest to Europe until the British government decided that it would be a good place to which to send criminals because British prisons were becoming crowded. So in 1788 in the south-east corner of Australia, known as New South Wales, a penal settlement (a settlement for punishing

A penal settlement in New South Wales, Australia
Initially such places had a predominantly convict population with a few overseers and a governor responsible to the British government.

prisoners) was opened. Not surprisingly this was not a very auspicious start for a colony and life was hard. Soon, however, free settlers began to arrive. In 1794 sheep farming began and the colony began to grow rich by exporting wool. Other settlers went to open up new areas of Australia and by the middle of the nineteenth century several colonies were flourishing. In 1850 the British government gave the Australian colonies complete self-government. In the very next year gold was discovered in Victoria and there was another rush of settlers to Australia. It was not until 1901 that the various colonies united to form the Commonwealth of Australia.

New Zealand

In spite of visits by Abel Tasman, Captain Cook and other sailors in the seventeenth and eighteenth centuries, New Zealand was almost completely ignored by Europe for many years. The British government—the only government likely to be interested in colonizing New Zealand—did not want to add another country to its empire. The British had no desire to interfere with the people of the islands, the Maoris, who were a fine warrior race. But groups of Europeans went to New Zealand as traders and settlers and by the 1830s there was serious trouble between the Maoris and the newcomers. Meanwhile in England the government was being urged to take over New Zealand as a new settlement area for British emigrants. Gibbon Wakefield (who was a firm believer in imperialism) formed the New Zealand Association and threatened to found an unofficial settlement in New Zealand if the British government did not act. But only when they learned that France was planning to colonize part of the country did Britain's leaders formally claim New Zealand (1840).

The development of New Zealand was rapid. The climate was well suited to European settlement and soon flocks of fine sheep and healthy herds of cattle were grazing the hills and valleys of the new colony. But what of the Maoris? When they agreed to British settlement they had no idea of the number of foreigners who would be coming to their country. Soon there were arguments about land, and arguments led to war. The war lasted for five years. The Maoris fought bravely but at last had to accept the rule of the white man. When the fighting was over they quickly adapted themselves to European ways and settled down to become equal partners in New Zealand's new way of life. So peaceful and prosperous was the country by 1852 that Britain was able to grant the colony self-government. In 1907 New Zealand became a dominion, like Canada.

South Africa
From 1820 there was a mixed white population of Dutch and British settlers in South Africa.

Emigration
Earlier on it was stated that the increase in population was the most important factor in modern history. It was one reason for the continuance of colonization. Growing population led to increased poverty and unemployment in Europe. Many people believed their only chance of a better life lay in emigrating — especially to new colonies such as Australia and New Zealand. This picture from a British magazine of 1848 shows the contrast (as people imagined it) between the conditions of a poor family in England and the conditions of that same family living as free farmers in one of the colonies. Special emigration societies were founded by men like Gibbon Wakefield, who was largely responsible for the settlement of New Zealand.

The Great Trek

When Britain abolished slavery throughout her empire in 1833, the people who opposed it most strongly were the Boers of Cape Colony. Rather than give up what they believed were their 'rights' to dominate the Africans, they moved north out of Cape Colony across the Orange river. This movement was known as the Great Trek. It brought the Boers into fresh conflict with other groups of Africans and it did not rid them of British control. There were to be conflicts between the British and the Boers right up until the end of the nineteenth century.

There was always trouble between the two groups. Their ways of life were different and so were their attitudes towards Africans. When, in 1833, the British abolished slavery, many of the Boers decided they would not stay any longer in British territory and they moved northwards, first across the Orange river and later across the Vaal river. But the British would not allow the Boers to form independent states based on slavery. They claimed control over the new Boer lands. This led to a series of conflicts between the two groups which lasted the rest of the century. Whichever side won or lost a particular dispute or battle, it was always the African peoples who came off worst. In most other areas where Europeans had settled in large numbers there were few local people to stand in their way. As the British and Boers pushed farther and farther into Africa they came up against the Zulus and other Bantu peoples. Thousands of Africans died resisting the white men and some groups were almost completely destroyed.

Britain's determination to rule the whole of South Africa became stronger after the discovery of diamonds and gold in the Boer areas (1867 and 1886). In 1899 the South African War (sometimes known as the Second Boer War) broke out. It was a final struggle between two different kinds of colonialism: the Boer idea of complete white domination and the British idea of responsibility for the development of all races and eventual equality of black and white. The British won (1902) but were generous to the Boers, after a few years allowing them self-government. The result was that relations between the two groups improved and in 1910 the various states came together in the Union of South Africa, another dominion within the British Empire.

These four 'white' dominions (together with India, see Part XII) were the heart of the second British Empire. Though they were almost entirely independent of Britain they had very close ties with the mother country. This was shown most clearly during the First World War. When Britain was fighting for her life against Germany all the dominions sent soldiers, money and goods to her aid.

The New Imperialism
By 1880, then, Britain was the only nation with a large overseas empire and most of that empire consisted of self-governing states. Most European statesmen disliked the idea of taking over

The Battle of Omdurman, 1898

No picture could show more clearly the spirit of the new imperialism which inspired many Europeans in the last quarter of the nineteenth century. In 1898 the British (who already controlled Egypt) decided to conquer the Sudan. They fought their way southwards and nothing could stop them. Here you see them fighting against a Sudanese army at Omdurman.

new colonies which would have to be ruled directly from the home country. Such colonies were too expensive to maintain. They were prepared to encourage traders to do business in Asia and Africa, but that was all.

But about 1880 a new 'imperial age' began in Europe and within a few years the leading nations were rushing to gain new colonial territory wherever they possibly could — mostly in Africa.

One reason was commercial. By 1870 the nations of Europe had overcome most of their own problems and were beginning to share with Britain a time of peace and industrial growth. As their industries grew these countries began to look for new trading areas. British merchants in Asia and Africa suddenly found themselves faced with French and German rivals. This rivalry sometimes led to clashes. Occasionally the merchants would ask their governments for help.

Another reason we may call social. There was a growing interest in the few remaining areas of the world unknown to Europeans. These areas were mostly found in Africa and South-East Asia. More and more explorers, missionaries and travellers visited these lands as the nineteenth century went on. They regarded the people of these lands as 'backward', 'uncivilized', because they were not Christians and were not technically as advanced as Europeans. Some men began to put forward the idea that it was the white man's responsibility to 'civilize' the peoples of Africa and Asia. This responsibility became known as 'the white man's burden'.

But the most important reason was nationalism. During the nineteenth century two new European nations — Germany and Italy — were created. The Germans and Italians were very proud of their countries and eager to show the world their new-found strength. The French people, too, were very proud. France had once had a great colonial empire but had lost it because of her eighteenth century wars with Britain. Now, many Frenchmen believed that the time had come to show French greatness by building up a second empire.

Thus, between 1880 and 1914 the leading nations of Europe took part in a 'scramble' for colonial territory. By 1914 entire new empires had been created and most of the people of Africa, South-East Africa and the Pacific Islands found themselves under European rule.

Part IX America, the Birth of a Democracy
Chapter 39 Independence

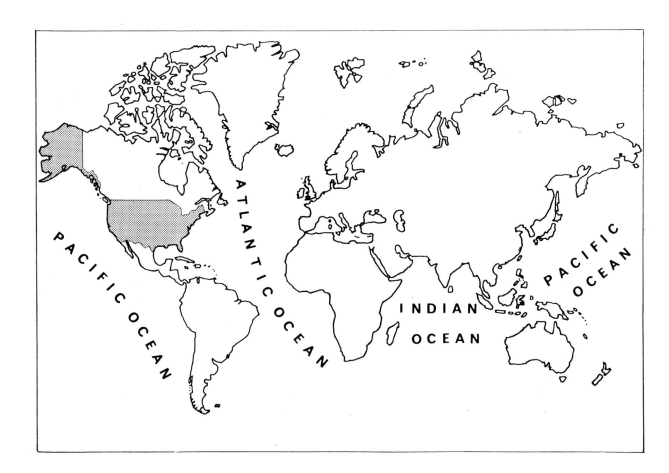

4 July 1776 is one of the most important dates in all history. On that day one of the world's leading nations, the United States of America, was born. This is how it happened.

The Thirteen Colonies and Britain, 1763–75
The settlers in the thirteen colonies along the eastern American seaboard were mostly British. They spoke the same language as people in England, they thought in much the same way. But they (or their ancestors) had deliberately left Britain to start a new life. Some of them, whose families had been in North America for perhaps as much as a hundred years, no longer felt very attached to their old country. They were beginning to think of themselves not as British subjects, but as Americans. Of course, they had been very happy to be protected by British soldiers during the Seven Years War, but now that there was no more danger of French interference, they wanted the British government to leave them alone to manage their own affairs.

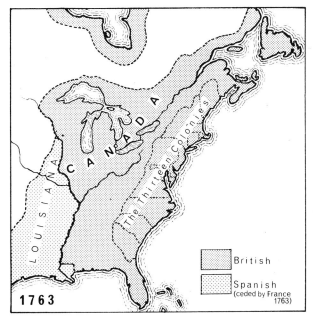

European settlements in North America

As we saw in Part II, after the Seven Years War Britain controlled most of the eastern part of North America. The rest of the continent was largely unknown to Europeans at that time. With the French out of the way the British government looked forward to being able to exploit their American colonies fully. But, as you will see in this chapter, the settlers of the thirteen colonies had other ideas.

The British government did not take the same view. The Seven Years War had cost them a great deal of money and they thought it only right that the colonists should pay taxes to Britain to help pay for the war. They also believed that colonies existed chiefly for the benefit of the mother country (Britain). So, they controlled North American trade to make sure the colonists did not buy or sell goods to other countries. They also controlled American industry to make sure that the colonists did not compete with British manufacturers. They found the growing independence of the Americans very annoying and tried, by imposing taxes and laws and by appointing governors who would rule firmly over the colonies, to control them from London.

But London was 3,000 miles away. The rulers of England who made decisions about the colonies had never been to North America and did not understand the situation there. Naturally, the colonists objected to having their lives controlled by these far-distant ministers. Above all they resented not being consulted about the laws that affected them and the taxes they had to pay. These matters were decided in the British parliament and the colonists were not represented

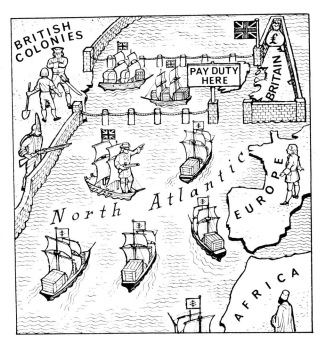

England controls all trade with the American colonies

The American colonists were expected to trade with Britain first. The Navigation Acts had been passed by the British Government to control trade with all other countries. By this means Britain made a profit on everything the Americans bought or sold.

237

Boston Tea Party

The incident shown here is known as the *Boston Tea Party*. The American colonists resented paying import taxes on goods which came from Britain or other British colonies. In 1773, to show what they thought of taxes on tea, a group of Americans, disguised as Red Indians, boarded a tea ship in Boston harbour. They seized the tea chests and flung them into the sea. This was one among many acts of defiance which led to the American War of Independence.

there. Their attitude was summed up in the phrase 'No taxation without representation', which meant that they would not pay taxes which they had not had a share in deciding.

The American colonists strongly resisted the attempts of the British government to control their way of life. They were so firm in their resistance that they managed to make the British leaders change their minds. Between 1766 and 1773 all the taxes which had been imposed on the thirteen colonies were removed – except one. Just to show that Britain had the *right* to tax her colonies, the Americans were required to pay a duty on all imported tea. But the determined colonists would not compromise. 'No taxation without representation' was their motto and they stuck to it. So when loads of tea arrived from British plantations in India they refused to buy it. In several places chests of tea were broken open and their contents scattered, while at Boston there occurred the famous *Boston Tea Party*.

The English King, George III, was furious. He ordered Boston port to be closed and British soldiers to see that all resistance was stamped out. This was not the first time the British had tried to enforce their will on the colonists at gunpoint. In 1770 blood had been shed when troops in Boston fired on a crowd of Americans, killing several. This *Boston Massacre* had not frightened the citizens into submission. They resisted all the more. As the number of British soldiers increased, so tension in the town and surrounding countryside mounted.

Lexington: the beginning of the American War of Independence

The event that sparked off war came in April 1775. General Cade, the British commander, heard that the colonists had been gathering a supply of arms at Concord, near Boston. He decided to make a night march to Concord to capture the weapons. But the people of the countryside around were warned of his approach and turned out to block his path. A small battle was fought at Lexington in which men on both sides were killed. The British were forced to withdraw. The thirteen colonies now recognized they would have to unite to resist the British. The British realized they would have to send a bigger army to force the Americans to submit. Thus the skirmish at Lexington became the first battle of the American War of Independence.

The Continental Congress and the Declaration of Independence

In September 1774 the colonists had begun to organize themselves for resistance. They called a meeting in the town of Philadelphia, which was attended by representatives of 12 colonies. This first Continental Congress agreed to resist taxation imposed by Britain, but did not even consider the possibility of breaking away from the mother country. But by the time the second Continental Congress met in May 1775, blood had been shed at Lexington and the delegates agreed to form an army to enable them to resist the British more effectively. By now a number of delegates were demanding complete independence from Britain. After long discussion, argument and careful planning, the great Declaration of Independence was signed by representatives of the territories which no longer called themselves 'colonies' but 'states of the Union'. The Declaration was more than a document which announced America's independence: it set out the principles on which the new nation should be governed. It stated, '... all men are born equal, ... they are endowed by their Creator with certain unalienable rights ... among these are Life, Liberty, and the pursuit of Happiness.' It said that it was the government's job to defend these rights, that the people must have a share in government (i.e. by elected representation) and that if a government failed in its duty it was the right of the people to abolish it. Such were the democratic ideals established by the founders of the United States of America for themselves.

George Washington

The man chosen to lead the American army was George Washington. The new general came from an old settler family in Virginia. He had already fought in wars against the French and Red Indians and was an experienced soldier. He was a brave man and an excellent commander. He never despaired and his courage and confidence in-

Paul Revere's Ride
On the night of 18 April 1775, the British troops set out to make a surprise raid on Concord to capture the colonists' supply of arms and ammunition. An American, Paul Revere, got to hear of the attack and rode hard through the night to warn the farmers and villagers to be ready to meet the British. Paul Revere's ride has become a favourite story in the U.S.A. and became the subject of a poem by the great American poet Longfellow:
'... A hurry of hoofs in a village street,
 A shape in the moonlight, a bulk in the dark,
 And beneath, from the pebbles, in passing, a spark
 Struck out by a steed flying fearless and fleet;
 That was all! And yet through the gloom and the light,
 The fate of a nation was riding that night ...
 So through the night rode Paul Revere.'

Signing the Declaration of Independence
On 4 July 1776 the Declaration of Independence was signed by the delegates of the Continental Congress. The Declaration had been drafted by a young lawyer, Thomas Jefferson (2nd row, first on the left). The man in spectacles in the front row is Benjamin Franklin, another American famous as a scientist and politician. The first man to sign was the President of the Congress, John Hancock of Massachusetts. He wrote his name in large letters so that 'George III might read it without his spectacles'.

spired his countrymen even when the war seemed to be going against them.

The American War of Independence

The British generals were facing a very hard task in trying to reconquer America. This was not like any other war they had known. If they could have faced their enemy in a few major battles, they would probably have won easily. Instead they met only small American forces, which disappeared into the hills and woods the moment a battle turned against them. The colonists spent most of their time attacking small groups of British soldiers and stealing or destroying British supplies. The British would have needed a large army to control the American colonies

The American War of Independence

and this they never had. So the war dragged on.

The British made three main attempts to reconquer their colonies. The first attempt, in 1775, was to subdue the northern colonies (New England) where the trouble had begun. Here, General Gage found it quite impossible to bring the people under control. In 1776 Gage was replaced by General Howe. He decided to attack the 'middle states' of New Jersey, Delaware, Maryland and Virginia with a much larger army. He captured New York and defeated Washington's army at Brandywine. He marched into Philadelphia and the members of the Continental Congress had to leave the town hurriedly. The British plan was for Howe's army to link up with another under the leadership of General Burgoyne. But Burgoyne had not enjoyed the same success as General Howe. Marching south from Montreal he had defeated all American opposition until he had to go through the thick forests of New York State. There the colonists successfully cut off his supplies and forced him to surrender at Saratoga.

The third British attack was launched against the southern states in 1779. The army sailed to Charleston, South Carolina. Under the leadership of General Cornwallis, the British crushed American resistance in South Carolina, North Carolina and Virginia before retiring to Yorktown. In spite of their lack of overall success, the British could have gone on fighting for a long time if it had not been for another circumstance. They were dependent on getting supplies by sea. In 1778–9, France and Spain, still angry over their defeat in the Seven Years War, sent their navies to help the American freedom fighters. This was the turning point in the war. By 1780 France had control of American coastal waters and the British army's links with England were cut. Cornwallis's force in Yorktown held out until October 1781. Then it was forced to surrender to Washington's invading army. This was the end of British military action and the war was really over.

The Treaty of Versailles 1783

It was not until 1783 that peace was formally made between Britain and America. Then at Versailles, in France, a treaty was signed by all the nations involved in the war. By this treaty Great Britain accepted the complete independence of the United States of America. A new nation was born.

Chapter 40 The New Nation Grows

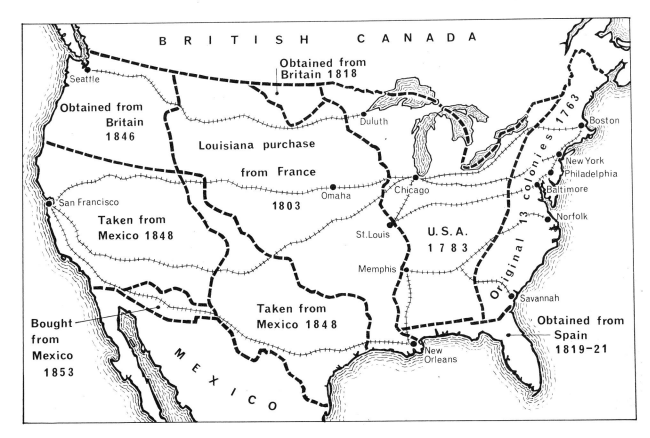

America spreads westwards

After the War of Independence the Americans occupied only a small area of eastern North America. By war, agreement and purchase they gradually extended their territory towards the Pacific Ocean. Railways (or, as Americans call them, 'railroads') were soon built to carry new settlers and supplies to the 'Mid-West' and the 'West'. By the middle of the nineteenth century, the United States of America had almost reached its present-day limits.

The American Constitution

The United States of America was a recognized nation in 1783 but it was not until 1789 that it became a united nation in fact. This apparent contradiction came about in the following way. In 1776 thirteen British colonies had banded together to obtain their independence from Britain. From then on they became thirteen American states united against a common enemy. After the war they had to organize themselves as a united nation *without* a common enemy. At once differences and disagreements appeared. Some Americans believed that there should be one strong central government (a *federal* government) representing all the states. This body would make all the important decisions. Others believed that the rights of individual states were more important. It is always difficult for states or tribes or kingdoms to band together into a federation. Each state has to give up some of its rights and powers to a central government which is by no means easy to achieve.

Representatives of the thirteen American states met together at Philadelphia in 1787 to make a federal constitution. They argued about import and export duties between states, they argued about money (each state had been making its own coins and banknotes). They argued about the numbers of people who should represent each state in the federal government. They argued about great western lands which would, in the course of time, become new states. They argued about the relationship between state laws and federal laws. Yet, at the end of only 16 weeks, they managed to agree on a constitution for the United States of America.

In a democratic nation two things must be very carefully balanced: strong government and individual liberty. Neither must be over-stressed at the expense of the other. If strong government is made more important, there soon comes a time when people are arrested without trial, when elections cease to be free, when criticism of the government is not allowed and when men and women cannot live the sort of life they wish to live. Such is the situation under dictatorships and in communist countries. If individuals are allowed too much freedom the police force fails to keep order, life and property cannot be protected, trade unions and other minority groups can exercise too much power and threaten the whole life of the nation, rioting and disorder can lead to the complete collapse of government.

In America a right balance was achieved by the Constitution and the Bill of Rights. The Constitution as it was originally drawn up in Philadelphia made clear the relationship between the federal government and the state governments. The central government was to make laws for all Americans (though states might have their own internal laws, as long as they did not contradict federal law), was to be in charge of foreign affairs, was to regulate all trade, was to impose federal taxes, was to approve the only legal American currency, was to be responsible for the supreme courts of justice and to have responsibi-

lity for all affairs that were too 'big' for individual states to handle. Many Americans, when they had a chance of studying the Constitution, said 'This is all very well, but it says nothing about the rights of the individual.' They insisted that a Bill of Rights be drawn up and attached to the Constitution. And so additions were made to the original document. These guaranteed the basic democratic 'freedoms': freedom to hold public meetings, freedom of worship, freedom of the press (that is freedom to publish whatever opinions one likes without one's books or newspapers being stopped or 'censored'), freedom from arrest without trial, freedom of speech (that is freedom to express honest opinions without being arrested or punished for doing so), and the right to trial by jury. Thus altered, the Constitution was accepted by the thirteen states. On 4 March 1789 the representatives of the new central government met in New York. On 30 April, the first President, George Washington, took office.

America grows

It was a good thing that a federal constitution had been worked out so peacefully, because the number of states in the Union soon began to grow. As you can see from the map at the beginning of this chapter, in 1783 the United States made up only a small part of the continent of North America. Vast areas of land to the west and north belonged to Britain, Spain, France and Mexico. But although these lands were claimed by the nations mentioned, they were largely empty territories. The various peoples who lived in the Mid-West and West of North America were all known by the Europeans as Red Indians. Apart from the scattered settlements of these people, the only other signs of life were a few European and Mexican forts and trading posts. From the earliest days, European settlers had ventured westwards in search of land for planting or grazing.

George Washington takes the President's oath
When it came to electing their first President the American people had no doubt about the man they wanted. They unanimously chose the champion who had led them through the War of Independence to lead them in the years of peace – George Washington. Here the First President of the United States of America is seen taking the oath of office on the balcony of a building in New York. The excited crowd cheer and wave the new United States flag – thirteen stars and thirteen stripes, to represent the thirteen states of the Union.

Red Indians

The original inhabitants of North America, all known by Europeans as Red Indians, came thousands of years ago from Asia through Alaska. There were many different tribes scattered across the continent. The way of life of the various tribes differed, but basically they were hunters and simple farmers. Very fine hunters they were too, as you can see from the picture. Young Indian warriors (known as 'braves') are attacking wild buffalo with bows and arrows. These Red Indians bitterly resented the white men coming to take their land. Many tribes fought fiercely and long to repel the newcomers.

Now the government encouraged citizens to travel into the unexplored lands and 'open up' North America. Thus, the colonists who had, only a few years before, broken away from the British Empire, now set about building an empire of their own. They claimed and settled territory in the West and Mid-West and conquered the original occupiers of the land.

The Louisiana Purchase

The first, and largest, addition to United States territory came in 1803. An enormous tract of territory covering most of the central part of the continent was called Louisiana by the French explorer, La Salle, who claimed it for France in 1682. France had done very little to develop the area (and had even, for a time, given it to Spain). But at the beginning of the nineteenth century, the French dictator, Napoleon Bonaparte, decided to make use of his colonies and send settlers to Louisiana. The American President, Thomas Jefferson, was horrified. If the French occupied the region, all hope of United States' expansion to the West would have to be given up. He urgently sent representatives to France to discuss the problem with Napoleon.

The Americans dared hope for nothing more than the purchase of the port of New Orleans. But one day the French Prime Minister suddenly asked the American representatives, 'What will you pay for the whole territory?' Napoleon had changed his mind about Louisiana and was prepared to sell. Hurriedly the sum of 15 million dollars was agreed on. On 30 April 1803, with one stroke of the pen, the size of the United States of America was doubled. New settlers poured in and soon discovered that the central prairies provided some of the finest farming land in the world—worth many times more than the 15 million dollars the government had paid for it.

War with Mexico

In 1821 Mexico won its independence from Spain. The territory of the new republic extended from Central America right up into the south-western region of North America. Much of this land was undeveloped and the Mexican government was only too pleased to allow settlers from the U.S.A. to enter the territory and start farming. The land-hungry Americans flocked, in ever-increasing numbers, into the region known as Texas. Too late, the Mexicans realized they had made a

244

mistake and tried to stop the settlers coming in. The Americans revolted and declared the whole of Texas an independent state. There was some bitter fighting in 1836 but eventually the Americans won and Texas became independent. In 1848 it joined the Union.

The official recognition of Texas by the United States government and its inclusion in the Union angered Mexico and, in the same year, war broke out between the two countries. The Americans welcomed this, because they had long wanted to get control of the land west of Texas, and now was their chance. The war was quickly over and at the end of it Mexico had lost all her North American territory to the expanding new nation. By this time America had gained, by agreement, land in the North-West from Britain and in the South-East from Spain. In 65 years the original 13 colonies had grown to 30 states and the United States of America stretched from coast to coast.

The Pioneers

The brave men and women who 'opened up' the new territories were called 'pioneers'. They crossed thousands of miles of rough country. They took their few possessions with them in covered waggons. They risked death from starva-tion, attack by Red Indians, disease and exhaus-tion. Why? Because they were looking for somewhere to make a fresh start in life. When they found a suitable place, they bought a piece of land and struggled for years to raise crops or animals on it. Some opened shops and businesses. Others were content to work on the land as labourers. Conditions 'out West' were very hard. In many areas there was little law and order. Soldiers had to be sent to protect the settlers from Indians, bandits, and sometimes from each other. Many pioneers died or gave up, but those who carried on usually lived to see success, for there were plenty of opportunities for men to make fortunes in the fertile new territories.

The Gold Rush

Many fortunes were made in the California gold rush. No sooner had this territory been added to the Union than a man, James Marshall, clearing some ground to build a saw mill found some gleaming objects among the earth. Examining them more closely, he could scarcely believe his eyes. He had discovered gold! The news quickly spread all over the United States. Men sold everything and rushed to California in the hope of making a fortune. Some did. Many did not.

Pioneers

Communications in America

North America developed so rapidly that new means of transportation and communication could not be found fast enough. Steam power was extremely important in opening up the West and the Mid-West. In the background of this picture you can see a Mississippi steamboat and a steam railway engine. Between 1830 and 1850, over 14,500 kilometres of railway track were laid. On the wide rivers like the Mississippi large steamboats driven by stern paddles were a common sight. They were particularly useful for carrying cargoes of cotton down to the ports, such as New Orleans. The man in the foreground illustrates the invention of the telegraph. By this means messages could be sent quickly across America. The steamboat, the steam engine and the telegraph were all invented in the first half of the nineteenth century, and played an important part in the expansion of America.

Towns sprang up round the gold mines and a new state was born. Later other minerals were discovered: coal, copper, silver, lead, zinc, and, in Texas and Pennsylvania, oil. The new lands were incredibly rich in raw materials.

Rarely in the history of the world has a country grown, developed and become rich as rapidly as the United States of America did in the nineteenth century. But in these years America also had its problems. In the 1860s the fine new Union almost split into two nations, as we shall see in the next chapter.

Growth of a frontier farm

Here are seen four stages in the development of an American pioneer's farm. First he had to make a clearing in the forest and build himself a log hut. Then more land had to be cleared for planting and grazing. There soon came a time when he had to fence his land to keep animals in and other farmers out. He now began to prosper and could afford horses, carts and simple farm machinery, for which he had to build a barn. Then, when his farm had grown quite large and he was earning more money, he was able to pull down the log cabin and build a large stone house. The whole process probably took twenty years or more.

246

Chapter 41 Latin America Breaks Free

By 1700 the vast continent of South America had been divided up by the rival claimants, Spain and Portugal. However, this does not mean that the entire continent was effectively ruled by these European nations. Large areas of forest and inaccessible mountain regions were quite unknown to the conquerors. Indeed, there are still to this day areas where no white man has ever set foot. As you can see from the map, the greater part of Brazil and large parts of Chile and Argentina were unexplored. Even within the colonies lack of manpower and money often reduced the administration to a mere token presence in remoter areas.

Spanish America

Spanish territories were ruled directly by the king through the Royal and Supreme Council of the Indies. For administrative purposes the enormous area under Spanish control was divided into three viceroyalties—New Spain, New Granada, and Peru. In 1776 the Viceroyalty of La Plata was constituted to incorporate territory conquered from the Spanish base at Buenos Aires. Each viceroyalty was further split into a number of kingdoms each under a governor who was helped by an advisory council known as an *audiencia*. This hierarchical structure of control might have worked well had authority been delegated to the men on the spot. In fact, all important decisions were made in Madrid. The Royal and Supreme Council worked hard and kept itself as well informed as possible but because of the distance of Spain from South America, delays, frustrations and wrong decisions were frequent. Nor did the Council fully trust the men they appointed to rule in the king's name: they encouraged members of the *audiencias* to send reports about the viceroys direct to Madrid and they occasionally sent out secret agents to report on the situation and officials in the colonies. Despite the obvious weaknesses in this system it worked reasonably well and maintained law and order for over three hundred years.

Latin America in the 17th Century
The map illustrates the distribution of vast areas of South American soil between three major European powers, Spain, Portugal and Britain. In the beginning of the period these nations were profitably exploiting the country's wealth—be it silver, gold or diamonds, coffee or cocoa.

For the rulers of Latin America religion and politics were bound up together. Officials gave the Roman Catholic priests every assistance in rooting up the old religions of the people and implanting Christianity. By 1700 millions of Indians had been baptised. But the religion which evolved in South America was not the pure Roman Catholicism which the original *conquistadores* had brought with them; it was mingled with many pagan beliefs and ceremonies. However, it became the official religion of the colonies, and helped to unite rulers and ruled. In one area the Church failed badly. This was education; very little instruction was given to the people. Attendance at mission schools was virtually restricted to the children of Spaniards and wealthy natives who lived in the towns.

The basis of the economy of Spanish America was the mining of silver and, to a lesser extent, gold. The Europeans brought new techniques with them. They prospected for precious metals, discovered hitherto unknown deposits and dug new mines. Most of the mines were situated in Mexico and Bolivia but gold and silver were discovered over a surprisingly wide area and other deposits were worked in Colombia and Chile (N.B. used here are the modern names for these territories; these states, of course, did not yet exist in the eighteenth century). The output from the mines of Spanish America was enormous; by 1800 they were producing 90 per cent of the world's gold and silver. Much of the profit from the mines went to the royal treasury but there was enough left over to enable many impressive towns, churches and public buildings to be built.

From the beginning the Spaniards encouraged agriculture in their new possessions. The government gave settlers land and helped them to establish themselves. Many areas proved suitable for the growing of a wide variety of crops. As well as indigenous crops such as maize, potatoes, melons, pumpkins and tobacco, the settlers grew plants introduced from Europe and other parts of the empire, such as sugar cane, wheat, rice, coffee, cocoa, apples, grapes and citrus fruits. The newcomers revolutionized farming by the introduction of the plough and draft animals. They began to rear sheep, cattle, goats and chickens. This agricultural expansion enabled the colonies to be self-sufficient as far as food was concerned, to expand their frontiers and to add other exports to the precious metals traditionally sent to Europe.

South American Church in European style

Market scene, 1827

248

The trading fleets which crossed the Atlantic to Europe were richly laden with a variety of goods. No wonder they frequently fell prey to pirates.

Society in Spanish America was separated into rigid class divisions. The top strata was made up of Spaniards born in Europe. They were the only people trusted by the Madrid government and they held all the best jobs. Below them were the creoles, pure whites born in America. Though racially no different from the Spaniards, they were barred from important positions. Most of them were farmers and traders but some had sunk to the status of peasants. Next down the scale were the people of mixed race, the *mestizos*. They were exempted from the restrictions applied to the Indians and were employed largely as overseers and muleteers. The Indians remained, for the most part peasants and labourers in their own land, But even they were better off than the negro slaves, brought over from Africa to do the hard work on the plantations and in the mines. They had no rights, were owned totally by their masters and received scant protection from the law.

Portuguese America

The situation in the Portuguese Viceroyalty of Brazil was in many respects similar but here the settlers and officials had a more difficult task in taming the country. Farmland had to be won from the forest and white settlement was fiercely resisted by the Indians. One settler complained to the government, 'The land you granted us in leagues we have had to conquer in inches'. This work of steady conquest was still going on in 1700. The main export of the colony was sugar, grown on plantations worked by African slave labour. But in 1692 gold was discovered in the southern part of the country and in 1729 diamonds were found. The prospect of wealth brought a rush of new settlers. Many of the newcomers, having failed to make their fortune in mining, went into farming.

The leaders of Brazilian society were not as strictly controlled as their Spanish counterparts. Estate owners ruled as kings, often treating their African and Indian slaves terribly. Many Europeans who had no land owned slaves and lived off their earnings. As territorial expansion continued so did the conflict between natives and settlers. Slave revolts also occurred from time to time. Some slaves who escaped fled into the

Pirates
Colonial governments enlisted the services of buccaneers in the war against Spain.

jungle and there set up settlements called *quilombos*. These could grow to a considerable size (one had over 20,000 people) and be a serious menace to the colonial rulers. In addition to these troubles the Portuguese had to face frequent border disputes with Spain. For all these reasons Brazil was less stable and prosperous than Spanish America. But there were serious stresses and strains in both societies and by the end of the eighteenth century the days of colonial rule in South America were numbered.

The Growth of Nationalism

Effective resistance to colonial rule came not from the most down-trodden groups in society but from the locally born white population—

the creoles and their Portuguese counterparts. These were the educated members of colonial society whose advancement was blocked by officials and wealthy landowners born in Europe. As time went by the numbers of the creoles increased. Many of them travelled to Europe or were educated there. These men came into contact with the revolutionary ideas which were sweeping through the Old World in the second half of the eighteenth century. News of the successful revolt of Britain's North American colonies was not slow in reaching Latin America. As in the North, the peoples of this area now thought of themselves not as Europeans but as Americans. Their resentment of control from Madrid and Lisbon was increased by the fact that it was sporadic. At times when Spain and Portugal were at war the colonies were largely left to solve their own problems in their own way but once the mother countries were free to do so they re-asserted their authority, often reversing decisions which had previously been made by officials on the spot.

From time to time discontent showed itself in open revolt. Sometimes the native population, anxious to throw off foreign oppression, joined in these risings, though they stood to gain little from changing one white master for another. The most notable native revolt was led by Tupac Amaru a descendant of the Inca rulers of Peru, 1780-2.

All the eighteenth century revolts failed but early in the next century something happened which gave the Latin American freedom fighters a new determination. In 1806 Napoleon Bonaparte, Emperor of the French, conquered Spain and set his brother Joseph on the throne. The colonists rejected French rule and most of them declared their allegiance to the deposed King, Ferdinand VII. But since Ferdinand was in no position to rule effectively the colonies were left almost entirely to their own devices. The monarchy was not restored in Spain until 1814 and even then the government was hampered by considerable internal strife. The colonists had by now proved that they could manage their own affairs, but the home governments were determined not to lose their grip on wealthy Latin America. It was this situation which led to the wars of independence.

The Wars of Independence in Spanish America
The Spanish colonies achieved independence

between 1809 and 1825. In place of the four vice royalties there came into being sixteen new states. The struggle for independence was continuous and widespread. Here is an outline of the main events. The conflict in La Plata began in 1806 when Britain (currently at war with Napoleon and his Spanish allies) tried to seize Buenos Aires. The viceroy fled and it was the creole militia which defended the town against the invader. A junta was established to rule in the king's name but was not accepted by all parts of the viceroyalty. Paraguay broke away from Spanish control in 1811 and two years later set up a republican government. But a similar movement in Uruguay did not achieve lasting success. By 1814 the Uruguayans had successfully thrown off Spanish rule but in 1816 their land was invaded by Brazilian forces and incorporated into the Portuguese colony.

Meanwhile fighting between republican and monarchist forces continued throughout La Plata. The viceroyalty was divided into provinces and a number of governments rose and fell. Then, in 1816, Juan Martin de Pueyrredon was named supreme dictator of the United Provinces and declared their independence from Spain. But the new state was far from secure. The Viceroyalty of Peru and the southern part of the old La Plata Viceroyalty were still in Spanish hands and from these strongholds colonial forces threatened to re-conquer the United Provinces.

It was at this point that José de San Martin was appointed to the leadership of the army of the United Provinces. This brilliant general decided that there was only one way to prevent his country being conquered from Peru and that was for Peru to be conquered by his country. He gathered his forces at Mendoza and crossed the Andes in 1817. He defeated a Spanish army at the battle of Chacabuco. This enabled the people of Chile, under their leader, Bernardo O'Higgins to proclaim their independence. O'Higgins now provided a fleet to take San Martin and his 6000 men northward. They landed on the Peruvian coast near Lima and besieged the capital in 1820. After a ten month siege Lima fell in July 1821 and San Martin was proclaimed the protector of a new republic. But the great general was no politician and he found it impossible to govern the rival factions competing for power in Peru. He turned for help to the most famous man in the Latin American independence movement—Simon Bolivar.

Simon Bolivar was a well-educated Venezuelan creole who had travelled widely in Europe and been deeply influenced by the revolutionary ideas circulating there. In 1811 a junta declared Venezuela independent. Bolivar became one of the leaders of the army which was under the command of Francisco Miranda, Venezuela's dictator. But Spanish forces mounted an active campaign of reconquest and in 1812 Miranda was forced to surrender. Bolivar now assumed the leadership of the freedom fighters. In exile he gathered forces for the liberation of his country but failed in successive attempts. In 1817 he began to collect another army on the Orinoco plain. This time he decided to prepare slowly and painstakingly and to choose the time and place of his onslaught with great care. When all was ready he marched his men 960 kilometres across the Orinoco plains, crossed the Andes into New Granada, and defeated the unsuspecting Spaniards at the battle of Boyaca.

Bolivar now proclaimed Venezuela, New Granada and Ecuador to be a united, independent state, Gran Colombia. During the next two years he disposed of the last traces of Spanish resistance. It was then that he received an appeal from José de San Martin to help in Peru. He took over the government in Lima while his general, Antonio José de Sucre, took military action against Bolivar's opponents. However, he could not prevent southern Peru breaking away to form a separate republic (eventually called Bolivia). Like San Martin, Bolivar discovered that it is easier to lead a revolution than to rule a people. Only with great difficulty did he succeed in establishing a stable government. Meanwhile, the united state of Gran Colombia was breaking up. In 1826 Bolivar returned there but failed to prevent the drift towards separation. In 1830 Gran Colombia broke up. Shortly afterwards Simon Bolivar died of tuberculosis. He had not succeeded in all he wished to achieve but by his steady determination and brilliant leadership he had finally broken the power of Spain. Not without reason is he remembered as the *Liberator of South America*.

In New Spain (Mexico) the first move against Spanish rule was led by a creole priest, Miguel Hidalgo y Costilla, who raised a vast army of Indians. In 1810 they captured the city of Guanajuato. Their indiscriminate slaughter of all white men turned creoles and Spaniards against them and the revolt was quickly put down.

Map of South America after Independence

Another priest, Jose Maria Morelos y Pavon, now took up the struggle. Using the remnant of Hidalgo's army he overran much of Mexico and declared the country independent in 1813. Freedom was short lived; a royalist force defeated Morelos in 1815 and returned Mexico to its Spanish allegiance. After five years of colonial rule a strange thing happened; the royalist government itself broke away from Spanish control. This was because it did not like the policies of the Madrid government. Royalist Mexicans joined forces with a guerrilla army under Vicente Guerrero and occupied Mexico City in 1821. The following year the royalist general Augustin de Iturbide was elected emperor.

Independence in Portuguese South America
The underlying causes of the revolt of Brazil were much the same as those which drove the creoles to seek independence. But the sequence of events which broke the bonds between Brazil and the mother country was rather different.

In 1807 Napoleon invaded Portugal and the royal family fled to Brazil. With the aid of his powerful ally, Britain, King John VI worked hard to improve conditions in the colony. In particular he turned Rio de Janeiro into a splendid capital. In 1816 he proclaimed the union of Portugal and Brazil as a dual monarchy in which each country was equal.

Despite this there was growing discontent in the country. Conflict between Portuguese and locally-born whites, resentment at British economic domination, and the spread of republicanism all contributed to an atmosphere of growing tension. The situation grew worse when King John returned to his liberated country. In 1821 the government in Lisbon introduced a new constitution which had the effect of making Brazil once more a dependent colony of Portugal. This was the last straw for the Brazilians. They complained to the regent, Prince Pedro, who had been left to represent his father. The prince fully associated himself with his people and refused an order to return to Lisbon. He also refused to allow any orders from Portugal to be enforced without his consent.

By September 1822 the whole country had united behind Pedro. On the seventh while travelling beside a stream called the Ypiranga, he received fresh instructions from Lisbon. Angrily he responded by tearing the Portuguese emblem from his tunic and crying out 'Independence or death!' This is still known as the Cry of Ypiranga. This impromptu declaration of independence was immediately ratified by the government and in October Pedro was proclaimed constitutional emperor.

The Aftermath of Independence

Freedom from European control did not solve the problems of Latin America. In all the new states there were deep political and racial divisions running through society and the existence of a powerful church posed other problems. For over twenty-five years rival factions fought for power. No one thought of consulting the people to discover their wishes. Often the most powerful men were the leaders of armed bands, these people were known as *caudillos*.

In some states — notably in Chile, Argentina, Brazil and Mexico — a measure of stability and peace emerged during the second half of the nineteenth century. With the aid of foreign capital the agricultural and mining potential of South America were more fully developed. In order to encourage foreign businessmen and investors, governments were obliged to maintain law and order. They were largely successful and the period from 1850-1914 saw some remarkable economic development. Large areas were cleared for farming. Harbours were improved. Railways were laid. Millions of people emigrated to South America. Thanks to the discovery of refrigeration Argentina became one of the world's major suppliers of meat. Brazil exported more coffee than any other country. Nitrates were mined in Chile and Mexico produced vast quantities of petroleum.

Economic development brought social and political change. South America's cities grew rapidly into vast, sophisticated centres of international commerce. People flocked into them because that was where the money was. The rural areas became depopulated and remained backward. Many areas did not share the advantages of the town dwellers. Improved educational facilities produced a new generation of politically active young men, many of whom resented the dominance of old families, the economic control held by foreign companies and, in particular, the fact that the U.S.A. had become the 'policeman' of the western hemisphere. Through its capital investment and its ownership of the Panama Canal, the United States controlled much of South America's economic destiny.

The republics of South America (Brazil was the last state to give up a monarchical constitution in 1889) were not the only ones to find that, as producing countries, their economic fate was largely controlled by the manufacturing nations of Europe and North America. But they had laid a solid economic foundation from which, in the fullness of time, they would be able to make a bid for economic as well as political independence.

Chapter 42 A Divided Nation

The North and the South

In such a large country there were bound to be different ways of life but the contrast between the landowners in the southern states and the small farmers in the North was very great. In the North farmers worked hard on quite small farms to earn a living from the soil. They lived simply and, if they wanted labour, they had to pay a reasonable wage. The South soon produced an aristocracy, a ruling class, of large landowners. Cotton was in demand all over the world and fetched high prices. The cotton was grown on large estates worked by negro slaves, who cost their owners almost nothing to keep. It is not surprising these 'cotton kings' were able to build fine houses and live in great luxury.

Thomas Jefferson, 1801–9, and James Monroe, 1817–25

The United States of America has always prided itself on being the home of freedom and democracy and the defender of liberty. This has not always been a fair claim. As we have seen Americans fought against Mexico and drove Indians from their ancient hunting grounds in their fight to colonize most of North America. We shall see how slavery became an accepted part of American life for many years. Yet there is some truth in the boast. For many years the U.S.A. welcomed new settlers, particularly those who were fleeing from oppression in their own country. From very early in its history the United States also supported small states against larger ones.

In 1800 Thomas Jefferson wrote to a friend, 'I have sworn upon the altar of God eternal hostility against every kind of tyranny over the mind of man.' The next year he became the third President of the United States. We have already referred to his drafting of the Declaration of Independence and his purchase of Louisiana from France. Much of his time as President was taken up with keeping America out of war. France, under Napoleon Bonaparte, was fighting against Britain and other European nations and both sides hoped for American support. Jefferson kept America neutral, believing that Europe's troubles had nothing to do with the U.S.A. But the British and French navies began to stop and search American ships trading with Europe and popular opinion forced the government to go to war against Britain in 1812.

Neither side gained from the war but it did make quite clear to the world that the new nation was prepared to fight to defend its interests. It also made it possible for the fifth President, James Monroe, to challenge Europe in a memorable way in 1823. Spain, which had in recent years been forced to give up its colonies in South and Central America, wanted to recover them. Some other European nations encouraged this ambition. In order to stop Spain the British Foreign Secretary asked the American government to make a joint statement with the British government refusing to allow Spanish colonization of the Americas. President Monroe went farther. Brushing aside the British offer of joint action, he declared: 'the American continents, by the free and independent condition which they have assumed and maintain, are henceforth not to be considered as subject for future colon-

Slaves being driven to the South to be sold in the slave market

A slave sale in the South of America

In the southern states the most important crops were cotton and tobacco. These had to be grown on large plantations and needed a huge supply of labour. The southern farmers found slaves to be the answer. For hundreds of years negroes had been captured in West Africa and shipped to the West Indies and the colonies of the American mainland. The plantation owners bought them at sales like cattle. Slaves belonged to their masters completely and had no rights: they might be underfed, illtreated and whipped; if they escaped they might be brought back dead or alive. There were no laws to protect them. One historian has described their conditions thus: '... the negroes lived in filth and wretchedness in villages of huts. Their clothing was made of ... the cheapest material that could be had; their food was almost exclusively corn meal, which they prepared in addition to the day's toil, often exceeding fifteen hours in the field ...'[*]

---

[*]H. W. Elson *History of the United States of America*, New York, 1918, p. 557

254

ization by any European power.' He warned Europe that any nation trying to found new colonies in the Americas would run the risk of war with the U.S.A. This Monroe Doctrine, as it is called, prevented a scramble for colonies in South and Central America in the mid-nineteenth century (like the scramble that took place in Africa). It also stopped Russia trying to claim parts of the American Pacific coast. What Monroe, in fact, told the other major powers was, 'Keep out of the Americas and we will keep out of European affairs.'

Slavery

By this time a serious problem was beginning to appear *within* America, which was of greater importance than the U.S.A.'s relations with other countries. In the days before 1783 all the thirteen colonies had employed African slaves. Yet many Americans felt unhappy about slavery. They believed that it was not in harmony with the spirit of freedom of the new nation. George Washington wrote a special clause in his will freeing his slaves. Thomas Jefferson made several attempts to get a law passed against slavery. In the northern states, where most people were occupied in small farming and industry, there was little need for slaves and one by one state governments abolished slavery. By 1800 there were no slaves north of Maryland. In 1808 the slave trade between Africa and America was made illegal. The Colonization Society was founded, with the object of taking freed slaves back to Africa and settling them there. In the 1820s the West Africa free state of Liberia was founded and for many years Americans helped the new nation to get established.

But in the southern states of America feeling was very different. Here the large cotton and tobacco estates had come to depend on slave labour. They firmly resisted any attempt to abolish slavery. So America was divided into 'free states' and 'slave states'. In the North an anti-slavery movement began and rapidly grew in strength. Members of the movement helped runaway slaves to escape. They made use of the democratic rights of free speech and free press to publish their views and more and more Americans were won over to their way of thinking. But the *real* clash began when new states were added to the Union. The abolitionists wanted the new states to be free, so that slavery would gradually die out in North America. The southerners refused to be made into a minority. If they moved into

John Brown, fighter for freedom for slaves

In 1859 an event occurred which drew wide attention to the question of slavery. John Brown was a strange man but a firm believer in abolishing slavery. He travelled over much of America to win supporters to the anti-slavery cause. He organized an escape route for runaway slaves. In the summer of 1859 he went to live in a farm house near the village of Harper's Ferry, Virginia. In Harper's Ferry there was an arsenal—a storehouse of arms and ammunition for the army. Brown planned to seize this and steal the weapons for his anti-slavery fighters. On the night of 16 October, Brown and his men easily captured the arsenal, but they were trapped there by the arrival of soldiers. They fired from the windows while troops battered the door down. John Brown was captured, tried, condemned on a charge of treason and hanged. But he was regarded by many in the North as a hero and a martyr. Soon a new song was being sung by the enemies of slavery:
'John Brown's body lies a-mouldering in the grave,
But his soul goes marching on.'
In Britain William Wilberforce campaigned for the abolition of the slave trade and slavery. In 1807 the actual traffic in slaves was abolished. Wilberforce's political agitation led to the legislation of 1833. This did not become effective in all subject colonies until 1834. Slavery itself did not, of course, disappear overnight.

the new territories they wanted to be able to take their slaves with them.

There was another difficulty which caused hard feelings between the North and the South. As industry developed in the northern states the businessmen and factory owners wanted their wares protected from competition. So the government put import duties on some goods coming from abroad. This made these goods more expensive and so helped American industry. But the southerners objected to having to pay high prices for imports.

Throughout the 1840s and 1850s the situation grew worse. Southerners began to talk about *states rights*. Though the relationship between the federal government and the state governments had been settled in the Constitution, there was still argument about exactly how it should be applied. Now the southern states declared that whether or not to allow slavery was a matter for each state to decide. This was rejected by the central government. Then the southerners began to think seriously about *secession* — that is breaking away from the U.S.A. to form a separate nation. Events like John Brown's attack on Harper's Ferry increased the bitter feelings on both sides and a conflict became inevitable. It was the election of Abraham Lincoln as 16th President of the United States of America in 1861 that started that conflict.

Abraham Lincoln

Lincoln, throughout his political career, had made it quite clear that he believed in two things above all else: the abolition of slavery and the preservation of the Union. In 1858 he had stated:

'A house divided against itself cannot stand. I believe this government cannot endure permanently half slave and half free ... I do not expect the Union to be *dissolved* — I do not expect the house to fall — but I *do* expect it will cease to be divided.'

Lincoln knew that the slavery problem had to be solved. But before he had even taken office the Southerners had made a move. First one state, then another, left the Union. Eventually 11 states broke away (or *seceded*) and formed the Southern Confederacy. President Lincoln solemnly warned them what the results of secession would be:

In *your* hands, my dissatisfied fellow countrymen, and not in *mine*, is the momentous issue of civil war. ... *You* have no oath registered in

The young man from the backwoods becomes America's most famous President

Abraham Lincoln was born of poor parents and spent most of his early life in the open air, clearing forest and farming. His father moved from place to place, ever seeking new land, never able to settle. Abraham had no proper education but learned to read and eagerly read every book he could find. Later he became a shopkeeper and then a lawyer. He settled, finally, in Springfield, Illinois. Early in his life he saw a slave sale in the South and was horrified by it. He entered politics in 1846 but was not much noticed until 1858 when he spoke with great vigour *for* preserving the Union and *against* slavery. The South then recognized him as a powerful enemy and did all they could to prevent 'Honest Abe', as the tall, Springfield lawyer was known, from getting elected to the Presidency. But he *was* elected, by a very narrow majority, at the end of 1860.

Heaven to destroy the government, while *I* shall have the most solemn one to preserve, protect and defend it.'

But the southern states would not give way and in April 1861, the United States of America was plunged into civil war.

The American Civil War

All the anger of the past 50 years was now unleashed as Americans fought Americans in a most savage war. The Union armies had great advantages: more soldiers, better weapons, plentiful supplies and a navy which was able to blockade Southern ports. But they suffered from bad leadership in the early days of the war and the Confederate forces were able to win some important victories. But, at last, Lincoln found a fine general in Ulysses Grant. At Gettysburg in 1863 the Confederate army was stopped and retreated on to Southern soil. 51,000 men were left dead or wounded on the famous battlefield. A few months later President Lincoln travelled to Gettysburg to dedicate the battlefield as a cemetery, honouring those who had fallen on both sides. He made a short but very famous speech, which ended with these words:

'...we here highly resolve that these dead shall not have died in vain, that this nation under God shall have a new birth of freedom, and that government of the people, by the people, for the people, shall not perish from the earth.'

Lincoln frequently offered the South generous peace terms. He had no wish to take revenge on the Confederate states. He wanted to forget the past and rebuild the Union. But the southerners carried on fighting for another two years after Gettysburg; two years during which southern towns and villages were burned, bridges smashed and farmland trampled into a wilderness.

On 9 April 1865, almost exactly four years after the first armed clash, the main Confederate army surrendered and the war was over.

Death of President Lincoln

Now Lincoln could really start planning for peace and recovery. The slavery question had already been settled. In 1863 Lincoln had issued an emancipation order, freeing all American slaves. While the North rejoiced at the Confederate defeat, Lincoln and his ministers considered how to replace slave labour in the South, how to rebuild towns, how to restock farms and bring torn land back into cultivation. He was perhaps the one man capable of bringing the two sides together again as a united nation. His belief had been expressed in 1864:

'With malice toward none; with charity for all ... let us strive ... to bind up the nation's wounds; to care for him who shall have borne

Assassination of President Lincoln

On 14 April 1865 President Lincoln drove to Ford's Theatre in Washington to watch a special performance of a play, put on to celebrate the ending of the war. He arrived late, having been working hard on government business. He was shown to a private box in the theatre, but as soon as he was seen the play stopped. Actors and audience cheered the man who had brought peace *and* preserved the Union. The play resumed and Lincoln relaxed – something he was rarely able to do. But there was in the theatre a man who did not share in the general rejoicing. John Wilkes Booth, an actor, was a supporter of the Southern cause. He and some of his friends believed they could help the Confederacy by killing Lincoln and other ministers. Booth made his way to the door of the President's box, opened it silently, and, from only a few feet away, shot Lincoln in the head. Then, amid the screams and confusion, he jumped on to the stage, waving his pistol, and escaped through the back of the theatre. Meanwhile President Abraham Lincoln was dying.

the battle, and for his widow, and his orphan ... to do all which may achieve ... a just and lasting peace among ourselves and with all nations.'

But at the moment of victory, just when he had begun to put his ideas for a reunited nation into practice, he was shot by an assassin on 14 April 1865. He died early the next morning.

Assassination never solves anything. By removing the nation's respected leader the murderer made the task of America's recovery from the war much more difficult. Twelve years passed, years of continued bitterness and misunderstanding, before the nation really settled to the task of reconstruction.

Industrial Development, 1880–1914

But when the U.S.A. did settle down, its rate of industrial development was astonishing. More roads and railways were built. Mines and oil wells made possible the building of iron and steel mills, hardware and textile factories, dams, electric power plants, etc. By 1914 America had become the world's largest producer of coal, iron and steel and was exporting grain and refrigerated meat all over the world.

Many Americans made important inventions and developed new techniques. In 1877 Alexander Graham Bell showed the public a strange new invention. People laughed and said it was only a toy. What was it? The telephone. In 1879 Thomas Edison invented the electric lamp. The petrol engine was first developed in Germany and Britain but it was an American, Henry Ford, who first began the mass production of motor cars. In 1903, the Wright Brothers made the first ever aeroplane flight. As we shall see in Part XI, American merchants took the lead in opening up Japan and other lands across the Pacific Ocean to western trade.

By 1914, the United States of America had become one of the most industrialized and wealthy nations in the world. It had achieved this by working hard to solve its own problems and by following the policy, laid down a century before by Jefferson and Monroe, of not getting involved in the affairs of Europe. But when in 1914 the leading nations of Europe went to war, many Americans began to ask whether the U.S.A. ought to remain neutral.

Two American brothers invent the aeroplane

Wilbur and Orville Wright were fascinated by the problems of flight, and began to study them seriously in the 1890s. By 1903 they had developed a two-winged aeroplane (biplane) with a petrol engine. They then had to see if it would fly. Choosing a large open space at Kitty Hawk on the coast of North Carolina, the brothers carried out tests on 17 December 1903. To their excitement their machine rose into the air and

stayed there for 59 seconds travelling at 48 k.p.h. Man could fly! They now worked hard to improve their aeroplane and, in later years, toured Europe with it. Wilbur died in 1912, but his brother lived on until 1948 and saw his invention developed enormously, with aeroplanes flying at speeds and heights that Wilbur would never have thought possible. The picture above shows Orville at the controls of an aeroplane in 1910.

Part X Russia under the Tsar
Chapter 43 The Expansion of Russia, 1700-1855

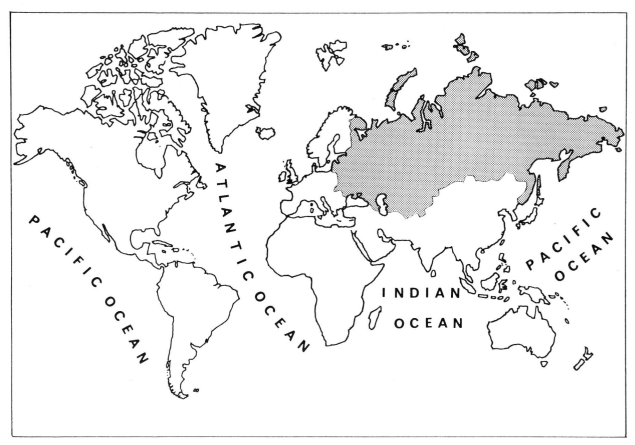

From North America we return to the large land mass of Europe and Asia. We have already seen some of the important changes taking place in Europe between 1600 and 1914: the Industrial Revolution, the formation of overseas empires, the growth of trade with distant parts of the world. In later chapters we shall see that, for most of this period, the leading countries of Asia were isolated from the rest of the world, preferring to follow ancient, well-tried ways of government and daily life. But between Asia and Europe there was another country, part Asian and part Euro-

pean. Its ruling people were Slavs from Eastern Europe but they had come to rule over millions of Asian people to the east and south-east of their homeland. It was a large country, most of whose people were peasants. Like most Asian countries it was largely cut off from events in Europe. The people lived as their ancestors had lived for centuries. Their clothes, their food, their village customs, their farming methods, their way of government, their religion, had all remained unchanged for hundreds of years. Yet their kings (or *tsars* as they were called) and their leading men dressed in European style clothes, spoke French at court, read English and German books, studied new political ideas and industrial techniques from the West and occasionally led their country into European wars. In the years after 1700 this country played an increasingly important part in the affairs of Europe and the world. Today it is one of the richest and most powerful of all nations. It is the Union of Soviet Socialist Republics-Russia.

The Expansion of Russia

The map below illustrates clearly two important points. The first is the very great expansion of Russia between 1450 and 1914. In the early fifteenth century 'Russia' did not exist. Muscovy was just one among a large number of north-Asian states. But under the rule of such tsars as Ivan the Great, Ivan the Terrible, and Peter the Great, all the Russian lands were brought under Muscovite rule and the new Russia began to con-

quer and colonize new lands. By 1700 the land of the tsars stretched from the Baltic Sea to the Pacific Ocean.

The second point to learn from the map is that, though by 1725 Russia had a large coastline, it was of little value to her. For parts of the year the coastal waters are frozen solid. Even the ports of the Baltic Sea are ice-blocked for much of the European winter (December–March). The Arctic Ocean and the northern Pacific Ocean are plagued by dangerous icebergs and ice-floes. Thus, in order to increase its contacts with the outside world and to take a share in international trade, Russia had to continue to expand until she had 'warm water' ports for her ships.

A third significant fact concerning Russia is not shown on the map. That is the political and economic conditions of most of the Russian people. The peasants, working on the land, had not been influenced at all by the new political and economic ideas from western Europe. Most

Russia expands her frontiers

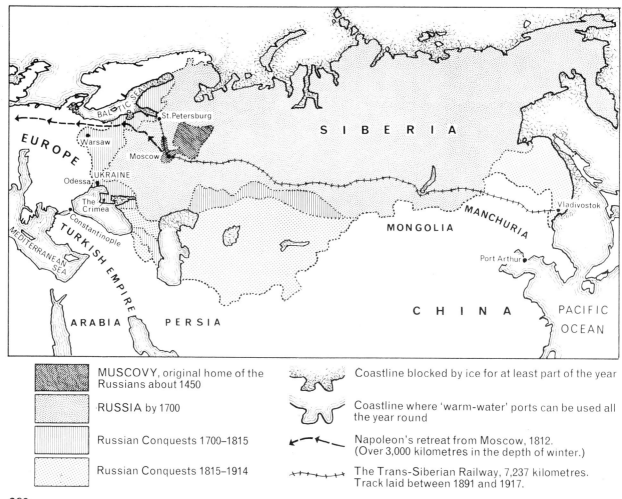

MUSCOVY, original home of the Russians about 1450

RUSSIA by 1700

Russian Conquests 1700–1815

Russian Conquests 1815–1914

Coastline blocked by ice for at least part of the year

Coastline where 'warm-water' ports can be used all the year round

Napoleon's retreat from Moscow, 1812. (Over 3,000 kilometres in the depth of winter.)

The Trans-Siberian Railway, 7,237 kilometres. Track laid between 1891 and 1917.

of them lived and died as *serfs*. That means that they were the property of powerful landlords. They had to work on their master's land and, in return, had small strips on which to grow their own crops for their families. A serf had almost no rights. A law of 1754 stated that the landlords had 'full power without exception' over their peasants. That meant they could make them work long hours, buy and sell them, punish them (they were only prevented from torturing or executing serfs), take them away from their families, prevent them from marrying and send them away to serve in the army (where the period of service was 25 years). By contrast the Russian noblemen and gentlemen lived a life of luxury and ease. They had estates in the country, where they spent the summer, and town houses in Moscow and St Petersburg, where they passed the winter months, going to parties, dances, gambling clubs and theatres. Life for the wealthy was very pleasant in Russia and they wanted to keep it

that way. Powerful groups of nobles always resisted (and sometimes killed) tsars who were making unwelcome changes.

Peter the Great, 1682–1721

One tsar whom they hated for making changes but who proved too powerful to resist was Peter the Great. No single ruler of Russia did more to modernize and improve his country than Peter Romanov (Romanov was the name of the ruling family in Russia from 1613 to 1917). He came to the throne at the age of ten and, when little more than a child, had to fight against powerful ministers and members of his own family in order to make his position secure. Peter hated much of what he saw in Russia. He thought his people were backward and not nearly as progressive as the nations of western Europe, which had fine modern cities, large ships sailing all over the world and powerful weapons of war. Most earlier tsars had not even been able to read and write.

Russian noblemen gambling their serfs
The noblemen of Russia cared nothing for the serfs whose lives they completely controlled. In this picture noblemen are gambling their serfs, represented by the bundles of dolls. The one who loses the game of cards will give all his serfs

to the winner. The serfs will be sent away from their homes and families and the land they farm, and their whole lives will be changed by a few hours of pleasure for their owners.

Peter patiently taught himself these skills and went on to learn many others: arithmetic, boatbuilding, gunnery and geography. When he could learn no more in his own country he travelled in western Europe, sometimes visiting foreign courts, sometimes disguising himself as a peasant to learn skills from simple workmen.

But if Peter wanted to bring Russia into closer contact with western Europe he also wanted to make western Europe aware of Russian power. The years 1698–1721 were largely devoted to war with two great neighbouring powers, Sweden and Turkey. By his successes in these conflicts, Peter at long last gained for his country outlets to the Baltic Sea and the Black Sea. By his defeat of the Swedish King, Charles XII (one of Europe's greatest generals), Peter had shown the western world that Russia was a power to be respected. To make it quite clear that Russia was now one of the world's leading nations, he built a strong, ocean-going navy, took the title of 'Emperor', and built a beautiful new capital city, called St Petersburg, on the shores of the Baltic.

Catherine the Great, 1762–96

For 40 years after the death of Peter the Great, Russian life and progress were disturbed by a series of struggles for the throne. Then, in 1762, another remarkable person seized power. She was Catherine II, known to history as Catherine the Great. Catherine was one of the 'enlightened despots' of Europe. That means that she wanted to use her power as absolute ruler not only to make her country stronger and greater, but also to improve the conditions of her people. She improved the organization of both central and local government. She encouraged the building of roads, canals and schools. She encouraged improved farming methods. She built a public library in St Petersburg. She founded a college of medicine and two hospitals. To show her faith in new medical ideas she became the first Russian to be vaccinated against smallpox.

She often declared her sympathy with the conditions of the serfs and tried to help them. But many of her planned reforms were never carried out. Catherine, just like earlier rulers, relied on the support of the gentry and nobility and they would not allow their power over the peasants to be limited. In fact, during the reign of Catherine the Great, the gulf between rich and poor grew wider. Towards the end of her reign

Peter shaving a courtier's beard
Peter the Great openly showed his contempt for many traditional Russian customs. For instance, he decided that the long beards traditionally worn by wealthy noblemen were a sign of backwardness. Western Europeans were either clean shaven or wore small, neat beards. So he ordered his courtiers to shave. If they would not he took a pair of scissors and cut their beards himself.

Catherine the Great

Catherine also began to change her mind about giving the peasants their freedom. Many of them had joined in a revolt against her, which nearly overthrew her government. Then, in 1789, the French Revolution broke out and Catherine, like many other European rulers, became frightened when she saw the lower classes of one country (France) seize power, kill their king and many of their noblemen, and threaten the peace of neighbouring states.

In foreign affairs Catherine continued to expand Russia's boundaries. In wars with Poland and Turkey she added large areas of eastern Europe to Russia, including the valuable, wheat-growing region of the Ukraine. Most of the northern shores of the Black Sea were won from Turkey, including the Crimea, and an important Russian naval base was established at Odessa.

Alexander I, 1801–25

Alexander I, who came to the throne in 1801 after the murder of his father, was yet another tsar determined to free the serfs and improve the conditions of all his people. He did away with the secret police, which all earlier tsars had used to control their people. He gave complete freedom of education and allowed young Russians to travel in western Europe, where they came into contact with new political ideas. He spoke of freeing the serfs and of setting up a new kind of government in which *all* Russians would share.

He was not very interested in war, or adding to Russian territory, but events in Europe forced him to play a leading part in international politics. When Alexander came to the throne, Napoleon Bonaparte of France had already made himself the most powerful man in Europe. Russia joined with other European powers in trying to stop Napoleon's career of conquest. All that happened was that Russian armies were defeated and thousands of Russian soldiers killed. So Alexander I signed a treaty with Napoleon in 1807. But it proved very unpopular with Alexander's people and by 1810 France and Russia were enemies again. In 1812 Napoleon invaded Russia with an army of between 400,000 and 600,000 men. But, for the first time in his career, the French Emperor suffered a very serious defeat and reached France again with only 20,000 members of his original army.

In the next two years Alexander played an important part in the final defeat of the French dictator. As a reward he claimed a large part of

The battle of Borodino, 1812
In this terrible battle, the last on Napoleon's march to Moscow, over a third of the Russian army, and a quarter of the French army, were killed.

The burning of Moscow

263

Napoleon's retreat from Moscow

It was Russia's climate rather than Russia's army which defeated Napoleon. As the Emperor made the long journey into Russia, Alexander's army only fought one important battle with him, which it lost. After that, the Russian generals retreated and retreated, making the French follow. Napoleon's men were short of food but hoped to find plenty when they reached Moscow. Napoleon believed that in Moscow, the second city of Russia, Alexander would surrender. But rather than let their beloved city fall into the hands of the enemy, the Russians set fire to it and retreated farther. Without food for his men Napoleon could not even spend the winter in Moscow and was forced to return home. The severe Russian winter killed thousands of the French soldiers on that 2,000 mile march and the Russian army, now following the retreating enemy, made frequent attacks on Napoleon's men.

Poland. This carried the Russian boundary well into central Europe. Fresh wars with Turkey added more of the Black Sea coast to Russia.

Alexander now tried to carry out his dreamed-of reforms. His Polish subjects were given their own parliament and much political freedom. New laws permitted landlords to free their slaves (very few did so). Political societies were allowed and journalists might write what they liked about the government. But things went wrong. The Poles demanded still more freedom. In Russia, there were plots to overthrow the government. Journalists and authors severely criticized the tsar and his ministers. Frightened by this, Alexander changed his mind about reform, set up the secret police again, closed newspapers, controlled education and forbade political societies.

Nicholas I, 1825–55

Nicholas I, the next tsar, decided that Russia needed strong rule. He stopped any political activity among the people. He sent possible troublemakers to prison in the distant, eastern part of Russia known as Siberia. But throughout his reign discontent increased. Foreign powers, also, were worried about the turn of events in Russia. Nicholas continued to expand Russia's frontiers at the expense of Turkey and of Persia. He was also trying to obtain more territory on the Pacific coast and to gain allies in the Balkan states. The leading European nations thought that Russia was becoming too large and too powerful. When Nicholas died in 1855 his country was fighting a war in the Crimea with England and France who were determined not to let Russia take any more land from Turkey.

In 1855 Russia had two large, unsolved problems. There was the growing political discontent at home. There was also the growing hostility of other countries towards Russia.

264

Chapter 44 Alexander II, The Tsar who tried to reform Russia

Alexander II
Alexander II came to the throne in 1855 at the age of 36. One of the greatest rulers of Russia, he had a deep love for his country and his people. He worked hard to try to solve the great problems facing Russia. In the end, after a reign of 26 years, those problems proved too great.

Alexander II took his father's place on the throne of Russia while his country was fighting one of the most wretched and unnecessary wars in modern history. The suffering of the soldiers on both sides was terrible. They fought in freezing snow and clinging mud. They endured hunger and thirst because their food supplies were so badly organized. They battled for month after month with poor weapons and under bad generals. The siege of the Black Sea port of Sebastopol alone cost over 400,000 lives and lasted almost a year. It was the sort of war that neither side could win. Bravery, endurance and heroic death were all wasted in this pointless conflict.

In September 1855 a tall, slim figure in a simple soldier's greatcoat moved among the frozen, weary troops at the battle-front. It was the new tsar. Though he spoke words of encouragement, congratulation and cheer, Alexander felt far from encouraged and cheerful. The men who lay around him, broken and dying, were Russian peasants, forced against their will to leave home and to fight for the tsar. As he looked at them, Alexander knew that not only must an end be put to the war but that the serf problem must be finally solved.

The Peace of Paris, 1856

The war was soon ended, at great cost to Russia's pride. Alexander let it be known that he was prepared to discuss peace terms. As a result all the countries concerned sent representatives to Paris, the capital of France, in February 1856 and a peace treaty was signed. By the treaty Russia gained nothing from two and a half years of war. Britain and France continued to support Turkey. Russia was not allowed free entrance to the Mediterranean Sea and her influence in the Balkans was reduced. The position of power and respect that Russia had enjoyed since 1812 had been challenged. Many of the tsar's people felt very bitter about this blow to their pride.

It took Alexander II exactly six years to get rid of slavery (for the serfs were no better than slaves). During those six years he had to force his will on his advisers, the representatives of the Russian nobility and gentry. They disliked the idea of change. They did not want their ancient power over the serfs taken from them. They warned the tsar that liberation of the serfs would lead not to the peace and contentment of the Russian people but to fresh disturbances and demands for even more changes — in fact they

Soldiers at camp in the Crimean war
Alexander II quickly ended this war when he saw how the troops suffered. They had to fight in severe weather without proper food, clothes, military supplies and medicines.

Estate serfs being freed
In 1861 Tsar Alexander II ended serfdom in Russia and 40 million serfs became free peasants. The ceremony shown below took place in the homes of many Russian landlords. While the nobleman and his family look on, their serfs kneel before them for the last time. They then arise as free men and drink to the health of the man who has set them free.

believed it would lead to revolution. But Alexander was determined. On 3 March 1861, the sixth anniversary of his accession, the emancipation law was published.

Whatever the landlords thought of the new law, most of the tsar's people were overjoyed. A writer who was alive at the time has described the feelings of Alexander and the citizens of St Petersburg:[*]

'... the Emperor came riding back to the Palace from St Michael's Riding School. At once hats and caps flew in the air ... and it seemed as though the very ground under our feet was shaking – so thundering were the cheers and hurrahs ... No pen could describe the rapture of those people as the Tsar rode past.... On his return to the Palace, the Emperor went to his little daughter's rooms and, his face radiant, kissed her and said: "Today is the happiest day of my life".'

As the news spread throughout the vast Russian empire, the peasants rejoiced. They were soon calling Alexander the 'Tsar Liberator'. They all knew that the emancipation law marked a turning point in Russian history.

But it was not the sort of turning point that Alexander II had hoped for. Soon rejoicing turned to angry demonstration, and cheers to shouts of protest. The trouble lay in the terms of the emancipation. The peasants were allowed small pieces of land to farm but this land had to be bought from the landlords. The division of farmland between the peasants and their former masters led to disagreements and riots. The peasants complained that they were given only the worst land, that the boundaries were not marked out fairly, that prices were too high. Usually they complained in vain and were forced to accept the terms laid down by the landlords. As a result many of them found themselves with small plots of poor land on which they could scarcely grow enough food for their own families. Yet they also had to earn enough money to make annual payments for their land. If there was a bad harvest or if the animals fell sick, the free peasants suffered terribly. Many of them were worse off than they had been before. Some moved to Siberia to make a fresh start. Others sold their farms and went to live in the towns in the hope of finding jobs. Some took their families away from Russia and began a new life in a new country – such as the United States of America.

Revolutionaries

It often happens that when a government begins to introduce changes in a country there is an immediate demand for more changes. So it was in Russia. Alexander believed that the emancipation was the first step towards reforming his country into an efficient, modern state. He wanted to go on from there to introduce other reforms – slowly and carefully. But there were some men who refused to wait – revolutionaries. There were many of them and they had many different ideas of what was best for Russia. Some wanted an elected parliament under the tsar. Others believed that only when the tsar and his government were overthrown could a new and better Russia be created. Alexander had done away with the censorship imposed by his father on books and newspapers, so these revolutionaries were able to publish their ideas for other people to read. Educational reforms had provided schools and more and more of the peasants were learning to read. In a very short space of time, revolutionary clubs had been formed which were joined by discontented men and women from all classes of society. In 1863 the tsar's Polish subjects revolted in an attempt to free their country from Russian rule. Alexander was willing to improve the lives of all his people but he was not prepared to give them complete political freedom. He certainly would not allow Poland to break away from the empire. He sent troops who put down the Polish revolt with great cruelty.

Other Reforms

Faced by the growing discontent of his people and the increasing demands for a freely elected parliament, Alexander began to wonder whether he had been mistaken in removing some of the harsh conditions placed on Russia by earlier tsars. Yet, for the time being he continued with his policy of reform. Earlier tsars had made strict rules for the running of universities, so that students could not learn or discuss subjects which the government did not like. In 1863 Alexander II removed these rules and the universities became, as they should be, places for the free discussion of *any* matters. Two years later the censorship of newspapers and magazines was eased and, as we have seen, Russians could read

---

[*]Quoted in E. M. Almedingen, *The Emperor Alexander II*, p. 166.

criticisms of the government. Another reform which gave the people more freedom was the reform of the law courts. Before this reform, peasants dared not accuse a landlord or gentleman in the courts. The judges were usually friends of the landlords and could be persuaded or bribed by them to decide in their favour. Now, trial by jury was introduced. That meant that, instead of one man deciding the case, a group of men listened to the two sides and then gave their verdict. Their decision was much more likely to be fair than the decision of one judge. Another reform later in the reign made the peasant's life easier. This was the army reform. Peasants still had to serve in the army, but for a smaller number of years. All classes had to share the duty (previously the upper classes were not forced to do military service) and men who had to look after their families did not have to serve.

These reforms all gave the Russian people more freedom. There were two other reforms which helped them to improve their standard of living. In 1864 Alexander allowed local councils to be set up to administer many districts of the empire. Local people were represented on these councils which were not under government control. They were able to carry out much-needed reforms in roads, hospitals, schools, etc. In 1870 similar councils were permitted in many Russian towns. One of the responsibilities given to the new councils was that of building schools where these were needed. There was still no system of state education in Russia but at least more people now had the opportunity to learn how to read and write.

Famine strikes the Russian peasants
Russia's new free peasants faced terrible suffering in times of famine. It was important to keep the animals alive, for without them the fields could not be ploughed. Here peasants take the thatch from their house to feed the horse (already thin and weak from hunger). Another house is being chopped up for firewood. If the people do not keep warm they will die in the freezing Russian winter.

Alexander II's attempts at 'reform from above'

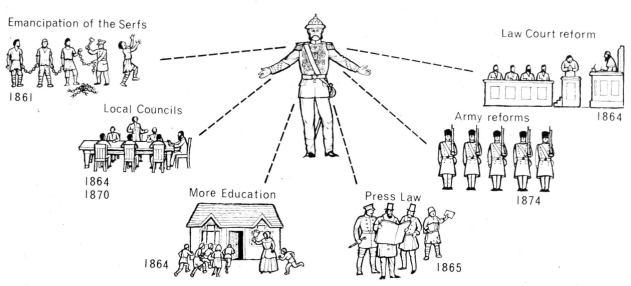

Emancipation of the Serfs
1861

Local Councils
1864
1870

More Education
1864

Press Law
1865

Law Court reform
1864

Army reforms
1874

Alexander changes his policy

One April day in 1866 the Tsar, with some members of his family, had left his palace to take a walk in one of the public parks in St Petersburg. As always, a small crowd had gathered to cheer him. As he left the park and walked towards his carriage a young man pushed his way through the crowd and, from only a few paces away, fired a pistol at the Tsar. Just in time another member of the crowd saw what was happening. He grabbed at the assassin's arm and the bullet just missed Alexander. The Tsar's life was saved but the experience was a great shock to him. He was at last persuaded that he *had* gone too far with his programme of reform. The assassin was a student and a member of a political club. His crime led to strict rules being imposed on all students once more. Clubs were closed. Newspapers and magazines were stopped. The government took severe measures to stop all political activity among the people and to suppress criticism. Although Alexander II never ceased seeking the good of his people and trying to modernize and improve his country, he no longer believed that the way to do this was by rapid reform. During the last fifteen years of the reign many Russians lost the freedom and advantages which had been granted to them during the first ten years of the reign. Suspected troublemakers were arrested and either imprisoned or sent to Siberia. The secret police entered people's houses and enquired into their private lives to seek information against enemies of the government. This only led to more bitterness among the people. Political clubs that had been banned, now met in secret. The spirit of revolution spread.

Foreign Affairs

While Alexander was facing these problems at home, his agents were continuing to build up one of the biggest colonial empires the world has ever seen. Turkey, Persia, Turkistan and China all lost territory to the advancing Russians. Many small Asian tribes and states lost their freedom and became Russian subjects. But these conquests did Russia little good. They had two main effects: they cost the Tsar's government a great deal of money and they made other European countries even more suspicious of Russia than they had been before. In 1877 war broke out with Turkey again. The Russian armies won some victories and marched almost to the gates of the Turkish capital, Constantinople. But then Britain,

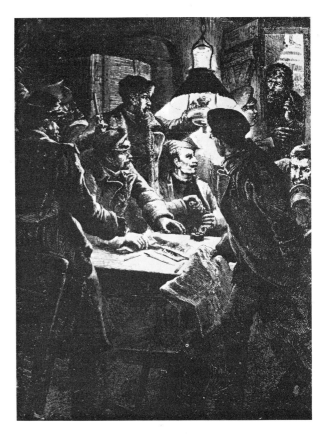

Revolutionaries meeting in secret

As Alexander II's reign went on the number of political and revolutionary clubs increased. After 1866 the government tried to destroy political activity among the people but this only forced the clubs to meet in secret. Here you see a group of 'Nihilists', men who believed in overthrowing the government by violent means because they disapproved of any kind of authority. We can see gentlemen in top hats. Other members of the group are soldiers and students. Most revolutionaries were members of the upper classes at this time. As they sit drafting a political pamphlet in the lamplight, a friend appears at the door to warn them that the police are coming. Immediately the men jump to their feet. They quickly gather up their papers and pens. A hand goes up to turn out the lamp. In a few seconds the police will arrive—to find an empty room.

Germany and Austria interfered. They forced Russia and Turkey to accept a peace treaty signed at Berlin. As a result of this treaty Russia gained almost nothing from an expensive war. Once again Russia was checked and humbled by other nations as she had been by the Treaty of Paris in 1856. Many Russians felt bitter about the Treaty of Berlin and felt that their government should not have signed it. They joined the growing number of people who were criticizing the Tsar and his ministers.

Revolutionaries and critics of the Tsar's government were few in number. Most Russian men and women loved Alexander and were loyal to him. To the end of his life Alexander II tried to combine continued reform with strong rule. But revolution and violence spread. Though the police arrested and punished thousands of the Tsar's enemies, several attempts were made on Alexander's life. Alexander himself felt more sorry than angry about these revolutionaries. He refused to make sure of his own safety by keeping away from his people. He thought of himself as 'the father of the Russian people' and delighted to show himself to them and make plans which he believed were for their good. At the beginning of 1881 Alexander and his ministers planned an important step forward in the political life of Russia: they proposed to let the people elect representatives who would help to make the laws of the country.

Death of Alexander

On 13 March Alexander had the document containing the new constitutional scheme in his pocket as he set off on a drive through St Petersburg in his carriage. Suddenly the horses reared as a bomb exploded close beside them. Another attempt had been made on the Tsar's life by a revolutionary. Alexander was unhurt. He stepped from the wreckage of his carriage to give what help he could to the injured. He even spoke, not unkindly, to Rysakov, the young man who had tried to kill him. 'Thank God your Majesty is safe,' said a member of the crowd. 'I am, thank God,' replied the Tsar. Just then another young revolutionary stepped through the crowd. 'Rather too early to thank God,' jeered Rysakov. The newcomer hurled a second bomb, which exploded at Alexander's feet, filling the air with smoke. When it cleared another 20 bodies lay on the ground and Alexander, his legs shattered and blood streaming down his face had only enough strength to murmur to his attendants, 'Take me home – to die.'

That afternoon the Tsar Liberator died and with him died any hope that Russia's rulers would be able to reform their country from above. From that moment revolution was only a question of time.

The assassination of Alexander II

On 13 March 1881, Tsar Alexander II drove back to his palace through the streets of St Petersburg. The route was carefully guarded by police but, because the Tsar was in a hurry, the driver took a short cut along an unguarded road. The Nihilists had already attempted to kill Alexander. Now one of them, Rysakov, siezed his opportunity. He flung a bomb at the royal carriage. Several of the Tsar's soldiers were killed or wounded but Alexander was unhurt. Minutes later a second assassin, Grinevetsky, hurled another bomb, which tore the Tsar's body to pieces. Thus died the one Russian tsar who had really tried to improve his people's conditions of life.

Chapter 45 The Last Tsars

Alexander III

The new Tsar, Alexander III, was understandably frightened and worried as he took the place of his murdered father. He had no desire to die in the same way and he also wanted to put a stop to the growth of revolutionary activity. He decided to rule firmly, to punish severely anybody who opposed him and to put an end to the reform movement. During his reign press censorship increased, justice and education came more and more under government control. It became clear to many Russians that the choice before them was between oppression and revolution. Plots against the Tsar's life were frequent. Frightened to go out into the streets and the countryside, Alexander III became almost a prisoner in his own palace. Though he escaped assassination, he wore himself out in the struggle against his enemies and died in 1894.

Industry

One good change that Alexander and his ministers had brought about in Russia was a great increase of industry and trade. In 1891 the first rails of the Trans-Siberian Railway were laid. This was to be one of the world's great railway lines, stretching right across northern Asia from Moscow to Vladivostock on the Pacific coast (see the map on Page 260). Alexander's government encouraged rich men to build factories and start trading companies. Moscow and St Petersburg grew as men flocked in from the countryside in search of work. But the industrial revolution brought more problems for the government to face. The factory hands often lived and worked under dreadful conditions. Many of them had nowhere to go at nights and had to sleep by their dirty machines. They were usually underpaid, but if they tried to band together to ask for more

Karl Marx

Frederick Engels

These two men, Karl Marx and Frederick Engels, wrote a book which has had more influence on the world than any other in modern times. The book was called *Das Kapital*. It was first written in German (both Marx and Engels were German) but soon appeared in other languages. The Russian version was published in 1872. The authors condemned capitalism, the system whereby rich men own factories, shops, etc. and pay other men to work for them. They predicted that the workers would soon rise up against their employers and establish a socialist state in which government and industry would be controlled by the workers. Neither man lived to see these ideas tried out but revolutionaries in many countries studied *Das Kapital* and some of them later organized workers' revolutions to overthrow existing governments and set up socialist or communist states. The first successful communist revolution occurred in 1917 in Russia.

wages their employers would not listen. The men grew angry with their wealthy masters and

discontented with the Tsar's government. Revolutionaries and political troublemakers found ready listeners in the factories of Moscow and St Petersburg.

Lenin and the Social Democrats

By the early years of the twentieth century the political opposition to tsarist government had become much more organized. Most revolutionaries realized that bomb-throwing and terrorism were not enough and worked out what sort of government they wanted to replace the existing regime. The moderate politicians were prepared to allow the Tsar to remain in power as long as he was guided by a parliament in which the people were represented. Others, however, wanted to replace tsarism by a socialist government. The most important socialist group was the Social Democrats. They based their beliefs on the ideas of Karl Marx and wanted a complete change in Russia's system of government. But not even all Social Democrats agreed on how to get what they wanted. In 1903 the party split into two groups: the Bolsheviks (which means 'the majority') and the Mensheviks (the minority). The Bolsheviks believed that only by revolution would political change be achieved but the Mensheviks hoped to obtain their objects by more peaceful methods.

The leader of the Bolsheviks was a remarkable man by the name of Vladimir Ulyanov. He was born in 1870 and early developed an interest in

The Tsar and his people
Towards the end of the nineteenth century the gulf between the tsar and his people widened. The royal family was surrounded by wealth and luxury. Here you see the Tsar and his family, beautifully dressed, watching an opera in the luxurious Imperial box. But the peasants lived in terrible poverty, even after the reforms of Alexander II. Conditions in the factories were particularly bad. Workers often had to sleep in narrow wooden boxes, as in the picture above, because they had nowhere else to go. Resentment grew and more and more people began to agree with the revolutionaries who told them that the tsar's government had failed and must be overthrown.

politics. When he was 16 his elder brother was executed for being involved in a plot on Alexander III's life. Young Vladimir swore to get revenge. He took a false name (as most revolutionaries did) — Lenin — and became an active Social Democrat. He was arrested and spent three years as a prisoner in Siberia. When he was released he continued his political activity and, in 1900, he had to leave Russia to escape fresh arrest. For most of the next 17 years he lived in various countries, organizing the work of the Bolsheviks from abroad. The Bolsheviks worked hard to recruit and train the industrial workers. In the factories they formed small groups of socialists, which were known as *soviets*, and as ill-treatment by government and employers grew, so did the size and number of the soviets.

Many workers joined the Bolsheviks because there was no other way they could improve their conditions. If they held demonstrations they found their meetings broken up by the Tsar's soldiers. If they went on strike they usually lost their jobs. The worst clash between demonstrators and troops came on 20 January 1905. It was a Sunday and many priests and workers decided to use the holiday to make a peaceful protest. They marched quietly towards the palace in St Petersburg to ask the Tsar to call a parliament and to grant shorter working hours to factory hands. As they walked towards the palace gates, there was suddenly a sound of rifle shots, followed by screams. Men and women lay dead and

Cossacks riding down strikers
When factory workers tried to draw attention to their grievances by strikes and peaceful demonstrations, the government's answer was to send soldiers to scatter them. Represented here in the film, *Dr Zhivago*, is a party of cossacks, the tsar's special cavalry soldiers, beating strikers with swords and whips.

dying as the soldiers fired again and the demonstrators struggled and fought to get away. This terrible event horrified people at all levels of society and turned many against the Tsar. The anniversary of *Bloody Sunday* is still commemorated in Russia.

Nicholas II

By this time there was a new tsar on the throne. Nicholas II became tsar in 1894. He was a handsome, charming man, not as harsh as some of his predecessors. But he was weak and allowed policy to be made by bad advisers and by his wife. They urged him to be firm and not to yield to the demands of the socialists and other politicians.

Russo–Japanese War, 1904–5

The first real crisis of Nicholas's reign came in 1904–5 and was a result of foreign policy. Russia was still trying to expand her boundaries in the East. This brought her into conflict with Japan who, like Russia, wanted to obtain control of Korea and the coast of Manchuria. In 1904 the two countries went to war. Everyone expected the tiny Japanese nation to be completely beaten by the mighty army and navy of Russia. But first the Russians were defeated on land and then their Pacific fleet was destroyed. Determined to win, the government ordered the Russian Baltic fleet to sail half way round the world to teach the Japanese a lesson. After a seven months voyage the Baltic fleet faced the enemy ships off the island of Tsushima. Almost every Russian ship was sunk. The suffering and loss of life among the Russian crews were very great and the country felt ashamed at the defeat.

The First Revolution and the Dumas

By now all sorts of people were against the Tsar's government. In 1905, for instance, the sailors of the battleship, *Potemkin*, mutinied. Sailors, soldiers, students, peasants, workers, doctors, lawyers, businessmen, all were demanding that Nicholas II should share the government of Russia with representatives of the people, that he should call a parliament. At last the Tsar gave way—a little. He agreed to the election of a body of advisers, known as the Duma. Between 1906 and 1917 four different dumas were called. They might have solved Russia's problems if they had been allowed to work properly. But Nicholas refused to trust them. He ignored their

Rasputin
Nothing made Nicholas II more unpopular than the support he gave to this man, Gregory Rasputin. He was known as 'the mad monk'. He was dirty and his habits were unpleasant but he exercised a strange power over the Tsar and his wife. In 1905 he is supposed to have healed Nicholas's son, Alexis, of a disease. Thereafter the royal family listened to everything Rasputin said. The Tsar even took his advice on government business. He urged Nicholas not to listen to other advisers and to be firm with the dumas. Rasputin became very unpopular with the Tsar's ministers and courtiers, and it was a group of them who murdered him in 1916. But by then it was too late to save the Tsar from disaster.

Russians reading the newspapers in September 1905
The news that these men are reading so eagerly is of the peace with Japan and the formation of the Duma.

decisions, forbade them to discuss certain matters, arrested some of their members and, when they still refused to obey him, he dismissed them.

The First World War

It was the Tsar's foreign policy which led to real revolution in Russia. In 1907 he made a treaty with Britain and France, promising to help them if ever they went to war with Germany (which even then seemed quite likely). In 1914 such a war *did* break out (see Part XIV) and, though the Russian armies were badly equipped, Nicholas, in support of his allies, declared war on the central European empires of Germany and Austria–Hungary. Millions of troops were marched westwards to face the enemy. The Germans were the best trained and equipped soldiers in the world at this time. The Russians fought furiously, but they did not have enough guns and ammunition to withstand the German attack. Within a year Russia lost nearly 4,000,000 men in the fighting. As the armies fell back, the Germans occupied large areas of Russian territory in the west and south-west. The roads were full of defeated soldiers and homeless peasants fleeing from the enemy back towards Moscow and St Petersburg.

In the cities things were almost as bad. Government inefficiency had resulted in severe food shortages. Thousands of civilians were starving, while their sons and brothers were dying on the battle fronts. Meanwhile the government fell more and more under the control of the Tsar's evil and unpopular adviser, Rasputin. While Nicholas was away commanding the army, the Empress and Rasputin made policy, dismissed ministers, controlled the Duma. At last, in December 1916, a few Duma representatives and courtiers could tolerate Rasputin no longer. They invited him to a party and put poison in his drink. He did not die. They gave him more poison. Still nothing happened. In desperation Prince Youssoupoff drew a revolver and shot the monk. Rasputin leaped about the room in pain — but he still lived. He dashed out into the courtyard. Only after four more shots had been fired at him did he fall in the snow — dead.

Lenin

Vladimir Ilych Ulyanov, better known as Lenin, is regarded in Russia and elsewhere as the second founder of world Communism. (The first was Karl Marx.) He is represented here in the film, *October*, addressing a meeting of soldiers and workers in 1917 during the October Revolution which swept the Bolsheviks into power.

Nicholas II and his son Alexis
Nicholas II was devoted to his family and sometimes neglected state business to be with his wife and children. He foolishly allowed his wife to dominate him and urge him to harsh measures when he should have been moderate. After the Revolution of 1917 Nicholas and his family were held as prisoners by the Bolsheviks. At last, fearing that his supporters might try to put Nicholas or one of his children on the throne, the revolutionaries shot the whole family all together in one room.

The March Revolution

On hearing of the death of his friend, Nicholas left his army and rushed back to the capital. But matters were getting beyond his control. On 11 March 1917 hungry citizens and strikers in St Petersburg marched through the streets with banners demanding an end to the war. They were fired on by the soldiers. The next day there was another demonstration, but this time the soldiers refused to fire. Instead, they joined the demonstrators. By midday disorganized groups of soldiers and workers were wandering through the capital with stolen guns, opening the prisons, killing members of the secret police, attacking government offices. To restore law and order the Duma took over the government under the leadership of a socialist named Kerensky. Tsar Nicholas once more left the war to return to the scene of the revolution. But on the way he learned to his horror that most of his generals suppor-

ted the new government. On the night of 15 March 1917 Nicholas II abdicated his throne. He was the last Tsar ever to rule over Russia. The tsarist system had come to an end after hundreds of years.

Defeated Russian soldiers persuading new recruits to fight for the revolution

After many months of terrible suffering in the war against Germany, the Russian soldiers, half-starved, wounded, exhausted and defeated, turned back for home. On their slow march back they met with new recruits marching to the war. They persuaded them that their real enemy was not the Germans, but the Tsar who kept them in such misery. The new soldiers returned with the deserters and used their weapons to overthrow the Tsar in the March, revolution (representation from the film, *Dr Zhivago*).

Part XI Eastern Empires: China and Japan

Chapter 46 The Great Days of Imperial China and Japan

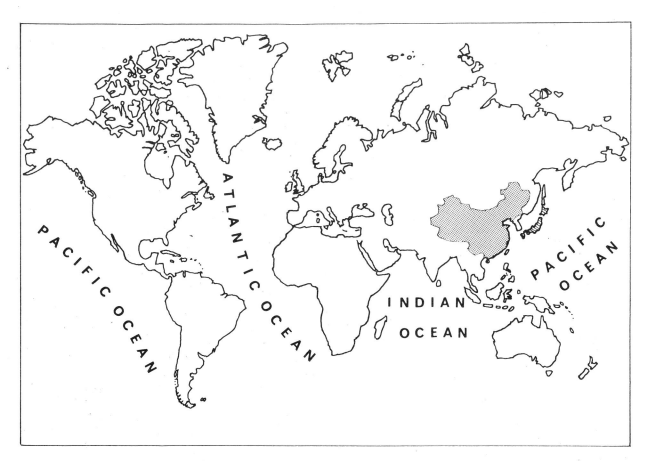

The Manchu Conquest of China

The Chinese, as you will already know, have a very old and highly developed civilization. The ancient Chinese peoples are known to us as the inventors of paper, silk, fine porcelain and gunpowder; they were the first to develop the art of printing; they were skilled also in politics, administration and philosophy. During the passing centuries many different *dynasties* (ruling families) had ruled China. Some, like the Mongols, had come from outside the country and established their dynasties by force. But all of them had been impressed by China's culture and way of life. Very few invaders had changed the ancient, well-proved customs of the people. So China remained much as it had been for centuries; a country proud of its traditions, practically closed to foreigners, having very little to do with the outside world.

Of all the dynasties which ruled China, that which seized power in 1644 was to prove one of the greatest—and the last. The Manchus came from Manchuria, the cold, mountainous country to the north-east of China. The peoples who lived to the north had frequently given trouble to the rulers of China. The Great Wall had been built centuries before to keep out the Mongols and the Manchurians, but as the Mongols broke through the Wall in the thirteenth century, so the Manchurians did in the seventeenth century. In 1644 the last Ming emperor was overthrown and the first Manchu emperor ruled in the capital city, Peking.

Growth of the Empire under Manchu Rule

The addition of Manchuria to China greatly increased the size of the Empire but the new rulers carried their conquests even farther. In the eighteenth century, Turkestan, Korea, the mountainous country of Tibet, the island of Formosa and large areas of Mongolia were added to the empire, while Chinese armies frequently raided southwards into Burma and Nepal. With these additions the Chinese Empire reached its greatest size ever.

The Manchu Emperors and their People

There were two great emperors of the Manchu Dynasty: K'ang Hsi (1662–1722) and Ch'ien Lung (1736–96). As you can see, each of them ruled for a very long time. As well as adding new territory to the Empire, these men ruled firmly and wisely. They appointed trusted governors to the distant provinces. They crushed rebellions swiftly and without pity. They kept to the old traditions of government and thus avoided angering people by the introduction of new methods — but they stopped officials being dishonest and made government administration more efficient. This meant that from the middle of the seventeenth century to the end of the eighteenth the Chinese people enjoyed peace.

But that was not the whole story. Life for most Chinese was harsh and cruel. Most of the people lived in the south and east of the Empire where the best farming land was to be found. In other regions there was desert, forest, barren mountain and rough pasture. But even in the agricultural area the people had a hard life. Most of the land belonged to a few wealthy landowners. The peasants hired their plots from these landlords at very high rents — as much as half of their entire harvest for the year. When the crops failed the rent still had to be paid and the poverty and suffering of the peasants were terrible.

Education

Yet in one way the Chinese peasant was better off than peasants in other countries of the world.

The Manchu Empire

Chinese painting of the Manchu dynasty
China has produced many very skilled artists. During thousands of years painters, sculptors, poets, musicians as well as makers of porcelain, silk-weavers and architects have built up a very fine artistic tradition. During the Manchu dynasty some forms of Chinese art reached their highest level. But then art began to decline, largely because artists continued doing things in the old, familiar ways, instead of thinking of new ideas. The same thing happened to the dynasty. Because the emperors refused to accept change they gradually lost their power.

This was in the opportunity to obtain education. The Confucian religion laid great stress on education and both the government and private individuals built schools. These schools were open to the sons of rich and poor alike. In most other countries only the sons of noblemen, landowners, or rich merchants had any chance of obtaining leading positions in the state. This was not true in China. All administrative officers were chosen on the results of a public examination. Any educated man who was clever enough or hard-working enough to pass the examination could become a civil servant. This system was not copied in Europe and elsewhere until late in the nineteenth century. It is just one of the many things that China has taught the world.

The one great mistake made by the rulers of China was their refusal to have anything to do with other countries. The emperors had always thought of themselves as superior to all other kings and princes. Since they refused to deal with foreign rulers as equals, there was, naturally, very little contact between China and the outside world. This, together with the mountains, deserts and seas which bordered the Empire, helped to keep it isolated. It is usually trade which brings different countries together, but the emperors were not very interested in buying goods from other lands. Chinese earth and Chinese skill produced everything that the Empire needed. Why should China, therefore, open her ports to merchants from Europe and America who were anxious to do business with her?

For centuries the people of China lived like this. Dynasties rose and fell but the old religion, the old traditions and the old attitude towards foreigners remained. From about 1750 this situation began to change. There were three reasons for this: population growth, foreign interference and weak rulers.

Population

The Chinese Empire was large and included people of many different races and tribes. The population of the Empire was also large but not until recent years *too* large. When the Manchus seized power in the mid-seventeenth century there were 108,000,000 people in China. During the next hundred years this increased slowly to about 143,500,000. But, during the next century the population more than doubled to 300,000,000. This, of course, meant that there was less land and less food for each Chinese man and woman.

The Emperor of China's Summer Palace at Peking
This beautiful example of Chinese architecture was raided and sacked by British soldiers in 1860. All the many treasures of Chinese art kept there were destroyed or stolen.

Ch'ien Lung, Manchu Emperor, 1736–96

A Chinese opium den

Here you see Chinese men smoking. But the stuff in their pipes is not ordinary tobacco. It is opium, a powerful drug that sends the smoker into a pleasant kind of trance. Millions of poor peasants in China smoked opium in the nineteenth century. It helped them to escape for a while from their misery and hunger. But the drug had other effects. It weakened the body and the mind of the smoker. Eventually it killed him. The Chinese government was very worried about the effects of opium on the people and did everything possible to stop its sale.

Once again it was the peasant who suffered the most. Discontent spread and the imperial government, which was quite unable to solve the problems of poverty, hunger and population growth, found itself facing outbreaks of rebellion and revolution.

Foreigners

Before the eighteenth century the only foreigners allowed on Chinese soil had been the Portuguese, who had a settlement at Macao. Then, in 1715, after many unsuccessful attempts, Britain gained permission for some of *her* merchants to trade in the port of Canton and to build a depot or *factory* there. Throughout the following years trade increased and both European and Chinese traders grew rich. Yet there was little sympathy or understanding on either side. The European seamen and merchants were often rough and ill-mannered towards their hosts, while Asian officials looked down on their visitors and allowed them little protection and few privileges. The situation was not too bad while the Emperor Ch'ien Lung lived, but after his death in 1799 (he actually stopped being emperor in 1796 but he remained the real leader of China until he died) the government was weakened, officials became dishonest, ill-treatment of merchants was frequent and relations between hosts and guests worsened.

Europe was now feeling the effects of the Industrial Revolution. More and more traders were looking for overseas markets. Because there was a great demand for the luxuries which China produced — tea, porcelain, furniture, silk, carpets, jewelry, fans and wallpaper — European merchants were determined to increase their trade with the Empire whether the Chinese government liked it or not. But, as we have seen, there were two problems to be overcome: the opposition of the Chinese government and the fact that China did not need foreign goods. The first of these problems, as you will see in the next chapter, was overcome by government pressure and force. The answer the merchants found to the second problem was opium.

Opium is a powerful drug made from the poppy flower. It has important medical uses but is also smoked by drug addicts. When Chinese people discovered that by smoking opium they could enjoy a pleasant 'happy' kind of trance and so 'escape' for a while from the harsh and unhappy world in which they lived, the demand for the drug grew. Most opium was produced in India and Turkey. European merchants began carrying it from these countries to Canton and Macao. But opium is a very dangerous drug. It has a bad effect on people's health and can also send them mad. Therefore the emperor's government tried to stop the opium trade. In 1729 the sale of opium was forbidden. In 1800 the importation of opium was declared illegal. But, instead of stopping, the trade increased. In 1800 5,000 chests of opium were sold in Canton. By 1840 this had increased to 30,000 chests. While Chinese men and women died of opium poisoning, while the government passed new laws and while officials searched

A battle with Chinese war junks during the Opium War

ports and warehouses for stocks of opium, Chinese and European merchants grew rich, the power of foreign traders increased and they began to demand the opening of more ports.

The Later Manchu Emperors

After the death of Ch'ien Lung, a series of weak emperors occupied the Chinese throne. The government's attitude to foreigners did not change and therefore relations with European traders, who were more numerous and powerful every year, grew worse. Within China civil servants became more open to bribery and corruption and the emperors lost control of their own government officers. No one in authority seemed able to produce any answers to China's growing problems. As the mid-nineteenth century approached, so did disaster.

The Opium War

In 1839 merchants at Canton and Macao were forced to stop opium trading. Then a Chinese was killed in a fight with some English sailors. When the British authorities refused to hand the sailors over, the imperial government ordered all British subjects to leave the mainland. As the situation worsened the British government ordered two naval ships to Canton to protect their

countrymen. On 3 November these warships were attacked by a fleet of armed Chinese junks. This event sparked off the Opium War. Now the Chinese were faced, not with a few European traders, but with the British government and the British navy, the finest navy in the world at that time. The warships attacked ports along the Chinese coast until, in 1842, the emperor was forced to ask for peace.

The Treaty of Nanking marked the end of Chinese isolation and the beginning of real European influence in the Orient. It was agreed: that four ports, as well as Canton, should be open to British trade; that Britain should have the island of Hong Kong as a naval base; that the opium trade should be made legal; that relations should be established between the governments in Peking and London as equals. Other western governments were not long in demanding similar concessions from the Chinese.

Manchu Emperors, 1796–1875

After the death of Ch'ien Lung, China's problems piled up and the later Manchu emperors were unable to deal with them. The growing population created economic difficulties. Harsh landlords provoked minor revolts among the peasants. There were racial clashes in some provinces. Everywhere people grumbled about increased taxes and dishonest officials. But not one of the four emperors who ruled between 1796 and 1875 was able to reorganize the administration. The imperial system of government was old-fashioned and incapable of reform.

Throughout the nineteenth century there were a number of serious rebellions. The most important of all was the T'ai P'ing Rebellion. In south China disorder, banditry and lawlessness were particularly bad. Then, in the 1840s, a new religion began to sweep the area. The leader of the movement was a young man called Hung Hsiu-ch'üan and he taught a faith which was a mixture of Christianity and Chinese religion. As the number of his followers grew, so the nature of the movement changed. From being a peaceful religious movement, it became a militant sect, the T'ai P'ing, armed and organized for rebellion. By 1853 the rebels controlled a large area of southern China including the important town of Nanking. The government had, of course, tried to suppress the revolt, but its armies had been completely defeated by the rebels. Not until 1864 did the emperor regain control of southern China and then only with the help of foreign troops.

So, the second half of the nineteenth century saw the emperor of China humbled by foreigners and troubled by his own rebellious subjects. The situation was similar to that faced at the same time by the tsar of Russia. Was the Manchu dynasty, like the Romanov dynasty, about to collapse?

The T'ai P'ing rebels attacking a gun boat at Nanking

Japan

Off the eastern coast of China lies a group of islands making up the nation of Japan. It is one of the most ancient nations in the world. According to Japanese legend, the emperor is descended from the sun goddess. Whoever the first emperor was, he certainly ruled long before recorded history. Since the time of that first, unknown emperor, the same family or dynasty has ruled in unbroken succession to the present day. The Japanese, therefore, can claim to have the oldest ruling family in the world, perhaps as much as 2000 years old.

But by the eighteenth century the emperor had long ceased to be the real ruler of Japan. He was recognized as the leader of the nation and enjoyed the respect of the people, but, in fact, his authority was wielded by someone else. That 'someone else' was the *shogun*, a military leader whose position depended on the support of the army and the nobility. The shogun ruled from the capital city of Yedo (now called Tokyo) while the emperor kept his court and performed ceremonial functions in the old town of Kyoto.

Japan was a feudal nation. Most of the land was held by wealthy nobles (*daimios*) who also kept troops of soldiers which had to be ready at all times for the imperial service. Beneath the noble and military classes were the class simply known as the 'common people'. They were peasants, traders and workmen—people with few rights and privileges and no social position.

> 'So long as the sun warms the earth, let no Christian be so bold as to come to Japan, and let all know that if the King of Spain or the Christians' God or the great God of all violate this command, he shall pay for it with his head.'*

This was an order made by the reigning shogun in 1640. For many years European traders and missionaries had been welcomed in Japan. But as time went by the government became more and more worried about the power and influence of the foreigners. The white men brought guns and gunpowder with them. Sometimes they used these weapons to kill Japanese people. They also sold firearms to some of the great nobles and the shoguns were afraid that these men might become too powerful. The Christian missionaries also created a problem: large numbers of Japanese

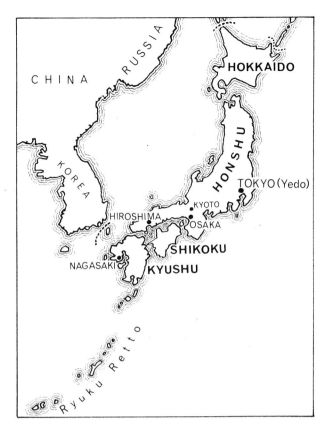

Japan

were converted (they changed their religion) and their loyalty to the traditional way of life and to the government was weakened. So the shoguns gradually broke off Japan's links with the outside world. In 1636 the following orders were issued: no Japanese ship might sail to a foreign port; no Japanese might go abroad; no Japanese already abroad might travel home; all Christians were to be arrested. These were soon followed by orders forbidding foreigners to trade in Japan. When, in 1640, the king of Spain sent an embassy (an official mission) to the Japanese court, 61 of the European representatives were murdered, their ship was burned, and the remaining 13 men were sent back to their master to tell him that the shogun of Japan meant what he said. For 213 years Japan remained completely cut off from the outside world.

Or almost completely. The Japanese rulers, though they were determined not to allow foreigners or foreign customs to influence their people, realized that they must keep *some* contact with the outside world, so they allowed Dutch merchants to carry on trading with Japan. But only on very strict conditions. The merchants had to

---

*Quoted in M. Edwardes, *Asia in the European Age*, p. 44.

stay on the tiny island of Deshima, surrounded by a high fence of sharp, pointed stakes. No Japanese were allowed on to the island and the only approach to it was heavily guarded by soldiers. The Dutch were only allowed to remain at all because the government wanted two things from them: European goods and news. Once a year the leaders of the Dutch community were taken, under heavy guard, to Yedo, where they had to give the shogun a report on everything important that had happened in the outside world during the previous twelve months.

So, for over two centuries, Japan was a group of 'closed' islands. It was as though a great wall had been built round them. No one outside knew anything about the firm, harsh rule of the shoguns or the backward way of life of the Japanese people.

Just as the Chinese emperor found it impossible to go on suppressing his people and keeping out foreigners, so did the Japanese shogun. By the middle of the nineteenth century the position of the shogun had been weakened by popular movements aimed at restoring the ancient Shinto religion (in place of the official Confucianism) and the power of the emperor. At the same time European nations were beginning to demand

A Japanese painting of foreign ships in Tokyo Bay
On 14 July 1853 foreign ships anchored in Tokyo Bay. As the astonished Japanese watched, several boats were rowed towards the shore. When they landed hundreds of smartly-dressed—and well armed—soldiers and sailors stepped ashore. The leader of the expedition was Commodore M. Perry of the United States navy. The picture below shows him about to present to the shogun's representative a message from the United States' president. On the far right of the picture you can see rows of armed American troops.

284

that Japan should open her ports to foreign trade. The government heard with alarm the results of the Opium War and realized that more and more foreign ships would now be sailing in eastern waters. The Dutch reported on the amazing machines which were now being built in Europe and America—particularly steamships. The shoguns were worried, but still they refused to allow foreigners into Japan—until 1853.

Commodore Perry

In that year a force of four armed ships was sent to Tokyo by the United States government. The expedition was under the leadership of Commodore M. Perry and he was ordered to present a message from the president of the United States requesting the shogun to open Japanese ports to trade. America was particularly anxious to 'open up' Japan because her whaling fleets, which spent many months every year in the southern Pacific Ocean needed ports where they could obtain fuel and supplies. The Japanese could not ignore Perry's show of force. When the American Commodore returned six months later—this time with *ten* ships and 2,000 men—the shogun agreed to sign a treaty which allowed American ships to use two Japanese ports. Determined not to be left out, Russia, France, Holland and Britain made treaties.

There now followed 15 years of disturbance in Japan. The government and the daimios were divided into two groups—pro-foreigners and anti-foreigners. There were incidents between Japanese people and European merchants. On more than one occasion British ships shelled a coastal town in order to revenge some Englishman who had been killed. Many Japanese nobles and officials blamed the shogun for admitting the foreigners and bringing all these troubles on the country, and Japan was divided between the friends and the enemies of the shogun. This confused situation came to an end in 1868, when the Emperor Meiji decided that he would no longer be a mere figurehead. He announced that he was taking over all the powers of the shogun. He left Kyoto and moved to Yedo (which he renamed Tokyo). He also announced that from that time onward Japan would take her place among the nations of the world.

This great political change is known in Japan as the *Restoration*. It marks the beginning of Japan's truly remarkable modern history. The country which, a few years before, had been backward, feudal and cut off from the rest of the world, immediately began to transform itself into the modern, wealthy, democratic, industrial nation it is today.

Chapter 47 The End of Imperial China

During the second half of the nineteenth century European influence in China grew. More trade agreements were forced on the Emperor's government until, by 1895, foreign treaty ports had been established all along the coast and even inland along the river Yangtze. Nor were merchants the only foreigners living in China. Missionaries were active in many parts of the country, teaching, not only Christianity, but also western languages and customs. European officers served in the emperor's army and European officials held important positions in the administration. British, French and Russian companies were given permission to build roads and railways in China. The imperial government could do nothing to stop this spread of foreign influence. To many educated Chinese it seemed that in a few years the Russians, Americans, French, Germans, British and Japanese would have divided up the Empire between themselves and that China would have ceased to exist.

Sino-Japanese War, 1894–5

The weakness of China was shown up most clearly in the war with Japan which broke out in 1894. Following a remarkably successful policy of rapid westernization (see next chapter), Japan had emerged from centuries of backwardness and feudalism as a modern, trading nation. Like other trading states, Japan decided that she, too, wanted bases on the Asian mainland. The territory that interested the Japanese was Korea. But China also claimed to control Korea. In August 1895 the two empires went to war. Within weeks, the Chinese army and navy had been crushed. Japanese troops invaded not only Korea, but Shantung and Manchuria. By capturing Port Arthur and Wei Hai Wei, Japan controlled the sea approaches to the Chinese capital, Peking. The Chinese government agreed to peace terms.

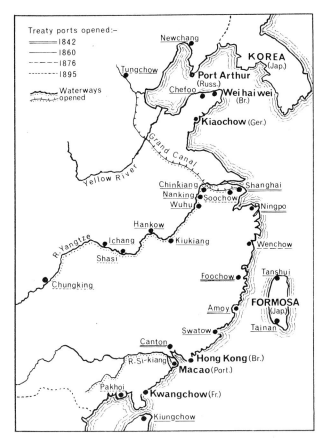

The treaty ports of China
Canton was a British treaty fort before 1842 and Hong Kong was ceded to Britain in 1842.

A battle between Japanese and Chinese soldiers in Korea, 1894

Korea was recognized as independent (though, in fact it was, and remained, under Japanese control). Japan obtained treaty ports and the islands of Formosa and the Pescadores. Japanese gains would have been even greater if European powers had not interfered in order to stop Japan becoming too powerful.

Sun Yat-sen

By this time there were many Chinese people, especially among the educated classes, who were alarmed by the corruption and inefficiency of the government and the increasing power of the foreigners. Some of them agreed with the Empress Dowager that the answer to China's problems was a return to the old ways. Others believed everything would be all right once the foreigners had been thrown out. But there were a few who saw that the only way to build a new China was to learn from the Europeans all about modern military, economic and political techniques. Once learned, these techniques could be used to overthrow the government and get rid of the foreigners. One man who thought like this was a young medical student, Sun Yat-sen.

Sun was the son of a Chinese peasant. From a very early age he was familiar with the poverty and misfortune endured by most of the Chinese people. He saw how they suffered at the hands of landlords and government officials. When he was twelve years old, Sun was sent to the Pacific island of Honolulu, where he was looked after by an elder brother. There he learned English and discovered — what he could never have learned in China — that the Europeans had developed economically and politically far beyond his own people. This knowledge made him angry and scornful of the Manchu government of China which refused to allow modern reforms in the country. When he was 20, Sun went to Hong Kong to learn medicine in an English-run college. In 1894 Sun Yat-sen returned to China as a doctor and began work in Canton. Already he was the leader of a small revolutionary group, who, because they were determined at all costs to bring about reforms in China, called themselves the 'Dare-to-dies'. When the Japanese war broke out and the government was busy trying to stop the invasion of China, the 'Dare-to-dies' decided the time was ripe for a revolution. Unfortunately the plot was discovered. Sun was lucky to escape from the group's headquarters just before government troops broke in and arrested several of his friends. While Sun was hiding in Hong Kong he heard that four of his friends had been executed.

The next five years Sun spent in exile in Europe. Wherever he went he tried to get money and foreign support for his cause. During this time he kept in touch with the 'Dare-to-dies', whose numbers were steadily growing. He also worked out his plans for a new China. These were contained in his book, *The Three Principles of the People*. Sun's 'Three Principles' were nationalism, socialism and democracy. He planned to found an independent nation in which the people would own the land and have a share in the government. 1899 found him in Tokyo from where he organized a number of unsuccessful revolutions in China.

The Boxer Rising

Meanwhile the Ch'ing dynasty was at last losing its control of the country. The event which more than any other marked the downfall of the Manchus was the Boxer Rising. The Boxers were wild, semi-religious bands of fanatics who supported the traditions of old China and pledged themselves to overthrow the foreigners. Violence began in 1899 with the murder of European missionaries and Chinese Christians. The foreign diplomats became alarmed and began to move more troops into China. The Empress Dowager thought the moment had come to rid her country of the foreigners and gave her support to the Boxers. This was the last great act of folly committed by a Manchu ruler. The foreign diplomats and their staffs took shelter in their own quarter of Peking and, after eight weeks, were rescued by foreign troops sent up from the coast. The Boxers dispersed. The government fled from the capital. Peking was looted by foreign soldiers. European armies penetrated deep into China to destroy surviving groups of Boxers. And the Chinese had to accept yet another treaty forced on them by the Western powers. It provided for the punishment of some of the officials responsible and memorials to those killed. Other measures strengthened the safety and status of foreigners.

The Government Attempts Reform

Now, even Tz'u Hsi recognized that the policy of shutting out the modern world from China was mistaken. Her government began to introduce reforms. Education was remodelled on western lines. Long-needed changes were made in the law-courts. The system of government was examined and the Empress Dowager promised that, in a few years, a parliament would be called and the people would have a share in the running of the

British troops defending the Legation during the Boxer rising
During the Boxer rising frightened foreign diplomats and their staffs took shelter in the Legation buildings in Peking. There they resisted several Chinese attacks for 55 days before they were rescued by European and Japanese troops.

The Empress Dowager of China, Tz'u Hsi
From 1861 to 1908 the real ruler of China was the Empress Dowager Tz'u Hsi. After 1861 the heir to the throne was a child and Tz'u Hsi took over as regent. In 1875 the new emperor died and was again succeeded by an infant, and Tz'u Hsi remained regent. She was a forceful woman who believed that China could be saved only by the old traditional ways. Without her courage and strength of character, the Manchu dynasty would probably have collapsed sooner than it did.

country. But, as in Russia so in China, reforms introduced by the government were too slow and too late. Revolutionary movements were growing in strength year by year — including the 'Dare-to-dies'.

The Double Tenth

10 October 1911 is known in China as the *Double Tenth* (the tenth day of the tenth month). It is the day when Sun Yat-sen's followers began the revolution which was to sweep the Manchu government from power. Sun himself was in America (he was a hunted man throughout Asia) when his general Huang Sing seized the town of Wuchang and then persuaded a large part of the Chinese army to join him. The success of the revolution was immediate: town after town, province after province joined the 'Dare-to-dies'. In December Sun returned to China, ready to become President of the newly-founded Republic.

Yuan Shi-Kai

But there was still a problem to be faced. Part of China, including Peking and the young Emperor, were under the control of a powerful general, Yuan Shi-Kai. Rather than continue fighting, Sun Yat-sen offered to make terms with Yuan. The two leaders at last reached an agreement. The Republic was to be officially proclaimed. The Emperor would be persuaded to resign. A National Assembly would be set up and the government would be in the hands of a prime minister and a cabinet. The head of state would be a president with no executive powers. The first president would be Yuan Shi-Kai. Sun Yat-sen was quite prepared to retire from politics after he had organized the National People's Party, the Kuomintang. So, in March 1912, the new Chinese constitution came into existence. Sun Yat-sen left the work of government to Yuan Shi-Kai and himself took the post of Director-General of Railways.

Failure of Yuan Shi-Kai's Government

But Yuan Shi-Kai had been too well trained by the Manchus to be able to accept the idea of a republic. Within four years he had dissolved the National Assembly, outlawed the Kuomintang, obtained money from abroad to finance a new dictatorial regime and proclaimed himself, first, President for life, then Emperor. Sun Yat-sen returned to political life to oppose the new tyrant but the 'Second Revolution' was easily

An agent recruiting for the 'Dare-to-dies'

Yuan Shi-Kai

Yuan Shi-Kai, to whom Sun Yat-sen entrusted the presidency of China in 1912 was a cunning and untrustworthy man. He had served long under the Manchu rulers and had risen to be Chief Minister of China. On more than one occasion he had betrayed his friends or his emperor to gain personal advantage.

289

overthrown by President Yuan in 1913. Yet the Kuomintang did set up a rival government at Canton. By now, however, they were not the only opponents of the government; China was full of rival revolutionary groups. This was the position when Yuan Shi-Kai died in 1916.

The First World War

By this time China had other urgent problems to face. In 1914 the First World War broke out. China took no part in this war but Japan, seeing the opportunity of increasing her empire in Asia, joined Britain and France in declaring war on Germany. In 1915 Japanese troops attacked the German treaty port of Kiachow and positions in Shantung province. Her stated aim was to hand this territory back to China, but, once it was safely in her grasp, she kept it and also made a series of commercial demands which the weak and divided Chinese could not resist.

Beginnings of Communism in China

Widespread protests swept through China and added to the political confusion in the country. At Peking various generals or 'war lords' fought for the control of the government. At Canton Sun Yat-sen had been appointed President of the Chinese Republic but he had support only in the South. Sun realized that he would never reunite China without outside help. Most of the major powers supported Japan's control of Shantung province. There was one nation which did not—which was in fact, an enemy of Japan, and which had, like China, just overthrown an ancient and corrupt regime. This was Russia, where Lenin and the Bolshevik party were establishing a communist state.

In 1923 the Russian leaders sent a man called Borodin to help Sun Yat-sen reorganize the Kuomintang party. Soon other Russians followed. As a result of their influence the Kuomintang made an alliance with the small Chinese communist party. Using modern methods, this new political force gained in strength but, even at the beginning, there were divisions between the Communists and the followers of Sun Yat-sen.

By 1925 China was in a pitiful state. Roads and bridges needed repair. Towns and villages were plundered by rival armies. Young men were taken away from the land and made into soldiers. Crops went untended and the people starved (remember, also, how rapidly the population of China was rising). In 1925 Dr Sun Yat-sen died. He had given his life for China and he did not live to see the birth of the new nation for which he had worked so hard. He was never interested in winning fame or wealth for himself and he died a poor man. After he died, a crumpled piece of paper was found beneath his pillow. It said, 'I beg Ching-Ling, my wife and comrade, to accept my books, my old clothes and the house in Shanghai, not as a bequest—because my few possessions cannot be called an estate—but as a souvenir'.

The burial of Sun Yat-sen
Not until 1929 was it possible for the Chinese people to give Sun Yat-sen's body a suitable resting place. Then a special tomb was built for it on Purple Mountain, outside Nanking. His name is still honoured in China as the founder of the revolution.

Chapter 48 Japan copies the West

One of the most amazing aspects of modern history is the change which came over Japan between the middle of the nineteenth century and the early years of the twentieth. We have seen how Japan was a closed, backward society. We have seen how America and Europe forced the Japanese to open their country to international trade. The same things happened in China and there the result was political confusion. But in Japan the story was quite different. The Japanese made up their minds to learn all they could about western industry and commerce. They sent their young men abroad to be trained in Europe and the U.S.A. They adopted western political ideas. They changed their educational system. They equipped their army with modern weapons. Within half a century of Commodore Perry's visit to Tokyo, Japan had become the most advanced and the most powerful nation in the East and had begun to build up a large empire.

A New Kind of Government
The group of men that helped the emperor to regain full administrative powers in 1868 immediately set about completely changing the political life of Japan. They started by breaking the power of the daimios. In 1871 feudalism was brought to an end. The noblemen were no longer able to keep private armies, maintain their own law courts and behave like kings in their own territory. They were allowed to continue administering their former lands but now they did so as paid officials of the emperor.

In 1889 the first real step towards democracy was taken when a written constitution was introduced. This stated that Japan was to be ruled—under the emperor—by a parliament consisting of two chambers. This parliament was closely modelled on the English pattern. The upper house consisted of noblemen and gentlemen—

the wealthy classes. The members of the lower house—the House of Representatives—were elected by the people. But not by *all* the people; only property owners were allowed to vote. This first Japanese parliament had very limited powers. The country was really ruled by a cabinet of ministers.

This setting up of representative government without any kind of revolution or popular struggle is unique in modern history. In most countries ordinary men and women have had to fight to gain their political freedom from a king, a powerful class or a colonial regime. In Japan, the constitution was the 'gift' of the emperor and his advisers to the people. It shows how very strongly the Japanese were influenced by the western world. The new government, determined to modernize their country, examined western political systems and simply decided to 'adopt' parliamentary democracy.

The new government changed the system of land ownership and tenancy and introduced a completely new system of taxation. These changes were resisted by noblemen and peasants alike but the government—and the army—proved too strong for them. Within a very few years the government was shown to be right. Japan had a healthy economy and could afford to pay for industrial and agrarian expansion.

The Industrial and Agrarian Revolutions
A hundred years after Europe's industrial revolution had begun industrialization took place in Japan. But it took place much more rapidly than it had done in the West. Most of the new factories and businesses were set up by the government, sometimes with money borrowed from abroad. Others were founded by private individuals with government encouragement and help. Traditional Japanese crafts, such as

silk weaving, were mechanized but steam-powered factories were also built to produce cotton cloth, paper, steel, chemicals, glass and cement. Mines, ammunition works and ship-yards were also opened. By 1890 over 200 factories had been built and the number was still rising. Public buildings, large shops, wide roads, street lighting and trams appeared in Tokyo and other towns, which now began to look like European cities.

Modern communications were vital to the new Japan. The first railway was built in 1872. It ran from the capital to Yokohama and was financed by the government. By the end of the century a network of state-owned railways had been built. In 1886 an efficient postal service, including a telegraph system, was created. By 1900 Japan had begun to build its own steamships. To pay for all this expansion Japanese finances and currency or money had to be placed on a sure foundation, and so the Bank of Japan was created in 1881 and the nation's currency was completely changed.

You will remember how in eighteenth century Britain, the Industrial Revolution speeded up the Agrarian Revolution. This happened in Japan also. Population increase and the growth of towns forced the Japanese to modernize their farming methods. Students were sent abroad to learn modern agricultural methods. They came back and applied in their own country what they had learned about mechanization, fertilizers and pest control. As a result the production of rice — the most important food in Japan — increased enormously. Unproductive land was brought under the plough. Peasants were also encour-aged to produce other foodstuffs. Along the coasts, for instance, a thriving fishing industry was established.

Education

Japan's eagerness to learn showed itself in a completely new education system. In 1872 com-pulsory primary education was introduced and, within a few years, secondary education, too, was obligatory. Colleges and universities followed. Teachers were brought from abroad. Western languages were taught to Japanese children. European books were translated into Japanese. The government was determined that as many people as possible should learn everything that the West had to teach.

Japanese warriors of 1868

Japanese soldiers in 1904
Note the contrast between these Japanese soldiers of 1868 and the new Japanese army below. The new Japanese army was an extremely fierce and efficient fighting force. It com-bined modern training and equipment with the traditional, fanatical loyalty to the emperor. Japanese soldiers thought it an honour to die for their country. Defeat was a complete disgrace for a Japanese officer. Rather than face it, he would fight until he was killed. Rather than surrender he would commit suicide. No wonder the Japanese army was so terrify-ing — and successful.

Military Expansion

But Japan's modernization had a more evil side. In the new regime the military leaders had considerable influence and independence. They were determined to provide their country with a powerful army and navy, for which there are several reasons. Military training had always been important in Japan. Samurai and other soldiers had to submit to the most strict discipline in order to make themselves tough. In the army there was a strong tradition of absolute loyalty to the emperor. A young soldier was happy to die, if necessary, for his country. National pride demanded that if Japan was to have an army and navy, they must be the finest army and navy possible.

But there was another reason. Many Japanese leaders were determined to extend their country's influence. In fact, they wanted to create a Japanese empire. They argued that all the neighbouring islands where Japanese people lived should be under the emperor's control. They also said that Japan needed new lands to which part of the nation's growing population could emigrate. They claimed that countries like China and Korea should be forced to open their ports to Japanese traders. Above all they felt that, as the leading nation in the East, they should take their place among the other great nations of the world. The creation of an empire would show just how powerful and important Japan was.

In 1872 the military reforms began. First of all conscription (compulsory military service) was introduced; men of twenty years of age had to serve for three years. Then the army leaders looked around for someone to help them train their troops. They saw that Germany had the best army in the world and so they hired German officers to advise them and they bought German guns. To help redesign the navy, Japan's rulers sought the aid of the world's leading naval power, Britain. By 1890 Japan was spending a third of its annual budget on the armed forces. She was soon to test her new army and navy in war.

War with China, 1894–5

It was natural that Japan should look first to Korea, the nearest country on the Asian mainland, to become a trading partner. In the 1880s she obtained treaty ports on the Korean coast and began to exert influence over the Korean government. But China also had considerable influence

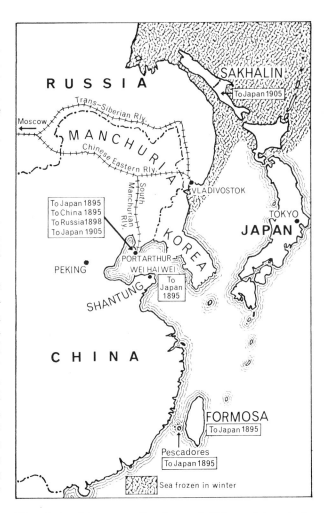

The clash of Japanese, Russian and Chinese interests in Korea, 1880–1905

Jap the Giant Killer

The western world was astonished by the Japanese defeat of the mighty Chinese empire in 1894–5. This was the first time that Japan's military strength had been realized. The European nations began to be worried by what they saw and persuaded Japan to give up some of the gains she had made by the Treaty of Shimonoseki.

293

in Korea. She considered Korea vital to Chinese security and greatly resented Japanese interference. So relations between the two empires grew unfriendly. There were frequent diplomatic clashes and open fighting between the two countries in 1884. But war did not break out until 1894. Japanese troops were sent to the Korean capital. The Chinese moved their army into the country, only to be defeated by their enemy. Soon they were thrown out of Korea and saw Japanese armies gathering on their frontier, threatening to invade China. They had to make peace. By the Treaty of Shimonoseki, Japan gained the commanding influence in 'independent' Korea as well as the possession of the island of Formosa and the naval base and harbour of Port Arthur, and some Chinese treaty ports.

War with Russia, 1904–5

But China was not the only mainland power Japan had to face. Russia, as we have seen was expanding eastwards in search of warm-water ports. As soon as news of the Treaty of Shimonoseki reached St Petersburg, the tsar's ministers discussed the situation with other European diplomats. As a result of their discussions, Japan was asked to give Port Arthur back to China. She did so – angrily. She was even more angry when, in 1898, the Russians took over Port Arthur themselves. As China collapsed into anarchy, Russia and Japan, like the western powers, were both hoping to grab territory for themselves. Russia built the Trans-Siberian Railway and the Chinese Eastern Railway. By the turn of the century she was in a position to control Manchuria and it seemed only a matter of time before Russian troops overran Korea. This Japan was determined to prevent, since it would put an end to her own ambitions on the mainland.

The two nations now raced each other in the building of warships and both tried to obtain diplomatic support from other powers. In 1902 Japan made an alliance with Britain. In 1904, choosing what seemed to be a good moment, Japan attacked Port Arthur, without making a declaration of war. We have already discussed how the Japanese army and navy were completely victorious in this war and how two Russian fleets were destroyed by Japanese warships. By the Treaty of Portsmouth (1905) Japan gained Port Arthur, the southern half of the island of Sakhalin and became the controlling power in Korea and Manchuria. The country was exhausted by the war but at last the Japanese felt that they had proved their right to complete equality with the world's leading nations.

Extension of the Japanese Empire, 1910–18

Japan was now ready to take advantage of any favourable circumstances to extend her empire. In 1910 the emperor of Korea was forced to abdicate (i.e. give up his throne) and his country became part of the Japanese Empire. In 1914 all the world's major powers (except the U.S.A., which did not join in the war until 1917) were involved in the First World War. Japan believed this was an excellent opportunity to push the boundary of her empire still farther. She made an alliance with Britain, France and Russia. First she took over the German treaty port of Kiaochow (saying that she intended to hand it back to China) and then, despite Chinese protests, she seized the province of Shantung. The next step was still more bold. In 1915 Japan made 21 demands of China. They included recognition of Japanese control in Shantung, more commercial rights for Japan and the provision of Japanese advisers to 'assist' the Chinese government in all its affairs. What they amounted to was the establishment of a protectorate* over the whole of China. China could do nothing but agree to most of the demands but other nations protested and began to be very worried about Japanese power.

In 1917 Japanese military leaders urged their government to take advantage of Russia's difficulties. After the Bolshevik Revolution, Russia was in a state of civil war. Japanese troops invaded Vladivostok and marched deep into Siberia. After the First World War, Japan received by treaty the right to administer several Pacific islands, formerly owned by Germany.

This was the height of Japanese power for the time being. As other nations recovered from the war, her gains were questioned. America particularly was becoming very worried about Japan's power in the Pacific. In 1921 Russia regained control of Siberia. In the same year an international conference persuaded Japan to withdraw from Shantung. Japan had been finding it impossible to administer her large empire but she resented being forced to give parts of it up. Like a lion whose dinner has been taken away, Japan was angry – and dangerous.

---

*This is the authority assumed by a strong state over a weak one without taking direct control and full possession.

Part XII India, the Jewel of the East
Chapter 49 Collapse of an Empire

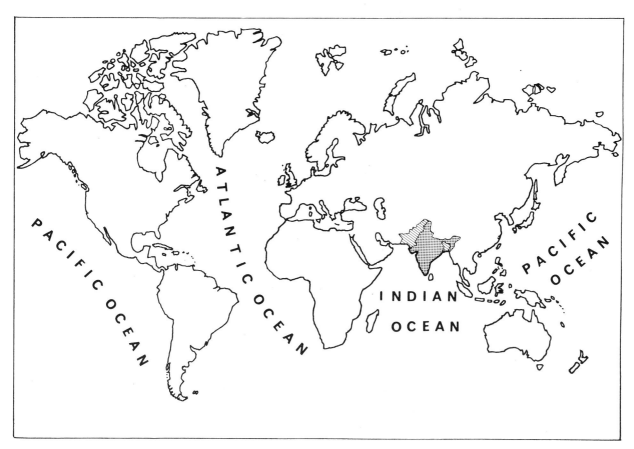

The Mogul Empire

India is many different lands in one. In the North there are deserts and snow capped mountains. To the south of these lie fertile plains and fertile river valleys. Much of Central India is covered with impenetrable forest. The grasslands of the South yield pepper, spices and other valuable crops. South and North India, roughly divided by the river Narbado, have rarely shared the same history, but both have attracted foreign invaders. The fertile lands of the North were frequently plundered and sometimes settled by men from the barren plains of Central Asia. The spices and pearls of the South were eagerly sought by European merchants who established coastal trading posts. In the face of these invasions, India was never able to unite from within. It was a land of many kingdoms and states—each one jealous of its own independence. So the history of India until very recent times is the story of foreign domination over all or part of the land.

At the beginning of the seventeenth century the Mogul Empire was at its height under the leadership of the greatest of its emperors—Akbar. The Moguls were a part of the great Mongol race

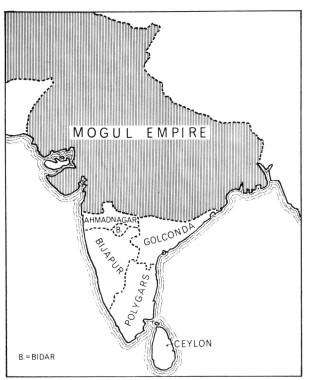

India in 1605   India in 1761

The Mogul Empire in 1605 and the divisions into which it had split by 1761

which conquered a vast area of Asia between the twelfth and fifteenth centuries. Akbar ruled over the whole of northern and part of central India. He was a wise and able emperor. Although himself a Muslim, he tolerated Hinduism (the other great religion of India) and all other religions and philosophies. It was his dream to establish an empire in which there would be no religious differences; in which all men would seek the truth.

But Akbar had managed to hold his large empire together only by launching frequent campaigns against groups of rebellious minor kings. After his death in 1605 his successors had increasing difficulty in preventing the empire from splitting up.

Aurangzeb

There were other reasons for the decline of the Mogul Empire. For one thing members of the royal family and important ministers were always plotting against the reigning emperor. The throne very seldom passed peacefully from one ruler to the next. When Aurangzeb came to the throne in 1658 it was only after a bloody struggle with other members of his family. In a letter to his

old teacher, Aurangzeb explained how he had been 'compelled to fight with my brothers, sword in hand, for the crown, and for my very existence. Such, as you must well know, has been the fate of the children of almost every king of Hindustan' (North India).

Aurangzeb was one of the most gifted rulers the Mogul Empire ever had. He did not, as some of his predecessors had done, pass his days in idleness and luxury. He was a devout Muslim. He spent his time in prayer and fasting and working hard at the administration of his empire. Yet it was during his reign that the Mogul Empire collapsed. As a ruler we must regard him as a failure. Why was this? The answer lies in Aurangzeb's character. Like many kings whose courts are riddled with intrigue, he trusted no one. He took too much work upon himself and refused to let others advise him. But the real cause of his failure was his religious policy. He refused to follow the path of Akbar the Great, who had won the support of his subjects by tolerating all religions within the empire. Aurangzeb persecuted Hindus. He taxed them heavily and took away many of their privileges and rights. He also tried to destroy those Muslims who belonged to different sects (for Aurangzeb himself belonged to the Sunni sect of Islam). This, of course, encouraged his subjects to revolt and to fight for their religion. One interesting result of Aurangzeb's policy was the boost it gave to the Sikh religion (a form of Hinduism) in the Punjab.

The most serious rebellion Aurangzeb had to face was that of the Maratha tribes, led by Sivaji. For 30 years the Emperor and his generals fought against the Maratha, only to see more and more of their land falling to the enemy. After Sivaji's death Aurangzeb was able to reconquer some of the lost territory.

The half century after Aurangzeb's death were years of immense misery for India. The Mogul Empire itself, under a series of weak rulers, existed in name only: regional governors and petty kings fought among themselves, their armies destroying towns and trampling the crops of the peasants. Meanwhile the struggle between the Empire, the Maratha Confederacy, and the Sikhs of the Punjab continued. There were frequent wars, none of which did anything to bring political stability (freedom from change) to India, though they brought death to thousands and suffering to millions. During these terrible years the Mogul capital, Delhi, was attacked and looted three times by the Marathas or other invading armies. By 1761 the Mogul Empire had ceased to have any real meaning. The title was preserved for another century but it carried no power with it.

Meanwhile the Maratha Empire had also run into difficulties. At the Battle of Panipat in 1761 the Marathas, trying to extend their territory into the distant north, came face to face with the Afghans — fierce warriors from the mountainous country beyond the river Indus. The Marathas were defeated. This defeat not only put a stop to their conquests but led to the break up of the Empire. The name of the Maratha Confederacy was kept but less and less attention was paid to the head of the Confederacy in Poona. After 1761 the Maratha Confederacy like the Mogul Empire was nothing more than a loose union of states which were often at war with one another.

British and French Interests in India

By this time other influences were at work in India which were to shape the history of the country far more than Muslim emperors or Hindu princes. You will recall that ever since

The Taj Mahal
Shah Jahan had this splendid tomb built as the burial place for his favourite wife Mumtaz Mahal.

Aurangzeb
Aurangzeb ruled the Mogul Empire from 1658 to 1707. He was a most pious Muslim and determined to do everything possible to spread Islam in India, even though most of his subjects were Hindus. He worked extremely hard and if he thought something was right he did everything possible to see that it was done. Yet he saw his empire crumble, and died a sad, defeated man. His last words were, 'My years have gone by profitless . . . . I have greatly sinned and know not what torment awaits me.'

297

the fifteenth century European traders had been interested in India. Portuguese, Dutch, French and British traders had established trading posts (known as 'factories') at points on the coast with the permission of the emperor or local ruler. The trade in pepper, spices, tea (a great luxury in the eighteenth century) and precious stones was very profitable and the merchants were extremely worried to see it threatened by the disturbed political situation of the mid-eighteenth century. By this time France and Britain were the two most powerful trading nations established in India. The British East India Company had bases at Surat, Bombay, Calicut, Fort St David, Madras and Calcutta. The French East India Company had established important posts at Surat, Pondicherry, Masulipatam, Chandernagore, Balasore, Kasimbazar and Mahé. Both companies had extended their authority beyond the fortified walls of their factories over the surrounding countryside.

Like all businessmen the French and English merchants were determined to gain as much trade as they could for themselves and do everything possible to hinder their rivals. There were many clashes between French and British soldiers and both sides were delighted when, in 1744, the opportunity came for open war. This came because the governments of the two countries had declared war on each other in Europe. A French fleet was sent to attack Madras and successfully captured the town. During the following months British possessions in southern India were reduced to Fort St David. However, when peace was signed in 1748 France returned Madras to Britain.

Meanwhile, in India, the two European companies had started a life-and-death struggle. In 1748 the Indian rulers of the Deccan and the Carnatic died. There was the usual struggle among rival claimants to the throne. In the hope of increasing their influence, the French and British supported different claimants. At first, Dupleix, the French Governor of Pondicherry was successful. The princes he supported gained their thrones and supported him against the British. It seemed as though the British East India Company would be thrown out of southern India. Then, in 1751, the tide was turned by a junior British officer. Robert Clive, with only 500 men, captured the capital of the Carnatic, Arcot, and successfully defended it against an Indian and French army of 3000. The British

The Koh-i-noor diamond

The Peacock Throne

Among the greatest treasures of the Mogul emperors were the Peacock Throne and the Koh-i-noor diamond. The former was a magnificent object decorated with hundreds of precious stones, in the design of a peacock's tail. The latter was (and still is) one of the largest diamonds in the world. In 1739, the ruler of Persia, Nadir Shah, taking advantage of the weakness of the Mogul Empire, entered Delhi (which had been the Mogul capital since about 1650) and plundered the city. Among the many precious and beautiful items he took back to Persia with him were the Peacock Throne and the Koh-i-noor diamond.

298

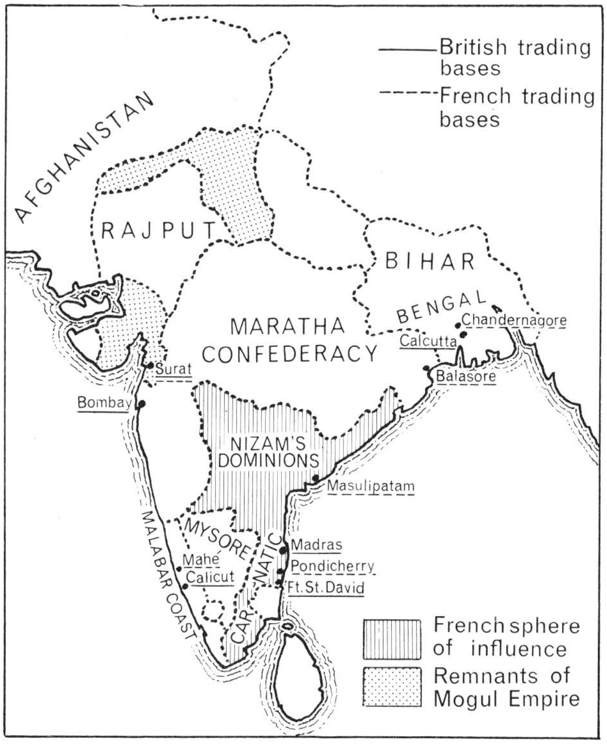

India in 1751

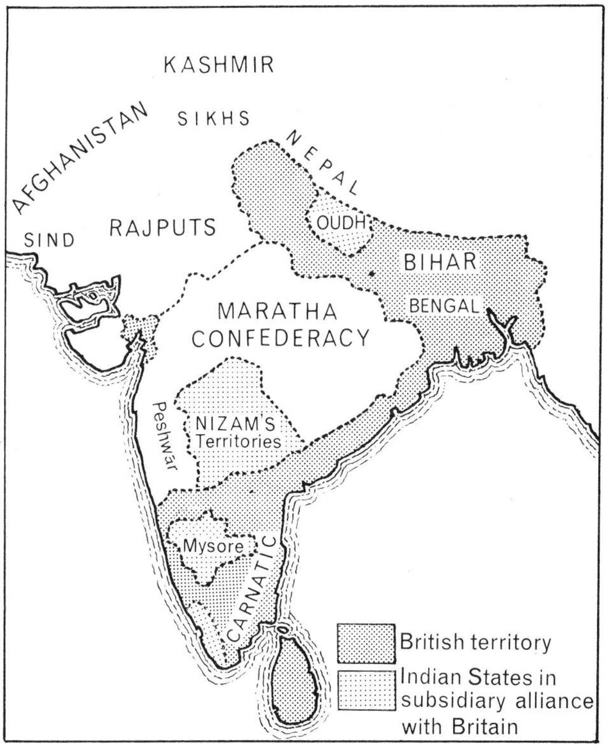

India in 1805

now went on to win fresh victories and, as a result, their friend Mohammed Ali became Nawab of the Carnatic. In 1754 Dupleix was recalled by the French government and hostilities between the Europeans ceased—but not for long.

Other Indian rulers did not simply sit back and watch the Europeans' struggle for power and influence without concern. In 1756 the new ruler of Bengal, Siraj-ud-Daula, decided that the British were becoming too strong. He ordered them not to fortify their base at Calcutta. When they took no notice he seized the town and plundered the English houses there. A few months later an English force recaptured Calcutta. By this time France and Britain were at war again (see below) and the French, naturally, aided Siraj-ud-Daula. Intent on destroying the power of the French *and* the Nawab of Bengal, the British, again under the leadership of Robert Clive, captured the French port of Chandernagore and then defeated the Nawab's army at the Battle of Plassey (1757). Siraj-ud-Daula was put to death by a rival—Mir Jafar. Then, after paying an enormous sum of money to the British, Mir Jafar was recognized as the new Nawab of Bengal. Henceforth the rulers of Bengal relied on the British to keep them on the throne.

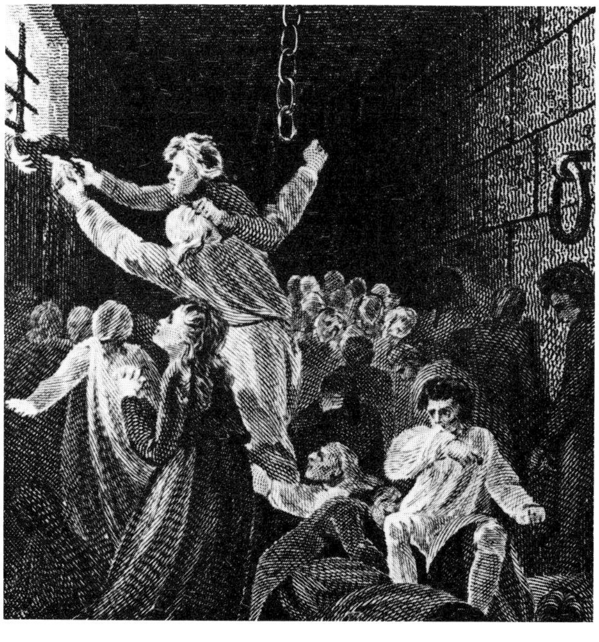

The Black Hole of Calcutta
When Siraj-ud-Daula's forces captured Calcutta, all the English prisoners (146 of them) were crowded into a tiny room and locked up for the night. Because of the intense heat and the lack of air and space, only 23 Englishmen were still alive in the morning. The British believed this incident proved the cruelty and barbarity of Siraj-ud-Daula. In fact the bad treatment of the prisoners was more the result of stupidity and inefficiency on the part of Siraj-ud-Daula's officers.

The Seven Years War, 1756–63

In 1756 Britain and France went to war again. Battles were fought in Europe and (as we have seen) in North America. The struggle was also renewed in India. After the Battle of Plassey, British troops were sent to invade the Northern Circars—states on the east coast under French influence. This finally convinced the Nizam of the Deccan that a British alliance would be advisable. The last major battle between the European rivals was fought at Wandiwash in 1760. This was won by the British who captured the major French fortress of Pondicherry a few months later.

After peace with France was signed in 1763 the British were masters of the greater part of India. They ruled, either directly or indirectly, Bengal, almost the whole of the eastern coast, the Carnatic, the Deccan and ports on the west coast. The French were allowed to keep trading posts at Surat and Calicut but no longer had any armed force in India. Proof of British power came a year later when the rulers of two north Indian states determined to stop the advance of the foreigners. At Buxar the British won a long and bloody battle. The Battle of Buxar was the foundation-stone of the British Indian Empire.

But India was not ruled by the British government as a colony. All the conquests and treaties had been made by the East India Company, which was still in purpose a trading concern. But now the Company had to spend more and more time and money on administration. Large armies were kept and Indians were trained to fight in them (Indian soldiers were known as *sepoys*). Company officials acted as advisers to Indian rulers. The Company levied (imposed and collected) taxes. The Company laid roads and put up buildings. Yet the British government could not allow the administration of most of India to be controlled by a few businessmen. So they made sure that they were represented on the Board of Control of the East India Company and that any important decisions made by the Directors were approved by the government. In fact British India was an *unofficial* colony.

'Pacification' of India, 1764–1819

The task of successive governor-generals during the half-century after the Battle of Buxar was to make British rule strong, firm and just. This involved occasional wars against rebellious Indian princes and strict control of British officials.

Joseph Dupleix

When the French and British went to war in the middle of the eighteenth century and fought each other for control of large areas of India, great responsibility fell on the leaders of each side. The French commander was Joseph Dupleix and the British leader was Robert Clive. Both were remarkable men. Dupleix, who was determined to create a French empire in India, often dressed and lived like an Indian prince in order to win the support of local rulers. He was a master of intrigue, scheming in secret to harm an opponent. He spent all his own money in the service of his country but in 1754 he was recalled to France. His government refused to repay his services and he died a poor man. Clive, a wild, strong-willed and obstinate man, rose from lowly rank to be leader of the British forces. He was brilliant as a military leader and did more than any other man to establish the British empire in India. The picture below shows the Emperor Shah Alum handing over to Clive the right to collect all the revenues of Bengal, Bihar and Orissa for the East India Company. Clive made a large fortune but it did not bring him happiness. He committed suicide in England in 1774.

Indian Wars

During the period when British power was being established the Maratha Confederacy was weakened as a result of internal divisions and its wars in north India. Later it recovered and its leaders made a number of attempts to break the British hold on central India. The East India Company had to fight three wars with the Marathas (1779–82, 1803, and 1817–19). In the last of these wars the Confederacy was completely crushed, their territory was split up into a number of small states, some were annexed (taken possession of) by the British, their ruler was deposed—in short the Maratha Confederacy was dead. Thus perished the last great Indian empire.

Another state which gave the British considerable trouble was Mysore. Hyder Ali, the ruler, invaded the Carnatic in 1781 and, despite his defeat, took every opportunity of opposing Britain. Both he and his son, Tipu Sultan, intrigued with the French, who, under the great dictator Napoleon Bonaparte, were trying to re-establish their overseas empire. In 1799 Tipu was defeated and killed in battle. His kingdom was greatly reduced in size and was 'given' by the British to a new ruler. Parts of Mysore were retained by the East India Company and parts were given to their allies. With the opposition of the Marathas and Mysore crushed, the whole of India, except the extreme North and North-West, lay directly or indirectly under British control.

Administration

As the East India Company controlled more and more Indian territory so the task of administering it became more and more difficult. Governor-generals, like Warren Hastings, did a great deal to make the collection of taxes, the enforcing of law and order, the administration of justice both efficient and fair. But there were many Indian and English officials who took advantage of their position to make themselves rich. Yet, it is undoubtedly true, that the coming of Company rule was an advantage to those parts of India that had previously been torn by war and anarchy (lawlessness). In 1813 the British government took away the East India Company's monopoly. That meant that for the first time other merchants were allowed to trade with India. After this the Company concentrated more and more on administration, its profits coming from taxation. The British government now had even greater control of the Company's affairs but it did not take over full responsibility for India for another half century.

The capture of Tipu Sultan during the battle of Seringapatam
One of the most troublesome of all Britain's opponents in India was Tipu Sultan of Mysore. He was trained as a soldier and, as a young man, gained considerable experience fighting against the Marathas and the British. He became Sultan of Mysore on the death of his father, Hyder Ali, in 1782. He spent most of his remaining years fighting and intriguing against the East India Company. In 1790 he tried to overthrow the ruler of Travancore (a British ally). He made an alliance with the French who were trying to restore their Indian empire. He was captured and killed in 1799 during the British siege of Seringapatam.

Chapter 50 The Rule of the East India Company

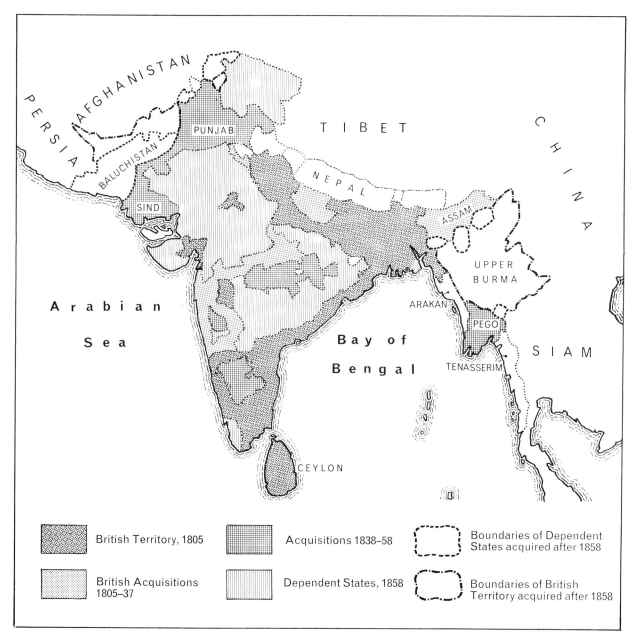

India, 1819–58.

Between 1819 and 1858 the East India Company's rule over India was extended. During these years also the Company did its best work. The chief problem for the various governor-generals was how much independence to allow to the princes who were their allies. Sometimes Indian rulers tried to throw off British control. When a prince died there was nearly always a dispute about who should take his place and frequently British soldiers had to be sent to help decide the question. All these affairs disturbed the peace of the country. Some governor-generals believed that friendly princes should be kept in office. In fact one of them looked forward to the political development and even independence of India. The day this happened, he said, 'will be the proudest day in English history'. But, as we shall see, there were more officials who believed that peace and prosperity could only be assured by increasing British possessions in India.

The Problems of the Frontiers

Another problem faced by the Company was that of stopping invasion across the northern frontiers. To the north-east lay Burma and to the north-west lay Sind, the Sikh state of the Punjab and Afghanistan. Trouble in any of these states might be a threat to the border states of British India. Britain was particularly worried about the north-west frontier because she feared that Russia might extend her influence over Afghanistan and use it as a base for attacking India. Two wars were fought against the king of Burma (1823–6 and 1851–2). As a result large areas of Burma were taken over by the British and the Burmese were no longer a threat to the Company.

Wars on the North-West Frontier

In 1839 events on the north-west frontier looked very dangerous to the Governor-General, Lord Aukland. The ruler of Punjab, Ranjit Singh, a faithful ally of the British for many years, died and there was a conflict over the succession. The Russians made a treaty with the ruler of Afghanistan, Dost Mohammed. Aukland, fearing the collapse of British influence in the North-West, sent an army to invade Afghanistan, remove Dost Mohammed from the throne and place on it a puppet king, Shah Shuja. Not surprisingly, the fierce mountain tribesmen of Afghanistan resented this. They rose against Shah Shuja and his foreign supporters and forced the British to retreat. During the retreat through the icy-cold mountain passes the army was destroyed. This was one of the worst disasters in British military history. Another force was sent to punish the Afghans, which it did, but it soon withdrew and there were no more attempts to extend British influence or control to Afghanistan.

The same was not true of Sind and the Punjab. After the Afghan expedition the governor-general decided that Sind must be brought under British control in order to safeguard the frontier. So, in 1843, an army was sent to conquer Sind. There was no excuse for this open, warlike act – but it was successful. The Sikhs of the Punjab were alarmed by this. They thought that the British were about to attack them. So they attacked first, in 1845. There followed a series of bloody battles in which many men were killed on both sides. At last the Sikhs were beaten back as far as their capital, Lahore, and were forced to surrender. The British put their own candidate on the

A Sikh horse soldier
The Sikhs are among the finest fighters in the world. Expert horsemen and fanatically brave, they proved very hard to defeat in the two Sikh wars. Later the people of the Punjab became very loyal to the British. Over many years Sikh soldiers fought in the British army, not only in India, but also in Africa and elsewhere.

throne and set up a protectorate over the Punjab. But after two years the people of the Punjab tried to regain their independence and the Second Sikh War broke out. Another year's fighting followed before the Sikhs were once more defeated. This time their country was taken over by the British.

Annexed territories

It was Lord Dalhousie (Governor-General from 1848 to 1856) who finally subdued the Sikhs and the Burmese. It was Dalhousie, also, who pushed British India to its farthest limits. In many of the states where Indian rulers were kept in power by the British, conditions were terrible. Since European soldiers would come to their aid if they faced any trouble from inside or outside their territory, the princes took little trouble to govern well. Their subjects were overtaxed and ill-treated, justice scarcely existed, while the rulers themselves enjoyed wealth and luxury.

Dalhousie was convinced that the people of such states would be better off under British rule. He took every opportunity to take over Indian states. When a prince had no children he had the right to choose his heir before he died. Dalhousie stopped this and ordered that such states should be taken over by the East India Company. Some states where the administration was corrupt or inefficient were simply annexed. In this way many new territories were added to the Company's possessions.

Reforms

Dalhousie knew that India was not just so much land to be brought under the Company's control. It was also millions of people, who were now his responsibility. He worked extremely hard to improve the conditions of the people. He worked very long hours and there was no feature of government or administration to which he did not give his attention. He urged the building of

An Indian mail cart
One of the many services introduced into India by the East India Company was a regular postal service. The carts were driven as fast as their drivers could make them go so that the letters could be delivered as quickly as possible. This made

it necessary to have good roads and frequent changes of horses. These mail-carts were the only means of communication in India before the coming of the telegraph system.

roads and railways. Before his departure he saw the opening, in 1853, of the first short railway line, the Grand Trunk Road from Calcutta to the Punjab and many other smaller roads. Dalhousie introduced an efficient, country-wide, postal service and the first electric telegraph. Where road-building was difficult he encouraged the building of canals. His engineers introduced Indian peasants to new irrigation schemes, which enabled them to make better use of the land. In 1854 he began to set up a new education system which provided Indian-language and English-language schools in all districts, as well as colleges and universities. To control all these services central and local boards were set up and a completely new and efficient system of government began to appear.

Dalhousie believed firmly that the British way of life was better than the Indian. Though his reforms brought obvious benefits to the people his attitude was resented. He ignored the fact that India had an older civilization than Britain and that Hindus and Muslims were not prepared to change their ancient customs because their new rulers disapproved of them. Some changes, such as ridding India of *thugee* were accepted as good. The British also rid India of another evil — *suttee*. This was the Hindu custom of burning a prince's widow with the body of her dead husband. The British army and law courts put an end to these practices.

But understanding and sympathy between Indian and Englishman were decreasing. There were a number of reasons for this. In the early days of the Company British officials had lived in close contact with the Indians. They had learned much about the customs and beliefs of the country. As the administrative system became more complicated, contact between Indians and Englishmen grew less. Too often the people of India were thought of by young British officials as savages who needed to be taught superior British ways. As time went on more and more Englishmen brought their wives with them. These *mem-sahibs* were even worse than their menfolk in refusing to understand Indian ways. As the nineteenth century wore on more and more Christian missionaries travelled to India. They did a great deal of good work but they also aroused considerable opposition among devout Hindus and Muslims who did not want to be converted to the Europeans' religion.

The speed and completeness of Dalhousie's

Thugs about to attack a group of travellers
Members of the thugee sect joined groups of travellers, and when they rested on their journey, they attacked them. The man kneeling on the left is about to strangle the rich merchant, and the two men behind will attack the others.

Mutinous sepoys pursued by the cavalry
The Indian Rebellion started in 1857 as an army mutiny, when sepoys refused to use cartridges coated in animal fat. They fled to Delhi, savagely pursued by the cavalry.

305

The massacre at Delhi

When the mutinous sepoys reached Delhi, they attacked the English population there, killing men, women and children. A few months later, a small British army took a terrible revenge: they recaptured Delhi and destroyed houses and stole everything of value. They killed hundreds of innocent men, women and children who had had nothing to do with the mutiny. The Indian Rebellion is an example of the ugly bitterness aroused on both sides when a ruling group have no sympathy or understanding of the way of life of the people they rule.

reforms further upset many Indians. They resented his taking over Indian states, his imposing English-style education and his encouragement of missionary work. They thought that he was trying to 'Christianize' and 'Europeanize' them. By 1856, when Dalhousie left, some regions were in a state of near rebellion and only kept under control by the army. But most of the soldiers were sepoys (Indian troops). Perhaps it was dangerous for the British to rely too much on their loyalty.

The Indian Rebellion or Mutiny, 1857–8

In May 1857 the Indian Rebellion broke out. It started as a mutiny among some of the sepoys and is often called the Indian Mutiny. We have already seen most of the causes of ill-feeling between the British and the Indians. What finally started the rebellion was the issue of new, Enfield rifles to the sepoys. In order to load the guns the soldiers had to bite the ends of the cartridges. The cartridges were covered in animal fat which came from the pig or the cow. Muslims refused to do this because to them a pig is an unclean animal. Hindus refused to do it because to them a cow is a sacred animal. The sepoys were convinced that this was another British attempt to insult them and destroy their religions. Some of them, therefore, revolted at Meerut, killed their officers and marched to Delhi. There they captured the Mogul emperor, Bahadin Shah II, and made him their leader. This was to give the mutiny the appearance of a nationalist rising.

The rebels were joined by some of the north Indian princes who had lost territory to the British. One of these was Nana Sahib, a descendant of the last Maratha ruler. Bengal, Oudh and several of the central states joined the revolt but southern India and the Punjab remained on the side of the British. The rebels were disunited and did not pursue a single course of action. Therefore the British were able to reorganize themselves and fight back. Delhi was recaptured in September 1857 and, one by one, the rebel strongholds were taken. But it was not until June 1858 that the last important battle of the Indian Rebellion was fought. Even then guerilla warfare continued until well into 1859. The rebellion had resulted in enormous suffering on both sides. Both British and Indians had been guilty of great cruelty. Now, the Rebellion was

The Nana Sahib

The Nana Sahib, heir to the last ruler of the Maratha Confederacy, saw the Mutiny as his chance to regain power. He led an attack on the British garrison at Cawnpore and captured the town. He proved cruel and treacherous to the British who surrendered to him. Having agreed to let them leave by river, he had the men killed as they were climbing into the boats. He took the women and children prisoner too. Later he murdered them also and threw their bodies into a well. Cawnpore was recaptured but Nana Sahib escaped and disappeared without trace.

over and firm peace had to be restored. The ringleaders who had been captured were executed but most of the rebels were treated without severity. More British soldiers were brought in so that the government did not rely so much on sepoys.

Results of the Rebellion

But there were greater changes. First of all the rule of the East India Company came to an end. From 1858 onward India came under the direct control of the British government. The country was now ruled by a viceroy responsible to the English monarch. This direct rule by Britain is sometimes known as 'the British Raj' (*raj* is Hindi for 'rule'). Dalhousie's policy of taking over Indian territory was reversed and every effort was made to co-operate with the ruling princes. A new period of Indian history was beginning.

Chapter 51　The British Raj and the first stirrings of Nationalism, 1858-1914

The 50 years after the Indian Rebellion were, for the most part, years of peaceful progress. There was further fighting in Afghanistan (1878–81) and Burma (1885) but these were the only major conflicts to disturb imperial India. Now that the country was under the direct control of the British crown, administrators had two motives: the development of India for the commercial and military benefit of Britain, and the well-being of the Indian people.

Agricultural and Industrial Development

The economic development of the country was of great importance to Britain. The traditional crops of tea, pepper and spices were produced in greater quantities. In the 1860s farmers began to grow cotton on a large scale and this soon became an important export.* Moreover cotton mills were built at Bombay. Ever since that time cotton cloth has been one of India's most important exports. The opening of the Suez Canal in 1869 made the journey from Europe to India much shorter. As a result more and more businessmen invested in the country; that is, they provided money for new businesses from which they hoped to make a profit. The railway system was considerably extended. Small industries were set up.

To understand the political and social developments in India at this time you must realize that there were two different ways of thinking among British people. There was the real imperialist attitude which thought of the Indian as backward, believed he should be Europeanized, and was convinced that he would never be able to govern himself. Then there was what we can call the liberal attitude which respected the

traditions of the Indian people and, while believing that British rule was good for the Indians, thought that they should share in and, perhaps, one day take over the government of their country. One or other of these points of view influenced British political activity at different times, depending on what group of politicians was in power.

Social Reforms

Now, for the first time, modern science could come to the aid of India. The growing of crops and the raising of cattle were improved by government regulations concerning irrigation and treatment of diseases. Human diseases such as smallpox, cholera and dysentry were treated by European doctors. The conditions which create disease were dealt with as towns and cities were modernized, proper drains laid, overcrowded slums destroyed and replaced by new homes. Laws (factory acts) were introduced to regulate conditions and hours of work in factories. A frequent disaster in India is famine, due to the failure of the monsoon rains. Government action here did a great deal to relieve suffering. Money was set aside for a special famine relief fund so that when famine struck, food could be rushed to the needy area by rail. In this way many lives were saved.

Education

Education was now taken very seriously by the British. The number of schools was increased and their quality improved. The viceroy's government was especially interested in training Indian rulers and their sons. From the time of the Rebellion it was British policy to co-operate with the princes of semi-independent states. Now special schools were set up to train future Indian rulers in western ways. The results, as far as the British were concerned, were highly successful. The

---

*Cotton growing began when the American Civil War stopped the supply of cotton from the southern American states.

princes became thoroughly Europeanized, lost touch with their Indian culture, administered their states efficiently, and were completely loyal to Britain. The schools also trained men for government service. They, too, formed a class of westernized Indians.

But the imperial government could not change India by creating a westernized ruling class. In fact this class simply became a barrier between the British and most of the Indians. Instead of changing and modernizing their ways, most Indians turned back to their own religions, cultures and traditions. The Mahasabha, a Hindu society, and the Muslim League were founded to encourage loyalty to the old religions and to resist Christian, European influence. This return to old traditions was one kind of nationalism.

The Beginnings of Nationalism

In most colonized countries two kinds of nationalism appeared. There were some people who simply wanted to reject everything European and fight for an independent nation based on the old traditions of the people. There were others who wanted to learn all they could from the Europeans so that they could use their knowledge to compete with the white men, to prove that they were just as 'civilized', and to persuade the colonialists to grant independence. They wanted to build a new nation based on the best of their own traditions *and* the best in European culture (as the Japanese did). In India the Muslim League and the Mahasabha represented the first kind of nationalism. There were other great Indians of the period who did a great deal to nurse Indian culture – men such as Ramakrishna and Keshar Chandra Sen who modernized Hinduism.

The second attitude can be traced back as far as the beginning of the nineteenth century. It was then that Ram Mohan Roy realized that the British could not be thrown out of India. Instead, he asked the new rulers to open English-speaking schools so that Indians could learn as much as possible about the western world. He encouraged his own people to give up customs like *suttee* and even tried to do away with the caste* system, which prevented most Hindus from improving their position in life.

---

*An Indian's caste (the four main ones were priest, warrior, merchant or farmer, worker) was inherited and involved strict rules of behaviour.

The Delhi Royal Durbar, 1911
India in the second half of the nineteenth century remained Britain's most important overseas possession. One politician referred to it as 'the brightest jewel in the British crown'. In 1911 a reigning British sovereign visited India for the first time. This was King George V, Emperor of India. In Delhi a large meeting, known as a 'durbar' was held, at which the King received the homage of thousands of his subjects. The King is riding in the carriage inspecting the troops. This Delhi Durbar is often thought of as marking the peak of British imperialism. From about 1911 onwards the empire began to decline.

Economic life in India
In spite of changes in crops and the introduction of scientific improvements, most farming methods in India are still primitive. The people are poor and few of them can afford tractors. In many areas the land is still turned with wooden ploughs drawn by cattle. Yet the hard-working Indian farmers produce impressive crops of tea, cotton, rice and wheat.

Indian Political Development

As more and more Indians went to school and learned about western history and political development, they began to want a share in the government of their country. The first really important Indian political movement was the Indian National Congress, founded in 1885. It was an unofficial body which met to discuss political issues. The viceroy approved of it as long as it conducted its business quietly. He was even prepared to grant requests for reforms if they were 'reasonable'.

In the second half of the nineteenth century important political changes did take place. In 1882, the Viceroy, Lord Ripon, began to plan changes which would give the Indians a greater share in local government. In 1892, the Indian Councils Act introduced elected Indian representation on both local and central legislative councils. This was an important step because it created a class of professional Indian politicians, who could learn the arts of government and become the leaders of their country. But in all their work the viceroys found themselves hampered by Englishmen who thought change was too rapid and Indians who thought it was too slow. For instance, in 1883 Lord Ripon introduced a law which would place foreigners under the control of local Indian magistrates. This met with so much opposition from Englishmen that the new law had to be changed.

In the 1890s different groups began to appear within the Indian National Congress. This body had increased in size since 1885. In its early days under the leadership of Krishna Gokhale it had been moderate in its ideas and methods. Now there was a more extreme and violent group within the Congress. They were dissatisfied with the pace of political change. They were particularly discontented because there were not enough jobs in the administration for educated Indians.

The extreme group was led by Bal Gangahdar Tilak. In his newspaper and his speeches he stirred people to hatred of the British and to violent action. In 1897 he was imprisoned after some of his followers had killed two British officials. But he was soon released, and he continued his political activity. His movement spread and attacks on British people and property became more frequent.

Between 1907 and 1910 the Viceroy, Lord Minto tried to deal with Indian grievances. The Morley-Minto Reforms, as they are called, intro-

Rabindranath Tagore

Jagadish Chandra Bose

Two of the greatest Indians of modern times were Rabindranath Tagore and Jagadish Chandra Bose. Tagore was a poet and author. His books were read all over the world and did much to help outsiders to understand the Indian way of thinking. In 1913 he won the Nobel prize for literature—the highest such award in the world. He used the money to help run a school for Indian children. Bose proved to the western world that Indians could become leaders in the scientific world. He trained in England as a physicist and made a great contribution to man's knowledge of electricity. In 1917 he founded a scientific research institution in Calcutta. He, too, took every opportunity to explain to outsiders how Indians thought and felt.

duced more Indians to central and local government. But these changes were not enough to satisfy Tilak's followers. Violence, riots and assassinations continued until 1914, when India became involved in the First World War. The Muslim League, also, began to urge rapid political change. There was a widespread popular movement not to buy British goods. But not all Indians were extremists; most were content for a gradual move towards independence. When the new King of Britain, George V, paid a state visit to India in 1911 he was very warmly received. In the following year, Delhi, capital of the old Mogul Empire (the title of Mogul Emperor ceased after the Rebellion) was made the new capital of India.

The man who was to become India's greatest nationalist leader was not even in India at this time. M. K. Gandhi was an Indian lawyer who had trained in Britain. In 1893 he had gone to South Africa on a law case and, horrified at the way Indians were treated there, had stayed on to fight for them against injustice. He founded the first Indian political party there. Until 1914 he used every peaceful means to improve the conditions of his fellow countrymen in South Africa. Then he returned to India, to find that his services as a nationalist leader were needed there also.

Gandhi
Mohandas Karamchand Gandhi (1869–1948) was born a fairly low caste Hindu. He went to Britain to study law and there he was impressed by the struggles of trade-unionists and social reformers to improve the conditions of working people. He was, above all else, a man of great human sympathy. He rejected some Hindu beliefs he considered inhuman. He was impressed by some Christian teachings. He tried to close the growing gap between Hindus and Muslims. Throughout his life he fought against suffering and prejudice.

A riot outside Bombay police court during Tilak's trial
When Bal Gangahdar Tilak was tried for writing seditious articles in his newspaper, his supporters rioted outside the court and attacked Europeans. Armed mounted police had to be called out to restore order.

Part XIII The Invasion of Africa

Chapter 52 African and Alien Societies before the Colonial Era

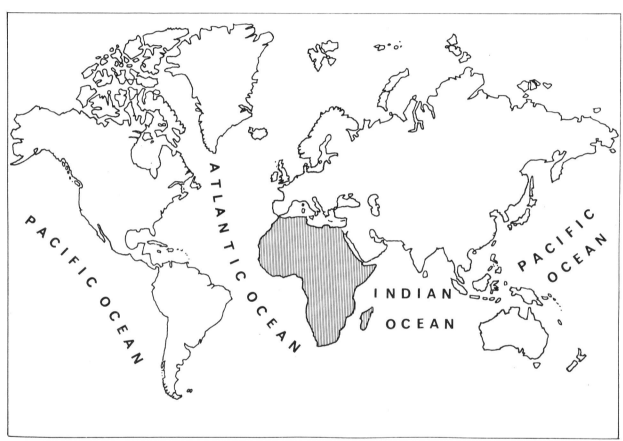

By the mid-nineteenth century Africa had suffered frequent invasions from outsiders but most of the invaders had failed to penetrate very far inland. The one exception to this was the Arab invasion of North Africa, which took place over a thousand years before our story starts. The Arabs spread all over Egypt and North Africa, bringing with them their way of life and their religion, Islam. They mingled with the African peoples. They crossed the Sahara and influenced the negroes of the western Sudan. By 1700 a way of life was established over most of North and West Africa which owed a great deal to Arab influence.

Arabs had also crossed the Indian Ocean from Oman and the Persian Gulf to set up trading settlements on the East African coast. From the fifteenth century onwards Europeans had established small settlements. Most of these were along the Guinea Coast of West Africa, where, by the eighteenth century, there were Portuguese, French, Spanish, British and Dutch factories. The Portuguese, also, were firmly established along part of the East African coast, south of

Cape Delgado. In the extreme south of the continent, where the African population was very small and where the climate was more moderate, the Dutch and British had set up trading and farming settlements.

Apart from these exceptions African societies developed completely uninfluenced by outsiders for thousands of years. As it would be impossible to mention all of these societies, we are going to think about just a few of the peoples of East Africa and then of West Africa.

Peoples of East Africa

From the map you see there are two main groups of people in East Africa. Most of the region is occupied by Bantu people who came originally from the west. Most of them are farmers. Parts of Uganda and the plains of Kenya and Tanzania are peopled by Nilotes who originated in the area between the Nile valley and Lake Rudolf. Many of them are also farmers, though some, like the Maasai, Turkana and Samburu, devote all their time to keeping cattle. The coastal belt, the region around Lake Victoria and the highlands of Kenya and Tanzania were mainly occupied by farmers. The plains were the home of wandering pastoralists and their cattle.

The East African Coast

The life of the coast was quite different from the life of the interior. In the villages the people grew their crops and kept a few animals just as the Bantu farmers of the highlands did, but it was the towns that were the centre of coastal civilization. There lived African and Arab merchants whose whole life was spent in trade. They bought animals, coconuts, skins and foodstuffs from the villagers. They bought ivory and copper from the inland peoples who came to the coast to sell. In exchange for these goods they gave cotton cloth, cowrie shells, and iron pots and tools. For their own use the rich merchants imported fine china (porcelain), silk and glass, rugs and beautifully-made daggers. All these goods were brought by Arab and Persian traders who travelled from the Muslim lands to the north-east in their dhows. It was the regular visits of these foreign merchants that made the east coast one of the most important trading areas of Africa.

At the end of the seventeenth century, the Sultan of Oman in south-eastern Arabia laid claim to the East African coast. He claimed it as he had driven out the previous conquerors,

The Great Mosque at Kilwa
Arab culture and religion have had a great influence on parts of Africa. Here you see the ruins of the Muslim mosque built in the Arabic style, at Kilwa, on the East African coast.

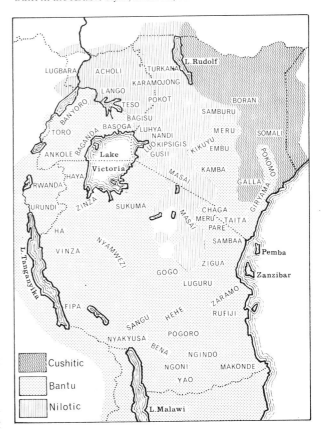

East Africa

the Portuguese. However, the coastal peoples had other ideas and for over a hundred years they resisted the Omani sultans with some success. It was not until 1829 that Sultan Said finally managed to defeat his enemies. In 1840 he moved his own capital from distant Muscat to Zanzibar and from that time until his death (in 1856) he personally supervised the development of his East African possessions. He caused cloves to be planted on Zanzibar and Pemba islands. He encouraged traders to venture deep into the interior in search of ivory and slaves. He built up trade with Europe, India and America.

Buganda

One of the most important states of inland East Africa was Buganda. Buganda began to grow powerful in the sixteenth century when the old empire of Bunyoro-Kitara, which controlled most of the area to the north and west of Lake Victoria, collapsed. The new state contained a mixture of Bantu and Nilotic people. From being a small country on the north shore of the lake it grew during the next 200 years into the most powerful state in the region. In the eighteenth century the Baganda began trading with African merchants who came to their land bearing strange goods from the coast. Later the Baganda themselves began to travel, taking loads of ivory across the lake by canoe to sell at Mwanza. In the 1840s Kabaka Suna welcomed the first Arabs to Buganda, and from then on an important trade route was opened by coastal merchants (Zanzibaris) who travelled across Tanzania and round the west side of Lake Victoria to Buganda. Suna and his successor, Mutesa I, kept the Arabs supplied with ivory and slaves (for which they raided their neighbours). In return they received cloth and guns. The latter were highly valued as they helped the Baganda in wars against their enemies.

The Maasai

By tradition the fiercest and most warlike people in East Africa were the Maasai. They originated in the region to the north of Lake Rudolf and moved southwards during the seventeenth and eighteenth centuries. By 1800 they had spread

Kabaka Mutesa of Buganda
One of the most famous rulers in East Africa in the nineteenth century was Mutesa I, Kabaka of Buganda, who ruled from 1856 to 1884. He was a harsh and ruthless king, but a very able one. He welcomed Arabs and Europeans to his kingdom because he hoped to gain their help against his old enemy, the ruler of Bunyoro. In this picture you see him receiving two British explorers in his court at Rubaga (modern Kampala).

over most of the Rift Valley, the Kenya Highlands and the plains as far south as northern Tanzania. Groups of Maasai warriors frequently made cattle raids on neighbouring peoples such as the Kikuyu. They were greatly feared and only people like the Kamba, who made special trading arrangements with the Maasai, dared to cross their land. Most of the Maasai were pastoralists, but there were some, on the Uasin Gishu plateau, in the Rift Valley and near the coast, who had taken to farming. These agriculturalists were known as *Kwavi* by the other Maasai. The two Maasai groups hated each other and, during the nineteenth century, they fought a series of wars which destroyed many of the *Kwavi* communities and left the pastoral Maasai very much weakened. For much of this period the pastoral Maasai were led by their great *laibon* (a man expert in religious ceremonies) Mbatian. Though they were successful in their struggle with the *Kwavi*, the Maasai had now passed their period of greatness. Weakened by war, famine and disease, they were no longer able to resist coastal traders who, by about 1880, had begun to cross their territory in search of a shorter route to Buganda.

West Africa
The climate and vegetation of West Africa very much controlled the way people lived. Behind the Guinea coast there is a thick forest belt. Here the people lived by hunting and farming in forest clearings. Beyond the forest lies a wide area of grassland, well watered by rivers. Here a great variety of ways of life were possible. Farming, herding and trade all flourished and there also grew up important towns. In fact this region, known as the western Sudan, has been the home of many flourishing African civilizations throughout history. To the north of the grassland lies the Sahara, a thousand miles of sand lying between the Sudan and the North African centres of population. You might think that this would cut the West Africans off from the outside world but in fact the Sudan was such an important trading area that busy caravan routes had been established across the Sahara and merchants were always coming and going between North and West Africa. With European traders established along the coast, with Arab and other traders travelling across the desert, West Africa was more influenced by outsiders than East Africa.

The Asante
The Asante Empire or Union came into being at the end of the seventeenth century. There were two main reasons for its formation. The Asante wanted to unite with other forest states in order to resist the attacks of powerful rivals. They also wanted to trade directly with the Europeans at the coast. This trade was almost entirely in the hands of the Fante with whom the Asante and other inland peoples had to deal. The Europeans wanted slaves, ivory and other goods. The Asante and their neighbours obtained these things but then had to sell them to the Fante for less than they could have got from the Europeans. During the next hundred years the Asante Union raided far and wide from its centre (Kumasi) until it controlled an area about the size of the modern Republic of Ghana. In 1806 the Asante were at war with the Fante. The latter called on their British friends for help and the Asante came to blows with Europeans for the first time. Other Anglo-Asante wars followed.

Oyo and Benin
Farther along the coast is the region of the lower river Niger. Most of this region was occupied by the Yoruba and Edo peoples, who had, by the end of the seventeenth century, built up very complex, town-based civilizations. As well as mastering the skills of farming and trade, they were fine craftsmen, highly skilled as workers of wood, bronze, clay, ivory and leather. They had trading links with the Hausa people and the trans-Saharan routes to the north and also with the European factories to the south.

The most important Edo state was Benin. From its centre in Benin city the empire spread over much of what is now southern Nigeria from about 1500 onwards. At its greatest extent it stretched from Badagri to the Niger. The *oba* (king) of Benin obtained most of his wealth from trade with the Europeans in pepper, slaves and palm oil. Benin city became a large, wealthy and impressive centre. A visitor at the end of the seventeenth century described it as a city with 30 straight streets all 40 metres wide. With his large army (he could put at least 20,000 soldiers into battle) and with guns supplied by the Europeans, the *oba* was able to dominate a large empire. But during the eighteenth and nineteenth centuries Benin grew weaker. There were civil wars and attacks by the Oyo Empire to the north. The last blow to the Benin Empire was the abolition of the slave trade. This led to later clashes with British forces.

The strongest Yoruba state at the beginning of the period was Oyo. From its centre in the grass-lands Oyo extended its control over most of Yoruba land. Its military power depended on excellent cavalry and, from about 1550, its kings extended their rule over a large empire. Oyo wealth came largely from trade with the Hausa, the leading merchants of the western Sudan. Early in the nineteenth century the empire began to split up. In 1817 a number of Yoruba rulers sent a message to the *alafin* (king) of Oyo to tell him they would no longer obey him. He replied by shooting three arrows to north, south and west and then making a terrible curse:

> 'My curse be on you for your disloyalty and disobedience, so let your children disobey you. If you send them on an errand, let them never return to bring you word again. To all the points I shot my arrows will you be carried as slaves. My curse will carry you to the sea and beyond the seas, slaves will rule over you and you, their masters, will become slaves.'*

His words were soon fulfilled, for parts of the empire fell under the control of the Fulani.

The Slave Trade and its Abolition
An activity which made a deep and tragic impression on many societies in tropical Africa was the slave trade. In West Africa the trade had been begun by trans-Saharan merchants in the distant past and was much increased after 1550 when Europeans came to buy slaves for the plantations of America and the West Indies. In the East it was mainly Arab traders from the Persian Gulf who were responsible for slave trading. However it was not until the middle of the nineteenth century that the slave trade reached its height. By that time Zanzibaris had begun to penetrate deep into East Africa. Many African peoples were turned into slave dealers and raiders out of greed for the goods the foreigners brought. In East Africa, the Yao, the Nyamwezi, and the Baganda were active slave traders. In the West almost all the coastal states had slave markets and the warriors of Asante, Benin and Dahomey (to mention only a few) travelled long distances on slaving raids.

*S. Johnson, *History of the Yorubas*, C.M.S., 1960.

Capture of a slaving ship
During the nineteenth century the British made great efforts to abolish the slave trade in East and West Africa. The navy patrolled the coasts and when they found a ship they thought was carrying slaves they ordered it to stop. If it failed to do so there would probably be a fight. In the picture you see a slaving ship which has been forced to surrender. A boat is taking British seamen to take over the ship. The slaves would then be taken to a friendly port, such as Freetown in Sierra Leone, and there the chains would be removed. They were free.

At the beginning of the nineteenth century powerful groups in Britain, which had been one of the leading slave-trade nations, successfully influenced the government in favour of abolition. After the loss of the American colonies, slavery was less important to British merchants and the establishment was more vulnerable to moral and religious pressures. From 1815 onwards Britain sent her navy to patrol the east and west coasts of Africa, made treaties with other countries to get them to stop slave trading and tried by persuasion and force to make African rulers give up dealing in slaves.

Anglo-Asante Wars
To see what this anti-slave trade campaign meant for some African peoples we will take two examples. First the Asante. By the beginning of the nineteenth century, the Asante had extended their empire to the coast and established their rule over the Fante people. All trade, including the slave trade, was now in the hands of the Asantehene. But when the British government decided to stamp out slavery they took over the control of some of the forts from the British merchants (1821) and decided that Asante power must be crushed. In 1823–4 the British

helped the Fante in a rising against their masters. But the Asante won and in the fighting the British governor was killed. This defeat stirred Britain to action. Fresh soldiers were sent out and in the renewed fighting the Asante suffered a crushing defeat (1826).

The Asantehene's empire was now cut off from the coast and, in the following years, he tried to find fresh outlets for the slave trade. Neither he nor his successors were able or willing to stop slave raiding and take up other kinds of trade. The effects upon the empire were terrible. It grew weaker and began to split up. Since slaves could not be sold, the practice of human sacrifice became more common. The more the British heard about Asante slave raiding and 'barbarity', the more determined were they to put an end to it. When, in 1873, the Asante tried to recover some of their lost southern lands they were beaten back by the British who captured their capital, Kumasi, and burned it down. This was a severe blow to Asante power, but they did not give up. There were further outbreaks of fighting before Asante was made a British protectorate in 1897.

Britain and the Sultanate of Zanzibar

Long before Sayid Said moved his capital to Zanzibar in 1840 the British tried to persuade him to restrict slave trading in his dominions. The Sultan was in a difficult position. He needed the help of the British navy in controlling his rebellious subjects and to rid his coasts of pirates. But he knew that any restriction of the slave trade would be resented by many of his subjects. Sayid Said *did* sign two treaties limiting the slave trade (1822 and 1845) but they were both very difficult to enforce. But the British were determined to stop the trade. In 1873, long after Said's death, their opportunity came. Zanzibar had just been hit by a hurricane and the ruling sultan needed the help and friendship of the British if his territory were going to recover. Britain now demanded that slave trading be ended completely and threatened to blockade Zanzibar harbour until the sultan agreed. The poor man had no choice. All slave trading on the East African coast was declared illegal. What Sayid Said had feared now came true. The sultan could not rule his angry subjects without British help. The British consul became the most powerful man in Zanzibar and it was not many years

A Yoruba king receives Christian missionaries
The religious revival in England led to a new interest in spreading the Christian message to the 'pagan' peoples of the world. The missionaries who were sent to West and East Africa not only tried to convert Africans to their religion but also to change their way of living.

before the sultan's possessions became a British protectorate.

Missionary Work

In the second half of the eighteenth century many new missionary societies were founded in Britain and a new wave of Christian missionary activity was directed towards Africa. In 1844, for instance, the first missionary arrived in Zanzibar. During the next 40 years many stations were set up in the interior as far as Lake Tanganyika and Buganda. The missionaries brought medicines, employment to Africans and taught a way of life that many African people have found satisfying. But they also brought problems. They interferred in tribal politics and if they were ill-treated they complained to their own governments and demanded protection.

Trade

The decline of the slave trade brought new merchants to Africa determined to encourage other kinds of commerce. The Niger delta, for instance, became a very important region for the production of palm oil. Governments encouraged

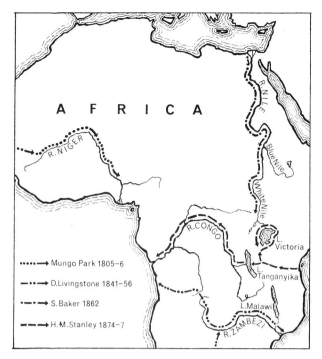

The great African rivers, the Congo, Nile and Niger

An explorer crossing the coastal mountains

merchants to penetrate into Africa in the hope that what was called 'legitimate trade' would replace the slave trade. The opening of the Suez Canal in 1869 brought more ships from Europe to East Africa. In the 1860s a British businessman, William Mackinnon, was helping the Sultan of Zanzibar to develop the coast and in 1872, a regular steamship service to Zanzibar was started.

Exploration

Of all the unknown regions of the world, none was more interesting to geographers than 'the Dark Continent' – Africa. What they particularly wanted to explore were the great rivers: the Niger, the Congo and, above all, the Nile. From the late eighteenth century onwards Europeans, usually with very small expeditions, set out to try to map accurately the course of these rivers. By 1830, the course of the Niger was known. By 1856 David Livingstone had completed his famous journey right across Africa and mapped the course of the river Zambezi. But it was not until 1876 that H. M. Stanley completed the work of earlier explorers by settling beyond doubt the source of the other two great rivers, the Congo and the Nile.

These journeys took white men into the heart of Africa for the first time. Explorers discovered, not only the geography of the continent, but the wealth of the continent as well. They began to urge their governments to send new expeditions into the country, in order to establish friendly relations with powerful chiefs. Traders and missionaries also were seeking official support from Europe. All this activity led to what has been called the scramble for Africa.

Chapter 53 The Scramble for Africa, and the Colonial Period in Nigeria

In Europe great changes had been taking place between 1815 and 1870. Two new nations, Germany and Italy, had been created and a war between France and Germany had left the former country defeated, angry and bitter. Britain, meanwhile, had been busy building up an overseas empire and establishing an enormous lead in trade over other countries.

After 1870 the other European countries were able to follow Britain's example and devote more money and energy to industrial and commercial development and ever more German and French businessmen travelled overseas to compete with British traders in foreign markets. These markets were vital to the continued commercial expansion of industrial nations.

Another reason for renewed European interest in overseas possessions was national pride. Germany and Italy were determined to prove their greatness to the rest of the world and were resentful of the colonial lead established by Britain. France, too, having been defeated in Europe, wanted to prove her power somewhere else.

That 'somewhere else' meant the China coast, South-East Asia, the Pacific and Atlantic islands and, above all, Africa—that large continent, from which explorers and traders were returning with such interesting stories. A few areas of Africa were, indeed, already ruled by foreign powers in 1884. Egypt and most of North Africa had for centuries been ruled from Constantinople by the Sultan of Turkey. In fact his control of these areas was weak and his agents had really established separate kingdoms there. In 1832 France had conquered the Turkish territory of Algeria. Portugal, the oldest European colonial power, still held territory she had conquered in the fifteenth and sixteenth centuries —Portuguese Guinea, Angola and Mozambique.

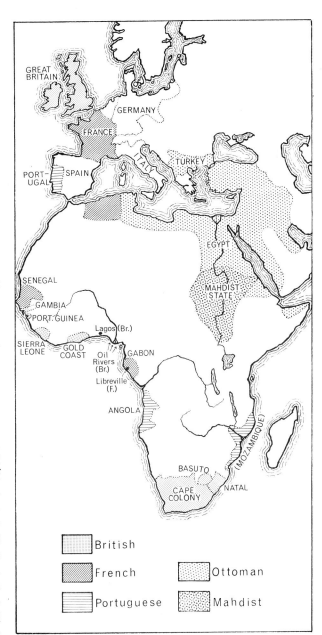

British
French
Portuguese
Ottoman
Mahdist

Europe and Africa in 1884

319

Britain controlled Cape Colony, but was having trouble with Dutch settlers there who were trying to gain their independence. In West Africa the British had set up a colony on the Gold Coast, because of their conflict with the Asante. Similar circumstances had led them to occupy Lagos. At the beginning of the century Britain had established her first African colony, Sierra Leone, as a settlement for freed slaves. In Senegal and The Gambia the French and British governments respectively had established protectorates in the interests of their traders. The French had also taken over part of Gabon. Apart from a few trading posts these were the only European footholds in Africa, and few of them stretched very far inland.

Rivalry in the Congo

After 1870 the leading European nations took a much more active interest in Africa and this led to rivalry between them. One area where different powers clashed was the Congo Basin. H. M. Stanley and other explorers reported that the region was rich in ivory as well as vegetable and mineral wealth. This greatly interested King Leopold II of Belgium, who wanted to enrich his tiny country by gaining overseas possessions. Concealing his real aims he founded an 'international' association for the exploration of the Congo. In fact, his agents were instructed to make treaties with the African rulers of Central Africa so that the whole region would be turned into a protectorate controlled by Leopold. When the French government realized what was happening they sent their own agent, de Brazza, to make similar treaties. Alarmed at this rivalry, Portugal and Britain signed a treaty aimed at giving the Portuguese strict control of the mouth of the Congo (thus making it very difficult for other countries to operate in the interior). In 1884, Leopold turned for help to the most powerful statesman in Europe, Chancellor Bismarck of Germany.

Rivalry in Egypt

Meanwhile there was trouble in Egypt. After the opening of the Suez Canal, Egypt became much more important to European nations which had interests in the East. They all wanted to see Egypt economically and politically strong. But the Khedive Ismail, who ruled Egypt, simply could not manage his financial affairs. He spent money on buildings, roads and personal luxuries.

Leopold II, King of the Belgians

H. M. Stanley
When H. M. Stanley, the explorer, completed his journey down the river Congo in 1877, one man who was very interested in his story was Leopold II, King of the Belgians. The King had been looking for an area to colonize and exploit and he hoped that the Congo Basin might be suitable. He sent Stanley back on further expeditions to the Congo and the result was the founding of the Congo Free State. In spite of its title this state was an enormous kingom ruled completely by Leopold, who made a fortune from it.

He borrowed enormous sums from foreign businessmen. He taxed his people until they could pay no more. By 1879 he had no money left to run the country, he could not repay the European loans and his people were about to rebel. The Sultan of Turkey deposed Ismail and a committee of European businessmen was appointed to try to solve Egypt's financial problems. Not unnaturally, many Egyptians resented the idea of foreigners controlling their affairs and there was a revolt, led by some army officers. The British Prime Minister, Gladstone, reluctantly agreed to send troops to suppress the rising. This was successfully done, but, once there, the soldiers could not leave for fear that trouble would break out again. So Britain was, in fact, in complete control of Egypt. France resented this and the French government sought the help of Bismarck in getting the British out of Egypt. Stirred by these and other clashes between rival colonising groups, Bismarck acted. He was not interested in Africa but he *was* concerned about the peace of Europe and he did not want European rivalries to grow into war. So he suggested a conference to meet at the German capital, Berlin, at the end of 1884, at which representatives of all the interested cour... ies could discuss their claims to various parts of Africa. As soon as European governments realized what was about to happen, the 'scramble' for Africa really began. They sent their agents hastily to Africa to make treaties and lay claims so that they would be in a strong position at the Berlin Conference.

The Berlin Conference, 1884–5

The Berlin conference did not divide up Africa into European colonies and protectorates. All it did was to draw a lot of (often very vague) lines on a map to mark out European 'spheres of influence'. It left large areas in the heart of Africa which were not 'given' to any European power. It was this which now set the nations of Europe 'scrambling' for Africa. Travellers, merchants, missionaries, statesmen began to develop their countries' spheres of influence and to press farther inland. This led to quarrels and treaties between the nations to define their boundaries more precisely. By 1914 there was very little of Africa which was not under the direct control of one or other European, colonial power.

In drawing these lines which often had no geographical or ethnic *raison d'être*, the European rulers were shaping the modern nations of

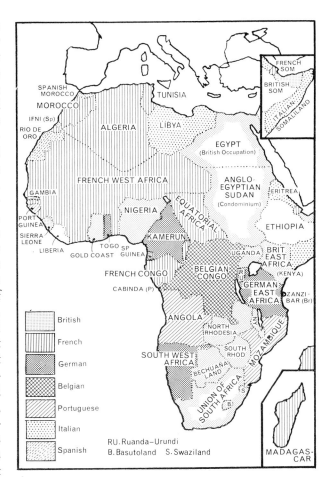

Africa in 1914

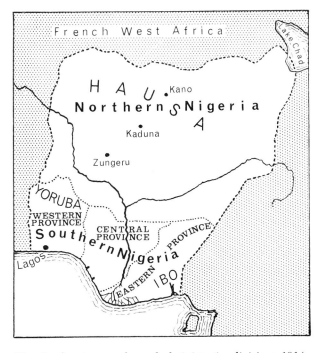

Nigeria, showing peoples and administrative divisions, 1914

321

Africa. To see what this meant for the peoples of Africa, let us consider Nigeria and Kenya.

At the Berlin Conference and in treaties which followed it, Britain maintained the right of her traders to exploit the lower Niger and most of the coastline of what is now Nigeria. Lagos and the area around it was already a British colony. The Niger delta region was occupied by a number of trading companies which received active support from the British Government. Farther up the river a large area was claimed as a British sphere of influence and here the Royal Niger Company was working. This company, rather like the East India Company, was responsible for administration as well as trade.

The Royal Niger Company made a treaty of friendship with the Caliph of Sokoto. British troops were frequently involved in the battles between rival states in the Niger delta. But most of the Yoruba, Edo, Ibo and Fulani peoples resented the white men who had come to their land without being invited. The coastal and riverside merchants did not like the foreigners interfering in their trade. Chiefs who made treaties for 'protection' by the British found that this really amounted to giving up their authority to them. So there was fighting. In this fighting the Europeans, with their modern guns and well-drilled soldiers, were nearly always victorious. The states of the delta became the Niger Coast Colony in 1900. In the same year the British government took over control of northern Nigeria from the Royal Niger Company, which had been unable to handle unfriendly Africans and a French advance along the Niger. In 1906 the whole coastal region was joined to form the Colony of Southern Nigeria. And in 1914 the division between North and South was removed when 'Nigeria' was formed. The new colony combined different peoples who had never been united before. Could the British develop Nigeria so that all the people would enjoy peace and prosperity?

How Nigeria was governed

The policy followed by Britain in governing Nigeria was 'indirect rule'. The newcomers tried to rule 'through' the local chiefs. The chiefs and their advisers continued to administer their own laws. They had also to administer *new* colonial laws, pass on and explain *new* colonial policies and collect *new* colonial taxes. There were times when traditional customs or laws had to be changed but the Europeans interfered as little as possible with African politics and society. This system did not work in all areas of Nigeria. For instance the Ibo had never had chiefs or kings and, when the British tried to make them recognize certain Ibo men as their leaders, they refused. Moreover, very few Nigerians were allowed to share in the government of the country as a whole, or to take top administrative jobs.

Nationalism

Some Africans gained a western-style education at mission schools only to find that their way to top jobs in commerce and administration was blocked by racial prejudice. Such men grew dissatisfied with the political situation in their country. Slowly, nationalism spread not only among the small educated class. As people learned a common language, English, and were able to travel to distant parts of the country by the new roads and railways, they began to think of themselves, not only as Yoruba or Ibo, but as Nigerian. The nationalist movement soon had local leaders, such as Herbert Macaulay and J. P. Jackson. It also had a great deal of support from outside. Negroes in the West Indies and the U.S.A. were struggling for the black man's rights. They pointed to West Africa as an example of a place where negroes were badly treated by white governments.

Very, very slowly the attitude of the Nigerian government began to change. One cause of this was the First World War (1914-18), in which Nigerians fought bravely for their British masters. During this war African soldiers realized that when it came to fighting they were just as good as, and sometimes better than, British soldiers. When they reached home again they began to demand political equality with the small white population. In 1920 the National Congress of British West Africa was formed to gain political rights for Africans. It immediately sent representatives to London to present demands to the British government. The British government took no notice, but two years later a beginning was made to encourage African political activity when some Nigerians were admitted to the Legislative Council.

Kenya

The scramble for East Africa began with the

visits of rival British and German expeditions in 1884. As a result, the region was divided vaguely into areas explored and exploited by the German East Africa Company and the British East Africa Association (later the Imperial British East Africa Company). Conflict between the two concerns led to the Anglo German Agreement of 1886 and the Heligoland Treaty of 1890, which divided East Africa into spheres of influence. The boundaries were roughly those dividing Kenya and Uganda from Tanzania. Zanzibar fell within the British sphere. The IBEA Company continued to administer British East Africa. But the financial strain proved too great. The Company sold out to the British government in 1894. In that year Uganda became a British protectorate. The next year the British East Africa Protectorate (Kenya) was set up.

Mumia, chief of the Wanga

Colonial Rule

The European officials who were now sent to East Africa found little difficulty in establishing colonial rule. They were interested only in certain areas in the early years of the twentieth century. In these areas they could usually find African rulers who were willing to co-operate with them. This was because of the rivalry that existed between various African peoples or because of disputes within certain communities. A chief was usually only too pleased to have the support of the white men and the white men's guns in his struggles with his enemies.

Among the Baluyia of western Kenya the British found a useful ally in Nabongo Mumia of the Wanga kingdom. His capital had an important position on the road to Uganda and the Europeans were anxious to have the Nabongo's support. Mumia needed the white men as much as they needed him. He was having trouble with powerful neighbours and with rivals for his throne. The British built a fort in his capital (which they called Mumias) and he supplied them with warriors who helped to suppress the northern Baluyia, Nandi, Luo and other peoples.

The Europeans were quite prepared to use force and treachery when they considered them necessary. These were the methods by which the British overcame Nandi resistance. Between 1895 and 1906 Nandi raids greatly annoyed the British. When the railway was being built groups of Nandi warriors would attack the depots and steal food, telegraph wire and equipment. If British troops pursued them they would dis-

appear into the hills they knew so well. Even when the British took hundreds of cows and goats as a punishment the Nandi did not give in. The turning point came one day in October 1905. The Nandi leader (Orkoiyot) Koitalel was asked to attend a peaceful conference with some British officers. As Samoei was greeting the white men he was shot dead. This act disheartened the Nandi but to make quite clear that further resistance was useless, a military force of over 3,000 men moved through the country, arresting or killing men, removing cattle and goats, emptying and destroying villages.

By all these different methods the new rulers established their authority in the areas that interested them and suppressed any resistance. But there were large areas of East Africa where the white men were never seen and where life went on just as before.

The colonial administrators were now faced with the problem of making their territories pay. They believed the first thing to do was to develop the trading possibilities of Uganda. Ivory was the most important product but the amount exported was limited by the long caravan journey to and from the coast. More could be sold more quickly if a railway were built. This was begun at Mombasa in 1896 and reached Kisumu on Lake Victoria in 1902. Now ivory and other goods could travel by lake steamer to Kisumu and by train to the coast.

The authorities had no specific plans for the development of Kenya. It was a large area mostly made up of barren, dusty plains. But somehow the railway had to be paid for and that meant that parts of the Protectorate had to be developed. Sir Charles Eliot, Commissioner from 1900 to 1904, thought he had found the answer in the Kenya Highlands:

'Here we have a territory (now that the Uganda railway was built) admirably suited for a white man's country...'*

Eliot encouraged European settlers to move to the Kenya Highlands to clear the forest and bush and to start farming. They came—from Britain, South Africa, Australia, Canada and other lands, rough, tough men prepared to overcome hardships *and* African opposition in order to make a new life for themselves.

Convinced that European settlement was the only way to develop the colony, Eliot granted away land in the Highlands and Rift Valley in defiance of the British government and against the advice of local government officials. The latter claimed that some of the land granted belonged to the Kikuyu, Kamba, Maasai and other peoples. African communities were moved into reserves and their lands were split up into large European farms.

Life was not easy for the newcomers, and only those who persevered through great hardships prospered. Wheat and stock farming proved very profitable. Some farmers began large-scale coffee growing and this crop rapidly became the Protectorate's most important export. By about 1920 it seemed as if Eliot had been right. Large farms, using modern agricultural techniques, were becoming the basis of the country's economy.

The government encouraged African farmers to raise cash crops for local sale or export. But the settlers did all they could to prevent the development of African farming. For instance, until the 1930s, they forced the government to forbid Africans to grow coffee. This was partly because they feared that African farmers would not be able to control plant diseases and also

The early days of tourism in East Africa
The Protectorate government were very anxious to encourage people to travel to East Africa so that money would come into the country. This was just one of the posters used in Britain to persuade wealthy Englishmen to visit East Africa as ivory hunters, game hunters or naturalists. In those days it was only the very rich who could afford a holiday in East Africa.

because they were afraid of losing their own farm labour.

The growing numbers and influence of the settlers spoiled relations between the government and Africans. Early in the century the settlers began to demand a share in the government of the country and in 1908 the government gave way and set up a legislative council. Settlers were represented on this body which advised the governor in the making of laws. Africans were not. The European farmers repeatedly demanded changes in the land and labour laws. By these laws the government strictly controlled the granting of land and the treatment of African farm workers. The settlers wanted the first claim on all land suitable for farming. They wanted Africans to be forced to work for them and they wanted the government not to interfere in the way they treated their workers. The government however were not prepared to give way very much on any of these points.

But the majority of the population was also becoming politically articulate. As in Nigeria so in Kenya a generation of Africans appeared who had received European education and who began to see that what they had learned might be used against the colonial rulers. In 1914 came the First World War and many East Africans were forced to serve the white men either in the army or the Carrier Corps. The horrors of mechanized warfare and their sufferings during the war helped to destroy the respect that many Africans had for the Europeans. While the older generation who had fought the colonial invaders in the early days tended to accept the rule of the more powerful white man, the new generation was determined to renew African resistance to colonial rule. This generation produced the nationalist leaders of the 1920s and 1930s.

*Quoted in G. H. Mungeam, *British Rule in Kenya 1895–1912*, p. 102. Oxford 1968.

UGANDA RAILWAY.

THE HIGHLANDS OF
BRITISH EAST AFRICA
AS A
WINTER HOME FOR ARISTOCRATS

HAS BECOME A FASHION.

SPORTSMEN in search of BIG GAME make it a hobby.

STUDENTS of NATURAL HISTORY revel in this FIELD of NATURE'S own MAKING.

UGANDA RAILWAY, BRITISH EAST AFRICA.

ARRIVAL OF THE FIRST COOK'S EXCURSION, AND THE RESULT OF CAREFULLY PRESERVING THE BIG GAME.

UGANDA RAILWAY Observation Cars pass through the Greatest Natural GAME PRESERVE in the WORLD.

For reliable information, etc., address:
PUBLICITY DEPT., UGANDA RAILWAY,
DEWAR HOUSE, HAYMARKET, S.W.

Interlude: The World in 1914

Indian troops at Dar es Salaam in 1915
This picture gives you some idea of the great changes that had taken place in the world between 1700 and 1914. In 1700 most of the peoples of the world knew little about other lands and peoples. But when, in 1914, Europe's leading nations went to war, a large number of other countries were involved. Here *Indian* soldiers are boarding a boat at Dar es Salaam in *Tanzania* to travel to Kilwa to help the *British* fight the *Germans*.

We have now examined separately and in some detail the course of events, the changes brought about through internal social and political developments and particularly the effects of Western European discovery, influence, interference and, in some cases, domination on the great land masses of America, Asia and Africa. In order to see history in perspective and to understand the motivating forces leading to the First World War, it is useful to survey the state of the world in 1914.

A smaller World

Earlier on the state of the world in 1700 was described as being rather like a row of locked houses —the people of one land knew little or nothing of the people of other lands. By 1914 this was no longer true. Countries like China, Japan, Africa and South America, which for various reasons had been closed to outsiders, were now 'opened up' to traders, travellers and colonizers. Men from India, Africa, Japan and other countries now journeyed to Europe and the U.S.A. as businessmen, students and statesmen. We sometimes describe this state of affairs by saying that the world had become 'smaller'. By this we do not mean that the size of the world had changed; we simply mean that people from different lands were now in much closer contact.

One reason for this was the changes that had taken place in the world of travel. Large steamships made regular voyages to all parts of the world and journeys which had taken months by sailing ships were now completed in days. In 1913 a man travelled completely round the world in 35 days. Railway lines crossed most of the large land masses, including Siberia, Canada and the U.S.A. Aeroplane travel was still very new but was developing rapidly. Flights had been made between Europe and Africa and the world's first airline had been started. Men could still not fly long distances over water but even this difficulty was overcome within a few years (the Atlantic Ocean was crossed in 1919).

Leadership of the Western World

At this time, as we have seen, Europe and the United States of America were technically the most advanced areas of the world. We usually refer to the U.S.A. and Western Europe as 'the western world'. You have seen how, because of their superior knowledge about ships, machinery, trade and warfare, men of the western world had come to control other parts of the globe. They had colonized parts of Africa and Asia. They had forced countries like China to trade with them. They had settled in every corner of the globe. By 1914 western languages were spoken, western ideas were adopted, western clothes were worn by the upper classes in many countries. It seemed as though the world was about to become 'westernized'.

Population

Large colonies of white people now existed in Africa, Australasia and the Americas. One reason for this was the growth of population. Europe had reached the stage, in the nineteenth century, where there were more people than there were jobs for them to do or food to feed them. So millions of men and women had moved to the empty areas of the world. By 1914 millions of square kilometres of waste land had been turned into farms and new cities such as Sydney (Australia), New York (U.S.A.) and Durban (South Africa) had sprung up. So the surface of the earth was becoming more and more filled with people. By 1914 man already occupied most of the areas where it was possible for him to live. But still the world's population was increasing.

Capitalism

The spread of western ways meant also the spread of capitalism. *Capitalism* is a term used very often by modern politicians (some of whom favour it, while others oppose it) so it is important

Mustapha Kemal – 'Ataturk'
One example of a ruler who deliberately 'westernized' his country was Mustapha Kemal, President of Turkey from 1923 to 1938. Kemal ruled Turkey as a dictator but he did a great deal of good and is thought of as 'the founder of modern Turkey'. He was determined to get rid of everything that was old-fashioned about the government and way of life of his people. He overthrew the old system of rule by sultans or caliphs who were also the leaders of the Muslim religion. He introduced the western alphabet and western forms of government. He even made a law that no one in the future was allowed to wear the 'fez', the traditional kind of hat worn by Turkish men. He used to go around the streets of the capital knocking off fezes whenever he saw them. Sometimes he was seen sitting in the roadway with groups of poor people teaching them to read. In this picture we see him teaching the new western alphabet.

that one can understand its application. Capitalism is the name for an economic system in which private individuals own *the means of production* (farms, mines, factories, etc.) and pay workers of various kinds (farm labourers, miners, factory workers, clerks, etc.) to work for them. In a capitalist state the government supports this system and interferes as little as possible with the running of business and the relations between capitalists and workers. People who oppose capitalism (mainly socialists and communists) believe that it prevents wealth being

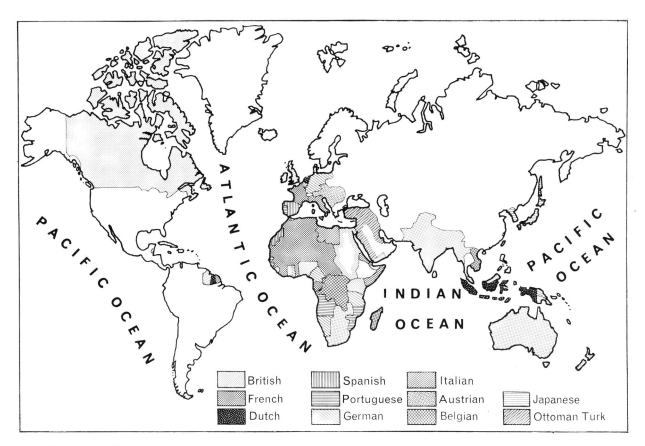

World Empires in 1914

shared equally among all people. They believe that government (on behalf of the people) should take over some or all of the means of production so that profits can be used for the good of the state as a whole and not just for the good of the capitalists.

The Peak Period of Imperialism

In 1914 most of the people in the world belonged to an empire. Imperialism had never been stronger than it was in 1914. Old empires like the Austrian, Russian and Ottoman empires still existed. They had been joined by new empires such as the German Empire, the colonial empires of Britain and France and the young empire of Japan. The great empire of China had just begun to crumble, as you have seen. Apart from that hundreds of millions of people were ruled by or in the name of a few powerful men such as the Tsar of Russia, the Sultan of Turkey, the Emperor of Germany and the King of Britain.

This, then, was the world in 1914. Since then things have changed very much indeed. Capitalism had already begun to be challenged by socialism and communism. This challenge grew stronger and the new economic ideas were accepted in many parts of the world. Empires crumbled as people all over the world decided they no longer wanted to be ruled by white men. New nations appeared in Europe, Africa and Asia—nations with a pride in their own traditions, who no longer wanted to live like westerners. At the same time Europe and America ceased to be the only great economic powers. In the last 50 years Japan, China, Australia, Russia and South Africa have grown into powerful industrial nations. Many of the world's smaller countries have also developed their own industries and are no longer dependent on the western world for many of their goods.

The world today is made up of many independent states. Instead of empires there are combinations of states, such as the Organization of African Unity, the Commonwealth of Nations and the Eastern Bloc countries. In many ways our world has changed more in the last 50 years than it did in the previous two centuries. What some of these changes were and how they came about we shall now see.

Part XIV The End of Western Leadership
Chapter 54 1914-1945, An Age of Violence and Fear

During the last 50 years contact between the peoples of the world has been so close that we cannot, in this book, consider the development of different countries in separate chapters. Events that happened in one part of the world affected other parts of the world. Important *international* movements began which involved peoples of many nations.

The First World War, 1914–18

The 30 years which we are thinking about in this chapter began and ended with war. Each war began in Europe. As we have seen, Europe by this time controlled or influenced large areas of the world overseas. For this reason other countries were also involved in Europe's wars. So we call these wars (from 1914 to 1918 and from 1939 to 1945) the First World War and the Second World War.

The First World War was the result of rivalry between the leading nations of Europe. Ever since about 1880 Germany, Italy, France and Britain had been quarrelling over colonial matters but by 1914 all these disputes were settled (although even in 1914 Germany and Britain were planning to take Portugal's African territories away from her). Yet there were still several purely *European* arguments which still were not settled. France was angry with Germany about land that Germany had taken from her in 1871. Austria and Russia both wanted to gain control of land in south-east Europe, where the power of the Ottoman Empire was collapsing. Germany and Britain were quarrelling about which of them should have the bigger navy. For 50 years and more the major European nations had been gaining power — economic power, colonial power, military power. They had used this power to obtain trade and territory throughout the world. And still they were not satisfied.

Tyne Cot War Cemetery in Belgium
Between 1914 and 1918 the world's leading nations were at war — the most terrible war the world had ever known up till that time. In four years over ten million people were killed and over twenty million were seriously injured. In this cemetery in Belgium there are 11,952 graves from the First World War. The suffering and destruction of cities, towns and villages were so terrible that men called this war 'the Great War' and 'the war to end wars'. They were determined that such a war should not happen again. Twenty-one years later an even worse war began.

They wanted more power. And so they had to fight each other.

The 1914–18 war was the first major war in Europe for a hundred years and it was quite different from any war that had ever been waged before. It was the first *mechanized* war in the history of the world. That means it was the first war in which much of the fighting was done with machines: automatic rifles and machine guns, large battleships and submarines, tanks and long-range field guns. Man is a very clever animal but, unfortunately, he can use his brains for evil as well as for good. We have already seen some of the momentous scientific and technical developments of the nineteenth and early twentieth centuries which were used for the benefit of mankind. The First World War showed that they could also be used for the destruction of mankind. Two examples are poison gas, which killed many soldiers and made others permanent invalids, and military aircraft which were also used in the fighting in Europe. These weapons were much more destructive than earlier weapons and made it possible (for the first time) for civilians far away from battle areas to be attacked.

In Europe Germany was faced with enemies in the East (Russia) and the West (France and Britain). For this reason she could not gain a quick victory in either area. But nor could Britain or France or Russia. So, for three years the war went on, with millions of men being killed and neither side gaining anything. Then, in 1917, as we have seen, there was a revolution in Russia, the tsar was forced to abdicate and the new Bolshevik government made peace with Germany (March 1918). With Russia out of the war the Germans believed that they could gain a quick victory but by this time the U.S.A. had joined in on the side of Britain and France. By the middle of 1918 fresh, well-equipped American soldiers were fighting in Europe. By the end of October Germany and her allies had been defeated. On 11 November fighting stopped.

The War in Asia and Africa
It was Europe's war and most of the fighting was done in Europe—but not all. As we have seen, Japan took the opportunity of occupying German bases in China and the Far East. There was conflict in Africa also. Germany owned four colonies: Togoland and Kamerun in West Africa, German South-West Africa and German East

The arrest of the assassin of Archduke Franz Ferdinand
By June 1914 the European nations were so close to war that it needed only a small event to start the war. On 18 June a member of the Austrian royal family, Archduke Franz Ferdinand, who was visiting Bosnia, one of the small states of South East Europe, went for a drive through the capital with his wife. As they smiled and waved to the crowds, a young man stepped forward, raised a pistol and fired several shots. The royal pair slumped forward, covered in blood, and died shortly afterwards. It was a terrible event, but it was not, in itself, very important. Yet within weeks Austria, Russia, Germany, France, Britain and Japan were at war. Other countries joined later.

A British tank used in the First World War
There were few weapons that could stop or damage these large, new, armoured vehicles.

Africa. The first three were easily taken over. Togoland was invaded from east and west by French and British forces and was conquered within weeks. Britain and France also joined to attack Kamerun but forest and swamp held up their advance and it was not until February 1916 that the colony was conquered. It was troops from South Africa who invaded German South-West Africa. They met fierce opposition which was not finally overcome until July 1915.

In East Africa it was different. The army leader in German East Africa, General von Lettow-Vorbeck, knew that he could not defeat the British, but he hoped that he could keep them busy for a long time so that troops would have to fight in East Africa who would otherwise have been fighting in Europe. His plan worked. British troops came from Kenya, Uganda, Nigeria, South Africa, Rhodesia, Malawi (then called Nyasaland) and India to fight against him. For over four years his army moved about East Africa, sometimes fighting the enemy, then withdrawing. Lettow-Vorbeck never let his army be destroyed or captured and, when the war ended in November 1918, his was the only undefeated German army.

Results of the War
The First World War was important because it hastened the decline of European leadership throughout the world. This was certainly so in many of the European colonies. The First World

New machines for war
All wars in the past had involved hand-to-hand fighting between soldiers of opposing armies. Now machines took some personal fighting out of war. Tanks were used by Britain in order to break through positions which the Germans had held for months. Submarines were used by the Germans to attack merchant ships and stop supplies of food and weapons reaching Britain. Aeroplanes were used mainly for spying on the enemy but they were equipped with guns and, sometimes, bombs, which were dropped over the side by hand.

African troops during the East African Campaign
African troops fought on both sides during the First World War. Here you see Nigerians arriving in Tanzania to fight for their British masters. The British also used Kenyans as carriers, and about 46,000 Kenyans died during the four years of fighting. The French sent 169,000 of their West African subjects to fight in Europe, as well as keeping thousands more for the African campaigns. The Germans also used African soldiers on their side of the war.

331

War was the turning point for imperialism. On the one hand it showed the strength of imperialism. Apart from armies from Australia, New Zealand and Canada, forces were sent from India and Africa to help Britain and France. The colonial troops did not all come willingly. Some were angry to know that they were expected to risk their lives for the white men. This anger grew stronger after the war when they went home to find that they were not to be rewarded in any way for their service. Though they might die for the white man, he still treated them as though they were inferior. Now that they had fought beside European soldiers, many Africans and Indians realized that they were *not* inferior to the white man. Europeans had often called coloured peoples 'savages' but these 'savages' had now seen Europeans behaving towards each other in a way that was just as savage as anything that happened in Africa or India. It is not surprising, therefore, that nationalist movements in Asia and Africa grew in strength and number after the war. (See Chapter 56.)

As a result of the war there was one less colonial power in the world. All Germany's colonies were taken away from her. But they were not taken over by other nations. Instead they became *mandated territories* of the League of Nations. That means that they were under the control of the League of Nations, an international assembly. One member country of the League was chosen to look after each mandated territory for the League. For example, Britain administered Tanganyika (previously called German East Africa) and South Africa administered South-West Africa.

The League said that mandated territories were to be run in a new kind of way: *trusteeship* was to be the guiding principle. (A trustee is somebody who is given the legal right to hold and administer property in somebody else's interest.) This meant that in each territory the interests of the local people and *not* the interests of white settlers were the most important. It meant that the League was going to look after these territories until the local people could rule themselves. So, as early as 1920, the *possibility* of independence for colonial countries was recognized.

This was the beginning of the decline of western imperialism. After 1918 two European empires disappeared completely. These were the Austro-Hungarian and the Ottoman empires.

A League of Nations assembly
In order to try to keep world peace, a new organization was founded in 1920 – the League of Nations. Many of the world's leading states belonged to it and it was supposed to be an assembly for discussing and solving international problems. The man most responsible for the founding of the League was Woodrow Wilson, President of the United States of America. Yet, strange to say, the American parliament did not agree with him and the U.S.A. was one of the few major powers which did not join the League.

In their place appeared a number of small, independent eastern-European states. American influence also played its part in encouraging the decline of imperialism. Until 1917, when she joined in the world war, the U.S.A. had been too busy developing its own industry and agriculture to bother much about the rest of the world. But from that time Woodrow Wilson and other leading Americans used their influence – and money – to help small, independent states and to encourage the imperial powers to give more freedom to their subject peoples. Americans never forgot that they had had to fight to free their land from the British.

America and the Great Depression

Another reason why the western world lost its leadership was the Great Depression. Before the war Europe had been the economic centre of the world. America was by then a great industrial nation and Japan was catching up quickly, but

Britain, Germany, France and Belgium between them still had most of the world's trade. Between 1914 and 1918 many European factories were destroyed, workers were killed, businesses were closed down. It took Europe a long time to recover from the war and during the 1920s much suffering was caused by unemployment and poverty. Europe's recovery, though slow, was partly due to help given by the U.S.A. After 1920 America went back to its old policy of *isolation* (not getting involved in international affairs) but it did help the countries of Europe to recover by lending them money and by investing in European business and industry.

The United States and Japan, the two industrial nations least affected by the war, prospered greatly during the 1920s. But even Japan could not equal the great expansion which occurred in America. There, industries and farms prospered, new businesses were founded almost every day. Millions of Americans were richer than they had ever been before. They had money to spare. Many of them invested this money in business and industry. So business and industry expanded even more. Everyone was happy. Until October 1929.

In that month the 'Wall Street Crash' occurred. Hundreds of companies went out of business. Thousands of people lost large sums of money. Millions more lost their jobs and had to queue in the streets for free bread. Faced with ruin Americans withdrew money they had invested in other countries. A great deal of business everywhere in the world depends normally on borrowed money. If lending money or giving 'credit' suddenly stops, the business man cannot buy materials or pay his workers. So, throughout the world, factories were closed, banks failed and businessmen lost all their money. The Great Depression had arrived.

Almost all countries were affected by the Great Depression. But those which had been the most advanced were the worst hit. Farmers could not sell their crops. Factory owners had to dismiss their workers. Governments could not deal with the great problems and were overthrown. The western world had to struggle to survive and could spare little time for leading the rest of the world.

As we have said, many European governments, unable to deal with the problems facing their countries, were overthrown. Leaders and political parties rose and fell. None of them, *using*

Adolf Hitler at Nuremberg

Adolf Hilter was a house-painter by trade until he took up politics. By his power of public speaking, by bribery and by murdering his rivals, he rose to leadership of the National Socialist (Nazi) Party in Germany. In 1933 he became Chancellor of Germany and was soon in a position of complete power. He used two methods to gain and keep the support of the German people: he stirred up national pride and race hatred. The picture above shows Hitler addressing a rally in Nuremberg. Here was built a special stadium where the people saw military displays and where they heard Hitler make long emotional speeches. The people got excited; they felt proud to be Germans and decided to follow Hitler — the Führer — anywhere. Hitler told the Germans that most of their problems were because of the Jews. Jews had their property taken from them, their businesses closed down; they had to wear special clothes or carry signs saying 'I am a Jew'. The picture below shows the sign outside the Nazi headquarters in Nuremberg; it says, 'By resisting the Jews, I fight for the Lord'. The Jews were herded into concentration camps where they were tortured and millions killed.

333

democratic methods, was able quickly to end unemployment and poverty. People did not know who to trust and they were ready to listen to anyone who would promise them work and food. For this reason cunning men were able to seize power in some countries and rule as dictators. These dictators often did solve the problems of unemployment and poverty — but not by democratic methods: they used violence and fear to achieve their ends.

Hitler and the Nazis in Germany

In Germany Adolf Hitler was the dictator. His supporters were the National Socialist Party (or Nazis). This was just a name: the Nazis were not socialists and they were more than a political party. They were a military organization. Their political rivals were dealt with by guns and knives, not by democratic means. Hitler solved the unemployment problem by setting men to build roads and public buildings, by building up a large army and by starting factories to make guns, tanks and battleships. He found the money for these things by taking it from citizens (such as the Jews) and by getting the support of wealthy businessmen. His financial advisers even tricked other countries into lending Germany money.

Mussolini and the Fascists in Italy

Things were not quite so bad in Italy where Benito Mussolini and the Fascists ruled. But even there individual citizens had few rights. They could be imprisoned without trial. They had to be careful what they said, because the secret police were everywhere. There was little individual freedom. Mussolini's government was only interested in the good of the state and not the good of the people who make up the state. By using methods similar to Hitler's, Mussolini helped Italy to recover from the Depression, though it is only fair to state that he did not find it necessary to murder thousands of Jews and other people.

By the mid-1930s Germany and Italy had become powerful states with large armies. Hitler and Mussolini had forced their will on their people. Now they thought they could force their will on other countries. Hitler began to say that Germans needed more 'living space' in Europe and Mussolini began looking for new colonies for Italy. So, Germany and Italy both began to bully smaller, weaker nations.

Japan's empire-building

But it was Japan which became the first country to break the peace. You will remember that Japan had been forced to give up some of the gains she had made during the First World War. The Japanese, and particularly the military leaders, were very angry about this. They wanted to be treated as equals by the big nations of the West but they were not.

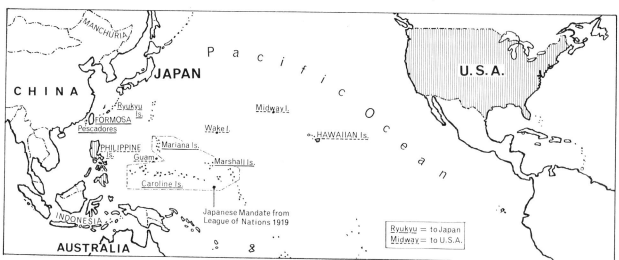

American and Japanese expansion in the Pacific

This map shows how Japan and the U.S.A. came into conflict. Japan was determined to build up an empire which would control all South East Asia. This included the Pacific islands between Asia and Australia. The United States, though in theory opposed to colonialism, had taken control of several Pacific islands, which she considered necessary as bases for her ships trading with Asia. America was afraid that Japan would block her trade routes. Japan resented America's economic strength and was determined to hinder America's trade with Asia.

Invasion of Manchuria

Japan had obtained the right to mine coal and iron in Manchuria, a part of China. Coal and iron were very important to the Japanese but they had some trouble in obtaining them because the people of Manchuria did not like working for Japan. In 1931 someone blew up part of the South Manchurian railway with a bomb. The Japanese used this as an excuse to invade the country. Within weeks Manchuria had been added to the Japanese Empire. In the following years Japan expanded the frontiers of Manchuria and attacked places along the Chinese coast.

Italy and Ethiopia

Japan's success in Manchuria encouraged the European dictators. In 1896, during the European scramble for Africa, an Italian army had invaded Ethiopia – and been defeated. This was the only European attempt at colonization which had been prevented by an African people, and Ethiopia had remained an independent state. Italy was determined to be revenged and to show the rest of the world that she, too, was a great colonial power. In 1935 Mussolini ordered the invasion of Ethiopia. Using modern guns, aircraft and poison gas against Ethiopian spears and shields, the Italians could not help winning and the last large free area of Africa came under foreign rule. Liberia was now the only independent African state.

German conquests in Europe

Now it was Hitler's turn. In 1938 a German army invaded Austria. In the same year the small European state of Czechoslovakia was added to Hitler's empire. In 1939 Germany prepared to attack Poland.

The League of Nations

Why did no one stop all these invasions? What did the League of Nations do to prevent free nations falling under the control of aggressive states like Japan, Italy and Germany? When Japan invaded Manchuria the League told her to withdraw. Japan took no notice. In fact, to show what she thought of the League, she left it in 1933. Shortly afterwards Hitler withdrew Germany from the League. In 1935 the League of Nations tried to make Italy stop her invasion of Ethiopia. It imposed *sanctions* on Italy (i.e. members of the League agreed to stop trading with Italy). But the sanctions failed. In 1936 Germany made treaties with both Japan and Italy. All three states now defied the League of Nations. The international organization had failed and from 1936 onwards no one took very much notice of it.

Events leading to the Second World War

One reason why the leaders of other nations did little to stop Hitler and Mussolini was their fear of war. They remembered the horrors of 1914–18 and above all else they wanted to avoid another world war. So Germany, Italy and Japan were allowed to take over foreign territory in the hope that they would soon be 'satisfied'. Even when, in 1938, the Japanese attacked an American ship on China's river Yangtse, relations between the two countries were not broken. But by 1939 the leaders of democratic Europe realized that Hitler must be stopped. Britain and France told Germany that they would declare war if Hitler's armies invaded Poland. On 1 September 1939 Hitler's armies *did* invade Poland. The Second World War had begun.

In the first year of the war Hitler and his allies overran most of Europe. His only real failure was his attempted invasion of Britain. All this was possible largely because he had made a treaty with Russia. In 1941 Hitler made the mistake of breaking this treaty by an invasion of Russia. Like Napoleon, Hitler failed to take account of the determination of the Russians to defend their homeland and of the severity of the Russian winter. By December 1942 the German invasion of Russia was stopped and Hitler's troops were forced slowly back towards the frontier. By this time German and Italian troops were fighting in Russia, Europe, North Africa and the Middle East. British and American aeroplanes were bombing German towns. In 1944 British and American troops landed on the mainland of Europe and gradually forced the Germans out of France and other occupied countries. Italy was invaded in 1943 and its capital, Rome, captured in June 1944. But the invaders did not capture Mussolini. He was caught by some of his own countrymen (who hated him for ruining Italy) shot and hung up by the feet in Milan for all Italians to see what happens to dictators. In April 1945 the end came for Adolf Hitler. In order to escape capture as British, American and Russian troops advanced on his capital, Berlin, the German dictator committed suicide. On 7 May 1945 the remaining German armies surrendered and the war in Europe was over.

The War in Africa

During the Second World War there was once again fighting in Africa. In July 1940 the Italians attacked Kenya across the Ethiopian border. Once again, as in 1914, East Africans were forced to join the army (the King's African Rifles). They were joined by soldiers from Nigeria, Gold Coast (Ghana), South Africa and India. The Italians were soon driven back and the invasion of Kenya became an invasion of Ethiopia. By the end of 1941 Ethiopia was reconquered and the Emperor Haile Selassie was once more able to lead his people. The Italians had also been defeated in Libya. But North Africa was very important to Hitler, who wanted to gain control of the Suez Canal and the oil-producing states of the Persian Gulf. So, in 1942, he sent German troops to reconquer North Africa and drive eastwards towards Egypt and the canal. Throughout 1942 there was fierce fighting in the desert. The German thrust was stopped and, in May 1943, the German African army was captured. Now Africa could be used as a base for attacking Italy.

Africans fought in other parts of the world as well as Africa. After the conquest of Ethiopia East African soldiers went to Madagascar (to protect it against Japanese invasion) and to Burma. In Burma they had to fight a long war against the Japanese in the hot, damp jungle.

The War in the East

By 1942 Japan had conquered a large area of China, Burma, Thailand, Indo-China, Indonesia and hundreds of the islands of the western Pacific Ocean. She was all ready for an attack on Australia. But then American, Australian and New Zealand forces began to fight back. Gradually the Japanese were forced out of many of their island bases but they fought very hard all the time. Meanwhile British, Indian, and African troops fought their way from India, down through Burma. By the middle of 1945, when the war ended in Europe, Japan had lost most of her empire and had little more than her own island home to defend. The Americans asked the Japanese emperor to surrender, but he was under the control of the military leaders who were determined to fight to the end. It was then that the United States' president decided to end the war quickly by using atomic bombs.

The Japanese attack on Pearl Harbour

Japan was delighted when war broke out in Europe. It meant that the French, British and Russians would have no time to defend their possessions in the East. The time had come for the Japanese Empire to be increased. The Japanese knew that this would mean war with America, so they decided to take the U.S.A. by surprise. On 7 December 1941, without declaring war, they attacked Pearl Harbour, an important American naval base in the Hawaiian islands, destroying many ships and killing hundreds of American sailors. This brought the U.S.A. into the Second World War.

New Weapons of War

During the Second World War scientists on both sides were busy inventing weapons that were more destructive than anything the world had ever known. Fighter and bomber aircraft were rapidly developed. Before the end of the war jet-propelled aeroplanes were being used. The Germans invented long-range rockets and flying bombs which needed no pilots and could be radio-controlled to land on their targets (cities where thousands of men, women and children lived). Tanks and guns, ships and submarines, all were improved. But the most terrible weapon of all was the atomic bomb. Scientists in many countries worked on the problems of nuclear and atomic power but the atomic bomb was finally developed in America. It was a terrible weapon, thousands of times more destructive than any ordinary bomb. One atomic bomb could destroy a whole town. Some scientists and politicians said that it was too terrible a weapon ever to be used. But on 6 August 1945 the Americans dropped one on the Japanese city of Hiroshima and three days later a second bomb was dropped on Nagasaki. In Hiroshima alone over 50,000 people were killed and another 100,000 injured BY ONE BOMB. A few days later the Japanese surrendered

Results of the War

In a little more than 30 years rivalries between the leading capitalist nations had twice plunged the world into war. By 1945 they were exhausted and had lost their position as world leaders. Some of them still had overseas empires but almost immediately after 1945 the colonies began to demand independence. Two other nations became world leaders: the United States of America and the Union of Soviet Socialist Republics (Russia).

As after the First World War, the statesmen of 1945 were determined, if at all possible, to prevent another major war breaking out. They thought that any future war would be fought with nuclear weapons. If one atomic bomb could kill 50,000 people, what would a nuclear war be like? So the United Nations was founded. Would it be more successful than the League of Nations?

The most important result of the Second World War was the really terrible loss of life and destruction it caused. Words cannot describe the horror of modern total warfare. Perhaps the best way to end this chapter is with these pictures:

The horrors of modern warfare

The top picture shows the enormous cloud of smoke and dust which rose thousands of feet into the air when the atomic bomb was dropped on Nagasaki, and the middle picture shows the terrible destruction of the city by this one bomb. Even now, over a quarter of a century after the bomb was dropped, people are still dying in Nagasaki from radiation sickness. The bottom picture shows the terrible sight that British and American troops saw when they reached one of the German concentration camps. Thousands of men and women had been starved to death and their bodies left unburied. These pictures show what 'civilized' man is capable of doing.

337

Chapter 55 Democracy and Totalitarianism, 1914-1949

Economic and Political Systems in some Countries

Economic System	1939	1949
Capitalist	Germany Italy Spain U.S.A. Japan Britain	Spain U.S.A. Japan
Moderate Socialist		Britain Italy W. Europe W. Germany
Communist	U.S.S.R.	U.S.S.R. E. Europe China

Political System	1939	1949
Dictatorship (totalitarian)	Germany Italy Spain Portugal Japan*	Spain Portugal
Parliamentary Democracy	Britain U.S.A. Most of Europe	Britain U.S.A. Italy W. Europe W. Germany Japan
Party Rule (totalitarian)	U.S.S.R.	U.S.S.R. E. Europe China

The chart above illustrates how various countries changed their political and economic systems partly as a result of the Second World War. Below are working definitions of the terms used.

Capitalism: Some private citizens own capital, in the form of money, land or factory machinery, etc. They employ other people to work for them. Because of their power and influence, capitalists may dominate society unless free elections and trade unions enable other classes to make their wishes known.

Moderate Socialism: Socialism is a system that permits the state to own the means of production (farms, factories, banks, etc.). In moderate socialist countries some of the means of production have been taken over by the state but private ownership still exists.

Communism: The community, i.e. the state, owns all property. The government, on behalf of the community, controls and organizes all property and labour.

Totalitarianism: Rule by a government that allows no political rivals or opponents to express their views or to try to gain power.

Dictatorship: Rule by one man who has complete power.

Parliamentary Democracy: Rule by the chosen representatives of the people. All citizens are free to express political views and to try to enter parliament. Governments are elected regularly.

Party Rule: Rule by one political party. Regular elections may be held but only candidates of the ruling party are allowed to be elected. Important jobs can be held only by party members.

---

*Japan was in theory a democracy but, in fact, the military leaders ruled the country through the emperor.

We read in the last chapter about the three great disasters that took place in the world between 1914 and 1945. Those disasters brought about very great changes everywhere. Not only did they cause great suffering to millions of people and lead to the decline of European leadership in the world: they also changed the way people lived and countries were governed. Of course, it was not only two world wars and a depression that brought about these changes (you have seen that revolutionary movements in China and Russia had already begun before 1914) but they were largely responsible for the enormous political and economic changes that took place. This chapter examines some of the more important of these changes and attempts to explain the complicated political and economic ideas and issues which brought them about. In the running of our modern world examples of every shade of the political spectrum can be found and these ideas seen in practice.

When governments are bad or weak (as in tsarist Russia and imperial China) or when problems are so great that governments cannot solve them (as in Europe during the Great Depression), people are ready for a complete change of government. There are two main choices open to them: democracy or totalitarianism. In Russia and China totalitarian, communist governments were set up. In Germany, Japan, Italy, Portugal and Spain totalitarian dictatorships appeared, but (except in Portugal and Spain) they did not last. In the U.S.A., Britain and other European states democracy survived the difficult years, though not without change. By 1949 most of the free nations of the world were either parliamentary democracies with a capitalist or moderate socialist economic system or totalitarian communist states. Let us now see how these changes came about.

Russia

There were two revolutions in Russia in 1917. The first one, in March, brought the Kerensky government to power, as we have seen (Part X, Chapter 45). With the tsar and his ministers gone, the people hoped for better government, reforms and an end to the starvation and suffering brought by the war. They were disappointed. The Kerensky government decided to continue to fight against Germany. There were few immediate improvements in Russia and the Bolsheviks, who had always said that Russia should keep out of the 'capitalists' war', gained in strength.

The Germans, as you can imagine, wanted Russia out of the war and did all they could to help the Bolsheviks. In April they provided a special train for Lenin to return from Switzerland to Russia. Under his leadership the Bolsheviks challenged the government in November. The revolution was soon over. Sections of the army joined with the Bolsheviks. Kerensky's government found few people ready to fight for it. Within a few days the ministers were in prisons in St Petersburg and Lenin set up a new government.

Soviet Russia

Russia now became known as the Union of Soviet Socialist Republics (U.S.S.R.). Lenin claimed that he and the Bolshevik leaders were ruling on behalf of the soviets—the groups of socialist workers (see Part X, Chapter 45) in Russian towns and villages. Soon the Bolsheviks began to call themselves communists. They abolished private ownership of factories, mines and farms. At first they encouraged peasants to seize land for themselves. The communists claimed that they had established the rule of the working class in Russia. In fact, what they did was to establish the rule of the communist party.

The new government had many opponents. Until 1920 the communists had to fight hard to overcome the resistance of the White Russians in many parts of the country. These were groups of men who disliked the new order because they still believed in tsarist government or because they did not want to lose the power and wealth they had previously enjoyed. They were helped by some European governments who were afraid that if communism were successful it might spread to other countries. The White Russians were defeated. But the communists were not so successful with the peasants. Communism believes that all land belongs to the state but in Russia the peasants had taken the land for themselves. The government, in order to win the support of the country people, had had to allow them to take over the estates of the old nobility and rich country families. After 1920 the government tried to gain control of the land or the crops. They failed. The peasants refused either to give up their land or to produce crops demanded by the government. Lenin and his supporters could do nothing—for the moment.

The attitude of the peasants, added to the

results of the war and the traditional backwardness of Russia, led to a period of great hardship and suffering. Factories closed, the peasants only produced enough food for themselves. People left the towns because there was no food there. 'Town markets became so empty that even dogs and pigeons stopped coming to them . . .'* In some districts bands of starving people wandered the countryside in search of food. Some of them even became cannibals. The U.S.S.R. had not made a very good start.

In the mid 1920s the position began to improve slightly. But this was only because the government largely gave way to the peasants and the factory workers (who demanded more pay). Real communism seemed to have failed in Russia. Another disappointment for the leaders of the Soviet Union was the failure of communism in other countries. Lenin, Trotsky and their colleagues believed that workers' revolutions in Europe and Asia would lead to the establishment of other communist states. They sent their own agents to other countries to stir up revolution. They encouraged and helped communists in other lands through the organization known as the Communist International. But in Europe capitalism and democracy proved too strong. Indeed, one of the reasons why Hitler and Mussolini were able to gain support was that the people of Germany and Italy were afraid of communist revolution. In China Russian agents had some success in the nationalist movement but then the leader, Chiang Kai-shek, dismissed his communist advisers and denounced their policies.

The Russian communist party was in trouble. It was losing support in the country and its leaders were always arguing with each other. Things grew worse after Lenin's death in 1924. There followed a five-year power struggle as politicians fought for leadership of the communist party and of Russia. The man who won this battle was Joseph Stalin. He was to rule the Soviet Union for 24 years. In theory the communist party governed Russia. In practice Stalin ruled as a dictator.

Stalin soon made clear what his aims were for Russia: 'We are 50 or 100 years behind the advanced countries. We must make good this lag in 10 years.' Stalin announced a 'five-year plan'. In it he outlined an enormous industrial and

Trotsky

Stalin

Both these men spent their youth fighting against the tsarist government, and suffered imprisonment and exile for their opposition. In 1917, Trotsky returned to Russia to help lead the October revolution, and for many years was second in command to Lenin in the communist government. But he made many enemies because his ideas did not agree with the 'official' communist doctrine. After Lenin's death, Stalin became a bitter enemy of Trotsky, because of their differences about world revolution. Trotsky believed that Russia should fight for communist revolutions throughout the world, whereas Stalin, more nationalistic than either Lenin or Trotsky, believed that Russia should concentrate her energies on making the revolution at home, to transform Russia into a great modern nation to prove to the world the success of communist economic doctrines. Only then would Russia be ready to fight for revolution elsewhere. Stalin could not bear to be opposed in his policies, and in 1927, Trotsky was thrown out of the party. Two years later he was exiled. He made his home in Mexico, but continued to oppose Stalin's policies. In 1940, an agent of Stalin found him out and killed him with an ice-pick.

*Sir Bernard Pares, *A History of Russia*, (1962 edition) p. 549.

agricultural development which was to be achieved in five years. This was only the first of many five-year plans. Factories and new factory towns were built. Millions of people were moved from the country to work in the towns. Peasant farms were taken over and became new state 'collective' farms.

How did the people react to this? Many of them disliked the violent changes Stalin was trying to force on them. But Stalin could deal with discontented people. They were thrown into prison, sent to Siberia or put into terrible work camps, where they often died of ill-treatment. There were many politicians and party members who also disapproved of Stalin's activities. These men could be dangerous to Stalin if they became leaders of revolts within the communist party. So he began a series of 'purges'. He removed from the party everyone who opposed him. He did this by having them arrested and tried for imaginary crimes. They were always found guilty and usually executed. In order to discover plots and discontented party members, Stalin relied heavily on the secret police. As in the days of Nicholas I and Alexander III the police spied on citizens, forced their way into houses at any time of day or night, arrested, imprisoned or killed without trial those suspected of disloyalty to Stalin. The only difference between tsarist government and communist oppression was that communist oppression was more merciless and efficient.

Communist government was also more efficient in bringing about improvements in Russia. At the close of the First World War Russia was a backward country: large areas were unoccupied, there was very little industry, farming methods were primitive. By the beginning of the Second World War Russia was among the world's top three or four industrial nations. Millions of people had been moved into the unoccupied areas. Collective farms using modern agricultural machinery could, in most years, feed the population. Twenty-seven new cities, each with over 200,000 inhabitants, were built. Mines, steel works, car factories, airlines, railways and roads appeared. No country has ever changed so much in such a short space of time. But the cost was enormous. Peasants and industrial workers were forced to co-operate. The Red Terror returned. Factories were built before houses so that the workers had to live in bad conditions. Stalin attacked the churches and did all he could

to stop people believing in God. Workers lost their jobs after one day's absence. If workers got together to claim better conditions they might be dismissed, imprisoned or sent to work camps. If the government were displeased with a town they might close all the foodshops for a few days to punish the townspeople. Schoolteachers had to make sure their pupils were taught communist ideas. University students could not read books which the government disapproved of. In other words every Russian was completely under the control of the government. He could not decide for himself where he would live, what work he would do, what he would believe, what he would eat or wear; he had no say in the education of his children. He could not travel to other parts of Russia without permission. He even had to be very careful about what he said to other people. He was not free.

Soviet Russia was not accepted as one of the leading nations of the world until the Second World War. When other European nations went to war Stalin was anxious that Russia should not become involved because it would stop the country's economic development. He signed a treaty with Hitler in August 1939. He divided conquered Poland with the German dictator and watched while Nazi Germany added Belgium, France and other states to its empire. Having succeeded so easily in the first months of the war, Hitler believed (like Napoleon) that he could not be defeated. In June 1941 he attacked Russia to set her free, as he claimed, from communism. The greater part of his army was involved in the invasion of Russia and it advanced towards Moscow, winning all its battles. Then Stalin called on his people to make a great effort to defend their capital and save their country. Near Moscow the Germans were stopped. Then the cold Russian winter set in and the determined Russian people fought back. Their greatest victory was at Stalingrad where after weeks of fighting the remains of two fine German armies surrendered to the Russians in February 1943.

Now it was Russia's turn to attack. The Germans were pushed out of Russia. Soviet troops occupied the countries in eastern Europe which had been conquered by the Nazis. Then they advanced—three million of them—on the German capital, Berlin. All this was possible because of the reorganization of the army and of industry carried out by the Soviet government. Russian soldiers in 1945 were not, as they had been in 1917, badly equipped and half-starved. So the war ended with all eastern Europe, including eastern Germany, under Russian control.

Stalin saw this as his opportunity to bring about the spread of communism and strengthen Russia from attack from the West. His armies kept control of eastern Europe. Some lands were added to the Russian empire. In others communist governments were set up and the states became dependent on the Soviet Union (these states are sometimes called satellites). You can see them in the map opposite. The wartime co-operation between Russia and the western powers soon broke down when Stalin's plans became clear. Britain and America sent help to Greece and Turkey to stop communist troops gaining control. Another cause of conflict between the major powers was Berlin. The German capital now lay inside the Russian controlled part of Germany but the western powers were determined not to allow the communists to control Berlin. So it was divided into Russian, French, British and American sectors. The Russians made several attempts to force out the western soldiers. But Berlin remains divided.

Russia's new empire
By 1945 the Soviet government ruled over an area bigger than anything the tsars had ever controlled. This new empire was firmly ruled from Moscow. The Soviet leaders spoke of the states of eastern Europe as free partners in the communist world but they were not free in any real sense. All government decisions had to be in agreement with Soviet policy. Travel between communist Europe and democratic Europe was very strictly controlled. As early as 1945 this barrier between the two parts of Europe was called an 'iron curtain'.

Nationalists and Communists in China
While communist rule was being established in Russia communism was struggling for power in China. When Sun Yat-sen died in 1925 he left General Chiang Kai-shek to carry on the task of uniting China under a nationalist government. Gradually Chiang overcame his enemies but he was only able to do this with the help of the communists. Chiang agreed on many points with the communists but he also realized that they were planning to take over the country in order to rule it the Russian way. Chiang, on the other

Russia spreads communism in Europe

hand, hoped to create a China modelled very much on western European lines. As soon as he felt himself to be in a strong enough position (1927) he broke off relations with Russia and dismissed his communist advisers. The next year he set up a nationalist government in Nanking.

The communists tried to gain the support of the peasants and soon had a number of small armies. Two men emerged as the leaders of the party in these difficult years: Chu Teh and Mao Tse-tung. Though they were good generals they were unable to avoid frequent defeats. Deep in the countryside, away from administrative centres, communism spread. But scattered communist groups would never be able to take over a country the size of China, as the party leaders and their Soviet advisers knew.

Meanwhile Chiang Kai-shek began to carry out reforms and reorganize the country. He might have succeeded and the communists might have failed if it had not been for the Japanese. As we have seen, the Japanese had not given up their hopes of a mainland empire. In 1931 and 1932 they invaded Manchuria and there was also fighting around Shanghai. In 1934 peace was made between China and Japan but the Japanese continued their warlike attitude. Chiang Kai-shek could not afford to fight both the Japanese and the communists so he tried to make peace with the communists.

In 1938 Japan captured Hankow and Canton, and Chiang Kai-shek was forced to move his capital farther inland. During the war with Japan (which after 1941 became part of the Second World War) both nationalist and communist armies fought against the Japanese. The invaders captured the coastal regions of China and travelled inland along the railways but they were never able to control much of the interior. If most Chinese kept their independence, that was about all they did keep. Because the Japanese controlled the ports and some of China's important farming land, they could stop supplies of food and other goods reaching the interior of China. Food became so scarce that it was worth three hundred times as much as it had been worth before the war. So the people starved and when the war ended China was a wasted country. For half a century the peasants had suffered. Armies had trampled their crops and looted their villages. It mattered little to them whether the armies belonged to the emperor or the nationalists or the war lords or the communists or the Japanese. It was always the peasants who suffered.

When the war with Japan ended the civil war went on. In 1945 the United States' leaders persuaded Chiang Kai-shek to agree to a new constitution which would recognize the communist party. But this arrangement did not last long. The communists had gained valuable fighting experience in the Japanese war and also had captured very many Japanese weapons. Their numbers had grown and they were particularly strong in North China. While the Red (communist) army grew and prepared for war, Mao Tse-tung by speeches and pamphlets tried to win over the Chinese people. He promised the peasants that they would rule the land. He promised the capitalists that their businesses would not be taken away from them when the communists came to power. He promised everyone national recovery, a united country and a good standard of living.

Millions of Chinese believed Mao Tse-tung and joined the communist forces. Between 1945 and 1948 the Kuomintang armies were defeated in battle after battle by the communists. Chiang Kai-shek was, at last, driven right out of mainland

Mao Tse-tung

Mao Tse-tung was born in 1893. He was very distressed at the confusion and misery in China during his early years. He decided that communism was the answer for China. He was one of the early founders of the Chinese communist party in 1921, and also joined Kuomintang. He realised, however, that the nationalists and the communist party were bound to split and began to train soldiers to fight for control of China.

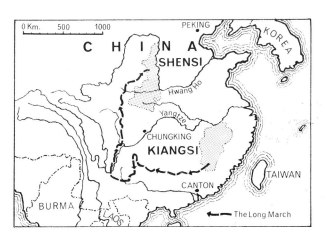

The long march

One of the most astonishing events in the history of Chinese communism occurred in 1934. It was called the long march. Communists trapped in the Kiangsi province of southern China by Chiang Kai-shek's armies decided that they would break out and link up with other communists nearer the Russian border. 100,000 Chinese communists marched for over a year to cover 9,500 kilometres. When they arrived in distant Shensi province, they set up a small communist state and waited for their chance to overthrow the government.

343

China and set up his government on the island of Formosa. His power was completely broken and only the support of the United States protected him from communist invasion. Yet he still claimed to be the true ruler of China. Meanwhile in September 1949 the People's Republic of China was set up with Mao Tse-tung as Chairman of the Central People's Government.

And so the world's largest nation (the population was over 500,000,000 in 1949) became a communist state. All businesses and land were taken over by the government. Enormous industrial development began. Men and women were moved from their homes to other areas to work on roads, factories, dams and railways. Contact with non-communist countries was cut to a minimum. All citizens were taught communist doctrines. People who refused to believe what they were taught were brainwashed. Only by completely controlling the minds of the people could the communists hope to rule and develop China. Churches were closed. Men and women suspected of not being good communists were put in prison or executed. The secret police and the army were vital instruments in the communist party's rule of fear. But the new totalitarian government was strong and under its leadership China began to recover from half a century of confusion.

Karl Marx had claimed that communism would eventually triumph everywhere. He said that all other forms of government would fail and that the rule of the working class would be established in all countries. With hundreds of millions of Russians and Chinese under communist rule it seemed that this might be coming true. But communism had only succeeded in Russia and China because imperial dictatorship had failed. In fact, in both countries communism only meant the replacing of one kind of dictatorship by another.

Western Democracy
How did the democratic countries of Europe and America face the bad years after the First World War? As you have seen Germany and Italy fell into the hands of dictators but after the Second World War democratic government returned. In other countries democracy survived but went through a very difficult period. In all western countries the hardships of the years between the wars led to a growth of socialism. This was because governments had to take action to decrease unemployment and suffering among the working class. That meant taking over some industries, giving money or food to the poor and controlling wages.

F. D. Roosevelt and the New Deal in the U.S.A.
In 1932 Franklin D. Roosevelt became President of the United States of America. It was the worst time of the Depression; the country had never been in a worse state. Roosevelt introduced the 'New Deal'. He started government building schemes which gave jobs to over two million people. He encouraged farmers to grow more food (they had been growing as little as possible because prices were low). 800 million dollars were set aside by the government to be given to the poor and unemployed. The last part of the New Deal was the devaluing of the United States dollar. This made it easier for people to buy food and clothes and to pay their debts.

Thanks to the New Deal, people were able to buy and sell more freely. Factories and farms started up again. More jobs were available. Slowly the U.S.A. recovered from the Depression. Many businessmen and politicians were angry with Roosevelt for introducing the New Deal. They were capitalists and they believed the President was bringing socialism into America. And, of course, they were right. By introducing state intervention in industry and strict rules which the capitalists had to obey, Roosevelt was introducing socialism. But it was a very moderate kind of socialism. In fact the history of the U.S.A. between 1932 and 1939 is an example of how a democratic, capitalist state could survive bad times without changing to communism or totalitarian government.

Chapter 56 Nationalism in Asia and Africa, 1914-1945

Wars and economic depressions were not the only reasons for the decline of European power and influence in the world. There was a growth of nationalism in many colonial territories. More and more people in Asia and Africa decided that they did not want to go on living under European rule. No country gained its independence before 1947 but the people and organizations which worked for independence began their activities many years before.

There were many reasons for the growth of nationalism at this particular time. Fine leaders appeared who were able to stand up to their colonial rulers and demand better treatment for their people. These same rulers explained to the people how they could get rid of the white men. Leaders were necessary because most ordinary people had given up all hope of gaining their freedom. There were some who benefited from colonial rule. They had gained land or jobs or money or education from the Europeans and did not want to see them go. Millions of Asians and African people were better off under colonial rule than they had been before. It was left to the small, but growing, nationalist movements to show the people that freedom, dignity and racial equality were more important than prosperity.

India
When the First World War broke out in 1914 most Indians felt loyalty towards Britain and were anxious to help her to win the war. Indian soldiers fought in many countries and so confident was the British government about Indian support that only about 15,000 troops were left in the whole of the country. If a rebellion had broken out it would have been very difficult to control.

There was no rebellion but the leading Indian political groups decided that it was a good time to make fresh demands on the government. In 1916 the National Congress and the Muslim League agreed under the terms of the Lucknow Compact to work together. It showed the government Indian determination to gain political freedom. The British acted quickly. They declared that it was their policy to give the Indians an increasing share in the administrative and political life of the country and to move *gradually* towards self-government. But the nationalist leaders were not satisfied. What did 'gradually' mean; 5 years, 10 years, 20, 100?

The Rowlatt Acts and Gandhi
In 1918 they began to demonstrate against the cautious British proposals embodied in the Montagu-Chelmsford Reforms. They wanted Indians to be represented in the central government and not just in local government. The British government was alarmed at these demonstrations and passed the Rowlatt Acts which gave the viceroy emergency powers to deal with any trouble. The nationalist groups responded by staging a number of demonstrations some of which led to riots. There were clashes between the nationalists and soldiers and police. Thousands of people were killed and wounded. Thousands more were imprisoned. Other Indian men and women were ill-treated by the authorities to terrify them into obedience to the government. This policy did not work; it only made the people more determined to gain their freedom.

It was in 1919 that M. K. Gandhi (usually known as Mahatma, the Holy One) became a leader of the Indian nationalist movement. Following the Amritsar massacre he organized satyagraha demonstrations throughout the country. The British found this very worrying but could do little to stop it. Even when Gandhi was put in prison in 1922 the satyagraha campaign continued.

In a country like India, containing different peoples and rival religions, it was very difficult to keep the nationalist movement united. Some leaders wanted complete independence from Britain, others hoped for dominion status, like Australia and Canada. Hindu and Muslim groups were often in disagreement. Another political force which appeared in the early 1920s was communism. The communists attempted to gain control of the working class and lead them in a workers' revolution.

As soon as he was released from prison in 1924 Gandhi called a meeting of most of India's political groups in Delhi and asked them to unite on a policy which had five main points. Firstly, co-operation between Hindus and Muslims; as a start Muslims were welcomed into the Indian Congress party which had been entirely Hindu before. Secondly, some of the worst aspects of the caste system were to be abolished. Thirdly, the status of women had to be improved. Gandhi knew that women, who at that time had few rights of their own, must be free to play a full part in the life of independent India. Fourthly, the trade in drugs and liquor had to be stopped. Drug-taking and drunkenness were two great evils in India which the British had done little to stop. Finally, India's economy had to be developed. A first step was the encouragement of home spinning and weaving. This provided thousands of families which had been almost starving before with the means of earning a living.

In 1927 an organization drawn from all India's political parties produced a draft constitution for India. After modification by the Indian National Congress, it was sent to England for approval. It seemed at first that the British government would accept the constitution and that India would move rapidly to self-government. Then, in 1929, the negotiations broke down. The Indian extremists insisted on demanding nothing less than full independence. The British government, which did not have a majority in parliament, faced defeat if it gave way to these demands.

A new campaign of satyagraha was begun. By the beginning of 1931 Gandhi, Nehru and over 50,000 demonstrators were in prison. Support for self-government did not only come from the poorer people. At a conference in 1930 the princes of the independent Indian states deman-

Holes in a wall from bullets fired in the Amritsar massacre
On 13 April 1919, a large crowd of unarmed nationalists gathered at Amritsar in North India to protest about the Rowlatt Acts. The governor of the Punjab sent troops to disperse the crowd. When the demonstrators would not go away, the soldiers were ordered to fire on the crowd. In the terrible massacre which followed over 400 people were killed and another 1000 injured.

Satyagraha
India's great nationalist leader, Mahatma Gandhi, was determined to resist the British rulers. But he had strong religious principles and refused to practise any kind of violence. How can you resist a government without weapons or fists? Gandhi's answer was satyagraha—passive resistance. It meant disobeying government orders, sitting down in the roads to stop the traffic, holding peaceful demonstrations—in fact any kind of action that would annoy the British rulers of India. This picture shows a demonstration parading a spinning wheel. Everybody is wearing home-spun clothes. This was part of a campaign to boycott foreign cotton. Satyagraha was kept up for many years and proved very effective in forcing the British to listen to Indian demands.

ded freedom for their country and a federal constitution. These demands from all levels of Indian society could not be ignored. In 1931 the viceroy had talks with Gandhi (now released from prison). The result was the Irwin-Gandhi Pact. The civil disobedience campaign was stopped, Congress agreed to accept Dominion status for India and Gandhi went to London for further talks about the future of the nation. Again there was hope. Again hope faded. The Depression and government changes in Britain brought into power men who were not sympathetic towards Indian nationalism. The result of the London talks was proposals which were unacceptable to most nationalists.

The India Act, 1935
Fresh riots and disturbances broke out. The British government continued to consider Indian problems without consulting the nationalists. In 1935 the India Act was passed. Each province was to have its own elected government and there was to be a central federal government representing the provinces and the independent principalities. Gandhi persuaded his party to co-operate and at the first elections in 1937 Congress gained control of over half the provinces. This provided very valuable experience of practical government for many nationalist politicians. But the decision to form a central government was never put into practice and India remained firmly under British rule.

India in the Second World War
In 1939 Indians were given no chance to decide whether or not they wanted to help Britain to fight the Second World War. The viceroy simply declared that India was at war with Germany. Indian soldiers fought in Burma, Africa and elsewhere. Industry expanded to provide weapons, clothing and equipment for the soldiers. The Congress leaders protested but Gandhi, who believed that Nazi Germany ought to be defeated, refused to do anything which would weaken Britain's war effort.

In 1942 in the hope of reaching agreement with the nationalists a British minister, Sir Stafford Cripps, was sent to India for talks with Gandhi. He promised self-government at the end of the war. Gandhi replied that India wanted self-government now. Nor was timing the only difficulty; Cripps could not get the Congress, the

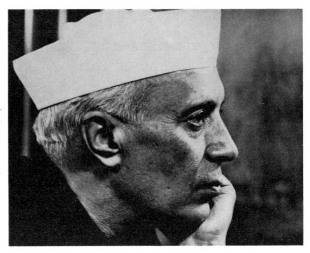

Pandit Jawaharlal Nehru
Pandit Jawaharlal Nehru was born in 1889 of middle-class parents and was educated in Britain. It was not until 1920 that he became really interested in politics. He came into close contact with the peasants for the first time and realized what a hard life they led. He joined Gandhi's satyagraha movement in 1921 and became a close friend of Gandhi. He was imprisoned and beaten by police and soldiers. In 1928 he became secretary of the Indian Nationalist Congress and in 1929 became its president. He led the group which demanded full independence from Britain. In 1947 he became India's first prime minister.

Muslim League and the princes to agree on a constitution.

Yet India *did* gain from the war. Indian soldiers fought bravely and loyally. This had a favourable effect on public opinion in Britain. Industry and agriculture expanded. More and more Indians received jobs in the civil service and, at one stage, 11 out of the 14 members of the Viceroy's Executive Council were Indians.

Nigeria
The National Congress of British West Africa demanded in the 1920s that Africans should have a share in the government of their countries. Nigeria was the first colony where this demand was met. In 1922 a new legislative council was set up. Out of a total of forty-six councillors four were to be Africans, elected by their people. These did not, of course, represent the whole country; three were elected in Lagos and one in Calabar. Herbert Macaulay formed the National Democratic Party to fight the election of 1923 and it won all three Lagos seats. This was an important beginning and it enabled the nationalist movement to make its demands known. But nationalist activity outside the capital was still restricted.

Country-wide nationalism really began among African university students. In 1925 Lapido Solanke founded the West African Students' Union in London. Though mainly a meeting place for West Africans in Britain, the W.A.S.U. was also a nationalist organization. It kept anti-colonial feelings alive among Nigerian students and, in 1936, the Nigerian Youth Movement was formed. The following year it came under the leadership of Dr Azikiwe, whose enthusiasm and ability transformed it into an active, nation-wide movement which the government could not ignore.

One reason why many educated Africans joined the N.Y.M. was because the colonial government treated them badly. Though they were as educated and cultured as most Europeans in Nigeria, they were unable to mix freely with them. More important still, they were not allowed to take important posts in the administration. There was certainly no question of an African being appointed to the governor's executive council. While the British claimed to believe in ultimate self-government for Nigeria, they also accepted Lord Lugard's policy: '... the interests of a large native population (should) not be subject to the will ... of a small minority of educated and Europeanized natives.' But if the 'educated and Europeanized' Africans could not be trained to form a government, who could?

Unfortunately, the bigger the nationalist movement became, the more divided it became. There were disagreements between moderates and extremists and there were also tribal differences —particularly between the Hausa people of northern Nigeria and the southern people (notably the Ibo) who had come to live amongst them. The only real advance towards self-government during the Second World War was the appointment of two Nigerians to the executive council in 1943. However, by 1945 the nationalist movement, though divided, was strong and the British government was forced to consider its demands.

Kenya

In Nigeria there were no foreign settlers. Europeans and European companies were not allowed to own land. This made possible good relations between the colonial government and the Africans. In Kenya there *were* foreign

Jomo Kenyatta

His Excellency Mzee Jomo Kenyatta was involved in the nationalist struggle in Kenya from its earliest days. He was one of the first members of the Kikuyu Central Association and in 1928 became its secretary. He edited *Muigwithania*, a Kikuyu magazine. In 1931 he went to Britain as a student. There he met other African nationalists (such as Kwame Nkrumah) and did all he could to make African grievances known to the outside world. His book *Facing Mount Kenya*, published in 1938, explained his people's way of life and their political hopes. He returned to Kenya in 1946 to become president of the Kenya African Union and to throw himself into the struggle for independence. During the years that followed he suffered imprisonment and many indignities before finally leading his people to full independence.

settlers and so the situation was very different. But they wanted more political power. They wanted Kenya to be like the 'white' dominions of Australia and South Africa, where European settlers elected the government and no one else had any influence. The Asians, who controlled the commercial life of Kenya, wanted political equality with the white men. They wanted to be able to buy land in the Highlands which was completely reserved for Europeans, and they wanted to be represented on the legislative council. Neither group paid much attention to the Africans.

Early nationalist movements

Yet a nationalist movement *did* begin. It began among the people of the Highlands, who came into closest contact with the Europeans. In 1920 the Kikuyu Association was formed by headmen who wanted to stop the settlers taking their land. After the war the government had encouraged more white men to come out as farmers, and had appropriated another large area of African land. But in 1921 a much more active group was formed. This was the Young Kikuyu Association and its leader was Harry Thuku. The Y.K.A. attacked not only the government's land policy but also its attitude towards the Africans, who were being made into servants and slaves in their own country. Soon a similar body, the Young Kavirondo Association was formed and it seemed as though the nationalist movement would spread rapidly.

The Kikuyu Association was no problem to the government, since it was moderate. The Young Kavirondo Association was turned into the Kavirondo Taxpayers' Welfare Association and came under harmless missionary control. But the Young Kikuyu Association was banned and Harry Thuku was deported to Kismayu. In 1925 the Y.K.A. was reformed as Kikuyu Central Association. It demanded the release of Thuku, the right to grow coffee, and African representation on the legislative council.

The K.C.A. gained in popularity and during the 1930s political groups were formed in other parts of the country. There were many clashes between these groups and the authorities. Such conflicts only led to an increase in the number of nationalist organisations demanding more freedom from colonial oppression. Trade unionism also began in the 1930s with the formation of the Labour Trade Union of East Africa. In 1939 this union organized a strike at Mombasa to force employers to improve the terrible working and living conditions of dock workers.

Had it not been for the outbreak of war in 1939 the government would have been forced to deal with the mounting nationalist activity in various parts of the country. As it was, all political groups were banned when the war started and thousands of young men, who had been members of these groups, had to go into the army.

Part XV Towards the Modern World

Chapter 57 The Rebirth of Independence in Asia and Africa

Kenya celebrates Independence, December 1963
Amid scenes of great joy, Kenya gained *Uhuru* on 12 December 1963. In the Uhuru Stadium, Nairobi, before a great crowd of over 250,000 people, the British flag was lowered and Kenya's new national flag of black, red, green and white flew for the first time. Kenya now joined the many African and Asian countries which had shaken themselves free from colonial rule. Her new leader was a man who had worked and suffered much for his people—Mzee Jomo Kenyatta.

The last part of this book considers the state of our world, its problems and advances since the end of the Second World War.

Anti-colonialism
One of the most important changes that took place after 1945 was the appearance of a large number of new, independent states—most of them in Asia and Africa. The colonial empires of Britain and France disappeared and in their place new nations, such as India, Pakistan, Kenya, Algeria, Ivory Coast and Nigeria emerged.

We have seen how nationalist movements in these countries had been working towards independence for many years, but there were other reasons why colonial rule came to an end when it did. After the war Britain and France were economically weak. They had to rebuild bombed houses and factories, restock farms and get peacetime industry and trade going again. To do all this they had to borrow from richer countries (mainly the U.S.A.). At the same time they had to spend more than ever before on their colonies. Yet many African and Asian leaders complained that the European powers were not devoting enough money to the development of colonial territories. Faced with these complaints and their own financial difficulties, French and British governments were more prepared to give up control of the colonies than they had been before the war. But they were not in a hurry to do so. They wanted to be quite sure that each of the various states was 'ready' for self-government before they handed over control. If, for example, Kenya and Nigeria had had to wait for Britain to decide that they were ready for independence, they might still be colonies today.

Pressure was also put on the colonial powers by other countries. After the Second World War the United Nations was formed to replace the old League of Nations (see next chapter). It was a meeting place for the free nations of the world and most of those nations were opposed to colonialism. The United States, in particular, did everything possible to urge the colonial powers to grant independence to their overseas territories. It was because of these pressures as well as the pressures of nationalism that freedom came to many of the peoples of Asia and Africa during the 20 years after 1945.

Independence and after in India and Pakistan

As the war against Japan drew to a close it was clear to the British government that Indian independence could not be delayed much longer. After the failure of the 1942 talks between Mahatma Gandhi and Sir Stafford Cripps there had been serious and prolonged disturbances which greatly annoyed the British and made it more difficult for them to fight the war in Asia. But was India 'ready' for self-government? She had some fine leaders in men like Gandhi and Nehru but her people were very divided. In 1945 a conference of leading Indian politicians took place at Simla to try to form a constitution. It failed. The Congress Party and the Muslim League could not agree on a constitution which would give equal civil rights to Hindus and Muslims. Meanwhile the viceroy tried to rule India with a few specially-chosen Hindu and

Muslim ministers but their authority was not recognized by the Congress party.

1946 was a year of violence and despair. The Muslims were now refusing to have any part in a united, independent India. They wanted their own state. The British government sent skilled representatives to try to bring the two sides to an agreement but after four months of talking they had to report failure. In August riots broke out in many Muslim areas. In September a new government was formed under the leadership of Pandit Jawaharlal Nehru. This was the first really representative government which was not firmly controlled by the British viceroy. But, as British power declined, the conflict between rival groups of Indians grew worse. Members of the government disagreed with one another and disturbances continued throughout the country. The people did not want British rule but they could not agree about what kind of rule they *did* want.

By this time the British government was determined to hand over control as soon as possible. In February 1947 the British Prime Minister, Clement Attlee, announced that his country would give up all authority in India by June 1948 at the very latest. Now all the Indian leaders realized they would have to reach agreement quickly. With the help of the last British Viceroy, Lord Mountbatten, Pandit Nehru, Mohammed Ali Jinnah (the leader of the Muslim League) and their colleagues agreed that the country should be divided into two states: India and Pakistan (a Muslim state). In June 1947 the British parliament approved these arrangements. At midnight on 14/15 August two new, independent dominions came into being — India and Pakistan.

But partition and independence did not put an end to the problems of the sub-continent. During the following months there occurred some of the most terrible massacres in the whole history of India. The trouble began because after partition many Hindus and Sikhs found themselves in Pakistan and many Muslims found themselves in India. Most of the trouble was in the Punjab, the homeland of the Sikhs, now divided between Pakistan and India. Soon, millions of people were fleeing from violence, often leaving their homes with few or no possessions. They wandered, without food or shelter, hoping to find friends who would show them kindness, cold and hungry but glad to be alive. By January 1948, when the riots were stopped, the two new nations were faced with the problem of finding homes for over 11 million people.

The northern hill-country of Kashmir also presented problems. On independence the various princely rulers of old Indian states accepted the control of the new central government. But the Maharajah of Kashmir was in a difficult position. He was a Hindu but most of his people were Muslims. His state lay between West Pakistan, India and China and therefore had great strategic importance. He was very unpopular with his people. Everyone waited to see whether Kashmir would join Pakistan or India. Then, in October 1947, civil war broke out in Kashmir. Frightened of his Muslim subjects, the maharajah offered his state to India and asked for protection. India took over Kashmir and sent troops into the country. But Pakistan also sent in troops. The Pakistan government claimed that the maharajah could not hand over his people to India without their consent. After peace had returned to Kashmir Indian and Pakistani troops stayed in the country and both sides claimed it. In fact Kashmir was divided into two when fighting stopped on 1 January 1949. And divided it has remained. India and Pakistan have quarrelled over Kashmir and the problem has been discussed by the United Nations assembly but no solution has been found.

But the main problems of India and Pakistan have been economic problems. India has the second largest population of any country in the world and, in spite of the efforts to introduce birth control, this population is growing rapidly. The solution of this problem is made more difficult by the attitude of many influential Indians who oppose birth control for religious reasons. How to feed the people is always the most urgent problem faced by Indian governments. Pandit Nehru's government decided to take over control of many industries and to set up a moderate-socialist state so that much of the profits of industry could be used for the good of all the people. India received financial and technical help from wealthier countries, particularly Britain and the U.S.A., but she was very careful not to take sides in the rivalry between the western nations and the communist world. India has always been neutral and non-aligned. Often she has acted as a peacemaker in disputes between other countries.

Neutrality has not always been easy. In 1950 Communist China invaded the mountain country

India and Pakistan

of Tibet, just across India's northern border. India protested and refused to recognize communist rule in Tibet. In 1954 Pandit Nehru had talks with the Chinese leaders. He withdrew his opposition over Tibet in return for pledges of peace. Even so there have been violent clashes between Indian and Chinese guards on the border. Though she has made considerable progress, India is still a poor country and she has to watch her northern neighbour very carefully.

It is very important that India should have strong, secure, representative government. In 1950 a new, republican constitution came into effect. India became a parliamentary democracy after the British pattern. The Congress party has been the ruling party since independence but the constitution allows for a parliamentary opposition and there is a number of smaller political parties represented. In the early 1950s communists tried to gain control of parts of India by force and by making promises of a better life to the poorer Indians. These attempts failed and the communists turned to constitutional methods. They now have a few members in the parliament at Delhi.

A democratic state, if it is to survive, needs four things: free, regular elections, so that the people may be properly represented in parliament; a well trained and uncorrupt civil service, so that people may have confidence in the administration; courts and judges which are free from political interference†, so that justice cannot be used by those in power against their enemies; armed forces and a police force loyal to the elected government, so that ambitious men cannot gain control of these forces in order to gain power for themselves. Because of developments during and after the colonial period India has these four things. The independence of women, though slow in coming, has made some progress. The outstanding example of this is Nehru's daughter, Mrs Indira Gandhi, who was appointed a Cabinet Minister in 1964 and afterwards became Prime Minister of India. Certainly such an appointment up till quite recent times would have been considered as quite an impossible one for a woman to hold in India. In addition to Mrs Gandhi there are at least two other women now prominent in Indian politics.

Pakistan was faced with many problems. Not only was there the refugee problem and the Kashmir dispute with India; there were problems arising from Pakistan's divisions. The country was in two, quite separate, parts—East Pakistan and West Pakistan—between which lay about 900 miles of India.

The work of government and business was made difficult and the people themselves disliked the arrangement. There was particularly strong ill-feeling in East Pakistan where a large Hindu population resented living under Muslim rule.

Another problem was political rivalries within Pakistan. In 1947 India already had a capital and an organized civil service. Pakistan had to start with almost no trained politicians and civil servants. One great exception, of course, was Mohammed Ali Jinnah, the first Governor General of Pakistan, who however, lived only for a little over a year after his appointment in August 1947. He was given the title of 'Quaid-i-Azam' which means 'the Great Leader'. Another experienced politician was Liaqat Ali Khan. When Pakistan was established the work of government was made difficult by bitter rivalries between different political parties. There were numerous changes of government until Field-Marshal Ayub Khan took over in 1958.

Ayub Khan
After serious disturbances in 1958, the president of Pakistan called on the help of the army, whose commander was Ayub Khan, to restore law and order. Realizing that the country needed a really strong man to lead it, the president resigned in favour of Ayub Khan, who ruled Pakistan with a firm hand for the next ten years. He resigned office in 1968.

To help in her relations with other countries and also to help with her internal problems, Pakistan has needed friends. At first she associated herself firmly with the western powers. After serious disturbances in 1954 the communist party was banned. Pakistan received considerable financial help from the U.S.A., Britain and Commonwealth countries, particularly during a serious famine in 1953. The people of Pakistan increased the export of their main products—cotton and jute. They started large new irrigation schemes, began new industries and greatly expanded traditional crafts, such as rugmaking. But, in 1970, many of Pakistan's problems still remained to be solved.

Nigeria
During the Second World War the nationalist movement in Nigeria was not very active. In 1944 Dr Nnamdi Azikiwe formed the National Council of Nigeria and the Cameroons (NCNC), the first nationalist party, which hoped to unite people from all parts of Nigeria. But the Nigerians were not alone in wanting political advance: the colonial rulers were prepared to give the African people more say in government. In 1946 the governor put forward a new constitution

---

†We call this 'an independence judiciary'

which would allow more Nigerians on the legislative council. It was unpopular with the NCNC because it did not go far enough but it was put into practice in 1947. It had two main aims: to preserve Nigeria's unity and to allow for different kinds of administration and political life in the different regions of the country.

It was differences and conflicts between the various peoples of Nigeria which proved one of the major difficulties in the struggle for independence. Since independence these same differences have contributed largely to tragedy in Nigeria. The British realized that Nigeria's leaders would not wait very long for independence and from 1947 onwards they made greater attempts to train Africans for government and higher civil service posts. They now decided the time had come to discuss the next constitutional changes. A conference was held at Ibadan in January 1950 at which all the Regions were represented. It was there that rivalries really began to come into the open. Hausa, Ibo and Yoruba delegates mistrusted one another and demanded a federal constitution which would give each Region considerable freedom and independence. New political parties were formed to oppose the NCNC, which was Ibo-dominated. These parties were the Action Group in the Western Region and the Northern Peoples' Congress and Northern Elements Progressive Union in Northern Nigeria. A new, federal, constitution came into being in 1952 and the first nation-wide elections were held.

The new constitution lasted little more than a year. The various parties and regional groups could not get on well together. In May 1953 there were riots in Kano during which hundreds of people were killed or wounded. It seemed that Nigeria was in danger of splitting into a number of small states all clamouring for independence. Again representatives from all Regions met at a conference — this time in London. As a result a new, improved federal constitution was introduced in 1954.

After these troubled years Nigeria now settled down to a period of peace. There were other problems to be faced before independence. Men had to be trained for positions in the public services of the national and regional governments. The Regions had to settle down to friendly relations with each other. So passed the next six years until on 1 October 1960 Nigeria became an independent federation. Sir James Robertson was the first Governor-General and Sir Abubaker Tafawa Balewa, a Northerner, the first prime minister. In 1963 Nigeria became a republic and Dr Azikiwe, who had succeeded Sir James Robertson as Governor-General, took the title of President.

The new government settled to the tasks of creating a prosperous and peaceful nation. Nigeria had begun to prosper during the Second World War when her exports were needed by Britain. After 1945 agricultural production increased, Nigeria's ports and harbours grew busier, new industries were founded. National and regional governments used their revenue to improve the living standards of the people by building schools, roads and hospitals.

But beneath the surface the old divisions remained. As we saw in the case of the U.S.A., it is difficult to make a federal constitution work. The Regions of Nigeria were dominated by different political parties each depending for support mainly on one of the larger tribes: the Hausas in Northern Nigeria, the Yorubas in the Western Region, and the Ibos in the Eastern Region. All of the parties mistrusted one another. There were arguments over the elections and arguments soon led to violence and riots in the Western Region. In January 1966 the crisis came. A group of Ibo army officers tried to seize power, and murdered the Federal Prime Minister, Sir Abubaker Tafawa Balewa, and the premiers of the Northern and Western Regions. But the rebellion failed, and to restore order the General Officer commanding the Nigerian Army, Major-General Aguiyi-Ironsi, himself an Ibo, became head of a military government which banned all political parties.

General Ironsi tried to solve the problems of regional rivalry by abolishing all the Regions and putting the whole country under the direct control of the government in Lagos, but this only caused fresh anxiety. The people of the Northern Region now feared they would be ruled by the Southerners, and especially by the Ibos. There was a second army rebellion in which General Ironsi was killed.

His fellow soldiers then asked an officer from one of the smaller tribes of Northern Nigeria, Lieutenant-Colonel Yakubu Gowon, to become Head of State and to try to bring peace to the country. He replaced the four Regions by twelve States. These States are too small to become a danger to the unity of the country but they are large enough for efficient government. Most people approved of the new constitution for it seemed to them that the new governments were more concerned with local problems than the old regional governments had been.

But the leaders of one Region did not like the new arrangement. This was the Eastern Region in which the Ibos were a majority of the population. Under the leadership of its military governor, Colonel Ojukwu, the Eastern Region acted more and more independently of the Federal Government. Other Nigerians became angry with the Ibos. Rioting spread through the Northern cities and thousands of Ibos were killed. Fearing for their safety, Ibos from all over Nigeria fled to their homelands. In May 1967 the Region broke away from Nigeria and Colonel Ojukwu proclaimed a new independent country, 'Biafra', with himself as Head of State.

General Gowon's Federal Government was determined to preserve the unity of Nigeria and crush this attempted secession. Civil War followed, causing great suffering. It is believed that hundreds of thousands of people were either killed in battle or died from starvation, as they fled from the fighting, leaving their homes and their land. Attempts by the United Nations, the Organization of African Unity and individual African states to end the war by negotiation all failed.

In January 1970 the Ibo leaders surrendered and the Federal Government was able to settle to the tasks of rebuilding the war-torn towns and villages and of creating a united nation. The Nigerian civil war is another example (like the troubles in India and Pakistan) of the truth that nations are not made by drawing lines on a map or by signing independence documents. It takes time for men and women of different cultural and tribal backgrounds to learn to think of themselves as one people.

The present

Not all of Nigeria was disrupted by civil war; indeed only a small area of the country was directly affected. Elsewhere progress in agriculture, industrialization, education and other social services has gone on steadily. One important modern industry which rapidly grew in importance was the production of petroleum oil. As Nigeria entered a new phase of political stability, it could also look forward to greater prosperity and social progress.

Victims of the Nigerian civil war

Kenya

Between 1945 and 1952 Kenya waited for some real move to be made towards greater political rights for Africans. But little was done. More African members were appointed to the legislative council. The Kenya African Union (KAU) was allowed to hold meetings. On the other hand, more European settlers arrived in the country and there was no move to deal with African grievances over land and political representation.

While KAU and other African leaders held meetings and made their demands peacefully, others turned to violence. In 1946 a number of young men returning from the army formed the Forty Group. They were determined to oppose the European government in every possible way. Working largely among the Kikuyu people of the Kenya Highlands, they persuaded or forced them to disobey district officers and to oppose white farmers. Within a few years this movement had grown into the Land and Freedom Army, an extremist organization which raided military posts and police stations for guns and ammunition, and forced thousands of people to take an oath promising support for its cause. Many European settlers reacted to this movement with their own kind of violence and extremism. There were cases of ill-treatment of Africans who were suspected of belonging to Mau Mau (as the freedom fighters came to be called) and the settler leaders demanded that Britain reject the nationalist demands and hand over power to a white government.

By 1953 the Mau Mau movement had spread throughout Kikuyuland and the colonial officials had failed to stop it. So the governor declared a state of emergency in Kenya. British troops arrived to fight the freedom fighters in the forests of Mount Kenya and the Aberdares. Many African leaders, including Jomo Kenyatta, were arrested and put in prison. Fighting took place for the next three years, and although most of the freedom fighters were defeated by 1956, it was not until 1960 that the state of emergency came to an end.

The Mau Mau struggle made many people in other lands realize that the African population of Kenya had real grievances and that they would not accept continued European rule. Slow constitutional change continued: there were more Africans on the legislative council and African political parties were formed. In 1959 nationalist leaders demanded an end to this slow change. They wanted a constitutional conference to consider Kenya's future. In 1960 a conference was held in London. It provided for elections to be held to a new parliament in 1961.

Two African political parties fought the election: the Kenya African National Union (KANU) and the Kenya African Democratic Union (KADU). Though KANU won the election, its leaders refused to form a government until Jomo Kenyatta was released. So KADU formed a government. During the colonial period it was the Kikuyu people who had come into closest contact with the Europeans. So it was they who had learned most about European ways, had become better educated and had led political and military resistance to the colonial powers. KADU drew support from a wider area and its supporters feared Kikuyu domination. Therefore the new government made plans for an independence constitution which would give some political freedom to the various regions of Kenya.

But this was not to be. In 1961 Jomo Kenyatta was released. In 1962 a second London conference took place to plan Kenya's independence constitution. In 1963 fresh elections were held and KANU, led by Kenyatta, won a clear majority of the seats. So it was Mzee Jomo Kenyatta, as Prime Minister of a KANU government, who led Kenya to Independence on 12 December 1963. One year later Kenya became a republic with His Excellency Mzee Jomo Kenyatta as first President.

In June 1963, as Kenya celebrated Madaraka (internal self-government), the Prime Minister spoke these words:

'... constitutional advance is not the greatest end in itself. Many of our people suffer in sickness. Many are poor beyond endurance. Too many live out narrow lives beneath a burden of ignorance ... as we make merry at this time, remember this: we are relaxing before the toil that is to come. We must work harder to fight our enemies – ignorance, sickness and poverty.'[*]

Inevitably the new government made many changes. British-style democracy was proved to be not the best political system. The upper chamber of parliament was abolished and when in 1969 the small opposition party was banned, Kenya became a one party state. Large areas of European farm land were taken over to be allocated to African owners or to co-operative schemes. These were not universally successful as the new farmers found the modern techniques difficult to master. Coffee continued to be Kenya's most important export but it was soon overtaken as a money-earner by tourism. Considerable investment was poured into hotels, game lodges and improved transport facilities and as a result Kenya was able to exploit fully its rich scenic and wildlife heritage.

Most serious posts in the administration were Africanized and thousands of Asians unwilling to adopt Kenya citizenship were expelled from the country. Kenya is not a rich country, but the development of a mixed economy enabled the government to bring education, health services and other benefits to the people.

---

[*]c.f. J. Kenyatta, *Suffering Without Bitterness*, EAPH, 1968, 207

Chapter 58 The Era of Confrontation, 1945-1970

By 1945 two terrible wars had been fought in one generation.

Within a few years the U.S.A., Britain, the U.S.S.R. and France all had stocks of atomic weapons. People realized that it was more important than ever before to prevent nations having disputes which might lead to war. Immediately after the Second World War relations between the communist and non-communist countries began to worsen. Soon relations between the United States and her allies and Russia and her allies were so bad that they were described as a 'cold war'. Yet *real* war never broke out between them.

At the same time as these conflicts between East and West, communists and non-communists, were taking place, there were other movements towards greater unity and co-operation in the world. Let us now look in detail at some of the examples of unity and disunity in the modern world.

Russian conquests in Europe

As we have seen, Russian armies occupied a large area of eastern Europe at the end of the Second World War, while most of western Europe was held by British and American forces. At a meeting at Yalta in February 1945 the leaders of the three victorious nations agreed to restore complete independence to all nations except Germany. But, within a few months, Stalin, the Russian dictator, insisted that Russia should be allowed to keep troops in eastern Europe for a short while. The British and American representatives reluctantly agreed.

Now, Stalin set about increasing the size of his empire. Estonia, Latvia and Lithuania had been occupied in 1940 and, together with other territory seized in 1940, became part of Russia. In other countries Stalin had communist govern-

ments installed which he could dominate. Germany was divided up into four zones: Russian, American, British and French. In 1949 a communist government was set up in the Russian zone, now called the German Democratic Republic (or East Germany). At the same time the other three zones were united into the German Federal Republic (West Germany), which soon had its own, freely elected government.

Clashes with the West

The old German capital, Berlin, lay in the Russian zone but as the other powers refused to let Russia control it, the city was divided into four sectors. Stalin was determined to force the western powers out of Berlin. In 1948 he closed all the city's links with western Europe—or almost all. The one way into Berlin which he could not interfere with, without risking war, was by air. Immediately the western powers began sending food and supplies by aeroplane into West Berlin. For over a year the 'airlift' continued until, at last, Stalin was forced to give in. But this was only the first of many Berlin crises.

What annoyed the Russian leaders most about Berlin was that people who did not like life in East Germany were going to Berlin, crossing into one of the western sectors and travelling from there to the West. Tens of thousands of refugees escaped from communist rule in this way. In 1961, in order to stop this, the Russians had a wall built dividing East and West Berlin. This cut down the number of refugees but there were many people who still risked their lives to escape from the communist world.† There have been

---

†It should be mentioned here that some people have gone from western Europe to communist countries but the numbers who have done so are small indeed compared with those who have fled from East to West.

Soviet troops in Hungary, 1956

In most countries of eastern Europe, communism simply means control by Russia. Yugoslavia is the only example of a really independent communist state in Europe. Twice since 1945 states have tried to break away from Russian control. In 1956 Hungary tried to assert independence. In 1968 Czechoslovakia tried to develop its own kind of

Soviet troops in Czechoslovakia, 1968

communism. The Soviet reaction was the same on both occasions: soldiers and tanks were sent in to 'liberate' these countries from 'western influences'. Many thousands of Hungarians and Czechs, realising that freedom was dead in their own countries, afterwards left home to live in western Europe.

many examples in history of nations which have built walls and stationed soldiers on their frontiers to keep enemies *out*. Never before has a country had to build walls and station soldiers on its frontiers to keep its own people *in*.

Having succeeded so completely in eastern Europe in 1945, Stalin tried to achieve the old ambition of the Russian tsars, that of gaining an outlet to the Mediterranean Sea. He helped communist revolutionaries in Greece and Turkey in the hope that they would overthrow the existing governments and set up communist states which Russia could control. But Britain and America helped the governments of these two countries to suppress the revolts. Since Yugoslavia, though communist, was under the rule of a dictator who refused to be dominated by the Soviet Union, Russia still had no direct way into the Mediterranean Sea.

It was during the struggle to preserve the independence of Greece and Turkey that the U.S.A. adopted a new policy. There were many Americans who believed that, now the wars in Europe and Asia were won, the United States should withdraw from these areas and leave them alone. In March 1947 President Truman announced a new policy (later known as the Truman Doctrine):

'I believe that it must be the policy of the United States to support free peoples who are resisting attempted subjection by armed minorities or by outside pressures.'

What this meant in practice was that America

was pledging herself to resist the spread of communism anywhere in the world.

In the following years a number of military alliances were formed between the U.S.A. and other countries interested in stopping the occupation of other countries by communist forces. Canada, Greenland, Iceland and a number of western European nations joined America in the North Atlantic Treaty Organization (NATO). To protect the Pacific area and Asia, the South-East Asia Treaty Organization (SEATO) was formed. A number of Middle East states signed the Baghdad Pact with the United States. Meanwhile Russia and her allies joined together in a military alliance known as the Warsaw Pact. So, by the mid 1950s, armed and united communist and non-communist groups of nations faced each other, and war (perhaps nuclear war) seemed a distinct possibility.

Communism did not have very much success in European countries where Russia was not able to force it on people. Communist parties existed in many west European countries. In no democratic state was communism prohibited. Yet in none of these countries have the communists been able to gain the support of the majority of voters.

Clashes outside Europe

Unfortunately the clash between the Soviet Union and the western powers was not confined to Europe. After the end of the Second World War there were American and Russian troops in the Asian country of Korea. The United Nations decided, in 1947, that all troops should be withdrawn and the Korean people should elect their own government. The U.S.A. agreed to this. The Soviet Union did not, so the country was split in two. South Korea became the democratic Republic of Korea. North Korea became the communist Korean Peoples Republic. All foreign troops were withdrawn. In 1950 North Korean soldiers crossed the boundary into South Korea, armed with Russian weapons. Within weeks most of South Korea was in communist hands. The United Nations sent an army, composed largely of American soldiers, to defend South Korea. China also sent troops to the aid of the Korean communists. As a result, the war dragged on for another three years. Fighting stopped in 1953 but by 1970 there was still no permanent settlement of Korea's problems.

There are few areas of the world which have not been affected by the rivalry between the United States of America and Soviet Russia. Both countries have tried to gain the friendship and support of developing nations by providing them with money, machines, technicians and advisers. (So have other communist and non-communist countries.) This help is desperately needed by many countries in Asia, Africa and South America, but governments accepting aid always need to be careful that there are no conditions attached by the givers which would enable them to gain power or influence in the country receiving the aid. When powerful nations use foreign aid to gain influence in poorer countries, they are said to be following a policy of 'economic imperialism'.

Conflict in the Middle East

Another troubled area of the world in this period was Palestine and her neighbouring countries. The basic population of Palestine was Arab but for many years Jews from various countries had moved there to set up a new nation-state under the terms of a League of Nations mandate. The two communities were armed against each other and only restrained by the mandatory power—Britain. Attempts to find a peaceful solution between 1945 and 1947 all failed. A UN plan for partition was rejected by the Arabs. Violence increased and thousands of Arab refugees fled to neighbouring states where they lived in 'temporary' camps pending the restoration of Arab rule in Palestine. In 1948 the British man-

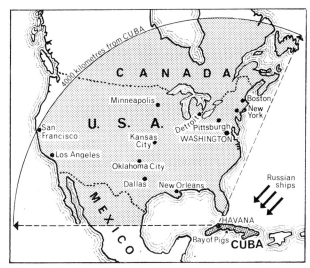

The Cuban crisis

In 1962 there was a clash between America and Russia which nearly led to nuclear war. In 1959 the West Indian island of Cuba came under the communist dictatorship of Fidele Castro. In 1961 some exiled Cubans tried to invade the island but were defeated at the Bay of Pigs. Knowing that the invasion had been supported by the U.S. government, Castro angrily turned to Russia for defence aid. In August 1962 the U.S. government learned with horror the type of weapons that the Russians were supplying. They were nuclear missiles with a range of 4000 kilometres. Cuba is only 144 kilometres away from the coast of North America. The U.S. President, J. F. Kennedy, threatened war if Russia did not immediately stop supplying these weapons. Meanwhile a further cargo was heading for Cuba in Russian ships. Anxiously the world waited to see what would happen. At last the Russian leader ordered the ships away from Cuba. Disaster had been avoided.

date came to an end and a Jewish provisional government immediately proclaimed the independent state of Israel. The Arab League declared war but open hostilities ended after a few months thanks to UN mediation. Terrorist activity and border raids, however, became a normal part of life in Palestine. Gradually the new state surmounted constitutional crises and economic difficulties to become a sophisticated modern nation with a well-equipped military strike-force.

Now the cold war reached the Middle East. In 1956 Russia supported the decision of President Nasser of Egypt to nationalize the Suez Canal, which had previously been under international control. At the same time Russia was providing massive armaments to Egypt, which had now assumed the leadership of the Arab world.

Israel felt herself threatened and invaded the Sinai peninsula to destroy military bases there.

Britain and France issued an ultimatum to both sides, and when this was ignored they sent troops to occupy the canal zone. This sparked off a major international crisis. Foreign troops were withdrawn; Israel evacuated most of the occupied territory, and UN forces were sent to patrol the troubled frontiers. More important were the determination of both sides to continue arming themselves and the increased backing by Russia and the U.S.A. for the Arab states and Israel respectively.

In 1964 various Arab liberation groups set up the Palestine National Charter and pledged themselves to regain control of Palestine. Terrorist activity increased, spreading beyond the Middle East in such actions as the hijacking of aircraft and attacks on embassies. In June 1967 a six-day war between Egypt, Syria, Jordan and Iraq on the one hand, and Israel on the other, left Israel victorious, having taken more territory and destroyed hundreds of Arab planes and tanks. During the conflict Egypt deliberately blocked the Suez Canal by sinking ships in it. Also the refugee problem was enormously increased. There were many attempts to create a permanent peace but they foundered on Israel's refusal to retreat from her 'secure boundaries' in the face of such securities offered, and the Arabs' fundamental refusal to recognize and negotiate with the state of Israel. So the basic problem remained unsolved and continued to claim many innocent lives.

Development of the U.S.S.R.

By the end of the Second World War the Soviet Union was one of the world's two leading powers. Its industrial and agricultural development under the leadership of Stalin had been astonishing. But the war had greatly slowed down Russia's advance. Twenty million Russians had died. Towns, villages and farmland in the west of the country had been laid waste. Stalin was determined that Russia must recover. He produced another five-year plan. Again people were moved to where their labour was needed. New factories were built. Small co-operative farms were combined into much larger state-owned units. Once again the Soviet Union developed at astonishing speed. Industrial production doubled in five years.

In 1953 Joseph Stalin died; the new rulers were not so harsh as Stalin and his supporters but the pace of development continued. The new Chairman of the Soviet Communist party,

Heavy Industry in Russia
Production of oil is a great economic strength. Here are oil rigs in the sea at Baku and huge drums at the railway awaiting transport. Note that the workers are women.

Nikita Kruschev, said:

'We want to compete with the capitalist countries ... let us see who produces more per head of population, who provides a higher material and cultural standard for the people.'
He was determined to prove to the world that communism was a better system than capitalism, by making Soviet citizens richer than American citizens. The resources of the U.S.S.R. are enormous, yet the living standards of the people still lag behind those in capitalist countries. Perhaps they will one day catch up. Yet there is something

more important than motor cars and refrigerators —freedom.

Science and Education

It is some of the more highly educated Russians who tend to feel the lack of freedom most deeply. Writers, painters and playwrights are not free to express themselves as they wish. Their work is checked by government agents. Some have been imprisoned and others have fled to the West. Yet Russia still has many very clever men in all branches of learning. By 1949 Soviet scientists had discovered how to make the atomic bomb and since then others have been to the fore in all kinds of scientific research. Soviet orchestras, musicians, ballet dancers and opera singers are among the finest in the world. Despite censorship, Russian authors have written many fine books.

The Russian leaders know the value of education. They set themselves a target to produce so many chemists, so many physicists, so many biologists, etc., each year. They have even founded a special city, Academic City, at Novosibirsk in western Siberia, where scientists and technicians live and receive training.

Communist China

The Soviet leaders were delighted at the establishment of communist government in China in 1949. Russia had given Mao Tse-tung's armies much-needed weapons and knew that for some time the Chinese would continue to need such aid. So Russia felt sure that China would continue to look up to her as the leader of the communist world. But Mao Tse-tung and his friends had other ideas. They gladly took the tanks, planes and ships that Russia offered but at the same time laid plans to become the leaders of communism in Asia.

They began to aid and encourage communist revolutions in other countries. In 1950, before they had gained complete control of their own country, they sent soldiers and equipment to Korea, as we have seen. At the same time Chinese communists were sent to British-ruled Malaya to try to bring about a revolution there. The struggle against these communist guerillas slowed down the movement towards independence in Malaya, which was not achieved until 1957. By then the people of Malaya had their own freely-elected government. It was not a communist government.

In 1950 China overran the mountainous country of Tibet. This gave China a long frontier with India and enabled her to interfere in the dispute between India and Pakistan over Kashmir. In 1962, there was a clash with India over their common border in the Himalaya Mountains. The Chinese soldiers had been specially trained to fight in mountain country and the Indian army was soon forced to withdraw, leaving China with a further 35,000 square kilometres of territory. Outside Asia, China has made a bid for the friendship of developing nations in Africa. Her greatest success has been in Tanzania where a large number of technicians and advisers have been sent to help with various development projects.

The Vietnamese War

China, which has become the most powerful Asian state, was behind almost all the communist activity in Asia. Non-communist states watched the growth of communist parties and the formation of guerilla bands with anxiety. They feared that, supported by Chinese money and armed with Chinese weapons, the communists would be able to take over one Asian country after another. That is why the Americans and their allies tried to stop the spread of communism in South Vietnam.

In 1954 the area known as Indo-China won its independence from the French colonial rulers and was divided into four states, Laos, Cambodia, North Vietnam and South Vietnam. Vietnam was divided into two parts because, like Korea, it contained communist and anti-communist groups. So, the north became a communist state, with a capital at Hanoi and the South a non-communist state with a capital at Saigon. It was agreed that, after two years, Vietnam would be reunited under a freely-elected government. But the communists did not wait. Communist guerillas in South Vietnam began to invade various parts of the country and aimed to overthrow the unpopular government (1955).

Alarmed by the successes of the Viet Cong (South Vietnamese communists), the government asked America for help. So United States soldiers arrived, but still the communists were successful. This made the U.S. government more determined than ever to defeat the communists, while North Vietnam gave increasing support to the Viet Cong, supplying weapons originally from China and Russia.

361

The war grew worse in 1964. Raids were made from North Vietnam. U.S. aeroplanes now began bombing military depots in North Vietnam. Still the war went on. After ten years of war the peasants, whose crops were trampled and villages burned, only wanted an end to the war. Probably they had ceased to care whether they were ruled by a communist or non-communist government.

The war became very unpopular in the West. Many Americans resented public money being spent to keep an unpopular foreign government in power. Public opinion in many countries was angered by reports of American bombing of North Vietnamese civilians, though it is clear that the communist forces were guilty of similar and even greater atrocities. Yet successive American governments continued the war because they were committed to supporting South Vietnam and because they were afraid that if the communists succeeded there, they would quickly overrun neighbouring countries. And so the war went on. In 1968 peace talks began in Paris but they made little or no progress.

China's internal development

As we have seen before, totalitarian governments and dictatorships can bring about rapid improvements in a country. This is because they can force people to go where they are most needed, they can take over privately owned land, factories and money, they can kill or imprison those whose ideas do not agree with their own and all their decisions can be made without the consent or knowledge of the people. So it was in communist China. The astonishing economic development in China since 1949 is sometimes called the 'Great Leap Forward'. State farms were created and new land cultivated. Within 20 years these measures had doubled China's agricultural production. China also developed as an industrial nation. Labour camps were set up and the people worked with their bare hands to build roads, railways, dams and factories. With Russian aid (in the early years) and their own hard work and skill the Chinese people set up industries for the manufacture of tractors and cars, aeroplanes and tanks, tools and ships, steel girders and machines, clothes and shoes. Full use began to be made of China's many mineral resources to make Chinese industry independent of other countries' steel and fuel. Many of China's rivers were dammed or

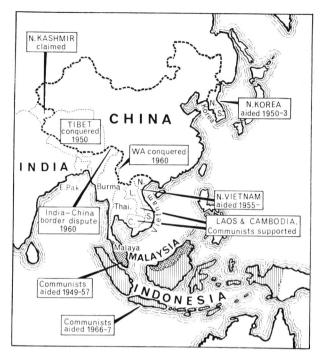

China's attempts to dominate South East Asia

re-routed for irrigation. Hydro-electric schemes were started to provide light and power for the new industrial centres. Communist China very soon discovered the secret of atomic power and in 1967 exploded its first hydrogen bomb.

Perhaps the greatest achievement of the communist government was in bringing a large degree of unity to the many different peoples of China. This has been done by improving communications, simplifying the Chinese written language, spreading information and propaganda through the thousands of state schools that have been built, and by the economic development of nearly all regions.

The communist party was all-powerful and its propaganda was spread in the them had had very little under earlier forms of government. The Chinese people had freedom but most of schools, by books and leaflets, by large posters in the streets and by radio. The people were taught, not only to support communism, but to hate the U.S.A. and other capitalist countries. The first great communist leader, Mao Tse-tung, was praised everywhere by communist agents and the people were expected to almost worship him.

Most of what happened in China was unknown to the rest of the world. The communist leaders put up what has been called a 'bamboo curtain' between their country and foreigners. Other powers were also guilty of isolating communist China. When the United Nations was formed, America and other leading powers still recognized Chiang Kai-shek and the Kuomintang as the real rulers of China. So nationalist China (Taiwan) was admitted to the organization and communist China was not. Despite the facts that communist rule in China was firmly established and that China had the largest population of any country in the world, it had still not been admitted to the United Nations in 1970.

Relations between the two great communist powers, Russia and China, gradually grew worse. They became rivals for the leadership of the communist world in Asia. Russian leaders made tours of Asian countries to try to neutralize Chinese influence. Both countries eagerly provided help to North Vietnam. In 1960 there came a real split between them when they disagreed over the meaning and application of communism. Both countries concentrated troops along their common frontier. Russia very anxiously watched China's development of nuclear weapons, especially as this development was centred in Sinkiang province, next to the Russian border. By 1970 it would be difficult to say whether China regarded Russia or America as its most dangerous enemy. But both these great powers, and many other countries, were by 1970 watching very carefully a nation of 700 million people (a quarter of the world's population) which was developing rapidly, which needed more land and food, which was trying to spread its influence in Asia and beyond and which had a supply of atomic weapons.

The Western World

In 1945 Europe was once again faced with the problem of recovering from a disastrous war. The European leaders also wanted to make sure that the Depression and economic hardships that had followed the First World War did not occur again. There was little thought this time of punishing Germany and her allies. The leading statesmen were concerned that *all* countries should recover as quickly as possible. America was the richest country in the world and her economy had not suffered as a result of the war. Many Americans believed that the country should return to a policy of isolation, (i.e. of not

Hongkong, a western-style Oriental city adjacent to communist China

being concerned in the problems of other countries) but their leaders realized that this was impossible. If battered countries were to recover, then America would have to help them. America saw this partly as a matter of her responsibility as the greatest world power, partly as a matter of self-interest.

In 1947 the American Secretary of State, General George Marshall, made a speech in Congress in which he said: '. . . the United States should do whatever it is able to assist in the return of normal economic health in the world, without which there can be no political stability and no assured peace.' He suggested that the U.S.A. should make large grants of money to Europe. His scheme was accepted and the help given became known as Marshall Aid. During the next few years the scheme provided £15,000 million for western European countries (eastern European states were not allowed by Russia to take part in the scheme). Thanks to American help and their own determination, these nations made an astonishingly quick recovery. Bombed cities were rebuilt, farms re-established, weapons factories converted for the production of peacetime goods. Within seven years the average man in western Europe was better off than he had been in 1939 and better off than the average man almost anywhere else in the world, except North America.

The war hastened political and economic changes in western Europe. Ordinary capitalist systems could not deal with the enormous problems of finding homes and jobs for millions of people, of caring for the war disabled, the unemployed and the homeless, of building a new society. Government planning and control was necessary.

The Welfare State

In Britain the suffering caused by economic depression and war made clearer than ever before the need for a fairer, more egalitarian society in which poorer and less fortunate people were helped with the resources of society as a whole. In 1942 the economist William Beveridge produced an official report on Social Insurance and Allied Services. In 1944 an Education Act was passed which introduced a new, integrated system of free state education to secondary level and provided financial assistance for university students. In 1945, to the surprise of many people inside and outside Britain, the Conservative party led by the wartime prime minister, Winston Churchill, was rejected by the electorate in favour of the Labour party which had promised a far-reaching programme of social reform. The outcome was the Welfare State. Earlier achievements such as old age pensions, unemployment pay and national health insurance were now integrated into a system of social welfare. Taxation was increased to pay for government housing schemes, a free health service, and educational opportunities at all levels. The government extended its socialist programme by nationalizing coal mines, railways, steel manufacture and road haulage. All this was done within the existing capitalist framework so that Britain came to have what is known as a mixed economy.

Economic Co-operation

As Europe and the world recovered from the Second World War and as many new African and Asian nations came into being, so world trade expanded at an astonishing speed. Many countries found it an advantage to combine together into groups for trade. In Europe two such groups were formed: The European Economic Community (Common Market or E.E.C.) and the European Free Trade Association (EFTA). In 1967 the East African Community was born.

The Commonwealth of Nations

The British Empire was unique among all the empires of history in the fact that its break up took place (for the most part) peacefully and that most of Britain's ex-colonies and dominions remained on friendly terms with her after independence. As each of the colonial territories achieved independence they were offered membership of the Commonwealth of Nations, a loose association of states acknowledging the British Queen as its head. Most of them accepted this offer. It is difficult to describe just what the Commonwealth is. All of its members have some things, such as parliamentary democracy, in common because they have inherited them from Britain. Many of them use English as a first or second language. Member states of the Commonwealth helped and advised each other in various ways and there were certain economic advantages of membership. At regular meetings of Commonwealth prime ministers matters of common interest and concern were discussed. Moreover, the Commonwealth stood for certain standards and ideals as was made clear when South Africa left the Commonwealth, realizing that its racialist policies were unacceptable.

The Organization of African Unity

As Africa's nations gained their independence in the 1950s and 1960s it was natural that they should want to band together in some form of union, but the various states could not agree on what they wanted. Some wanted to move rapidly to a single African nation. Others wanted to take immediate military action against the white-dominated states of Southern Africa. At last in 1963 at Addis Ababa representatives of all the African independent nations met to form the Organization of African Unity (OAU). The OAU concerned itself with all problems involving Africa. It proved to be a meeting place for rival groups and in its early years made useful contributions to the settlement of trouble in the Congo and made frequent attempts to settle the Nigerian civil war. But those who hoped for a really united Africa were disappointed: the leaders of the new nations became increasingly more concerned with their own problems and less interested in pan-African federation.

The United States of America

We have already mentioned a number of facts about the United States of America after 1945. Already the richest and most advanced nation in the world, she continued to develop rapidly. For example, by the late 1960s she was producing nearly half the world's steel and oil and more

grain than she could export at a profit. She gave
large sums of money in foreign aid, not only to
Europe but also to Africa, Asia and South America. She led the western world in the preparation
of its defence against communist attack. Her
soldiers fought in two anti-communist wars in
Asia.

Yet despite this expansion, this activity and
leadership in the world, the United States had its
own severe problems at home. The two largest
problems were racialism and poverty. In 1863
America's large negro slave population was set
free. In 1870 Congress changed the constitution
to make it quite clear that no American citizens
could be discriminated against, treated differently and unfairly, because of their colour or race.
But prejudice and race hatred cannot be got rid
of just by legislation. In the southern states
negroes and other coloured people were still
treated badly. Some states found ways of restrict-
ing the number of coloured voters. In Louisiana
at the beginning of the century there were
130,000 adult negroes. Less than one thousand
were allowed to vote. Coloured young people
were not allowed to attend the same schools and
colleges as young white Americans.

After the Second World War, when so many
negro soldiers gave their country devoted service, the federal government began to take steps
to make sure that all Americans really would be
equal. In 1948 racial discrimination in the army
was stopped. In 1954 separate schools and colleges for black and white students were prohibited. By this time the negroes had begun to
organize themselves into movements demanding
full equality (or 'civil rights', such as equal rights
to jobs, houses, etc.). The greatest leader of the
civil rights movement was Dr Martin Luther
King, a negro clergyman, who from 1955 organized peaceful demonstrations all over
America. He was assassinated in 1968.

The United Nations

On 26 June 1945 representatives of 51 nations
meeting at San Francisco in the U.S.A. signed the
Charter of the United Nations. The basic aim of
these representatives was: '. . . to save succeed-
ing generations from the scourge of war, which
twice in our lifetime has brought untold suffering to mankind, and to reaffirm faith in fundamental human rights, in the dignity and worth of
the human person, in the equal rights of men and
women and of nations large and small . . .' By
1970 over 120 nations belonged to the organiza-

The Ku Klux Klan

The Black Panthers
Racial tension in America led to the formation of extremist
groups. The Ku Klux Klan is a society of white Americans
who hate negroes. The society has a bizarre set of rituals,
including burning crosses and wearing hooded gowns, but the
society itself is anything but ridiculous. It has the sinister and
evil aims of stirring up race hatred, and uses violence and
murder in attacks on negroes and on whites who make friends
with negroes. Another extremist group is the Black Panthers,
who are small, disciplined bands trained to start riots and stir
up violence as part of a revolution to gain Black Power for the
black people of America. Neither the Black Panthers nor the
Ku Klux Klan believe that people of different races can live
in peace together, and both are a threat to the solving of the
racial problems of the United States of America.

tion and three quarters of the world's population was represented there. The countries which did not belong were communist China, colonial territories, disputed areas (East and West Germany, North and South Vietnam, North and South Korea) and Indonesia, which walked out in 1965 after being criticized in the UN General Assembly. All the member nations have, in fact, admitted that the world is so small that events in one country affect other countries, that different nations cannot ignore each other and that peace will only be preserved if the world's leaders can meet together to discuss their differences instead of fighting about them.

In its first 25 years the UN had to act in a number of difficult situations. It sent troops to Korea and the Congo. It intervened to try to preserve peace between Greeks and Turks in Cyprus and between Egyptians and Israelis in the Suez Canal area. It has not always succeeded in having its decisions obeyed. In 1965 the white-dominated government of Rhodesia illegally seized independence from Britain in order to keep itself in power and prevent the African people from ever taking over their country. The United Nations called on its members not to trade with Rhodesia. Rhodesia was placed in great difficulty but she did not give in. Sanctions failed because not all UN members enforced them. In 1968 the UN Assembly agreed that South West Africa (Namibia) should no longer be under the trusteeship of South Africa. The South African government ignored this decision. Short of using force there was nothing the UN could do.

But probably the most important work done by the UN was not connected with international politics. It was done by the various commissions and agencies which were trying to tackle the world's social and economic problems. Commissions were set up to deal with illegal drug traffic, with refugees, with the peaceful uses of atomic power, with world health, with the proper care of children, and other vital issues.

The United Nations
The world's first attempt at organizing an international assembly to keep world peace, the League of Nations, failed to prevent the Second World War. Thereafter a new assembly was formed, the United Nations with head-quarters in New York. UN agencies have been set up to tackle various problems. The Food and Agricultural Organisation (FAO), for instance, concerns itself with improving the world's food supply by increasing agricultural production.

The United Nations building in New York

UNESCO helps education
Newly-independent Nigeria was very short of trained secondary teachers. This well-equipped teacher training college, built with UNESCO aid, was an important contribution towards solving the problem.

Chapter 59 Detente and Development

The story of mankind has been brought almost up to date and as the point approaches where history merges into current events, certain questions arise. How has man benefited from his experiences? Has he learnt anything from the past? In the widest possible sense, are we developing into more civilized people?

In one sphere, that of scientific and technical advance, enormous strides have been made especially in this century. It would be impossible to catalogue all the inventions and discoveries which have changed our lives but we can highlight some of the significant developments of recent years which future generations will still regard as turning points.

Medicine

Today many people live normal, healthy lives who, a few years ago, would have died from or been crippled by such diseases as tuberculosis, polio, leprosy or diabetes. This is because many new drugs have been produced which can cure or control these diseases. Probably the most valuable kinds of drugs are those known as antibiotics. These are drugs obtained from living organisms which kill disease-carrying germs (*bacteria*, as they are called by scientists) and usually having no harmful effect upon the person taking the drugs.

Alexander Fleming, Penicillin and Antibiotics

The discovery of antibiotics began in the 1920s with a British scientist named Alexander Fleming. He was studying certain bacteria in his laboratory in London. To do so he had to grow the bacteria on glass dishes. One afternoon in 1928 Fleming was clearing up some of the dishes on which he had carried out experiments. He noticed that a mould had got on to one dish and that in the area round the mould the bacteria had not grown as rapidly as the rest. Fleming asked himself 'Could the mould be producing something which poisons the bacteria?' After several years of careful work Fleming and his helpers managed to separate out a powerful bacteria poison from the mould and, much to their astonishment and joy, it proved to be almost harmless to man. They named it penicillin after the mould from which it came.

For many years Fleming's marvellous discovery had no practical results. The reason was simple: penicillin could not be produced in big enough quantities for the regular treatment of human beings. It was not until 1941 that American scientists discovered a way of producing penicillin in large quantities. After the Second World War scientists did a great deal of research into substances like penicillin. They believed that if penicillin could cure some diseases, then similar drugs could cure other diseases. They were right. The study and production of antibiotics became an important branch of science. Now there are hundreds of antibiotics in regular use by doctors. Among the previously deadly diseases that can be cured by the new drugs is tuberculosis, now treated by streptomycin.

Modern Surgery: Transplants

In surgery, also, there have been remarkable developments in recent years. In December 1967 a South African doctor took the heart from a patient who had just died and put it into the body of a man whose diseased heart he had removed. This kind of operation is called a transplant.

For many years doctors in several countries had been carrying out experiments on animals and human beings. During the Second World War people who had been badly burned had damaged skin removed and replaced by good skin from another part of their own body. Later scientists were able to replace some diseased parts of the body with artificial organs. But often these man-made parts were not as good as the real thing. So, in the 1950s, a great deal of work was done on the problem of transplanting parts from one animal to another. By the mid-1960s enough progress had been made for human transplants to be begun. Kidney and liver transplants took place before heart transplant surgery began. Many patients still die as a result of transplants (some after several weeks or months) but a start has been made and every year transplant surgery becomes more successful. The time may be coming when hospitals will keep a stock of 'spare parts', both natural and artificial, ready to give to patients.

Transplant surgery is probably not as important as the work on new drugs. It needs great skill and technical resources which only the biggest hospitals will have. Consequently it creates a new and very difficult problem of deciding which patients should be given this special treatment. On the other hand, new drugs affect the chances of everybody to be cured of diseases. More important than either repairing or curing sick bodies is the job of preventing sickness. Great advances are being made in this respect too, so that we can expect that more and more people in the world will live longer and longer.

This brings us to the first great problem of today and the future.

Several times in this book we have thought about the problems of a growing world population. Today there are nearly four thousand million (3,828,000,000) people in the world. Half of them are underfed, but unless something happens to stop the present growth rate there will be twice as many people in the world in 37 years' time. In another 37 years the population will have doubled again—over 12,000,000,000! In Africa at present, 30% of children born do not reach the age of 15 but, even so, the population of Africa doubles every generation. As medicine and farming improve, fewer people will die of disease and starvation. But that will only mean *more* people in the world. Is it possible to feed, house and clothe all these thousands of millions of extra people? We cannot.

The only real answer to this problem lies in birth control. People must learn how to control the size of their families. Since 1945 scientists

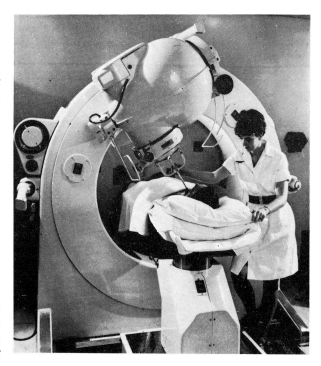

Treating cancer with gamma rays
One of the most terrible diseases today is a cancer. It is caused by a 'growth' which gradually increases in size inside a man's body and stops parts of his body from working properly. Death from cancer is usually very slow and painful. The study of nuclear physics has shown that certain rays, called gamma rays, given off by radioactive cobalt can kill the cancer growth. Here you see a man inside a cobalt unit about to be treated.

have done a great deal of work on this problem. They have discovered a number of very simple methods easily available to people to prevent them having too many children. Medical staff now go to Asia, Africa and South America to teach men and women how to use the new birth-control methods. But progress is very slow and, meanwhile, thousands of babies are born every hour.

This is a problem all countries have to face. Over-population in countries has often been a cause of war. Over-population in cities and towns is a cause of bad housing, poverty, crime and unhappiness. Everywhere it causes the natural beauty of our world to be destroyed. We hope that in future our numbers will not be reduced by great wars or by disease. So control of the size of families is essential.

Industry

Earlier on in the book we saw how industry developed in the eighteenth and nineteenth centuries. In Britain and Europe, then in North America, Russia, Japan and parts of Asia and Africa a whole way of life was changed as factories and towns sprang up. Now we live in a highly complex world in which almost every country has its manufacturing industries and competes with rival nations for a share in international markets. People who control large industries are always looking for ways of producing goods faster or cheaper or more efficiently and so more complex machinery is invented.

Computers and Transistors

The most complicated machine so far invented is the computer. This marvellous piece of equipment is a thinking machine—an electronic brain. An enormous amount of information is recorded electronically and stored in the machine. When a problem is given to the machine to solve, it immediately 'remembers' the necessary information and so produces the answer.

Computers can deal with problems far quicker than the human brain. To take a simple example: a computer can answer in less than a second an addition sum involving thousands of sets of figures. In industry, where a great many problems are dealt with every day, the computer is a great help. There are even some factories where all the machines are controlled by one computer.

There are few people today who do not know what a transistor radio set is. But what is a transistor? In the 1950s and earlier, radios were large objects which could not be carried around easily. Before they would work they had to be plugged into an electrical circuit. Inside there were many wires and valves (a valve is a glass tube with wires inside, looking like a complicated electric light bulb). In 1947 three American scientists discovered that the work of a valve could be done by a tiny crystal of germanium. Working on this discovery they eventually produced the transistor. A transistor is smaller, stronger, cheaper and more reliable than a valve. Its discovery made possible the making of radio sets which will fit in a person's pocket. But it had much more important uses than that. With such transistors can be made tiny hearing aids for deaf people, teaching aids for schools, complicated computers and the machinery necessary for space rockets and satellites.

Nuclear Power

The development of the atomic bomb and the

A laser

Have you ever burned a hole in a piece of paper by concentrating the rays of the sun through a magnifying lens? Scientists have now developed a machine that can produce a ray of light so strong that it will burn a hole in almost anything. Above, this machine, called a laser, is burning right through a sheet of aluminium, showering sparks of molten metal. Lasers are used in many kinds of engineering, for boring holes in rock or steel. They are also used in surgery. Doctors have joined together delicate parts of the human eye by using laser beams.

appalling destruction wrought in Hiroshima and Nagasaki terrified the world. During the period of the 'cold war' the nations of East and West developed still more devastating missiles capable of carrying nuclear warheads thousands of kilometres in order to hit targets in enemy territory. Vast sums of money were spent on the development and stockpiling of these weapons while, in many countries, groups of people campaigned for the total abolition of such weapons. In the event, these terrible tools of mass annihilation have never been used although many countries have developed their own missiles and have, to use the grim jargon of the press, joined the 'nuclear club'.

While the threat of a terrible holocaust hung over the world nuclear power was being put to more beneficial uses. It has been employed to drive electrical power stations. Although such plants are expensive to build they do not need to be sited near sources of water power (i.e. dams and waterfalls) and they do not use large quantities of precious natural fuels such as coal and oil. Atomic power and other types of radiation which have been studied as a result of nuclear research can be used to provide intense heat for industrial process, propulsion for ships, means of sterilizing food and of destroying bacteria and growths in the human body. In the 1950s many scientists believed that nuclear power was the golden key to unlimited sources of energy. It seems that they were wrong or, at least, that we shall not be able to use that key until we have solved the problems of obtaining nuclear power more cheaply.

Transport and Communications

In 1903 the Wright Brothers' aeroplane made the first successful flight. It was a light machine of wood, wires and canvas, with a tiny engine. Its great flight covered about 300 metres and lasted for less than a minute. Fifty years later aeroplanes were flying miles up in the air at speeds faster than the speed of sound. It was at the beginning of the Second World War that an Englishman, Frank Whittle, invented the jet engine and immediately his country started to make jet-propelled aeroplanes for use in the war. After 1945 his invention was put to peaceful uses. Large jet airliners were built which could carry people and goods from country to country faster and more cheaply than ever before. Nothing has done more than the jet aeroplane to bring peoples and nations into closer contact with each other. Politicians, businessmen and great numbers of ordinary men and women now travel to other lands and get to know them and their problems better.

It is not only travel between different countries that has become faster. As business and industry develop, so more and more goods have to be carried from town to town in lorries and vans. Businessmen need cars to take them about quickly. As soon as people have enough money they want to buy a car for their own pleasure. The manufacture of motor vehicles is now one of

A complicated fly-over road system
So many people have cars in America, that they have developed some complicated road systems to help the traffic to flow freely. In this picture, the minor roads sweep in wide circles, so that the traffic does not need to slow down to turn sharp corners, and then 'fly-over' the main twelve-lane highway to avoid dangerous cross-roads.

A Jumbo Jet
Below is a picture of the 'Jumbo Jet', the Boeing 747, first flown by Pan American. It is the largest aeroplane ever built, and holds 362 passengers. It takes only six and a half hours to fly across the Atlantic from New York to London, and its normal cruising speed is 1,006 kilometres per hour. In early 1976 Concorde, a joint Anglo-French venture, made her historic maiden flight—the first commercial aircraft to cruise at a speed greater than that of sound.

the biggest industries in the world. There is hardly a country in the world whose roads are not becoming busier and busier each year. This presents many problems. More cars on the road means more accidents. Governments have to try to find ways of making people drive safely and carefully. They also have to build better, wider roads so that motorists can travel quickly from place to place and prevent traffic becoming congested.

We should welcome developments which make it possible for more people to travel more easily but there are disadvantages which have to be overcome. Great cities like New York, Tokyo and London now contain so many cars that it is sometimes quicker to walk. All these cars poison the air with gas from their engines. Jet aeroplanes make so much noise that houses near modern airports need to be given special protection against sound. Either ways must be found of preventing these nuisances or we must decide to do without modern developments that make life uncomfortable or unhealthy.

Radio and Television

Like many other inventions television was first invented many years ago but did not come into everyday use until after the Second World War. It was in 1926 that a Scottish inventor, J. L. Baird, produced the first machine that could change a moving picture into an electric current, send that current along wires and then change it back into a picture again. But it was another 20 years before television sets could be made which were reliable and cheap enough for ordinary people to buy. Now it is the most important form of entertainment in the world. It brings pleasure and information to millions. It brightens the lives of sick people who cannot leave their beds. It is an important form of education and is used in many schools and colleges. It is yet another way in which we can learn of different peoples and lands. Unfortunately like most of the other developments we have been considering, radio and television can be used for the wrong purposes. They can be used to spread lies, mistrust, rumours and hatred. They can be used by governments and those in power to spread propaganda and influence the viewer as they wish.

Man in Space

Man has always been an explorer. In the past he

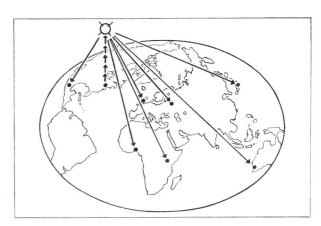

Communication by satellites

One of the most important results of the space race has been the development of satellites. These are small spacecraft carrying electrical instruments and machines which are carried into space by rockets and put into orbit around the earth. (That means that they continue to go round the earth, as the moon does.) Satellites were very important during the early days of space exploration because they gave scientists valuable information about the earth's atmosphere and the space which lay beyond. But satellites were found to have other uses. They can be used to send radio and television messages from one part of the world to another. Pictures and messages are sent from one place to the communications satellite, and from there can be relayed or sent to other places all over the world. They can be used to photograph the earth's surface and tell us about our continents and oceans. They can be used in weather research so that we can know far in advance if heavy rains or storms are coming.

The surface of Mars

In 1969 man's knowledge of the planet Mars was greatly increased. At its nearest point to the earth this planet is 56,000,000 kilometres away and the best photographs obtained of it were taken from Earth with the aid of a powerful telescope. But in 1969 an American spacecraft flew within 10,000 kilometres of Mars, and took pictures of the surface of the planet like the one shown above. From these photographs and other measurements made by the spacecraft, astronomers can work out what the surface of the planet and its surrounding atmosphere are like. At one time many people thought there might be life on Mars. Now astronomers consider this very unlikely.

The first moon walk: a photograph taken on the moon
In July 1969 two men, American astronauts, walked on the surface of the moon. This was the most astonishing of all human achievements up to that time. Ever since the end of the Second World War, American and Russian scientists had been working hard on the problems of space exploration, each country hoping to be the first to put a man on the moon. The successful moon flight took years of preparation and cost billions of dollars. Some people believe it would have been better to spend this money and effort on trying to solve some of the world's great problems, such as poverty and starvation. Others say that the moon flight was a great achievement and one all people should be proud of.

has risked his life to climb great mountains, to cross the oceans in tiny ships, to travel to every corner of the world. Now he has begun to travel outside his own world. One reason for the rapid development of space exploration was the political rivalry between Russia and America since the Second World War. Each nation decided to prove to the world how advanced it was by trying to be the first to put a man on the moon. (This rivalry was called the space race.) In April 1961 the Russians surprised the world by sending up a spacecraft with a man inside to travel round the earth. This first man in space was Yuri Gagarin. But that was only the first step and most people thought that it would be very many years before a man could land safely on the moon. In fact this was achieved a little more than eight years later, in July 1969, when two Americans spent several hours on the moon's surface and then returned safely to earth. And that was only the beginning. Rockets with cameras and other scientific equipment inside were soon being sent to the outermost parts of our solar system.

But just as some people were beginning to think that real space travel was only a few years away Russia and America began to slow down their space programmes. For years groups of people had complained about the expenditure of billions of dollars and roubles on such extravagances. They said that the money should be diverted to the fight against the problems of this planet such as poverty, disease and population explosion. At the very least, they suggested, Russia and the USA should pool their resources instead of competing in a ruinously expensive race to be the first to put a man on the moon or set up an orbiting laboratory in space.

In the early 1970s the sheer cost of space projects forced the politicians and scientists to take these complaints seriously. When the moon landing had been accomplished the competitive element in space research ceased. Scientists from East and West shared their knowledge and agreed to co-operate in future ventures. America sent three more manned spacecraft to the moon to collect rock samples and measurements and then announced that they had gathered enough information to keep scientists busy for years. There were to be no more manned flights in the foreseeable future. However, on 19 July 1975 occured an event historic both in the field of scientific and political achievement, two manned space craft orbiting the earth docked together successfully. The crew of one was Russian, the other American and their handshake and exchange of hospitality were televised to earth. At least in space East and West can still meet with good intentions and genuine co-operation.

It is important to realize that space exploration has already brought advantages to man. Spacecraft need a great deal of very complicated electrical machinery. Scientists exploring this problem have invented tiny electrical parts, such as transistors, which, as we have seen, have many other uses. Doubtless other useful by-products of space research will lead to new developments in communications, medicine, food production (astronauts have to have all their food in the form of fluids, tablets or compressed lumps) and many other aspects of human life. Apart from all this, it is important to know more about our universe and its changes.

Mechanisation and Technical Training

New techniques, new ways of doing things inevitably involve a challenge to manpower. The installation of computers and better machines in factories mean that fewer men are needed in those factories. Changes in manufacturing processes mean that workers have to learn new skills. In industry the unskilled workman is a thing of the past just as, in modern agriculture, the peasant farmer is obsolete.

These changes create many new problems. In industrial states employers and trade unions have had to think about unemployment, redeployment and technical training. Rather than cut down drastically on manpower, firms which have modernised their plant tend to employ more workers than necessary but for shorter hours. Even so, it has often been necessary to lay off some workers or insist that they complete training courses or move to new areas. Many workers, backed by powerful unions, resist such moves. They insist that every man has a 'right to a job'. The employers counter by claiming that unless they modernise their factories they will be forced out of business by more efficient competitors and then *nobody* will have a job. For these and related reasons industrial strife has become one of the features of modern life in the West. Matters are no better in the developing countries.

Unfortunately, the benefits of modern science are not shared equally by all the world's peoples. It is only the nations that are more advanced that can afford to train scientists and technicians. So the people of western Europe, the U.S.S.R. and the U.S.A. gain more from scientific advance than the peoples of Asia, Africa and South America. But the developing nations have gained something. Every year many communist and capitalist nations spend large sums of money on aid to developing nations. This may take the form of equipment or trained men. British and Italian engineers build an oil pipeline in Algeria. Russian generators are used in an Indian electrical plant. There are thousands of examples of new industrial nations learning from the old. In this way some enormous problems are being tackled: how to water large areas of arid country; how to prevent the spread of disease; how to make agriculture more efficient; how to use local water power for electricity.

But the pace of technical advance in the developed countries is so rapid the Third World simply cannot catch up. All producers are caught on a treadmill which is turning faster and faster. If they are to keep up with competitors they must be constantly modernizing and using the latest techniques. Industrial giants like ICI and Unilever spend millions every year on research into new products and improved industrial methods. Companies in Africa and Asia cannot possibly compete. They can only buy experience and machines from 'big brothers' of the industrial world.

Yet they are not entirely powerless and under certain circumstances they can exert considerable pressure. All world markets are so closely tied together that producers and consumers have vital need of each other. This was shown last dramatically in 1973-4. A period of industrial boom throughout the world had led to an increased demand for a wide variety of raw materials. The leading industrial nations had been used to fixing the price of commodities such as oil and copper by simply wielding superior economic power. But now the producers realized that they had their own economic power. They banded together and drastically increased the price of raw materials. The cost of crude oil from the Middle East, for instance, quadrupled in a year and a similar price rise affected sugar from the West Indies. This sparked off a period of wild inflation and industrial recession in the West. Unfortunately, the inflation and recession spread back to the raw material producing countries. They had to continue buying goods from the manufacturing nations but they could only do so at increased prices. Yet at least they had asserted their right to a more equal position in the economic world. They had shaken off the last vestiges of colonialism and would no longer be thought of as suppliers of cheap goods for the 'superior' white nations.

International Politics 1970-1975

Technical and scientific developments have radically changed the relationships between nations. In past centuries wars frequently broke out because rival states were not accurately informed about each other's intentions and because heads of government had no direct contact with each other. Now, thanks to modern transport and communications, the world's peoples know each other better and statesmen can be in almost instant contact with their opposite numbers. In the 1970s there has been a move away from confrontation and rivalry by the big powers towards co-operation and greater understanding—a policy sometimes called 'detente'. This new spirit has affected not only direct relations between the great powers

but has also spilled over into other areas of tension.

In 1969 the U.S.S.R. and the U.S.A. began a long series of discussions aimed at mutually reducing their level of armaments. These SALT (Strategic Arms Limitation Talks) meetings very slowly produced results. In the meantime America had, at long last, lifted her veto on mainland China's right to U.N. representation. Only in the 1970s did representatives of the Peoples Republic of China take their seats in the Assembly and the Security Council for the first time. Shortly afterwards President Nixon of the U.S.A. made a state visit to Peking, where he was warmly received by the communist leaders. Such a visit would have been inconceivable a few years before when large anti-American placards were seen in all China's main cities.

President Nixon had also pledged himself to ending the war in Vietnam. Peace talks in Paris had been going on intermittently for years without result. Now the Americans brought increasing pressure to bear on the negotiators and announced that there would be a phased withdrawal of U.S. troops. A treaty was patched up between the combatants and the last American forces left Vietnam in 1973. But the treaty was little more than a face-saving arrangement to enable the U.S.A. to disentangle itself from a war which was very costly and very unpopular. The Americans left their South Vietnamese allies well provided with military equipment but this did little to protect the non-communist state from the North Vietnamese who resumed their invasion almost immediately. Early in 1975 Saigon, the South Vietnamese capital, fell to the communists. The neighbouring state of Cambodia was overrun by 'red' forces soon afterwards. The American fear that all S.E. Asia would go communist seemed well on the way to being fulfilled. On the other hand, the tragic events of twenty years had proved that the Truman doctrine was inoperative, and that America alone was powerless to prevent the spread of communism.

This did not mean that America had ceased to be an influence in the world. The ability of U.S. statesmen was clearly shown in the Middle East conflict. After the death of President Nasser of Egypt in 1970 the tension between Israel and Egypt relaxed very slightly. The Arab states were reluctant to resume open hostility, but they were under constant pressure from the various Palestinian liberation movements. Arab terrorists continued to commit atrocities in many parts of the world and even took their conflict to the Olympic Games in Munich in 1972. There they murdered some Israeli competitors and more were killed during an attempt by the police to capture the terrorists. In 1973 Egypt and Syria launched a sudden attack on Israel. Egyptian forces recrossed the Suez Canal to establish bases in the Sinai peninsula which Syria invaded across her border. Though taken by surprise the Israelis fought back furiously and had regained much ground before international pressures forced the combatants to agree to a truce. After this conflict it was the American Secretary of State, Dr Henry Kissinger who took the lead in mediating between the two sides. He paid repeated visits to the leaders of all the governments involved and, though his efforts were not crowned with complete success, he did go a long way towards achieving detente in this troubled area. One positive result of his was the re-opening of the Suez Canal in 1975.

The tendency to look to the major powers for intervention in the real crises indicates the political role of the United Nations and the growing importance of large power blocks. The U.N. continues to be a useful forum for the staging of protests and the discussion of international problems. The secretary-general of the organisation continues to be a much respected figure whose opinion is listened to with attention. Yet the political resolutions of the U.N. carry little weight and largely for economic reasons U.N. peace-keeping forces have been less in evidence than in the first twenty-five years of the United Nations existence.

One area in which the U.N. failed to achieve political change was southern Africa. Trade sanctions against Rhodesia failed to dislodge the illegal white minority regime of Ian Smith and the Rhodesian Front party. The removal of South Africa's mandate over South West Africa (Namibia) did not prevent the territory being ruled from Cape Town. But other pressures did bring change to southern Africa. Years of persistent African guerilla activity in the Portuguese territories of Mozambique and Angola eventually brought colonial rule to an end. A coup d'état in Lisbon in 1973 overthrew the existing right-wing dictatorship and one of the

Israeli Withdrawal 1974
Last units of the Israeli Armed Forces are seen at their bridgehead on the west bank of the Suez Canal before their final withdrawal into Sinai over the Israeli-built causeway.

first moves of the new government was to announce the Portuguese withdrawal from Africa. Mozambique achieved independence in 1975.

The existence of a friendly neighbour had been vital to the Rhodesian government. Imports had reached the country along the railway lines from Mozambique. When it became obvious that such help would soon cease Ian Smith was forced to open negotiations with African nationalist leaders, some of whom he had previously imprisoned. South Africa, also, came under international pressures and began to modify its racial policies. For many years South Africans had suffered the exclusion of their sports teams by other countries. As more and more of Africa came under black rule the isolation of the republic increased. The government maintained a rigid adherence to the policies of apartheid but in practice these policies began to be slowly adapted.

The major communist and capitalist powers moved into a period of co-operation but this did not mean that the ideological struggle between the two politico-economic systems disappeared. Communism gradually became stronger in a number of countries such as Italy and France. The army group which seized power in Portugal in 1974 had a definite communist bias. In other areas communism lost ground. The most notable example was Chile. In 1970 Salvador Allende became the first ever *elected* communist head of state anywhere in the world. He set in motion a programme of political and economic reform, including nationalisation of large companies and distribution of land to the peasants. But in 1973 he was overthrown by a right-wing coup and most of his policies were reversed. European capitalism received a boost in 1973 when the European Economic Community was enlarged by the inclusion of Britain, Denmark and Ireland.

Terrorism

One feature of the 1970s affected western states more than communist countries. This was the growth and spread of terrorism. We have seen how the Palestine liberation movements resorted to terrorism on a worldwide scale. They used assassination, hijacking, occupation of embassy buildings and the siezing of hostages to attract attention to their cause, to force governments to pay ransoms or to secure the release of imprisoned comrades. These methods proved all too effective. When violent men held innocent people as hostages responsible governments had no alternative but to meet their demands. Other political groups began to use the same methods. Revolutionaries in South America kidnapped businessmen and officials. In Germany an anarchist organisation known as the Bader-Meinhoff gang commited many outrageous acts of violence.

This spate of violence spread to Britain in 1968 with a recurrence of trouble in Northern Ireland. The province had seldom known real peace because the Protestant majority and Catholic minority were often at loggerheads but violent civil rights demonstrations in 1968 heralded a new era of civil war. The Irish Republican Army (IRA), pledged to the re-uniting of the two parts of Ireland, began a campaign of arson, assassination and sabotage. The police proved unable to deal with the situation and troops were sent to maintain law and order. The government of the province collapsed and direct rule from Westminster was established. The Protestant side soon produced its own unofficial, armed groups and the situation degenerated into a sectarian bloodbath. The government took emergency powers and

hundreds of people were imprisoned without trial. Various attempts were made to find a constitutional solution to the problems of Northern Ireland but the demands of the two sides proved irreconcilable.

Violence and terrorism are evils which are difficult to combat in democratic states. In communist or other totalitarian states undesirable political groups are banned. People suspected of belonging to such groups are imprisoned or executed, usually without trial. In a democracy, freedom of speech and freedom of assembly are fundamental rights enjoyed by all citizens. No one can be imprisoned for his political opinions. Those who believe in the democratic process hope that freedom provides people with the opportunity to express their grievances and thus prevents them seeking violent solutions. Usually this works. When it does not citizens, and particularly prominent men and women, have little protection against the kidnapper and the assassin.

Democracies in which a free economic system operates are, in theory, also ill-equipped to deal with severe economic crises. We have seen how the Great Depression of 1929–31 brought governments crashing down in many western countries. Freely elected governments can seldom take the strict measures necessary to solve their problem since they lack the power to enforce unpopular measures and run the risk of being voted out of office. Totalitarian states do not have this problem. Yet western democracy survived the crisis of the 1930s and will probably survive the crisis of the mid 1970s.

The Future

Political and economic systems are of relative importance when set alongside the fundamental problems facing our planet. Over-population, wastage of natural resources, disease, famine and drought—these remain the real enemies of man. In the period 1970–75 there were severe droughts in India, Ethiopia and West Africa; an international commission reported that we were destocking the sea by reckless fishing; experts calculated that world oil resources will not last us very far into the next century. All the time the steady multiplication of humanity goes on.

Of course, considerable work has been done on the basic problems confronting us. Every year the number of killer diseases decreases as scientists discover new cures. Urgent experiments on alternative sources of energy are taking place. Perhaps in the future we shall be able to use not only nuclear power but solar energy (heat from the sun stored for use). The achievements of our scientists are quite astonishing. They may even be on the verge of creating life itself, for biologists have successfully identified the basic substance which is at the root of all living things. When they can make this substance in the test tube it may be only a short step to the creation of living organisms.

But the making of discoveries is not enough. Someone has to decide how and in what ways such discoveries shall be put to use. That is an enormous responsibility.

There is a European folk story about a magician who had an apprentice. One day the magician went out and left his apprentice to do the housework. The young man soon grew tired of his labour and thought, 'Why should I work when I can use some of my master's spells to help me?' So he took down the magician's big book of spells and he found a spell to make his broom do all the work. He ordered the broom to fetch water from the well to the house and the broom did so. The apprentice soon had all the water he needed but, unfortunately, he could not find a spell which would stop the broom. So it went on emptying bucket after bucket into the overflowing cooking-pot. Now the apprentice had to work harder than ever to try to clear up the mess. He could not do so and when the magician returned he found his apprentice exhausted and his house flooded.

Some people wonder whether modern scientists are not rather like the magician's apprentice —using discoveries and powers that they cannot fully control. Certainly science creates new problems, even though it does solve many old ones. It has given man the power to destroy the world with atomic weapons. It has made it possible for one nation to invade another with germs, so that all its people will be weakened by disease. Radioactive nuclear waste is another problem (material left over from nuclear-powered machines). It is very dangerous and can cause disease, deformity or death to men. How can this waste material be safely thrown away?

Satelites have many peaceful uses but they have also been used by Russians and Americans to take 'spy' photographs of each other's military bases. Such action could lead to war.

As we consider the advantages and disadvantages of modern developments, it is obvious that if we were really determined to do so we could have the benefits without the disadvantages. We could prevent the world from becoming too crowded. We could agree to use atomic power for peaceful purposes only. New methods of farming and water-supply could prevent anybody in our present world population from being hungry. We could do a great deal to prevent them from being ill. We could preserve the beauty of the world and its wild life for everybody's enjoyment. We could eventually reduce the amount of work people have to do and give them opportunities for spending leisure time in study, travel, sport, service to other people and hobbies.

But we do not do all these things. Why not? A great philosopher once said. 'Man is the glory and the scum of the earth.' Man is indeed the most advanced of all the animals, capable of inventing marvellous machines, composing musical symphonies, writing books, inspiring and leading his fellows; he is also greedy, selfish and wicked, capable of spoiling and even destroying the world in which he lives.

This study of the world has shown many examples of man as the glory of the earth and man as the scum of the earth. Education, nationhood, control of disease — in these and other aspects of human life, we have taken great steps forward. But everything still depends on that curious creature man, and that is why the story of the world is not one of unceasing progress. And when we talk about 'man', we do not just mean the leaders — the politicians, the generals, the scientists — we mean ordinary people. But how can we ordinary people influence the history of nations and of the world? We have made a very important start when we begin to understand ourselves. Alexander Pope one of the great English poets once wrote:

'The proper study of Mankind is Man'.

And that is what History is all about.

Index

383

384